The Long Way Home

The Other Great Escape

John McCallum

ISIS
LARGE PRINT
Oxford

Copyright © John McCallum, 2005

First published in Great Britain 2005
by
Birlinn Ltd.

Published in Large Print 2006 by ISIS Publishing Ltd.,
7 Centremead, Osney Mead, Oxford OX2 0ES
by arrangement with
Birlinn Ltd.

British Library Cataloguing in Publication Data
McCallum, John
    The long way home: the other great escape. –
    Large print ed. – (Isis reminiscence series)
    1. McCallum, John
    2. World War, 1939–1945 – Prisoners and prisons,
    German
    3. World War, 1939–1945 – Personal narratives,
    British
    4. Prisoner-of-war escapes – Czech Republic –
    Sudetenland
    5. Large type books
    I. Title
    940.5'47243'092

ISBN 978–0–7531–9370–9 (hb)
ISBN 978–0–7531–9371–6 (pb)

Printed and bound in Great Britain by
T. J. International Ltd., Padstow, Cornwall

Foreword

The Rt Hon. the Lord Robertson of Port Ellen KT GCMG Hon FRSE PC (Secretary of State for Defence 1997–99, Secretary General of NATO 1999–2003)

We all know the great war stories — the deeds of inspirational bravery which make movies to be seen over and over again. We recognise and revere the great war leaders and personalities. Their names are in lights, on books and on statues. We have whole libraries devoted to the origins of wars and the impact the conflicts have had on our history.

But wars affect ordinary people in extraordinary ways as well. Lives are disrupted, affected and even ended by forces far from the lives of the man or woman in the street. People are taken from their peaceful way of life and faced with challenges they could never imagine. Some of the greatest stories — about the ability of accidental heroes to rise to dizzy heights of achievement — are never heard.

Here is one such story: three telephone engineers are plucked from obscurity and thrown into a maelstrom of adventure. The story has all the ingredients of a modern airport novel — courage, daring, sex, love, cunning, innocence, humour and incredible luck. But this is not fiction — it is for real. The three Scottish heroes of the action then returned to obscurity after their amazing exploits. For decades, because of the Official Secrets Act, the story could not be told. Luckily, sixty years later, one of them has published this account.

When I read this book in manuscript, I could not stop turning the pages. The early events made the old Scottish word "gallus" come to mind, but as events unfold, you realise how determination, resourcefulness and sheer bravado can move mountains — or at least the bars of a prisoner of war camp.

Those of us who, almost every Christmas, watch *The Great Escape* would never have guessed that nearby three Scottish guys had been doing the same thing on the same day. And unlike the more famous escapees from Stalag Luft Drei, these three made it home.

At this point in history, anniversaries of the First and Second World Wars have brought home to a new generation how much we owe to those who gave up their comfortable lives so that we might live in peace and safety. Old men, and women too, with blazers and medals nowadays leaning on sticks are living legends. Ordinary people, like John McCallum, Jimmy O'Neill and Joe Harkin were called upon to do extraordinary things. And, collectively, they guaranteed our precious freedom.

This is a great tale — with a deep message. Read, enjoy — and reflect.

George Robertson

Preface

You've seen it on TV a dozen times, you may have read the book and, if you're old enough, you may have discussed it after it happened. When they filmed it, they called it *The Great Escape*.

What I cannot understand is who christened it with a name that is totally misleading. Rembrandt's painting "The Man in the Golden Helmet" is a great masterpiece, as is Tolstoy's *War and Peace* a great piece of classical writing. The list of Greats that spring to mind is unending, but most of them were successful achievements.

There are exceptions to everything in life, like the Great Plague and the Great War, neither of which could have been great to anyone who was involved in them.

The dictionary quotes "great" as meaning "large, big, important or distinguished". The Stalag Luft Drei escape was definitely big, but was only distinguished by the deaths of the fifty brave airmen who misguidedly made the attempt.

Truth being stranger than fiction, three Scots escaped from their camp at the same time as the sixty-seven airmen and, as luck would have it, they unfortunately chose a route which passed through the town of Sagan, which was the railhead for Stalag Three.

Just as the mass escape story is true, so also is the story of the three Glasgow men who escaped at the same time — they were my brother Jimmy, my friend Joe and myself.

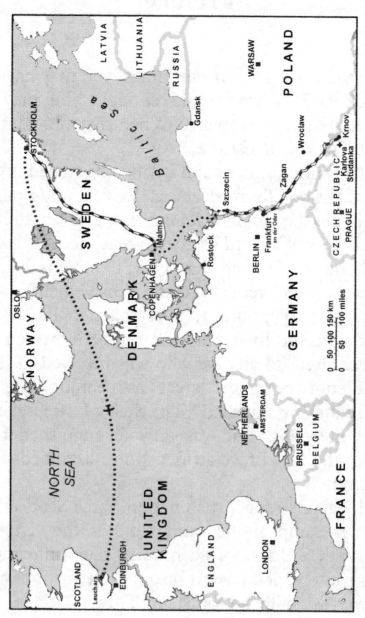

Map drawn by Mary Spence

CHAPTER
ONE

When I reached the glorious age of nineteen, I signed up as a Supplementary Reservist with the Royal Corps of Signals, whose Drill Hall was situated in Yorkhill in Glasgow. I was merely following a family tradition, as my two older brothers had set the pattern for me previously. My brother, William, had completed his service but my brother, James O'Neill, was still in. The three of us were telephone engineers in the Post Office, so it made good sense to give our services to the Signal Corps and this particular unit consisted almost entirely of Post Office personnel.

This was when I first met Joe Harkin, who was already a Reservist, and from this time on, as long as we were in uniform, we were almost inseparable — Jimmy, Joe and Johnny.

Joe was a slim good-looking young man with wavy brown hair, fairly energetic and a few years older than myself. At that time he was an external lineman and, as I had joined the Corps in this capacity, we had something in common, including a mutual liking.

Brother Jimmy was a different type of character from Joe — slightly older, reddish blonde hair, mainly cool good-humoured nature, but with a temper which could

1

flare and then disappear as quickly as it had come. He was the most solidly built of the three of us and, being the eldest, naturally assumed the lead figure in our trio.

I was the lightweight of the party in all departments — age, height and weight, with no distinguishing features that anyone would ever remember me by — which, in life, could also be an asset.

We were paid an annual bounty, which we received quarterly, and although it was not a lot, it did provide a new suit and a pair of shoes every year as long as you restricted yourself to the less expensive tailors. The money was laughingly referred to as "Blood Money". Much as I enjoyed spending this extra cash, little did I dream that the day of reckoning would come and that I would be called upon literally to repay in blood, with bullet-wound scars as a receipt for having paid up! But that, as they say, is another story.

It is strange to think that our lives are made up of stories of adventure, drama, romance and other things, and all these happenings are either gilded or eroded, sometimes enhanced, by our memory and imagination.

Jimmy, for instance, had spent some years in the Merchant Navy and so had a background of world travel, which stood us in very good stead later, as without his intimate knowledge of port operations and seamen's habits, we could not possibly have succeeded in our big adventure. After his time at sea, Jimmy took a job ashore and became a cable jointer with the Post Office, and this was the only difference between the three of us — Joe and I were external lineman and Jimmy was a cable specialist.

Being a lineman was, on the whole, very hard work. Imagine sitting at the top of a telephone pole in winter with a heavy safety belt supporting you and the steps cutting off the circulation to your feet, the wind and rain slowly freezing you, making for awkward cold hands. Yet I loved it: when my external training was completed, I was transferred to an internal section fitting switchboards. I wriggled, pleaded, cajoled and left no stone unturned to get back to the outdoor work that I so much enjoyed, but all to no avail. The rest of my time in the Engineering Department was spent doing work from which I derived no pleasure whatsoever.

However, the Royal Signals were willing to let me exercise my prowess at being a lineman. If I had thought that I had seen some hard times doing the job in a Scottish winter, what was still to come was devastating.

By the way, I suppose I should mention as background that Jimmy and Joe were both happily married and that I was a very inexperienced bachelor.

CHAPTER
TWO

In September 1938 our unit was taking part in the Regular Army manoeuvres which were taking place in Southern England and our performance during this period, we were told, booked us a place in the top bracket job of GHQ Signals. To my mind this was not surprising as we were, after all, employed daily in the business of telephones.

Towards the second week of manoeuvres we were told that we were on standby as it was touch and go whether the Second World War started now or a little later, but, as events turned out, it was to be the following September before we got our marching orders. War was declared on 3 September 1939 and by the middle of that month we were in France and billeted in a quaint little village called Dainville, just outside the historically famous town of Arras, which was now established as British Expeditionary Force GHQ. Our billet was in the local dance-hall, attached to the pub called Café Aeroplane, which was, of course, an excellent watering-hole for any of our troops who took a dram. They could really tank up and almost literally fall into bed. Needless to say, the troops made very good use of this facility. Being a non-drinker myself, I soon discovered that the cuisine side of the café was more interesting and that Madame made a wonderful omelette and chips which, strangely enough, never gave me a single headache or hangover!

Our unit had an outstanding reception in France as, apparently, we were the first complete outfit to arrive; at a very grand full-dress parade in the main square in Arras, we were presented with the flag of the Légion d'Honneur (I think). Before the ceremony took place we were warned there was to be no hilarity when the French officer kissed our officer on both cheeks, as this was only ceremonial and not affection. We were not convinced, but as the RSM had his beady eye on us, we behaved ourselves.

The weather was fantastic and we were amazed at the number of fruit trees that lined the highways and byways in our operational area. We seemed to be driving over apples everywhere we went that September.

We soon settled down to work in an area where, in the previous war, many huge battles had been fought. We ran lines over historic sites like Vimy Ridge and examined the old trenches which had been preserved to remind people of the horrors of the war which was fought to end wars. And here we were again, like a lot of kids, ready to do it all again. Unbelievable! How often will the politicians be allowed to sacrifice so many for the indulgence of so few? Why not follow the new government legislation and have a one-for-one ballot of the Electoral Register? I don't think we would need to be involved with any nuclear deterrents if we did that. How many mothers agree to their sons and daughters going off like animals to be maimed or slaughtered? Unfortunately men think differently, or don't think enough, and this was seen in the number of volunteers in the Second World War who were men who had served in the First World War.

Aided by the Indian summer of '39, we began to spread our huge spider-like network of lines of communication over the HQ area. We never really had the feeling of being on active service and the odd German reconnaissance plane did little to remind us that there was a war on. Unfortunately, the winter that followed was unfit for brass monkeys, let alone us, and turned out to be the coldest ever recorded in that part of France. Our particular job became a daytime nightmare. As we did our work, our Section Officer, although unable to help us physically, plied us with tots of rum which helped to keep our blood circulating. At times it was so bad that the linemen were being roped so that they could be lowered if necessary from the pole they were working on to the ground when they could no longer climb down on their own.

We struggled on until spring arrived. Then came the aftermath of the big freeze. The winter frosts had bitten so deep that, when the thaw came, the frozen moisture began to expand and the cobbled roads boiled up like rising dough and became impassable, although they were centuries old and had withstood the traffic of everything from horse to tank. This was an impressive natural obstacle to add to the rest.

CHAPTER
THREE

In early April I had a stroke of luck. I was picked to ride shotgun on one of our trucks doing a duty run to Paris to collect some essentials for HQ. Naturally, I was asked to make some purchases of items which could not be obtained in the north — such as campbeds for Jimmy, Joe and myself, as we were fed-up sleeping on palliasses stuffed with straw. The Signals had a slight degree of leniency that would not have been tolerated in an infantry regiment.

Paris was, of course, out of bounds to all troops unless they were in possession of a pass. At this time everything in Paris looked fairly normal. Having only seen cities like Glasgow, Edinburgh and London, I was not quite sure what to expect, but Paris in the spring exceeded everything I could have imagined. We had only two days to absorb it all, but Driver McLean had done it all before so I got the whole guided tour. I managed to lose my virginity to a young mademoiselle. I even remembered to buy the campbeds.

On our return to Arras we heard rumours of the first rumblings of the German war machine. Confirmation was coming through that the German preparations were complete and they would soon be on the move. The French army were girding their loins, so to speak, on the impregnable Maginot Line and all forces were on Red Alert. The contention was, of course, that there would be no Blitzkrieg in France as there had been in Poland earlier. I wonder where one should apportion the blame for what was to follow. Should Belgium and Holland have agreed to an extension of the defence line, which would have made any real invasion a non-starter? The cost of such an undertaking was probably prohibitive, but would it not have been cheaper in the long run?

The Maginot Line became the Imaginary Line, and the Blitzkrieg came after all, but through Belgium instead of France. When the breakthrough came, a Signal section was made up to establish communications from GHQ to the new front line using the French and Belgian telephone exchanges, which were rapidly being evacuated by their staff. Joe and I were part of this group but Jimmy was deployed to another detail. This was one of the few times that we were separated.

From Arras we linked up through Douai and then Tournai. By this time both towns were in flames and practically deserted as the Luftwaffe bombed and strafed the area almost unopposed. We were eventually stopped by our own troops, who kindly informed us that if we went any further on there would be no way back; they were blowing up the canal and river bridges as they retreated. A quick telephone call to HQ confirmed that we should get the hell out of it and return to our new coastal meeting point at Calais.

The roads were in a state of total turmoil on our way back. The gruesome scenes in the ditches — the dead lying where they had been thrown off the highway to make way for the traffic — should have disturbed us much more than they did. My personal lack of reaction to seeing men, women and, worst of all, children lying in a variety of death poses, like bundles of discarded clothing, surprised me very much indeed. I can only think that this was a subconscious protection of my sanity — that as long as we had no physical contact with the horrors we faced, we could not be adversely affected by them. The fact that all these people had proved to be mortal seemed only to enhance our own feeling of immortality.

Eventually we arrived in Boulogne, in the middle of a night bombing raid by the Luftwaffe. Hell had been let loose. The noise of the low-flying aircraft dropping bombs coupled with indiscriminate machine-gunning being answered by Bofors guns and anything else that could return fire created a real cacophony of soul-searing sound.

All this was, of course, taking place in a total blackout, with a huge conglomeration of traffic which slowly ground to a halt. The private car immediately behind us, for no apparent reason, switched on his headlights. This, quite rightly, brought roars of disapproval — as if a referee had refused a penalty claim at a Rangers/Celtic match. When the offending

9

lights were not promptly doused, Jock McGregor vaulted over the tailboard of our truck and with the heels of his number ten tackety boots smashed both head-lamps, in all probability saving the lives of all in the vicinity of those telltale lights.

CHAPTER
FOUR

We finally reached our projected meeting place with the rest of our Section, only to find that they had been moved further up the coast, probably to Calais, possibly to Dunkirk — each soon to become household words. Our orders now were to stay overnight in the Rest Camp at Boulogne and to join up with our unit the following day. We found the camp. Oh, the luxury of a proper meal! Although the air-raid was still going on, we just bedded down where we were, too tired to even think of going to the air-raid shelter.

An uncomfortable awakening came with the dawn, but after a hard-tack breakfast we felt quite refreshed and looked forward to joining up with our own outfit. But it was not to be. The Gods of War had decided that our adventure was not quite finished and had devised a nasty, untidy ending for our little group.

Our special Signal Section was assembled and preparing to leave the Rest Camp when a staff car pulled in and a captain wearing a red arm band bustled out and called everyone to attention. A short speech informed us that all transit personnel were being commandeered for special duties; a light armoured German column had broken through our main front and was believed to be heading in our direction. We would be used to set up road blocks at strategic points outside the town. When the emergency was over we could return to our normal duties. In my case, this turned out to be over four years later.

Joe and I, along with a few odds and bods, were put under the command of a Royal Army Medical Corps captain, whose name I never knew. Nor did we know that this little job was a death sentence for him: very soon he was to die just a couple of yards from me.

His first instructions were to set up a road block in the village of La Capelle, just outside Boulogne on the St Omer road. As we travelled towards our destination everyone seemed fairly cheerful, until a most disturbing incident took place which changed our mood to one of gloom and despondency and set our mission in its true perspective. Our vehicles were flagged down just outside the town and, because we were obviously going in the wrong direction, we were asked if anyone wished to be given the last sacrament by an army chaplain. Even the Catholics declined this kind offer, which I can understand, because to accept it was to admit that our new mission was possibly terminal.

This stoppage also shed new light on my own position in the party. Prior to leaving the camp, the staff officer had asked if there were any good rifle shots among us. Knowing I was in that category, my hand went up without thinking. In doing so, I broke the first law I had been taught after putting on a uniform: "volunteer for nothing". The result of my unthinking action was that I had to relinquish my rifle and take a bren gun in its place. After fiddling with it for a few minutes I was able to see how the bolt action worked and the magazine could be changed. I never dreamed that I would be called upon to use it. Volunteers usually get the heavy end of the stick, as in the case where a section sergeant asked if he could have six men who were interested in music and the men who responded had to shift a grand piano, which probably resulted in at least a couple of hernias. That damned bren gun was to get me into a lot of trouble very soon.

When we reached La Capelle there were all the usual routines to follow. Setting up a local HQ, finding a suitable place for the cookhouse, a place to bed down, latrine position and, of paramount importance, the siting of the road-block.

All sorts of ideas went through our minds as to how one would go about blocking a road, but the staff captain who was still with us at this stage had decided on a very simple method. You make up your mind where you want the rear of the road-block and then you stop all the traffic coming from the danger zone and place these vehicles crosswise on the road. There would be no exceptions.

That sounds simple until you see the people you are forcing to leave their vehicles: the old and infirm, pregnant mothers, cripples, nuns and so on. They all had valid reasons for not leaving the security of their transport, but their pleas fell on deaf ears. Any men of military age were escorted to the rear to be questioned, and if their answers did not satisfy the commanding officer, they were summarily dealt with behind the HQ barn. This was to avoid the possibility of infiltration by the Fifth Column.

CHAPTER
FIVE

Wars are remembered by famous actions and battles, for example the Battle of Hastings, where Harold took an arrow in the eye and made it easy for schoolchildren to remember him. Another example is the Charge of the Light Brigade, where almost everyone was gloriously and famously killed. Let's not forget Nelson being fatally wounded or what he said to Hardy as he died. All these and many other historical actions faded into insignificance for us when compared with "The Battle of La Capelle", which was about to take place.

The scene was set — our road block completed, traffic had dried up and one of those wartime phenomena took place for which these is no explanation. As if acting on a signal, the householders of the village came out and closed their shutters, top and bottom.

At this point, only Jimmy Strathearn and myself were at the front of the road block. I had to stop the German army with my bren gun and he had to carry the ammunition and keep me supplied with fresh magazines. The bren was sited in the middle of the road, with an ammunition box on either side, facing in the direction from which we expected the trouble to come. A hundred yards in front the road took a turn to the left and an empty car stood on the corner. Jimmy and I were discussing the strange behaviour of the villagers and wondering what it meant when the sound of a small plane caught our attention.

A few seconds later a single-engined monoplane approached us, flying fairly low. Seeing the black crosses on the underside of the wings, we realised that we were in the presence of the enemy. It was obviously a reconnaissance plane and offered no personal threat to us, but to Jimmy this was a chance to do battle and he insisted I "shoot the bloody thing down". I pointed out that the bren had a very low tripod and that unless the pilot flew at road level there was nothing much I could do. But Jimmy was not to be denied and insisted I use his shoulder as a high tripod. As I was quite keen to see if I had figured out the working of the gun properly, we did just that. These planes fly very slowly, which is just as well, otherwise this one would have been gone by the time we got organised. With Jimmy holding the tripod on his shoulder, I released the safety-catch, worked a round into the breach, aimed — allowing for speed — then squeezed the trigger.

Then came all the things that gave me satisfaction in shooting: the noise — which accounts for my being almost totally deaf in my right ear — the smell of cordite and the feel of the tightly-held gun butt bouncing on the shoulder. As I wasn't using tracers I couldn't tell how close I came but, judging by the pilot's reaction, it must have been good because he was off like a bat out of hell. Jimmy was jubilant, picked up one of the spent cartridge cases and put it in my pocket as a souvenir. He then decided he had seen some movement in an adjacent field and went off to investigate. He had just disappeared when the captain came forward to find out what the shooting was all about. When I told him, he decided to stay forward in case I needed any help. I had no idea how the others were deployed but it seemed awfully lonely up front.

Suddenly all hell broke loose. There was one huge bang and the car on the corner blew apart. Shrapnel zizzed all around us. It was obviously suspected of being an observation post and was completely wiped out. The captain and myself dropped to the ground, still in the middle of the road behind the bren. Before we could say anything, there was a loud rumbling and round the corner came one very large tank displaying a black cross on its turret. Fortunately, it stopped to survey the situation and gave me time to line up my sights on the driver's sight slit and to fire a burst from the bren. The captain had decided that our position was too exposed. The tank commander must have decided that we were no great threat to them but had given us the few seconds necessary to get off the road and into the nearest garden.

This is where fate took a hand in the proceedings. Opening the garden gate, the officer turned right and took up position with the rifle he was carrying, leaving me no option but to turn left and take position there with the bren. We didn't have long to wait. The tank rumbled towards us and took station just outside the garden. My mind was racing with the possibilities of what would happen next. I figured that the turret lid would open and a hand grenade would be slung into the garden, so I held the bren so that I could fire a burst at the lid to discourage them. Sure enough the turret began to swivel and I thought I had been right. My finger tightened on the trigger and I waited for the lid to open. Instead, the tank's machine gun raked through the garden. Shocked at being on the receiving end of gunfire for the first time in my life, I saw the captain's head sag as the burst hit him across the back. Then it was my turn. I was hit by lightning in my left leg. I remember thinking that a second burst would finish me off and my poor mother would never know what had happened to me, but it never came.

As the tank moved off I had a chance to evaluate the situation. My leg was completely numb; blood was oozing out of a wound in the ankle and this seemed to be the main damage, although about a week later a bullet was discovered lodged in my thigh bone. I checked the bren and found that a ricochet had damaged the breech, which also accounted for the blood on my left hand. The mopping-up troops were now visible through the hedge. A few minutes later I could have been finished off by the big German sergeant who came into the garden behind his threatening Luger. I closed my eyes as I didn't want to see the shot that killed me, but when I heard him shouting at me I opened them again. He was motioning for me to stand up. I pointed to my bloody ankle and shook my head, whereupon he went to the door of the house and hammered on it with the butt of his automatic.

When the door was opened he went in and reappeared carrying a chair, which he placed on the path near me. Then, with very little apparent effort, he picked me up and gently placed me on it. He then checked the bren and, on finding that the bolt was jammed, unceremoniously threw it in a corner. Opening one of his tunic pockets, he produced a packet of cigarettes and offered me one. When I indicated that I didn't smoke, he courteously offered me a bar of chocolate out of the other pocket. To this I said "Thank you, but no thank you". He now went into one of his trouser pockets and produced a field dressing; after removing the gaiter, boot and sock from my damaged ankle, he bandaged it. Everything was done with great care and consideration, yet the same man could just as easily have killed me and no-one would have been any the wiser. All very confusing.

He now did his level best to interrogate me as to the deployment of troops in the area. I don't think there could have been a less informed person than I. After he established that I belonged to the Signal Corps and not an infantry regiment, he relieved me of my pride and joy — my lovely chrome pliers which I carried in a holster on my belt.

This big gentle man then arranged transport to take me to the nearest German field hospital, where I was placed in a long queue awaiting field surgery. The real war had broken out down beyond our road block, with lots of different kinds of gunfire. Finally the Stukas were called in to dive-bomb the obstruction to the German advance.

About a year later Joe told me the rest of the La Capelle story. Apparently the lead tank which shot us went on down the road and straight over the road block as if it wasn't there, firing its machine-gun as it went. Joe said he had never seen our group move so fast as they dispersed towards the coast. He eventually met up with my brother Jimmy, who wanted to come back and look for me. The squad convinced him that I must have been killed and that there was no way back. The official verdict was "Missing believed killed in action". So ended my one and only go at fighting in the war.

CHAPTER
SIX

After a succession of dressing stations and hospitals I finally ended up in the British 21st Field Hospital in the town of Camiers. Although a British hospital, it was under German control. The hospital itself was under the command of Colonel Robertson, whose house I had worked in just before the war during the auto telephone conversion of the area he lived in. This connection was a stroke of luck.

I had been told I would never have full use of my ankle again and would probably need calipers to walk. At the hospital, however, there was Colonel Wilson, a brilliant surgeon, and Major Tucker, an outstanding bone specialist, both reputed to have practices in Harley Street. They decided that I should be able to use my ankle again, and after a great deal of pain and time this objective was achieved. Years later I was re-graded in an army medical and passed A1. It is strange to think that if I had not been channelled through this hospital I would very likely have been crippled for the rest of my life.

A few months later, a group of us who were just able to hobble about were assembled and put into a variety of French, Belgian and British uniforms and unceremoniously bundled into a freight wagon, whose doors were slammed and bolted. We spent three miserable days and nights in this hell-hole as the train was slowly shunted to Upper Silesia in Eastern Germany, close to the Polish border. Occasionally the doors were opened and some rations thrown in, but we were never allowed to get out. Someone enterprisingly ripped up a piece of the floor and this served as our toilet for the trip. I often have a quiet giggle to myself when I hear people complaining about the terrible inconveniences that they have had to put up with.

Eventually we reached our destination and were rousted out with lots of noise and shouting. To my horror, my walking stick, a necessity rather than an affectation, was taken from me and thrown aside, as were all the crutches and sticks of the group. We made a sorry spectacle as we shambled through the town, sore from the discomfort of our trip and unable to walk properly. We were not a pretty sight. The townsfolk must have wondered why the war was taking so long; if we were an example of the British armed forces then the Hitler Youth should have been capable of wiping us out without the might of the Wehrmacht.

After this degrading march, we were transported by trucks to Stalag VIIIB, Lamsdorf, where we were body-searched and then lined up. There were already thousands of British prisoners in this main camp and, of course, a batch of new arrivals created quite a stir, with people checking to see if any of their friends or buddies were amongst them. It just so happened that Joe was one of those. When he recognised me, he was quite overcome, and after an emotional reunion he told me not to go away as he had another surprise for me — my brother Jimmy. Apparently when he told Jimmy that I was there Jimmy grabbed him by the throat and said that if this was a joke it was in very bad taste. This was understandable, as he had come to accept I had been killed at the road block. After much persuasion, Jimmy came along to see for himself, and once again our trio was complete.

Jimmy managed to convince the guards that we were brothers and I was allowed to stay with them in the same hut. There then followed for me a welcome period of recuperation, during which Jimmy and Joe did everything possible to get me back in shape. I began to realise that, given time, I would be able to walk normally again. You can imagine the stories we had to tell each other. After having been separated and captured in different places, it was an amazing coincidence to be re-united in the same Stalag in Eastern Germany.

I was now an official POW and had my own number to prove it. My mother was notified accordingly, whereupon she wrote to Winston Churchill that he should take it upon himself to see that I was provided with proper footwear so that I could make a full recovery. Astonishingly, as a result, an extra pair of new boots was delivered to me every six months through the Red Cross, outwith the normal issue. I often wonder what would have happened if she had insisted that I be repatriated immediately.

CHAPTER
SEVEN

It was now catching-up time. Jimmy and Joe related their hair-raising adventures of how they had met again and been rounded up in the fort in Calais. They had no hope of being rescued from the beach there as the main retreat flotilla was concentrating on Dunkirk.

They and thousands of our other troops, still bewildered by the speed of events over the last few days and totally stunned by the outcome of the Blitzkrieg, were forced to march across France into Germany. This journey left scars on the minds of all those who took part in it and was always referred to afterwards as The March. No rations or drinking water were provided, and sleeping accommodation was simply the ground where they stopped for the night. Toilets were non-existent. This became a great problem as stomachs rebelled at what was being put into them — stagnant water from ponds and brooks, along with anything that looked edible. Naturally, all this took its toll and left them severely debilitated. We had been in reserved occupations at home and had, after all, volunteered. Nowadays when I see the commercials urging young men to join the Territorial Army, I feel they should be shown some of the horrors of war as well as the entertaining side of the army.

Over the next few years the amateur POWs arrived at the various Stalags which had been set up in Germany and Poland and, through bitter experience, became hardened professionals. Most of them had some untapped abilities of which they had not previously been aware. In their new life of enforced captivity there was time to think, listen, watch and learn — to try something new, to improvise and maybe succeed. Those who did not adjust to the new way of life became "Stalag Happy" and lost touch with reality. Thank God this didn't happen to many of them.

Jimmy and Joe were first-class survivors and worked very well together. When they arrived in Stalag VIIIB, they organised themselves into the plum job in the camp — the cookhouse. In no time after my appearance in camp, I also was elected to a post on this elite staff.

Now began a period of readjustment for everyone. No one could possibly forecast how long we were going to be "in the bag", and everyone was well aware that it had been said that World War One would be over by Christmas. We realised that it might be years more before it was over, so the word was "settle down, chaps, and make the best of it". This having been established, the organisers took over.

Slowly the birds of a feather flocked together. The music men found a place where they could talk shop and make plans; likewise the bookworms, the artisans and others who had similar interests. As time went on the German authorities co-operated as far as possible in providing instruments for the musicians, and books and writing materials for the studious; eventually there were bands and various types of learning classes leading to examination standards which were accepted at home.

There were, of course, the Escape Committees which no self-respecting camp should be without. One of the unwritten laws states that it is a POW's duty to escape from the enemy and that, if successful, he will not be returned to the same theatre of war. One presumes this is so that he can go through the whole bloody business again, only under different conditions.

The Escape Committee is a weird and wonderful organisation for which there are no known qualifications — they don't exist in the real world. This means anyone in the camp is eligible to become a member. Many escapes were made as there was a hard core of men who made escaping their full-time occupation, even though they were captured time and again. These were the ones that the Committee delighted in concentrating on. A first-time escapee would be told that beginners could not receive assistance. This was what happened to us when we made our one and only approach for help.

We three discussed the pros and cons of escape and decided that in the first year it would be impossible, as I had to rebuild strength and mobility in my shattered ankle. A prime requirement for such a venture is physical fitness. It is strange, however, how the mind works. During the next few years we listened carefully to any stories we heard of where the escapes went wrong and a pattern began to build up: the same mistakes were being made time and again. They kept trying to travel at night and, as there was a curfew on, they were easily picked up. Some contacted the Polish people for help and almost always were turned over to the Germans. Subconsciously, this type of information was filed for future reference.

The camp slowly assumed the identity of a small town and in time the layout became familiar to everyone. If you wanted to go shopping you went to the swap-shop area, where it was possible to barter one thing for another. In the beginning, the trading was fairly primitive, but as time went on it became more and more interesting, especially after the Red Cross parcels began to arrive.

On a good day you could take a walk up to the Canadian compound and enjoy hearing a change of accent or, if you were feeling naughty, you might slowly pass the Married Quarters compound, which always led to a heated debate about the problems of homosexuality. Thank heaven we didn't have AIDS to worry about in those days. The energetic could congregate at the football field and perhaps get a game. The less energetic could always watch. Quite often it was worth watching as many good players had been captured, including a number of professionals.

You could visit Johnny the Barber and get your hair trimmed. If you were lucky there might be a cup of tea thrown in. After a tidy-up, a visit could be made to the theatre area, where one of the bands might be practising a piece worth listening to. Failing all else, you could just sit around and talk about your favourite food and drink, which, considering the circumstances, was a pretty stupid thing to do — but it was indulged in with great gusto and relish. It certainly made a contrast with our daily diet of soup, three or four potatoes and three hundred grams of bread.

Writing about it may make it sound like a holiday camp, but there were drawbacks — barbed wire and armed guards, for example. The limitation on movement was the real soul destroyer. This was what drove men in the main camp to volunteer for working parties.

CHAPTER
EIGHT

After a desperately hard winter, in which we experienced the biting cold east winds from the Russian steppes blowing straight through us, came the slow, miserable, messy Silesian spring. The warmer weather brought the terrible affliction of "itchy feet". This was our first spring in prison camp so we had no precedent to compare it with, but as the years went by it became something to look forward to, wondering who it was going to strike and how it would affect them. There were those who began to huddle and plan escapes which never came to fruition, and others who wondered how to wangle themselves onto the repatriation list. Others decided to go out on a working party or to switch to a different one. It was like the restlessness nowadays when winter turns the corner, only our options were rather more restricted — no dithering between Majorca, the Costa Brava or Bournemouth.

Jimmy, Joe and I had a long and serious talk about the importance of the next step. Should we give up our cosy jobs in the cookhouse and gamble on one of the working parties? We could end up regretting our decision for the rest of the war. Eventually we decided to give it a go and volunteered to go out as replacements on an existing working party. We got a right kick in the teeth.

We ended up in a railway construction job on the Polish border: a more desolate area would be hard to imagine. I can't remember what kind of working party we were supposed to be joining, but the lure was usually that you were told you were going to a chocolate or jam factory, which invariably turned out to be something completely different and horrible. There were a number of other parties in the area and we were warned that when the overall control officer visited the camp and gave an order, we should obey it as fast as possible. He turned out to be a German Army Sergeant Major and obviously the job had gone to his head. He was so brutal that he achieved a place on the Black List back home. His nickname "the Killer" was given to him after two recaptured escapees were brought back to their camp where, in front of the other prisoners, he prodded and goaded them until one of them retaliated — whereupon he shot them in cold blood.

The work was hard and heavy. Handling the rail sleepers was back-breaking, with no machinery or equipment to help. Everything was done by muscle power, which wasn't easy on our type of rations. One consolation of this gruesome period was that we had never been so fit or healthy. I don't suppose it is so surprising, since we had no drink, drugs or fornication to upset our systems. Without fail, we were early to bed and early to rise. With our regular but limited diet, there wasn't a pot belly or spare tyre to be seen anywhere.

As soon as it was humanly possible we transferred out of this hell-hole. There followed a couple of other working parties, none of which could be recommended for food or accommodation. We soon realised that something was wrong, and the three of us sat down to work it out. We realised that we were operating at the wrong rank level: the answer to our job problem was that we would have to have Stalag promotions and become NCOs. So Jimmy was to be made a Sergeant and Joe and I would be made up to Corporals. This proved surprisingly easy. We were allowed to write a certain number of postcards home and we used them to tell our families to start using our new ranks when sending us mail, which they duly did. Slowly the new ranks became accepted and in time both the German authorities and we grew used to them. One of the advantages was that NCOs could, if on a working party, ask at any time to return to the main camp.

In 1942 we decided that we had done our share of work in the hard labour camps and that it was time to test our stripes, remembering of course that they were self-awarded and only on our uniforms. We duly applied for a transfer back to Stalag VIIIB and were quite astounded when we were returned without question.

CHAPTER
NINE

The three of us were in agreement about the strangeness of being back in total captivity again. On a working party you are almost out in the normal world, although not actually part of it, whereas in the main camp you suffer total segregation, which is a punishment that no one in their right mind would want. It was in Stalags like ours that the abbreviation BEF took on a new meaning. Properly, it stood for British Expeditionary Force, but to the fifty thousand left behind by Lord "Tiger" Gort, it now meant the Bastards England Forgot. It proves the adage that if you're stupid enough to get caught, then you must take the consequences, and that was exactly what we were doing. Next time we would be off like a shot and to hell with the barricades.

We circulated around camp for about three weeks renewing our contacts with Signal associates and all the other friends we had made in the last two years. They were glad to see us and there were interminable "bumming schools" as we brought them up to date about what happened to us on the outside. They, in turn, filled us in on the latest intrigues in camp, and so a few more hours dribbled through the time machine in this game of waiting for release.

But all good things come to an end and we began to attend to the purpose of our return to camp, namely to find a good NCO working party where we could live happily ever after. We were delighted to hear that twenty NCOs were required for a holiday village in the mountains. All the able-bodied men there had now been drafted into the army and the local jobs had to be filled to keep things going. To us it sounded very much like the old chocolate factory story, but there was only one way to find out if it was true. So we put our names down and were accepted — but for what?

About a week later our party was mustered and with all our worldly possessions in a bag we moved out, after having said our farewells again to everyone; parting in those days was often terminal.

It was a short trip from the camp to the railway station and by the time we were on the train we knew we were on our way to a place called Bad Karlsbrunn, which was indeed a holiday village in Sudetenland. We had heard many stories before the war about this country, which originally had been part of Czechoslovakia and later was colonised by the Germans, but we knew little of its real history. To me the name Sudetenland was a just a name like Persia, Albania or California — exotic places which I knew existed but were unlikely ever to be part of my world. Yet here we were on our way to a place which for two years became a real "Shangri La".

As the train laboured slowly southward away from the Silesian industrial belt, the landscape improved with every mile that we travelled until, on the horizon, the foothills and mountains of the Altvater range became visible.

You cannot imagine our feelings as the scenery became more and more like Scotland. The last part of the journey by bus from the railhead at Wurbenthal to Bad Karlsbrunn was a steady climb through the forest and halfway up the mountain. Finally, we reached our camp, which was sited at the side of the River Oppa, over two thousand feet above sea level.

CHAPTER
TEN

The number one man in our Bad Karlsbrunn working party was Sergeant Bill James — a famous surname you will remember from the main members of the notorious "James Gang", namely Frank and Jesse. They were reputedly the toughest outlaws who ever lived but, believe me, they would have been regarded as sissies compared with our Bill.

I first met him when we were both hospitalised after being wounded. He had suffered a nasty shrapnel wound which had cut across the Achilles tendon on one leg. For a while we were in the same boat, having to learn to walk again. He must have heard that I was a Scot and, having become mobile before me, became a regular visitor and taught me many card tricks, which I still produce to amuse and amaze my grandchildren. He was a very good friend and looked after my interests while I was immobilised. But I had no idea then what a tough cookie he really was.

Bill was born and reared in the Vale of Leven and boasted that there was only one person in the world who could get the better of him physically — someone who could actually punch harder and faster than him. Having seen him in action many times in the years that

I knew him, I had to ask who this man was. Without a blush, Bill admitted that it was his beloved mother.

It became apparent in the course of time that he had a strong aversion to bullies and braggarts. If anyone tried to throw their weight around, he always had to take them on and the result was inevitable, with the victim wondering how this eleven-stone pale-faced man could administer such punishment. Putting his knuckles back to where they should be after these bouts was always a problem, but they always healed in time to deal with the next offender.

Other Scots in the party, apart from Jimmy, Joe and myself, were Big John, Mully Mitchell, Phony and Young Alec. We also had two Kiwis and a genuine Maori, one Aussie, three Merchant Navy lads, one Air Force Brylcream boy and the rest a mixture of army units, which included Busty Waring of the Royal Artillery. Busty was the type you see at the Earls Court display lifting gun barrels and wheels over walls, so you know exactly how he looked. With it he was always bright and bouncy. Our Maori was called Charlie, and a more lovable character I have yet to meet, with a good singing voice and the ability to accompany himself on the guitar. When he sang the Maori farewell song "Now is the Hour", it was a very touching moment for everyone, though we didn't often indulge in the luxury of sentiment. Charlie's singing always made me reflect on what a hard-bitten crew we had become.

The personality mix of our party was intriguing. For instance, take our two Kiwis, who could not have been more conflicting in character — Jim Rowe was the perfect laconic colonial, who didn't sit on a chair but managed always to drape himself over it, perfectly relaxed, whereas his oppo, Davey Jay, was always ready to move at any given moment and, when he sat down, was like a coiled spring waiting to be released. Jim was blond and slim and sported a moustache, whereas Davey was clean-shaven and dark, slightly smaller and thick-set. Davey had been a fairly competent boxer at home, which, at a later date, almost cost him his life — it certainly cost him his sanity.

Mully Mitchell, or to give him his full title, Motherwell Mitchell, was a cheery dapper little Scot who was a friend of Bill James — another of the Argylls who had been left behind to fight the thankless rearguard action. Mully on the football field was every bit as good as Bill in a fistfight, but his greatest forte was as a naturalist. He showed me how to capture wild birds, examine them without hurting them and then release them. I had heard of the art of tickling trout but Mully was the first person to demonstrate it before my very eyes, again returning the fish unharmed to the river. He was a real charmer.

Our tame Australian was called Arthur and was a nice-looking bundle of raw muscle. To this day I can't make up my mind if most of his stories were boastful truth or sheer romancing. I didn't care as they were very entertaining, like the one he told us about the time he was driving a four-horse harvester in the wheat fields. The story goes that his team-mate on the other harvester hurt himself and a replacement couldn't be found in time to complete the contract. But all was not lost. Arthur had the brilliant idea of making a special rig so that he could drive the two harvesters and the eight-horse team by himself. If Arthur had said that the horses were slowing down and that eventually he had to pull the harvesters himself, I would have applauded him loudly.

Brother Jimmy had been a godsend over the last two years in all the camps we had lived in, as he had an almost phobic tendency towards cleanliness and keeping things tidy. He had imposed his strong will in this direction no matter how much opposition there was. Some of the squalor we encountered was quite unbelievable, but when we left a camp behind, thanks to Jimmy, it was always cleaner than when we arrived.

Not many POWs had the good fortune to have a big brother to look after them in such circumstances, and to think he was there because of me made me feel terribly guilty at times. Jimmy should have been at home working in his nice reserved occupation with a perfectly clear conscience, but when I decided to join the Reserves he re-enlisted to help me through the first couple of years. His reward for this brotherly love was four years behind barbed wire, doomed to spend the whole of the war away from his beloved wife.

The deprivation that the married men suffered was naturally more acute than that of the single men, and quite often I could see the effects of it on both Joe and Jimmy. Being such strong characters, they came through these spells with flying colours. On the other hand, the bachelors reverted to the roving eye technique, which was, of course, possible when you were out on a working party where you could look and let your mind wander. During the first two years in Silesia most of the female temptresses were dressed in oily boiler suits and were built like tanks. This wasn't surprising as they were doing the jobs of their absent husbands who had worked in the engine sheds and railway yards before being drafted, and only the strongest type of female could survive.

CHAPTER
ELEVEN

The camp was a wooden structure surrounded by a high barbed wire fence put there, I suppose, to protect us from wild animals or anything else that might harm us. It certainly wasn't there to keep us in, or if it was, it didn't work. We couldn't see the village from our compound; we were just around the corner from the main street and very close to the local farm.

Before we ever set eyes on the village, the question of allocation of jobs had to be settled. Jimmy pulled a job in the Spa bath-house, Joe became an assistant to the joiner and I became a plasterer's labourer — a fine re-allocation of three technicians.

Our bosses were supposed to wear armbands, showing them to be assistant guards. Their job was to collect us each morning and return us to the camp in the evening when we finished work, but both the armbands and the collection idea were soon given up and we were trusted to appear and disappear on time.

The plastering team consisted of the boss, one Herr Springer, who was an uncommunicative fifty-year-old with a bad tummy, and his number two, ragdoll character called Franz, who had lost all his toes in World War One and consequently walked strangely. He was also one of the nicest men I have ever met. When Springer wasn't around, Franz took it upon himself to try and teach me some German. He was so successful that years later I was asked where on earth I had learned such hillbilly German.

Bad Karlsbrunn itself is a small mountain spa village with healing peat baths and special spring water, which tasted awful but reputedly was good for the innards. If this was true, then why did Herr Springer suffer so much? The main business was the baths and all the rest was hotels, ranging from the top-class down to the ordinary ski hotels. The type of skiing was fairly restricted as there were no ski lifts of any kind and the only skiers around were the local children, who were very good and exciting to watch. This was hardly surprising as they started to ski as soon as they could walk. The slopes were also used by the German army and formed a training area for mountain troops.

Most of the residents in the village were involved in the holiday business, which was why the village existed. There were only a few shops on the main street, such as the butcher, the baker and the shop that sold everything, including souvenirs. In the beginning the locals were quite stand-offish. This was hardly surprising, since we were the enemy: all they knew about the British Tommies was what they had been fed through the powerful German propaganda machine. Suddenly here were twenty of them in their midst. Fortunately for us, we had now been supplied with new battledress and everyone looked smart and tidy. Those who wished also acquired shorts and shirts for summer wear, which looked great with our all-weather tans. As time passed the villagers realised we were successfully doing the jobs we had come to do. The general attitude became more relaxed and we began to blend into the scenery — so much so that some of the visitors who didn't know we were POWs would nod, smile and even pass the time of day, thinking probably we were members of the Pioneer Group of the Organisation Tod, whose dress was very similar to ours.

By now all the female talent in the village had been spotted, discussed and placed in order of desirability, which was, of course, only a mental exercise which could never be realised under our present circumstances. But, as they say in the song, you can't stop people from dreaming, no matter how you guard them. Some orientals say that the pattern of our life is made like a tapestry and cannot be altered. Some people disagree and say that if you look closely you can see where there are options to take a path less travelled. Here in Karlsbrunn I had a choice between having an easy life or one fraught with danger. This is what happened.

It was midsummer and all was right with the world. I was enjoying the physical labour of mixing cement and sand in front of one of the hotels where Franz and I were repairing the stairway and, as I stopped for a breather, caught sight of a blond mädchen watching me from one of the hotel windows. She was leaning on the window-sill and the sunlight was doing wonderful things to her hair. I looked away and then back again. Sure enough, she was still watching me and there was a hint of a smile on her face which looked quite lovely.

Although this was only visual contact, it was, nonetheless, extremely exciting, and mixing the proper quantities of sand and cement became of secondary importance. I returned what I hoped was a smile in her direction and this time her smile was unmistakable and definitely for me. Palpitations now set in, and I knew it wasn't sunstroke. When I looked up at the window again, the vision had vanished and now I wondered if I had really seen anything at all. Had I finally succumbed to frustration and joined the "Stalag Happy" brigade?

That evening I told Jimmy about the incident. In his wisdom he gave me various pieces of advice on how to deal the situation. The main theme was to exercise extreme caution, as the penalty for fraternisation with the enemy during hostilities was execution of both parties. The best thing would be to forget the whole thing had ever happened. He also said that if the young lady was a visitor to the hotel, she would soon leave. This was a possibility that I hadn't thought of, and it didn't appeal to me at all. Jimmy was right: proceed with caution and don't make any fast moves.

Next day I could hardly wait to get into the village. We were still working at the same hotel and the only thought in my mind was "would I see her again?" or had the bird already flown? The question was answered in the afternoon when she suddenly appeared from the rear door pushing a pram. This really set me back. Obviously she was a young married woman with a baby and her husband was fighting on the Eastern Front — or somewhere else — but she had more or less flirted with me the day before. How could she? But maybe that was all rubbish and it was her little sister or brother. Or maybe she was baby-sitting. When she spotted me staring at her, she stopped and fussed a bit with the baby, then straightened up and subjected me to that happy smile again. I was devastated to say the least. In her mountain dirndl she looked a real picture. I was in love.

In my return smile, I tried to say everything that I felt, but probably managed only to look soppy. Then she moved slowly away towards the village. It took me about a week to find out who she was and about another week to find out her name. Remembering Jimmy's advice about being circumspect, I found it difficult to ask questions without raising suspicions. For now, let us call her Traudl. She was the daughter of the caretaker couple in the hotel where I first saw her.

My German course with Franz now took on a new urgency and importance. I knew that if by any chance I ever made contact with Traudl, questions and answers would have to be dealt with in German. I worked hard on my side. I obtained a German/English dictionary and set myself the task of memorising two or three new words every day. For me, this was a considerable undertaking, but I had a powerful incentive to study — conversing with Traudl.

CHAPTER
TWELVE

The mood in our working party was extremely high. The pleasant surroundings were to our liking. After the horrors of Upper Silesia, this was a veritable holiday camp. After two years of misery, we were all set to enjoy the pleasant quirk of fate that had placed us here. There was not a single complaint about any member of the party not giving satisfaction on the jobs they were doing. Our food from the Kur Hotel was satisfactory and the Red Cross parcels supplemented our diet nicely. So what more could a body want?

Take twenty men, feed them, make them fit, lock them up every night after work and what have you got? Big trouble. All those healthy hormones being generated — and what do you tell them? Forget it and go to sleep? Unfortunately, hormones don't listen.

The German army guards were very understanding and allowed us to play football on a piece of spare ground adjacent to the camp as there wasn't enough room in our compound. On Sundays we would play for two or three hours at a time. Those who didn't want to play or watch were locked in the camp while the guards supervised the game. Football helped us to get rid of some surplus energy, but the underlying problem remained. The rooftop demonstrations we have nowadays in our prisons, the fights with wardens, prisoners taking hostages and other types of misconduct all stem from the same source — overactive hormones.

Some of the lads were working near a group of Greek girls in the village and found them quite receptive to their advances. There was, of course, no possibility of any contact with them during the day, even though the ladies indicated where their living quarters were. So began the first talks in the barracks of how to get out of the camp at night and, more importantly, how to get back in safely. Everyone agreed that a bolt-hole was a good idea, even if it was never used. The problem was to get from our bungalow into the compound without using any of the windows or doors. After a lot of discussion, a decision was reached which met with everyone's approval: using an existing trap-door in the floor of the kitchen. When we lifted the lid, it exposed a cavity under the floor about three feet deep, lined with wood, which had obviously been a cold store. Our planning experts removed the wood from the end nearest the wall and made a tunnel which came up through the floor of the outside toilet in the compound.

It sounds simple, but it wasn't easy to conceal. When it was finished, it was a first-class job and quite undetectable. The wooden floor in the outside toilet was also doctored. It became a lid which could be lifted and replaced easily when you knew how to do it. This made a good vantage point for checking whether it was safe to approach the barbed-wire perimeter fence, part of which could be lifted sufficiently above ground level to allow someone to crawl through, closing the wire behind him.

It was agreed that the use of the tunnel would be under the supervision of Bill James, who would decide when it was safe to use it and how many could go on the same night. It was also agreed that the tunnel would never be used for an escape "for real". In all working parties there was an unwritten rule that no-one should escape from a good camp, the proper procedure being to return to the main camp and then choose a camp where conditions would not be jeopardised by an escape. Shortly after its completion, another use was found for the mole-hole.

We were contacted by an escapee from another camp and agreed to put him up for one night. We asked a million questions, but his stock answer was: did we not get all this information from our radio? We didn't have a radio but it was then agreed that we should try to acquire one. The think-tank went into operation. We knew that if a radio was stolen anywhere in the surrounding area we would be the prime suspects, so we would have to go further afield. But how could we pinpoint a target in a strange mountain area? I finally came up with a possible solution. On odd occasions when I wasn't needed by the plasterers, I was used by the local van driver on trips to buy provisions for the village. This meant travelling to the nearest town, where we usually indulged in the luxury of an ersatz coffee at a gasthaus; on the sideboard of its sitting room lived a large radio.

It was agreed that the distance from the camp was about right to avoid suspicion, but could we cover the ten miles there and back, partly on the road and partly cross-country in the dark, lugging a heavy radio? Was it really a viable proposition, how many men would we need, when would we set out and how long would it take us? Every question required careful thought as our lives would depend on getting the answers correct. It was agreed that the prize was worth the effort. The next step was picking the team and setting the date, the latter being dependent on the weather, which would have to be good.

I would have to go, as I was the only one who knew the way; Bill decided he would be another and that he would make the entry with me and bring the set out. Another four stalwarts would be needed to cover us when we were inside. They would also be able to share the carrying of the radio back to camp. Jimmy was an automatic choice as one of the four, which made me feel a lot safer; we had a mutual understanding which did not require words and almost amounted to thought transference.

Such an undertaking showed the state of our minds after three years of war. In peacetime the whole idea would have seemed reprehensible, but here we were happily planning and discussing breaking, entering and stealing.

CHAPTER
THIRTEEN

Almost every working day now I saw Traudl somewhere in the village. In my heart I believed she went out of her way to make this possible. On my side, if a day went by without my seeing her I felt it was wasted. Then fate stepped in and the pace quickened. Herr Springer told the guard that they would be away on a certain day and could they please arrange for me to have some gainful employment elsewhere. I wasn't very pleased about this until I heard where it was: the basement of the hotel where Traudl lived. The job was to pick out the bad potatoes from the good ones in the hotel cellar cold store — a real stinker of a job in more ways than one, especially for a fresh air fiend like myself.

But this time I was more than happy to take on the chore. To have the chance of perhaps meeting the lady of my dreams gave me quite a tingle and also a chance to work on my thought transference technique. I have always believed in telepathy and on this particular day it worked like a charm. So if you ever want to try it, make sure you have some smelly potatoes around. Within an hour of my arrival in the cellar there was the patter of feet coming down the stairs from the hotel.

There she was — Traudl with a basket over her arm for the family's ration of potatoes.

Can you imagine the odds against such a situation? For a POW on a working party suddenly to find himself alone with the girl of his dreams, with no-one around to disturb or distract them, was quite amazing. Yet that is exactly what happened.

Traudl looked very surprised to see someone in the cellar, but when she saw it was me she gave me a big wide-eyed smile of recognition, which I happily returned. The next ten minutes were taken up with introducing ourselves, at first very tentatively, but a rapport quickly built up between us and ended with my suggesting we meet some night after dark at the edge of the woods near the hotel. She was naturally a bit sceptical about the idea but I worked hard at convincing her that I could do it and in the end she agreed. I was shocked at how limited my German was and decided to work much harder with my little dictionary. The strange thing is that if I had been in the main Stalag in Lamsdorf I could have taken a real first-class course in German under a proper teacher. On the other hand if I had been in the main camp there would have been no incentive to learn the language.

Three of the lads had already tried out the tunnel outlet a few times to visit the Greek girls at their quarters in the village. However, the strain had become so great on them that their outings became fewer and eventually died out altogether, they having decided in favour of a quiet and peaceful life. I confided in Joe and Jimmy about my proposed meeting with Traudl: they both agreed that I must be crackers to attempt such a thing, but they would give me all the help I needed. Dress was very important, nothing white or reflective, and shoes would have to be covered over with an old pair of socks to reduce noise to a minimum. The route I would take was worked out between the three of us and I was warned that after clearing the camp lights I would have to stop and wait until my eyes re-adjusted to the darkness.

I told Bill about my date and he wished me luck and said that I would be out on my own that night, which suited me fine as I had no wish to bump into any of my own pals. I was reminded by Bill that there was a curfew on, and if I got into trouble outside it would be disaster for the whole camp. So at all costs I must avoid trouble.

The next day Traudl appeared on her daily walk with the baby and I gave her a nod of confirmation that our tryst was on the agenda. She smiled her acknowledgement. Now my nerves began to jangle. What had I committed myself to, and would I be brave enough to see it through? The enormity of the whole idea suddenly came into focus. I was going to risk my life for the possible reward of a kiss and a cuddle — if I managed to make the rendezvous and if Traudl turned up. My head was telling me I had lost my marbles and should stay in bed after lights out, but my heart was shouting that I should give it a try. In this type of contest, I don't know of anyone who has listened to their head rather than their heart.

CHAPTER
FOURTEEN

The weather could not have been better for my first attempt at breaking out of camp. It had been a beautiful sunny day with clear skies and good visibility. I had also checked that there would be no moonlight that night.

My nerves were jangling like a fire alarm bell and the strain on my innards was horrendous. I knew that I couldn't show the state I was in or Jimmy would never have agreed to my going out. So there I was, looking cool, calm and collected until it was time to go. After work we all made our way back to camp for a wash and change of clothes. Believe it or not, hygiene standards were extremely high; we had all learned that hygiene was easier than delousing. We all followed our normal routine. The evening meal was collected from the hotel, pleasurably eaten; then followed the customary dish-washing and cleaning of the billet. After dinner everyone settled down to relating the adventures of the day or being bored to death listening to other people's stories, which of course we had heard time and time again.

At last the guard came to make the evening roll-call, which he did with his usual care and efficiency. Then we were safely locked in for the night, or so they thought. Timing was now critical. If the guard followed his normal routine, I had only ten minutes to clear the camp. Jimmy and Joe opened the trap-door in the kitchen while I was dressing, and with their best wishes ringing in my ears I went down the hole and through to the outside toilet before I could even think of changing my mind. I replaced the toilet floor carefully, quickly checked the coast was clear and, without further ado, ran across the compound to the barbed-wire fence. In a couple of minutes I got through Joe's cleverly prepared hook-on gate at the bottom of the fence, and after carefully replacing it I reached the safety of the trees.

At this point I should have been able to relax and prepare myself for the next part of the outing. Instead I had to move like lightning and drop my trousers as all the years of constipation that I had suffered came to an abrupt end. I had literally scared the shit out of myself.

By the time I regained my composure, the problem of adjusting my eyes to the darkness was completely overcome. The visibility made me move with less caution than I should have to the safety of the woods on the other side of the road and onto the path leading to the village. It suddenly dawned on me that I might not be able to negotiate the few hundred yards to the spot where I hoped Traudl would be waiting for me. The path was almost invisible and my feet were warning me when I strayed onto rougher ground or it became too grassy. I walked with my arms outstretched and hands clasped together so that twigs and branches couldn't blind me if I got too near the trees. My ears were working overtime but fortunately on this first trip there was no wind to create any strange noises to jangle my already overstretched nerves.

Hidden animal instincts must have taken over and soon I was moving more freely and, more importantly, faster. In the excitement of solving the early problems, I had almost forgotten the object of the whole operation. With the adrenalin flowing, it all came flooding back and elation set in. There was a break in the trees where it seemed to be very light compared with the blackness of the woods. Suddenly I had reached the rendezvous point. Standing still and watching for Traudl was a tremendous relief — a bit like having climbed a mountain and enjoying the moment you have reached the peak. A new thought came to mind: even if Traudl didn't turn up, this would be a night to remember.

A slight movement to my left alerted me, and Traudl and I were re-united. There is no need to go into details of the next hour. I am sure everyone can remember his or her first big date. It can be awkward under normal circumstances, but here was I in a village under curfew, in enemy territory, trying to communicate in a foreign language of which I knew only a few words. We managed so well that we decided our next meeting should be indoors, since courting in the great outdoors at this altitude in winter was not on. Traudl showed me where her bedroom window was, at the back of the hotel, and conveniently on the ground floor. When we had a date in future, this window would be left unlatched and it wouldn't matter what time I arrived. Likewise, if anything went wrong and I didn't arrive at all it meant that Traudl would not be at risk wandering around at night after curfew. After a prolonged goodnight kiss, we decided time was up and I had to start back to camp and embark on the part of the night I hadn't thought about — breaking back into camp. Now I realised why the other blokes had stopped going out — the mere thought of getting back into camp was quite daunting, perhaps more hazardous than breaking out.

Making my way back through the woods seemed more difficult than before, and seemed to take twice as long. Once misgivings had set in, I almost lost the path. Everyone else was tucked up in a warm bed snoring away and here was I in the middle of the bloody woods wondering if I would reach the camp before dawn and praying that our guard was a sound sleeper. Fear spurred me on a bit faster and eventually I reached the edge of the woods. After a carefully reconnoitre of the camp area, I made my way to Joe's trap door in the perimeter fence. The camp lights all seemed to be spotlights focused on me, but I forced myself to move through the gap, carefully closing it behind me. A slow crawl followed to the toilet hut door, which I inched open and then crawled in. Frantically lifting the trap door, I moved quickly down into the tunnel and replaced the floor above me. Then I fainted. The relief of not having to concentrate on my movements had finally caught up with me. I could have quite happily gone to sleep in this little piece of no-man's land. When I came to, I completed the operation and very quietly undressed and slipped into my bunk. In no time I had passed into oblivion.

CHAPTER
FIFTEEN

After the success of the first trip, the amorous outings became a regular routine. The only time they were curtailed in any way was due to weather conditions. When there was fresh snow on the ground after roll-call, it wasn't practical to risk making obvious tracks. After it had been well beaten down around the compound, however, I did go out in the snow. But when there was heavy cloud cover I also had to stay at home. One night I went out and everything went well until I entered the cover of the trees and it was totally dark — a blackness I had never experienced in my life before. It was like being inside a black velvet box inside a room with no windows or lights. After the first few yards of entering the woods I realised it would be impossible to go any further and when I turned round to go back I began to wonder how I was going to get out again. I had to resort to going down on my hands and knees and feeling for the path, then slowly inching forward until I was clear of the trees and the camp lights came into view.

Moonlit nights were also a problem as it could be too bright, and the combination of moonlight and snow made it impossible to go out. The best nights for travelling were the clear starlit nights with no wind, when visibility was fair and there were no strange noises to disturb my concentration. On such nights it was exhilarating to be on the move and clear of the camp and not to be a POW under constant surveillance.

It was on such a night that, having reached the shelter of the trees, I had the strangest feeling that something was wrong. I stopped, listening and watching for any movement, but everything seemed to be normal. The feeling persisted so I stepped off the path and squatted under a big fir tree and waited, breathing very gently. It didn't take long to spot the large man-sized shadow going along the path in the direction I should have been taking. My brain raced with possible explanations of this new development. The only solution was to wait a couple of minutes and turn back into camp. When I explained to Jimmy, Joe and Bill James what had transpired, we came to the conclusion that the guard had spotted me on one of my trips and, instead of doing a body-count in the barrack-room, had decided to follow and find out where I was going.

The guard in question at this particular time was a very nice bloke. Tall, good-looking and softly spoken, he had told us that he would do any boot repairs we required as this was a hobby of his. In return we were to give him no hassle. In fact he was so pleasant to have around that when we heard his wife was coming to visit for a weekend, we had a whip-round of odds and ends from our Red Cross parcels so they could have a tasty couple of days. It was strange to see this strapping big soldier with tears in his eyes, and it was worth it to see the smile of thanks from his wife. This same guard asked me to treat a nasty boil on his wrist because if he had returned to his Depot for treatment the chances of his being returned to our camp were slim. So, for both our sakes, I took on the job. In about a week, after treating it with a strong-smelling ointment, I extracted the big root, leaving a large hole which healed up nicely in about another week.

Having said all that, I have no doubt that he would have had no hesitation in doing his duty and reporting us to his seniors had he found us breaking any of the rules. So it was agreed that there would be no more "flying", as Bill called it, until further notice. It was during this time that it became clear what harm my love life had done to my nervous system.

Everything was fine for the first five nights that I stayed at home doing nothing but being bored. This should have had a good therapeutic effect on me but my hormones set up their own protest and almost killed me. We had turned in as usual after roll-call and I settled down to sleep after lights out, having spent a good healthy day in the beautiful mountain air. All went well until about two o'clock in the morning — the time I usually returned from visiting Traudl. Suddenly I was wide awake, but never in my life had I been so wide awake. The intense awareness of noises in the far distance was frightening and my whole body began to react to this super-sensitivity. Progressive palpitations followed and I felt that my heart was going to explode. Within seconds of waking I was in such a state that I felt that death could be the only conclusion of this attack.

But after reaching its peak, the attack slowly eased off and I lay in my bunk, drained both mentally and physically, and gradually slipped into a deep dreamless sleep. In the morning when Jimmy called me to get up, I told him what happened and asked him to report me sick as I felt totally incapable of work. However, after a day of complete rest, I recovered and almost forgot what I had been through. We discussed the possibility of restarting nocturnal outings but it was agreed that it was still too soon after the last incident, so I signalled this information to Traudl on her next walk through the village. To this she gave me an understanding nod and a disappointed pout.

Camp life went on as usual for another two humdrum weeks, and then, like a bolt out of the blue, in the middle of the night my eyes shot open and it happened all over again. This attack seemed worse than the first one. It followed the same pattern, leaving me totally wrung out and exhausted. The thought of these attacks recurring terrified me, and I felt from their severity that my body would eventually succumb. A side-effect was that I became afraid to go to sleep.

CHAPTER
SIXTEEN

Luckily, the acquisition of the radio intervened and took my mind off my own problems. It was the summer of 1943 and rumours were flying about regarding the state of the war. Up here in the mountains it was hard to believe that there was a world war going on. The weather was great, and we had plenty of food and acceptable clothing, but we always had a thirst to know what was going on in the real world. We felt the radio would be the answer, and if we were to start using the tunnel again it might as well be for the benefit of the whole camp.

The team having been picked, we decided to go out on the first clear moonless night. Most of the team had never broken out of camp before, so you can imagine the state of their nerves. Those of us who had been out before had to calm them down and convince them it would be a doddle. Personally, I wasn't looking forward to it one little bit. I knew my own capabilities in the dark, but how would the first-timers take to the new environment? It was a gigantic gamble, considering six men had to get out of camp and get back in again in a very limited time. We had all played games against the clock before for fun but this time we were laying our lives on the line. Was the prize really worth it? At least Jimmy and Bill were in the party, the other three being in the strong-man class. They were needed to carry the radio back over the mountain; Bill and I couldn't be relied on for this because of our gammy legs.

The weather held, the break-out sequence went like silk, the whole team behaving as if this was a nightly occurrence; with no untoward incidents we arrived at the target ahead of time. The gasthaus had just closed and the guests had all merrily departed. Bill and I reconnoitred the building to find a point of entry, which turned out to be a toilet window which had not yet been closed. After making sure there was no one in, we quickly and silently entered, knowing that Jimmy and the others were posted outside and would warn us of any danger if it came along. I had actually used this particular toilet on occasions and knew exactly where the room with the radio in it was. There was no-one in the passageway, so we moved on, and while Bill stood guard at the door with his right fist cocked, I rapidly disconnected the set. In a few seconds it was out the toilet window and into Busty's waiting arms.

The return trip to camp was made in a state of high jubilation, and the clear winter air at over two thousand feet lent wings to our weary legs. With everyone except Bill and myself taking turns at carrying our precious cargo, we made excellent time back to the camp. Speed was important in case the alarm was raised and our guard telephoned to check whether all his charges were safely tucked up in bed.

In the end, we never heard the theft mentioned in the village and we were never under suspicion. After all, who would think that such an escapade was possible?

CHAPTER
SEVENTEEN

Our triumphant return was greeted with great wonderment from the rest of the boys. After we had showed off our prize, it was stowed away in the kitchen tunnel entrance until we decided on a permanent site for it. We all agreed it wasn't sensible to keep it on the premises. Next night after roll-call, when we were safely locked in, the place was buzzing with excitement as we unearthed our newfound source of information and prepared to connect it up to our power source. Within minutes we discovered what Rabbie Burns meant when he wrote, "The best laid plans o' mice and men gang aft aglay". We discovered to our horror that our mains was at a different voltage from that in the village where we had stolen the set. The next step was to see if the whole of Karlsbrunn was on the same voltage as the camp. After a couple of days of asking around, we discovered that one side of the village was also on this different voltage. All we had to do was find a working point for the radio on the other side of the main road from the camp.

After various other possibilities were discarded, I suggested the cellar of the hotel where Traudl lived, depending on the availability of a power supply to operate the set. The outside door to the cellar was never locked but the door from the hotel to the cellar was locked and bolted from the inside. It was finally agreed to check this out as a first possible location, and within a couple of days we found out that there was a really archaic system of wiring in the cellar. There were no conduits at all and the various lights were fed from two insulated wires which ran along the arched roof. Halfway along the passageway we found a little empty room which didn't appear to be in use, so we decided that if we dug a hole and boxed it we could put the radio safely in there and make a lid which could be filled with earth, making it virtually undetectable. The insulation on the corridor wires would have to be tapped and two temporary leads connected to the set and removed after use.

Finally, the big night came when we were to test the set. Along with Vic, an air force bloke masquerading as army, I had the privilege of doing the initial trial run. I'll never forget that night. We went through the tedious rigmarole of setting everything up, switched on and Vic tuned in to Victor Sylvester at the Hammersmith Palais. He was ecstatic; I had difficulty convincing him he couldn't listen to the end of the programme.

A listening rota was set up — two men going out together — and so our BBC information service came into being. For the first time, the real news of the war was available to us.

CHAPTER
EIGHTEEN

It was around this time that we were told we would be taking part in a historic piece of remodelling of the Altvater mountain servicing. The electricity supply at the mountain top was from an old-fashioned generator and they wanted us to extend the supply cable from Karlsbrunn to the top of the mountain, about another two thousand feet. We were devastated and said that it would be an impossible task for our small working party. To our surprise, the authorities agreed and said they were going to supplement our workforce with a dozen ditch-diggers from the land of Oz.

The Aussies duly arrived and I have never seen such a hand-picked bunch of mobile muscle before or since. They were on a par with our own tame Aussie, Arthur. We had been told that there would be no mechanical help in the ditch-digging, but when we saw our new assistants, the job became a possibility. The work distribution was to be ten yards of ditch per day per man and everything worked out well, except when we struck solid rock. Then the dynamiter had to be called in.

Things didn't go too well with our new workmates, who tried to take over the nice quiet running of our camp. This led to continual resetting of Bill's knuckles as he dealt with them one at a time. But, just as all good things come to an end, so too did this bad job. Our gallant allies were duly returned whence they came and the normal routine returned. This also meant that I could safely resume my love life with Traudl, which had ceased on the arrival of the Aussies as they were never told anything of our nocturnal activities. We also suffered a news blackout during this period.

CHAPTER
NINETEEN

The war news was turning very much in our favour now and the effect was beginning to show in a variety of ways. Any mention of the Eastern Front brought a look of terror to the face of any German. The war was going badly in Russia and troops returning home on leave were telling horror stories of conditions at the front. The enormous numbers of wounded returning home also told their own story.

Can you imagine the impact of the loss of 240,000 men in the Stalingrad area alone through fighting, hunger, cold and disease? It was now January 1943. There was still no significant breakthrough and talk of a second front in France was still only talk. The death-toll continued to rise on all fronts.

The flags and banners with their Swastika inserts seemed to hang rather limply now, the German chins seemed to droop a bit and the buoyancy that had been there a couple of years before was missing. We were not having to endure the full impact of war because places like Sudetenland and East Prussia lived fairly comfortably off their local produce and were not strategic targets for the Allied bombers.

The war had no effect on my love life and I was seeing Traudl about once or twice a week, though how she put up with my immature lovemaking I'll never know. The snowy winters provided a number of problems for us. Our arrangements for my entry to the hotel, through her unlatched bedroom window, worked fine in beautiful summer weather but it was not feasible after a fresh fall of snow; the local gossips would have had a field day. Traudl decided to provide me with a front door key as there was always a well trodden path to the door. We agreed that if fresh snow fell after lights out, my visit would automatically be cancelled.

Since I had started making these night visits, I had learned how to move quietly, and in situations where there was total darkness to feel with both my hands and feet as I moved. Even to this day I get shouted at for creeping up on people because I move so quietly.

Traudl came up with a brilliant idea during our first winter in Karlsbrunn. The snow at altitude is perfect for much of the time, and like most of the villagers Traudl had been brought up on skis. She and her younger brother were about the most daring skiers in the village. Sometimes I could hardly bear to watch their dangerous antics through the trees, but Traudl just laughed and said there was nothing to it. When I remonstrated with her to be more careful, she suggested that the way to cure my fear for her was to learn to ski myself.

Traudl said that there was an old pair of her father's skis in the attic and she had spare sticks which I could use, so all we had to do was arrange a suitable day and time for my first lesson. The guard knew I had been having bad headaches so he was quite amenable to my having a day off. During his time off, I left the camp and went to meet Traudl on the mountain. After about two hours' tuition from an accomplished skier like her I was able to do the basic snowplough and eventually a pretty poor Christiana. Other lessons followed when possible, and eventually I could herringbone up the slopes and ski down them.

The skiing era didn't last very long, because when some of the other lads miraculously acquired skis, it didn't take long for the guard to ferret out the hiding places of all the skis, which then disappeared forever.

CHAPTER
TWENTY

Fate must have decided that we had had things too good for too long. Our nice guard was removed and replaced by two "Wasser Polaks". This happened about the beginning of 1944 and the new policy was a general tightening up as regards POWs. Their value was increasing as the German situation deteriorated. Apparently, if five or more prisoners escaped together, the matter had to be reported directly to the Führer. For us the holiday was over, and slowly a feeling of animosity crept in between the guards and ourselves.

This erupted violently one day. We were all returning to camp in the evening after work; as we entered the compound, the younger of the two guards decided to help matters along and pushed the prisoner in front of him through the gate. The unfortunate guard didn't know that there were two men in our camp you didn't push around, one being Bill James and the other Davey Jay. I don't know what Bill's reaction would have been but Davey's was instantaneous.

A quick shuffle of feet brought him round to face the guard, another fast adjustment to balance his body properly, then a lightning short right which hit the guard between the eyes with the full force of Davey's weight behind it. Another shuffle of feet brought Davey round again and he completed his entry into the barrack-room. Those of us who saw the incident were shocked at how quickly it happened and very smartly got into our compound, closing the gate behind us. We knew there would be an aftermath but none of us could have guessed just how horrible this would be.

Pandemonium reigned in our hut as word of what had happened went round the others. One of the lads watching at the window reported that the guard had crawled into his own hut. The calmest bloke in our hut was Davey, who sat on his bunk and tried to ignore all the fuss, though possibly he was going over in his mind the trouble that would arise from his uncontrolled action.

The waiting became intolerable. The guard who had been hit was trying to piece together what had happened when the other guard asked him if he had seen his damaged face, so he looked in the mirror. Right on cue we heard the screams of rage from the guards' hut. Within seconds, two very angry guards were in our hut and all hell broke loose. When we actually saw the damage that one punch from Davey had done we were shocked. Both the guard's eyes were rapidly discolouring and the bridge of his nose was swelling and taking on horrible rainbow hues. Somewhere he had lost his forage cap but in his right hand he had his unsheathed bayonet and his fellow guard had his rifle at the ready.

In a blind, mad rage the guard was swinging his bayonet in wide circles until finally he had Davey cornered alone. The other guard had the rest of us herded at the other end of the room and made it clear to us there was a bullet up the spout and the safety catch was off.

Davey was sitting on the edge of his bunk; the guard's vicious swing with the bayonet caught him unawares and hit him on the crown of the head. Blood spurted and we all shouted or screamed but the guard with the rifle again made his intentions quite clear. He would brook no interference in what was going on behind him. Davey saw the next blow coming and held up his hand to ward it off. The blade sliced down through his fingers, causing another surge of blood and more screams from us.

The sight of the blood must have helped to bring the guard back to his senses, and as suddenly as they stormed in they stormed out. First thing on the agenda was to tend to Davey's wounds as he was in a state of shock. Bill quickly decided that the Village Director should be notified and Busty was dispatched over the wire to attend to this. Davey required immediate hospitalisation, and God knows what the guards would get up to next. They might decide that, having gone this far, they might as well complete the job and wipe out the whole lot of us.

However, nothing further happened before the Director arrived. He promptly relieved the guards of duty pending their return to barracks and replaced them with temporary civil guards. He arranged transport to take Davey to hospital and then took a detailed report of the events. In one hour, our peaceful world had been turned upside down. The death knell had been sounded in our mountain Shangri-la, although we were lucky to have had two years of peace in this haven — especially when you think of the mass murder that was being committed all around us in the name of Christianity.

CHAPTER
TWENTY-ONE

Traudl and I were naturally devastated by the turn of events, as it now became virtually impossible for me to carry on with my night visits to the hotel. Our romance would now be restricted to the odd loving glance if we saw each other in the village. To my mind this was a sad end to a remarkable piece of wooing but, on the credit side, it would give my badly shredded nerves a chance to recover.

It didn't take very long before we were informed that the working party would be wound up and all personnel returned to the main camp in Lamsdorf. This was extremely sad news after a happy two-year break in the Altvater mountains.

Many people might ask why no-one had escaped from such an easy camp, but it would have been extremely unfair to destroy a good situation like Karlsbrunn for those who had no wish to escape. The recommendation to anyone wanting to make a break from a good working party, of which there were very few, was that they return to the main camp and go out to a camp where another escape wouldn't do any harm.

Jimmy, Joe and I talked the whole thing over again and decided that we should now do something concrete about getting home, as it really looked like the war could go on for many years yet. In our present frame of mind we were ready to face the risks this entailed rather than sit tight in a worsening situation. The three of us, individually and collectively, began planning the complicated business of leaving Germany and returning home. I managed to steal a few minutes with Traudl in the cellar of the hotel one day and told her of our plans. She immediately insisted that we include her as there were many ways in which her help would be invaluable. For example, she could give us up-to-date information on the route we would be using, as travel restrictions changed continually due to bombing and troop movements. All three of us agreed that Traudl's plan made the most sense. After we returned to the main camp at Lamsdorf, we would arrange to come back to Sudetenland on a bad working party, escape from there and make our way back to Karlsbrunn, where Traudl would arrange to hide us while we made our final preparations for the journey home.

Everything began to move quickly now and only a week later we were back in Lamsdorf renewing our contacts with our Signals friends and all the others we had come to know in the past few years. It took about a week to tell them our adventures over the past two years and for them to bring us up to date on what had been happening in the main camp. We then got down to the business of finding out who the contact man was for the escape committee, and Jimmy and Joe arranged an appointment with them. The result of this meeting was completely negative. We were informed that no help could be given to first-time escapees. Jimmy got quite annoyed with me when I raged on about this stupid policy of having to prove that you were a loser before they would help you, instead of encouraging people who might get home on their first attempt. Why would anyone in their right mind keep giving assistance and material help to a constant loser who kept coming back like a rubber ball?

This meant that we were now out on our own, and any problems that arose would have to be solved by ourselves. I was still very optimistic about what lay ahead of us. The next step was finding a job back in Sudetenland and, soon enough, our chance came along.

Three replacements were required in a factory in the small town of Jagerndorf, which was about ten miles from Bad Karlsbrunn and suited our purposes admirably. So we volunteered for the job, and were accepted. We told our friends of our intentions; they wished us luck and a safe journey home. They also voiced their opinion that three was a crowd for such a venture. We reassured them that as a team we had survived so far.

A couple of days later the guard who was to accompany us to the job picked us up and we were off on our travels again. The pleasure on entering Sudetenland again was as great as the last time, and the three of us felt like children setting out on a great adventure, the first chapter of which would begin when we arrived at our new camp.

We were marched in through the standard wall of barbed wire, which of course would be no problem to Joe's educated pliers. However, when we came face to face with the concrete blockhouse with iron-barred windows and barbed wire on the outside, you could have knocked us down with the proverbial feather. When the guard handed us over and we were allocated our bunks, we were then locked in until mealtime. Inside were concrete walls, concrete floors and a concrete ceiling — and those damned iron bars looked more horrible from the inside than they had from the outside.

CHAPTER
TWENTY-TWO

Being left alone inside this impregnable fortress was possibly the best thing that could have happened to us at this time. The three of us had all very different thoughts about the situation we were now in and had the opportunity to express our views in private. Jimmy was of the opinion that maybe we were being given the opportunity to call the whole thing off and, under the circumstances, I had to agree with him fully. Joe just couldn't believe that it could end with a whimper and not with a bang.

We agreed to discuss it with the camp leader and explain that we had come to this camp for the sole purpose of escaping and, if he had no objections to this, ask him if he had any ideas on how we might achieve a night escape from such formidable premises. This we did after having a meal and a natter with all the lads when they came in after work. His advice was to say nothing to anyone about the escape plans, with the exception of the two Glasgow men whom we had met with the others.

Over the years I have found that rather than rant at fate for being unkind at times, it is better to be a little philosophical and to count your blessings. It's amazing how often things come right in the end. Who would have believed that in the present circumstances there was any glimmer of hope that we would achieve our objective?

One of the Scots boys was called Danny and he almost ended himself with laughter when he heard that we had arrived in a strange camp on Friday and wanted to make our break on the Sunday night. He went on to explain that he and his friend had their escape planned for the coming June and that they had been setting it up for almost a year, so what was our hurry? We explained to him that four years had always been our target and that if we were prisoners as long as that, then we would have a go at getting home. Time was up.

Mentally we were prepared to have a go and the three of us felt that any delay at this time would probably erode our plans and let us sink into a state of apathy. Thinking about escaping and actually doing it were two very different things, which accounted for the small number of escapees. After all, you were literally laying your life on the line when you broke out of camp and not many were prepared to do that.

Danny and his friend had a quick pow-wow and told us that if we were so desperate to go now, we were very welcome to use the facilities they had set up. We naturally remonstrated with them that this would be detrimental to their escape later but they insisted so heartily that I got the impression they were glad to get the idea of them having to go brought to an end. They then proceeded in great detail to explain that their preparations were complete and drew us diagrams of what they had done and how they had done it.

As we agreed, a daytime break was out of the question because you need time to get clear of the area before the manhunt starts, whereas if you start after roll-call at night, then you have until the next morning to get clear. The two boys had worked this out correctly and came up with the most astonishing method of overcoming the problem of getting out of the barrack-room. They knew that the roof, the walls and the floor were out of the question, so it had to be through the windows, which to their minds were the weakest part of the set-up. They went on to explain how they dealt with the vertical iron bars set in concrete, passing through lateral flat bars also set in concrete.

The upright bar, which had to be cut, was pencil-marked above and below the two lateral bars. A rope was then tied around the upper laterals and wound tight until the mark to be cut was exposed, then, with a very fine-bladed hacksaw, the bar was cut through. When the cut was completed, chewing gum was inserted in the space and the rope was removed, allowing the lateral bar to return to its normal position. This cut was repeated on the lower part of the bar and again chewing gum was inserted in the space and the lateral bar returned to its normal position. We were invited to have a go at finding out which bar was the one to be removed, and though the three of us tried our damnedest, we had to admit defeat.

When we asked Danny to show us which one it was, he laughed and said that when we were ready to go they would take the bar out and when we were gone they would put it back. This worried me a little, as I would have liked to see that it actually worked; timing was critical once we started our break. However, it would probably have taken us the best part of a year to get to where we could have managed on our own, and here was Danny handing it to us on a plate. Joe said that he had total trust in our new friends and Jimmy said that it would be all right on the night. And none of us even dreamed of asking where they got the hacksaw!

CHAPTER
TWENTY-THREE

Our main objective now was to appear to be settling in to our new environment, and this we did thoroughly. In this we made a terrible, but simple, mistake, for which we were to suffer badly. Sunday was a day of rest for everyone, but as the football pitch was now clear of its winter coating of snow, the lads decided to have their first game of the season. When they found out that the three of us played, they were highly delighted as it gave them two full teams. In view of what we had planned, you might think that at least one of three sane men would have realised that this was not a sensible thing to do, but we indulged ourselves in a full ninety minutes of our favourite sport. The old adage about living and learning is a lot of rubbish.

Since we had arrived in the new camp, I had checked the star formations at night and had lined them up in the direction that we had to take to hit Karlsbrunn. I was, of course, presupposing that we would have a clear sky on the big night. I had acquainted myself with our route on the local maps we had but, of course, there was the black-out to be taken into consideration, plus the curfew, plus the Home Guard, plus dogs in kennels and farms that could raise alarms, plus the unknown and the unexpected. It would have been so much easier to sit and wait until our gallant troops came to relieve us — but, as I said, hormones don't listen.

That Sunday night we did our final checking and planning, and on Monday morning we went off and did a normal day's work. We were never inside the factory; it was said to be a parachute production outfit, though we couldn't verify this in any way because of the high-security conditions surrounding the area. Anyway, we were not going to be there long enough to find out.

The weather was at its very best, with a clear sky and a light spring breeze; if it lasted through the night, it would be perfect for our trip. I knew there would be no moon that night and it looked as if there would be no cloud cover either. At least the elements were working in our favour.

Finally, our working day was over and we were feeling no ill-effects from the football, so we returned to the camp in good spirits. We began to make the final preparations after our evening meal in order to be ready to go after roll-call, leaving no signs behind that we had ever been there at all. Danny and the others still had their doubts that we would really make the break, but we finally convinced them that we were leaving and that we would send them a postcard when we got home.

Jimmy, Joe and I had a final huddle to make sure that there were no last-minute second thoughts, as the effort had to be one hundred per cent, and the three of us confirmed that it was all systems go. Danny and his mate had the equipment they required to release the bar in the window, and we had the clothes we were to travel in safely out of sight. Our order of dress was normal underwear and shirt, boots and socks, dark trousers and a heavy dark pullover. Other than this, we would each carry a light snack to be consumed on the march. In addition Jimmy would have a first-aid kit, Joe would have his pliers and I would have my maps and a small battery torch I had acquired. The reason that we were travelling so light was that this first part of the break had to be successful. If it failed, then would come the time for improvisation.

CHAPTER
TWENTY-FOUR

Roll-call. The next half-hour could possibly be the most exciting time of our lives, or — with bad luck — it could be the end of our lives. This was always the alternative when you left camp without permission, and I knew the horrible feeling I had had in the pit of my stomach every time I had gone to see Traudl. I also knew that Jimmy and Joe must be going through hell at the thought of what was in front of them. Fortunately, they showed nothing of this while the guards went through their dreary routine of counting their flock for the last time that day. I can vouch for it that, on this occasion, everyone was present and correct.

Finally satisfied, the guards withdrew; as soon as the key clicked in the lock, Danny's team attacked the window that we were to go through. We three began to change into the clothes we were going to leave in. Time was now of the essence, as we knew that in about fifteen minutes the first perimeter patrol would begin and before that we would have to be completely clear of the camp.

All three of us hit the finishing tape together in our personal preparations and Danny signalled that the window was cleared for Joe to operate on the barbed wire on the outside — which he promptly did. Danny had told us that when we hit the ground on the outside we should get going immediately, and he would close up the wire and restore everything to normal. This was an amazing blessing with time so short. Jimmy was to go first as he was the biggest; if he got out safely, then our first problem was solved. He had worked out how he would make the difficult exit through the space in the bars. Joe and I watched him very carefully. In a few seconds he was out and dropped to the ground. Joe followed, and I was right behind him.

With a quick "thumbs up" to the boys watching at the window, we were off and running to the part of the perimeter fence that we had decided to go through. In about half a minute, Joe had cut enough barbed wire to let us crawl through, and half a minute later he had it resealed. This done, we stole away to the cover of some trees nearby. As soon as we were in cover, we silently hugged each other in congratulation, and then it became my problem to take the lead and guide us to the promised land which, in this instance, was Bad Karlsbrunn.

Away from the lights of the compound, the darkness became more intense, but our eyes rapidly adjusted and it was a beautiful clear starlit night — better visibility than many of the nights that I had already been out. The adrenalin was still running high, and we had to put as much distance as possible between ourselves and the camp. It took about five minutes before I picked up the road that would take us out of town and finally on to Karlsbrunn. Twenty minutes later we were almost clear of the last houses and reaching the open countryside. Our plan was to use the main road as much as possible, as this was the only way we could cover the distance involved and reach our destination before dawn. We removed the heavy socks that we had pulled over our boots when we were moving through the area with houses and would put them on again when we felt we were too loud. They would have worn through too quickly if we had kept them on all the time.

We kept silent while we were marching but stopped at odd intervals for a confab. We even had to stifle our giggles on the first rest when we all agreed that our eyes and ears felt ten times as big as normal.

Our first problem came when we approached a village right on the main road. How were we going to deal with it? The choice was either to walk straight through or go round it. For safety's sake we decided to take the long route. In daylight it might have been a simple detour, but at night we lost so much valuable time and got into such a mess that we decided to take the direct route in future. It began to dawn on us that at our present rate of progress we were not going to reach our target on time, so we agreed to step up the pace. This is when we discovered what our stupid game of football had done to us. Within an hour of going at the faster speed all three of us were feeling the effect on our leg muscles, and as we were almost continually climbing now, the strain was getting worse all the time. We knew that we had to be under cover before daybreak; the alarm would be raised by then, and to be out in the open would be fatal. I had no idea where we might hide safely for a whole day in the woods.

By my reckoning we still had about ten kilometres to go and dawn was only a couple of hours away. Normally this would have been no great problem, but with our leg muscles screaming for rest, it was becoming cripplingly clear that the odds were against us arriving on time. We stopped for a couple of precious minutes and talked over the situation. We decided it was a case of heads down and try our damnedest. Maybe the pains would go away. They didn't, but they didn't get any worse, and I think what saved us was that none of us wanted to be the one to say that he couldn't go on.

There were no more villages to go through, so it was a straight slog all the way now. The miles slowly rolled by and, in these final stages, I think our brains became numb, although I can't say the same for our legs, which continued to complain bitterly about their treatment. The sky was becoming noticeably lighter when we reached the top of our climb, and this was where we had to part company; Jimmy and Joe were to make their way to a hut in the forest which was once used by hunters. We had discovered it when we worked in Karlsbrunn and had stowed away a couple of blankets there, which would be very useful for the boys. I now had to make my way down behind the village to Traudl's hotel and see if it was safe to climb in the bedroom window which, God and Traudl willing, I might find unlocked.

We said our "auf wiedersehens" and arranged our contact times. We parted company, hoping that all would go well for both parties.

CHAPTER
TWENTY-FIVE

Jimmy and Joe were to keep under cover in the hut while I tried to forge some kind of travel documents for us. Without these it would be impossible to travel by train. From what we had learned over the last four years, rail was the only way we could possibly cover the distance from Sudetenland to the northern coast at Stettin. From Stettin we would try to stow away on a ship going to Sweden. To do a good job of the travel documents I would, of course, have to have warm comfortable surroundings and a source of the necessary materials. Traudl's bedroom was the obvious place, and the source was to be Traudl herself. How lucky can you get?

When I parted from the boys, I worked my way down to the rear of the hotel via the trees on the upper side of the village, and by this time it was almost daylight. After a quick look around to check that the coast was clear, and a smart walk with my heart in my mouth. I was directly under Traudl's window. With a prayer on my lips I jumped for the ledge below the window and pushed up the lower part of the window. It opened smoothly.

Seconds later, I was over the sill and safely into my favourite bedroom. Once inside, I watched intently for a while to see if there was any movement in the vicinity, but everything remained peaceful. The night-light at the bedside came on and Traudl was holding out her welcoming arms. In no time at all I was snuggled down and felt as if I would never get out of bed again. The euphoria didn't last long; Traudl whispered that it was time for her to go on duty and that when she left the room I would have to lock the door from the inside so that on-one could enter, even with a pass key.

This led to a very frightening experience for the poor girl, as it was twelve hours later before I heard her knocking to get in. When I opened the door she was in a terrible state; she had tried to wake me at various times during the day without success, and only at six o'clock in the evening did she succeed, finally delivering the meal that she had lovingly prepared earlier.

As she was now off duty, we had a long talk about all that had happened since we last met. Then we discussed what was to be done about the documents we needed. Traudl thought that the simplest solution would be for us to carry the normal German identity cards; when she showed me hers, I agreed that to copy them might just be a possibility, given that we could obtain materials to do the job. And so to bed.

Next day I began the search for paper as close as possible in texture and colour to the ID card that had to be copied. I finally found blank pages in some old books that would do nicely. Traudl produced a variety of pens and different inks because, apart from the print, there were also rubber stamps to be copied. Only when we had all the materials together did it finally dawn on me that the most important thing for an ID card was missing — our photographs. I nearly cried.

Traudl wisely pointed out that passport and ID photos were never really a close likeness anyway. She then produced all the photographs of men from the family albums that were approximately the right size. Not one of the photos looked like any of us three. We made a choice of three, on the most tenuous of grounds. One appeared to be blond, so that would be Jimmy. Of the other two, one couldn't possibly be Joe so he would have to be me. That left one, who must be Joe. In the end, it was all very simple.

I spent four tense and tiring hours working on the first ID card copy, but when I stopped and really looked at it, the result was so poor that it got torn up and thrown in the fire. Instead of feeling despondent about my first attempt, I buckled down to the fact that I would have to do better and in the next two days produced what I thought were a couple of masterpieces. Traudl agreed that they were not bad and came up with the brilliant idea of acquiring three plastic holders for them, which would help to disguise them a bit. At a quick glance, folded with the photo and identity particulars outward inside the holders, they looked quite authentic, we thought. Next day I finished the two pages that would be exposed on the third ID and decided not to bother with the eagle, swastika and other details on the inside as they wouldn't be seen. Thus I completed the third and final document.

At least that's what I thought. When the boys and I made our rendezvous in the woods that night and I explained to them what I had done, they were both adamant that the third card should be completed and it didn't matter how tired or fed up I was. So I had to go back to the drawing board. Their insistence on the completion of the third card saved our lives later, as it turned out. Next day, I grudgingly finished the job. We were now at the stage where we must move on, as we had endangered Traudl for far too long.

CHAPTER
TWENTY-SIX

Our next step was to collect the escape clothing that we had hidden away in Karlsbrunn previously, including the iron rations we would be carrying to help us reach our destination. These consisted mainly of chocolate and biscuits and a few tins of meat, all of which had been saved from our Red Cross parcels. Also included in this valuable hoard was the German currency that we had acquired from various sources. This was added to the money we had accumulated on our last visit to the main camp. Two old briefcases and an old rucksack completed our new civilian outfits, as all of the workmen carried these, or something similar, when they were on the move. Our shaving gear, plus a towel, soap and comb, had come with us from Jagerndorf and would naturally be included.

Traudl had been working hard to teach me the most likely phrases that might be required on the journey, such as buying train tickets or asking directions, or things you might want to ask in a restaurant. Her advice was that the best person to ask was a policeman. This made good sense to me as they have local knowledge. At home they're the most helpful of people and Traudl said they were the same in Germany.

We had been a bit concerned about the weather; there had been a slight flurry of snow on the day that we decided our preparations were complete. However, it cleared quite quickly and the spring sun shone again, so we made up our minds to get on with it. The decision made, we were off next day, at the ungodly hour of 2a.m.

This part of the journey required us to go on foot from Karlsbrunn, mainly downhill, some eight or nine miles to the railhead at Wurbenthal, the same station we had arrived at two years before when we came from upper Silesia, and also on our return to Sudetenland fairly recently. There was a local bus which made this run but, after working in the area for two years, we couldn't take the chance of someone recognising us.

Traudl and I said our final farewells, and after a tearful parting and a promise to return, I left to join the boys and continue our journey home. Since we had broken out of camp in Jagerndorf I don't think I ever entertained one negative thought about being recaptured. Even though we still had over two hundred and fifty miles to cover as the crow flies, I felt it was a one-way journey. It is just as well that we didn't know that fate was setting up one of the biggest booby-traps in history.

At two o'clock on the morning of 25 March we set off at a leisurely pace, knowing that at this stage there was no urgency. We had lots of time to reach the station and catch our train. March in the mountains could be very chancy for weather, but today there was a real touch of spring in the air, which transferred itself to our legs. We all felt fit after our enforced rest, but there was a touch of sadness at finally leaving Karlsbrunn, which had sheltered us from the horrors of war for two peaceful years.

The road we were now taking was reputedly traffic-free at night, and tonight was no exception. We knew there was only one small village to pass and our rapid downhill progress needed to be slowed down drastically. Our arrival at Wurbenthal had to coincide with the early morning movements of the local population. An old barn at the roadside provided us with the ideal shelter for an hour's rest. Joe had to move from the original heap of straw that he sat on when it began to move, but he apologised politely and found another unoccupied spot with no nest of mice. Once we set off, the aim was not to be furtive, but at all costs to avoid being conspicuous. When we finally entered the town, there was enough early morning movement to keep us comfortable as we made our way to the railway station.

I wonder if you can imagine how I felt when I had to approach that little window and ask for three tickets to Sagan. It would either be the beginning or the end of our journey. What would happen? Stagefright maybe, with no words coming out. Total loss of memory of the German phrases I had so painstakingly learned? Maybe Jimmy or Joe wouldn't mind going over and buying the tickets. It was the bren-gun situation at La Capelle all over again. Why couldn't I keep my mouth shut instead of saying: "All right, I'll do that!"?

When the dreaded moment came, I detached myself completely and watched from outside as my body went to the window, asked for the tickets, paid for them and received the change, then turned and walked away almost jauntily. Jimmy and Joe congratulated me on my cool behaviour, but I didn't tell them how it had been done.

CHAPTER
TWENTY-SEVEN

I thought that the most difficult part of the journey was over. The problem of buying the tickets had been giving me nightmares ever since I had been elected to do it. I had thought that three fit young men in civilian clothes would stick out like a sore thumb, when we should have been wearing a uniform of some kind — any kind. I can only imagine that we had spent so much time in France that perhaps we had picked up a slightly French aura. As the Laval scheme, which used French civilian workers, was in full swing, maybe we were mistaken for French.

Our train was due to leave in about five minutes, and a fair number of people were hanging about waiting to board, so we just followed the general trend of looking tired and fed up. Soon we were seated uncomfortably on the hard benches in the quietest part of the coach we could find. Following almost everyone else's example, we leaned back and closed our eyes as the train slowly and noisily left the station. It turned out to be one of those trains we had heard about — the kind you could get off to pick flowers while it's in motion and rejoin. It also seemed to stop at the least excuse and very often for no reason at all. But it was better than walking and there would be faster sections on the way north, we hoped. Otherwise, it seemed, we were doomed to spend the rest of our lives on this train.

Sagan surprised us at about midday, and quite a few passengers got off with us. We found ourselves walking stiffly, like John Wayne. Maybe he travelled a lot on the old trains with wooden seats. It certainly knocks hell out of your circulation.

If our intelligence information turned out to be correct, then there was a fairly large French civilian camp just outside the town, and this was our first target; we wanted to find out if their hospitality was really as good as we had been led to believe. Under no circumstances would we ever approach any Poles for help; all the escapees who had done so seemed to end up back in camp — though there must have been exceptions to this.

There seemed to be an inordinate number of people standing about but it could have been in aid of some sort of celebration or special market day. We shrugged off any thoughts we had about this and went on our way to find our French friends. How do you find a Frenchman in a country full of Germans? Our time in France must have helped us, because within minutes we spotted two blokes who just had to be what we were looking for. When we got closer and could hear them talking, we knew that we had hit the jackpot. We asked them to take us to their leader — or words to that effect — and, with the few French words that we knew added, they got the message and pointed out to us the man we were looking for in a shop across the road.

When he came out, we crossed over to introduce ourselves, but when we explained to him that we were three Scottish soldiers on the run from a prisoner-of-war camp, the poor man went very pale and almost wobbled at the knees. Thinking that maybe he had heard some strange stories about the Scots, we told him that we were only looking for some temporary shelter and perhaps a bite to eat. He was slowly regaining his natural sallow colouring and, having got over the shock of hearing who we were, told us in good and fluent English to please leave his presence at once as he did not wish to be seen speaking to us. This was not what we expected to hear from a gallant ally. As he started to move away, we more or less surrounded him and asked what his problem was; had we said something to offend him?

Realising that we wanted an answer, he quickly explained that a mass escape had taken place the previous day from the local RAF camp, namely Stalag Luft Drei, and that it could only be minutes before we were questioned and arrested. Now it was our turn to go pale. With a short apology for not being able to help us, the camp leader smartly disappeared. We looked at each other in stunned silence, and slowly a picture formed in my mind of all the strange-looking people we had seen in the railway station when we arrived. They began to take shape as members of the Gestapo, the German CID, and many other punitive organisations. They were all looking for escaped POWs — not us, necessarily, but that would make no difference. Short of carrying a placard stating that we had escaped from

Sudetenland and not from the RAF camp, there was no way out of this dilemma.

Our brains began to function again, and without a word being said, we slowly walked away from the station till we reached a nice quiet spot where we could talk safely. We agreed that we were in it right up to our necks and that there couldn't possibly be a way out; the whole area must be alive with forces with just one thought in mind.

Joe suggested that we head out into the open country and try to work our way north. I pointed out that we had made no provision for travelling in this manner and it would be far too slow. Apart from that, it would be very difficult to find places to stop for the night before curfew. Also, not having a detailed map of the whole area between here and Stettin made it virtually impossible. Jimmy quietly asked what I had in mind. When I told them, they both looked at me in astonishment, then all three of us burst into hilarious laughter at such a frighteningly stupid idea. My proposition was that we return to the station and carry on with our original plan of moving on to Frankfurt after our stop at Sagan.

The tall, lean French camp leader might have exaggerated the whole business and his idea of a mass escape might have been five or six airmen — in which case there was probably no need for our present panic. The only way to verify this was to return to the station. We kicked the idea around for a few minutes and came up with a unanimous decision to take the easy way out. As soon as we re-entered the station, we knew that the bloke had not exaggerated. Practically all the men in the station were being stopped and asked to produce their papers by a variety of stern-faced teams of two and three. I remembered something that Traudl had told me about coupon-free soup and, after we established that our train didn't leave for another forty minutes, we headed in the direction of the station restaurant and ordered three plates of the same. The waiter scowled at us in a most unfriendly manner, but I suppose it could have been because he had had a row with his wife or, even worse, his girlfriend. Half an hour soon passed and we prepared to leave. Just as we were going through the door, Jimmy turned round and, to our amazement, stared right at the waiter and rapped out a loud "Heil Hitler". The waiter reacted as if he had been shot but came smartly to attention and answered Jimmy's greeting. Outside we asked Jimmy why he had done it. He admitted that it had been totally spontaneous but he did feel that the waiter needed smartening up a bit and it would certainly remove any suspicion from his mind.

In fear and trepidation I now went to buy our tickets to Frankfurt. After paying for them I checked which platform we departed from. With the skin on my back crawling with fear, we headed for the platform, feeling we were never going to make it. Five minutes later the train pulled out; we hadn't been stopped. I could hardly believe our luck. We were not invisible, because I could still see Jimmy and Joe as large as life. We had sprung the booby trap and come out unscathed. Our problem now was to reach Frankfurt in time to find help before curfew. Would you believe it, the first thing we heard on our arrival at Frankfurt was the happy chattering of four Frenchmen, almost as if they had been waiting for us.

It took a few minutes to convince them of who we were. Retaining their happy mood, they escorted us to their camp, which was not very far away. The camp leader was a real charmer who spoke some English; he made a very thorough job of interrogating us. When he was satisfied, he agreed we could stay for one night — which was all we wanted. Then they generously gave us something to eat and turned down our offer of a couple of bars of chocolate in return, saying that we would probably need them before our journey was over. Conversation proved to be difficult so, when we were shown where to bunk down for the night, we gladly got our heads down. It took quite a while to stop our minds turning over the events of the day time and again. Exhaustion eventually won and a dreamless sleep ensued.

CHAPTER
TWENTY-EIGHT

All three of us woke next morning feeling fully recuperated and happily able to talk freely in English which, of course, we were unable to do most of the day. Fortunately, we had been living and working together so long that quite often a look or an inclination of the head could convey the message. Our telepathy was put strenuously to the test during our trip, but worked wonderfully well.

Over a cup of ersatz coffee and a roll, we went through the events of the previous day. None of us could come up with a plausible explanation of what had transpired in Sagan station. We had seen the Controls stopping people and checking their documents. Joe had also spotted the French camp leader in the station, no doubt waiting to see us being arrested. He too was probably left wondering why we hadn't been stopped.

Anyway, the next step was to wash and shave in comfort. After having thanked the camp leader for his hospitality, and accepted his kind offer of a guide to take us back to the railway station, we gave him a big Gallic hug. Then we moved back into the real harsh world outside, wondering what Fate had in store for us on this bright sunny day. We had decided to book all the way from Frankfurt to Stettin, not stopping at Angermunde as we had originally planned.

The train we were to catch was listed as an express; we had no illusions about what this meant, as we had been warned about long delays and possible diversions due to bombing raids. But suppose we were caught in a town which had just been bombed, where they were still digging out the dead and dying; what would happen to us? In our imaginations we thought we would be torn to pieces. This threat hung over every escapee. The moment you donned civilian clothes, you gave up the right to be treated as a POW and could quite correctly be prosecuted for espionage, which could carry the death penalty. If you were daft enough to escape and travel in your own national uniform, however, you would be safe if recaptured, as you would merely be returned to camp and punished.

Our biggest worry now was whether we would reach Stettin in time to make contact with our indispensable French allies before curfew time. The train left on time, so at least we were off to a good start, but we had only been travelling for about fifteen minutes when a heart-stopping incident occurred. The compartment was fairly full, with one small boy restlessly wandering up and down the aisle between the seats. After passing by several times he suddenly approached his mother, and pointing to us, told her that we were "Englanders". The three of us heard him quite clearly, and I'm sure that everyone could see the colour draining from our faces. I closed my eyes and waited for the inevitable to happen. Mummy quietly asked her son what gave him such a strange idea and his reply was that he could smell chocolate when he passed us. His mother gave an apologetic smile in our direction and told him to sit still and stop wandering about. They got off at the next stop.

We had failed to anticipate this method of being detected, but the remainder of the chocolate was wrapped more carefully, so that the smell didn't alert anybody else deprived of the taste. All the experience and knowledge we had accumulated in the past four years could have been nullified by a small boy who knew that the Englanders received chocolate in their Red Cross parcels. Someone probably told him this when they were explaining to him why he couldn't have any.

I glanced at Jimmy and Joe, who looked relaxed, yet my nerves felt completely shredded. I remember at one stage even thinking that if we were caught we could at least finally return to a normal way of living as POWs. Looking back on my nervous attacks in Karlsbrunn, which were still occurring but thankfully at longer intervals, I realised this trip could lead to a complete nervous breakdown. On the positive side, though, I was drawing strength from Jimmy and Joe all the time.

The landscape in this part of Germany was dull and boring, and we couldn't converse in English, so I spent most of the time with my eyes closed. Again and again my mind went back to Sagan station and the riddle of why we hadn't been stopped for a document check. The hypnotic rumble of the train finally helped me to come up with a possible solution. Supposing there had been someone in overall control of the checking operation and, again, supposing this person had seen us arriving on the train from the Breslau direction, then it would be noted that we were coming into Sagan and not trying to get out. Later, when we were leaving, this very efficient person remembered us and signalled that we were OK and not to waste time on us. Either that, or we had the luck of the devil.

I came back to reality with a bump as the brakes began to squeal in pain and we started the slow entry into Angermunde. The three of us exchanged smiles as this was the penultimate stop before Stettin. But we should have known better than to tempt Fate. Lined up on the platform was a group of German soldiers wearing "Kontrolle" shields round their necks. When our train stopped, they spread out and began to enter the different carriages. Jimmy quickly leaned forward and whispered that there were to be no heroics, and if anyone of us was caught, then all three of us would go quietly. We nodded and sat back to wait for the inevitable to happen.

CHAPTER
TWENTY-NINE

It was only now that I thought what a stupid waste of time the making of the identity cards had been. Although they had given us a sense of security, we never thought that if anyone seriously looked at them they could believe they were genuine. I remember feeling the whole thing was finally over, but we had acquitted ourselves well and at least the Escape Committee would have to take us seriously now. If they had helped us instead of the losers, the documents they would have provided might have seen us through this check. The little guard was slowly working his way towards us. He looked to be in his forties and was probably not physically fit enough to fight and die on the Eastern Front, but here he was about to recapture three British prisoners, for which he would probably be awarded the Iron Cross.

Finally, it was our turn and Jimmy cleverly fumbled a bit before producing his cellophane folder with his ID card in it. When I saw the uninterested look on the guard's face, I just couldn't believe it. He handed the card back and held out his hand for mine — a cursory glance later, it was returned. Joe was next, but here the pattern changed. In my head I was screaming that two out of three wasn't bad, but it looked now as if our luck was running out. The guard looked at Joe's card as he had looked at ours, but something about it seemed to disturb him. To satisfy himself he removed it from its folder, opened it up and examined the inside. When he saw the eagle and swastika insignia, he replaced it in the folder and handed it back without comment. He then moved on to the next seat. Was this the card that I hadn't wanted to finish? What made the guard want to check this one? Did he want to check to see if I had finished it?

The three of us sat in stunned silence, but it wasn't over yet. When the guard had finished his compartment check, the train started to move again and he came along and sat in the free seat next to Jimmy. We were so cocky that we had been mentally congratulating ourselves until this happened. Of course this clever little man had us spotted, and when the train stopped again we would be placed under arrest. And I had been thinking how stupid he was not to have seen that our documents were fakes!

We suffered silent torture for about another three miles and then the train began screeching, slowed down and stopped. The guard stood up and slung his rifle strap over his shoulder. This seemed to me to be a bit casual for an arresting officer as he should, of course, have had it at the ready in case there was any trouble. He didn't know that we wouldn't cause trouble. In fact, I was all ready to stand up and follow him at a nod of his head. But he slowly made his way to the door at the end of the compartment, opened it and left us without even a farewell.

When the train moved on, we looked at each other in total disbelief. We could see the guards who had been on the checking party assembling on the platform outside. I began to wonder if parts of this journey were real or just dreams that occurred when I dozed off. The compartment was almost empty at this time and the boys confirmed that I wasn't having nightmares. They had also thought that the guard had spotted us and had us under surveillance. More passengers came into our compartment at the next stop, which put an end to conversation, so we went back to our mental and physical relaxation positions in the hope of undoing the nervous damage we had suffered.

The feeling of tension was just beginning to wear off as we pulled into a small station near the end of our journey. Suddenly, a small girl on the other side of our compartment screamed "Englanders!" My hands almost involuntarily shot up in the air, but then I saw Jimmy standing up and pointing to a working party of British POWs walking along the platform outside. As everyone was looking in the same direction, they didn't see the shocked look on our faces. First, the little boy with the highly developed nostrils, and now a sweet little girl with a shrill voice . . . We considered ourselves extremely lucky that the adults in Germany were not as perceptive as their children.

Our so-called express continued to inch its way slowly along and finally arrived in Stettin. The only indication we had that our destination had been reached was the fact that the train stopped and everyone got off. When we stepped onto the platform, there was no sign of a railway station as such, just rubble, which until very recently had been the station. There was a small wooden hut on the platform, which was obviously for the use of the railway staff, but the rest was desolation. We quickly agreed that we didn't want to be captured in this town so soon after a devastating bombing raid. As we walked slowly into the city centre, the damage became more apparent, but then we came upon one of the freaks of such raids. Right in the middle of the town stood a beautiful big red building, completely untouched, like a monument in the desert. As we passed it, we discovered that the building with the charmed life was the Head Post Office.

All three of us were now on the alert for the sight or sound of some Frenchmen.

CHAPTER
THIRTY

A deep feeling of despondency seemed to affect the German people now. The war news from all fronts was bad and the number of wounded returning to the Fatherland was continually on the increase, especially from the Russian front, where the German troops were being mowed down by the thousand as they retreated. What with all this and the continual increase in the Allied bombing raids, it was becoming more evident that there could only be one outcome to the war. The Wonder Weapon had not materialised.

The Allies can only thank God and Werner von Braun and his team that they deliberately delayed their production of the first complete atomic bomb, otherwise there would probably, nay certainly, have been a different outcome to the war. However, with only conventional weapons, Hitler now had no hope of any kind of victory on land, sea or air. You would think that one look at a world atlas would have shown him the futility of trying to fight on so many fronts. On the other hand, he must have felt complacent about the way his troops swept through Poland and then pushed the British out of France (despite General Tiger Gort putting me in the front line as the final deterrent), and about the way his troops controlled the North African theatre of war for a period. Together with the toll that the U-boats took on our shipping, this must have convinced him and Germany that he could conquer the world. The euphoria of all the early successes had long since died. Now the reality of the mammoth task had become apparent, and the inevitable failure had to be faced — but could not be talked about, as this was forbidden. Hitler's pledge of total war had also been a dreadful mistake for the German people, as it left no loophole for a settlement, and could only end in unconditional surrender.

These thoughts ran through our minds as we walked through the town and absorbed the dismal mood of the people who, at the beginning of the war, would have raced from one street to another, just to get a glimpse of either Hitler or Göring. This enthusiasm didn't extend to Heinrich Himmler, however, as he preferred the streets empty and well guarded when he paid a visit to a strange town.

Soon these thoughts were interrupted by a very welcome sound: voluble French. We shadowed the two Frenchmen until they reached a convenient spot for us to approach them, then tried to make them understand who we were and what we needed. In the beginning there was the usual distrust, but then they felt our desperate need and finally agreed to take us to their camp, where their leader would make the final decision whether to help us or not.

This leader turned out to be a very charming man, and between his broken English and our almost non-existent French, we convinced him that we were genuine. He congratulated us on having come so far safely, and said that they would give us their wholehearted support and assistance. He pointed out that the toughest part of our journey was in front of us; he had never heard of anyone succeeding in breaking through the security cordon surrounding the port.

We were shown where we could have a bath, given a meal, and then shown where we could bunk down and have a good sleep in perfect safety. Next day, he told us, he would send someone with us to the dock area and we could make our first reconnaissance. From then on it would be entirely in Jimmy's hands. He had said all along that if we could get him to a seaport, he would get us out of it and home. So all he had to do was keep his promise.

When we saw the dock area next day, I began to have grave doubts. The actual shipping area could only be reached by crossing a bridge which, of course, was permanently manned by soldiers, and a special pass had to be shown by anyone wanting access to the docks. The boys suggested that we could swim over the river at some point, but not being a very strong swimmer, this didn't appeal to me one little bit. Jimmy decided that this was not an insurmountable obstacle and that first he had to find a seaman from a Swedish ship and find out when it would sail; then we could tackle the problem of getting into the docks.

That evening Joe and I were confined to quarters and Jimmy went off on his own. This was one of the few times during the war that we were separated, and Joe and I felt most unhappy about it, but Jimmy insisted that he had to do this on his own as it was safer. We could only sit, worry and wait, wondering if he would ever come back.

Three hours later we got the answer. Jimmy breezed in looking as if Scotland had won the World Cup, so we guessed that his mission had been successful. Sure enough, everything had turned out exactly as he had hoped, and as he regaled with us the details of his evening out, we realised that the final stages of our ambitious trip had become a possibility.

CHAPTER
THIRTY-ONE

Jimmy explained to us that when he went into town he had to find the club, pub or brothel that the seamen on shore-leave used, so his target area would be near the docks. When he got down near the harbour, he met what looked and sounded like a bunch of sailors having a good time. Reckoning that they must be coming from the place he was looking for, he moved on in the direction they had come from. Sure enough, there it was, in the middle of the next block, looking just as it looked in ports all over the world.

He went in and ordered a beer, but when the pretty brunette barmaid starting asking questions, he excused himself and sat at a nearby empty table. Luck took a hand when five minutes later the door opened and a blonde bloke of about thirty came in. After ordering a beer at the bar, he looked around and saw Jimmy, who was about his age and also blonde, sitting alone and perhaps of the same nationality. He came across and indicated a wish to join him. With a nod of assent and a wave to the vacant seat next to him, Jimmy couldn't believe his luck: if anyone was watching him, they would see that he hadn't made the first approach. The stranger introduced himself. He was a Swede from a ship in the harbour and spoke a fair bit of English.

Without getting involved in a lot of lies or fairy stories, Jimmy decided to go for broke and told the Swede who and what he was, tentatively asking if there was any possibility of his new friend helping him to stowaway on his ship when it sailed. He was amazed at the reaction to this request. The man's face broke into a happy smile and he said that he would be delighted to take Jimmy back on board with him immediately, as his ship sailed with the tide in the early morning. He also said they would have no trouble entering the docks because if one of them had a shore-leave pass, the guard would assume they both had passes.

Now Jimmy had to explain there were three of us. Then, of course, the deal was off. Under no circumstances would the Swede contemplate taking three men into the docks. His offer to Jimmy still stood, but only if he came alone. After explaining that he couldn't do this, he asked if it was possible to give him the berth number the ship was lying at. This information was given grudgingly, but he did allow Jimmy to walk to the entrance to the docks with him, where, with a vague wave of his pass, he went through the control point. This was when Jimmy realised how we were going to get into the dock area by ourselves.

Having told us his story, Jimmy now told us to get ready to move and to dump all our kit except the clothes we were wearing; this was the last step in our bid to get home. I felt quite frightened by the finality of it all.

118

With "Bonne Chance" ringing in our ears, we said our farewells and thanks yous to our French friends, and headed for the docks. Jimmy told us to pick an unobtrusive spot from which to observe the control point. When we saw some seamen approaching, we were to join them as they went through, keeping as far away as possible from the guard and waving folded pieces of paper of the correct colour. It seemed a very dicey manoeuvre to me, but less unappealing than swimming the river.

About five minutes later a group of five seamen arrived, and a nod from Jimmy confirmed to us that we were to join them when they entered. It went exactly as planned and suddenly we were through and walking towards the berth where our ship would be waiting for us. Throughout our journey, every success had been followed by a setback, and this was no exception. We had been congratulating ourselves on our brilliant success, but when we arrived at the berth where our ship was to be waiting, it wasn't there. Jimmy had mentioned that it had seemed awfully quiet for an area where a ship was due to sail, and now we knew why, but not where the ship had gone. Jimmy's years in the Merchant Navy paid off again; he remembered that ships waiting to sail with the tide were sometimes moved to mooring berths, to leave the loading bays free for other ships. He decided this must be what had happened, so we would have to look nearer the entrance of the docks.

He led us in the direction he reckoned it would be and we began to see signs of life, making it difficult for us to move freely. We could see the masts and funnels of at least three ships ahead of us. If Jimmy was right, one of them would be *Heros*, the one we were looking for. Joe was the first to spot the guard patrolling the quayside. Our problem was how to get near enough to identify which was the one that we wanted — if it was there at all.

CHAPTER
THIRTY-TWO

Despite strict blackout restrictions, there were lights along the dockside where the three ships were lying. The lighting wasn't brilliant but it was still going to make it difficult for us tonight. Railway lines ran the length of the dockside, so we retired to the shelter of some wagons near the ships. We talked over our plan of action and decided that, to save time, we would split up and each find out the name of a ship. Jimmy would take the one on the left, Joe the one on the right, and I got the middle one, which was actually the easy one. Thankfully it was a mild and cloudy night which meant, of course, that away from the lighting it was really dark. This would help cover our movements to a certain extent. When we were having our talk together about the quayside lighting, it had suddenly dawned on us that if there had been no lighting, we wouldn't have been able to identify the ships or see their names.

Our movements now had to coincide with where the patrolling guard was, so the one nearest to him stayed put and the other two had a bit of freedom. I decided that the best place would be under the railway wagons nearest to the ship. As I was crawling along beneath one of these, there was a sudden bump and the wagon started to move. My immediate reaction was to drape myself across the wheel axle which was quite near me, thinking that I would be safe there until the shunter stopped, when I could resume my crawling routine. The result of this was that I was whipped right over the axle and landed on my head, which luckily isn't the weakest part of my body, ending up flat on my back on the track. Before I had gathered my wits, the wagons were stationary again. This little incident taught me that the wheels and axle on this wagon were fixed and did not work independently.

The lighting seemed better at the stern of the ship so I made my way there with an eye on the guard. Eventually, I made out some queer name that looked Russian or Polish, but it wasn't the one we wanted. Returning to the rendezvous point was much easier and quicker. I was becoming better with practice and had a sore head to prove it. The biggest surprise was that the boys were already back and waiting for me. That seemed strange as they had both had further to go than me. I began to wonder if the axle business had knocked me out for a few minutes.

Jimmy had hit the jackpot in the "find the *Heros* competition", so we moved further back from the quayside towards the ship at the end of the line which, presumably, would be the first one out in the morning when the tide was right. We found a suitable spot in the darkness from which to watch the progress of the guard as he paced his beat on the dockside. Jimmy told us what the plan of action would be. He would wait until the guard was about halfway down his beat with his back to us; then he would walk over to the ship and board it. If all went well, he would signal to us that we were next, but we would follow only after the guard had returned and was again halfway down in the other direction.

There was a deadly stillness about the place, except for the odd bursts of activity from the shunting engine. It was two o'clock in the morning and people were in bed sleeping soundly. Again I fleetingly wondered if we would ever achieve the luxury of sleeping peacefully or in our own beds again. My reverie was rudely shattered when Jimmy said he was off. As he casually walked out into the light and across to the ship's gangway, I imagined rifle and machine-gun fire suddenly sweeping the dockside, but in fact nothing happened. Jimmy disappeared momentarily as he crossed the deck but very quickly reappeared higher up the ship, where he turned round and gave us the thumbs-up sign. Now Joe and I had to wait until the guard had returned and was again halfway down his beat. Time passed too quickly for me, as I felt safe and secure in the dark surroundings, but a touch on my arm put an end to that and we were off.

I felt sure that the guard would hear the thumping of my heart from where he was. Then we were climbing the gangway and all seemed to be going well, until Fate blew the whistle again. From somewhere on our left a voice hailed us and we saw the German guard on deck about twenty yards away. I almost imagined it was the little guard who had played cat and mouse with us on the train. Once again the years of working together paid off. Without even thinking about it, Joe and I both pulled our imaginary passes out of our pockets and waved them in the air, shouting "Crew" in German, and carried on to where Jimmy was waiting to pull us into a doorway, which he smartly closed behind us. The three of us now stood with bated breath, waiting to see what would happen next.

Nothing did, and Jimmy reckoned that when he came on board the guard must have gone for a pee and that was why he saw no-one. He commended us on how well we had handled a nasty situation. Our next step was decided for us because the door that we had come in by was opened by what looked like a cabin-boy. He didn't look unduly perturbed when he saw us, but this soon changed when he found we were strangers. Jimmy quietly and firmly explained that he was to go and tell the steward that he had met "Joe Bloggs" in the pub and that he was to come to us immediately. He did this using voice and sign language successfully; when he was finished, the young man indicated that he understood and repeated the message in Swedish, I think.

He went off briskly, closing the door behind him, and now we had a big discussion as to what he would do. I reckoned he would turn us in to my little friend, the guard who was going to haunt me for the rest of my life. Joe was willing to bet his first stop would be one of the ship's officers, but Jimmy just smiled and said the boy would do exactly as he was instructed. Anyway, we would know soon enough — the next time the door was opened. The young man must have moved very fast because about seven minutes later he returned and, thank God, Jimmy was right.

Jimmy's friend arrived alone and seemed dismayed about the three of us having made it this far. But he was as good as his word and in a strangled voice urged us to move very quickly because the whole crew would be on the move soon, preparing the ship for sailing. With him leading the way, we carefully and quietly followed him. This nightmare journey took us deeper and deeper into the ship's bowels. Eventually, we were ushered through yet another bulkhead door, but this proved to be the last one, and it was the coal-bunker. Our final instruction from our Swedish friend was to get into the bunker and as far away from the bulkhead door as possible, then to bury ourselves under the coal and to stay there quietly for as long as possible. We thanked him profusely and genuinely from our hearts, because his help could have cost him his life if we were caught. He smiled warmly at us, wished us "Bon Voyage" and then he was gone. It made me wonder why a total stranger would put his life on the line for people he didn't know and would probably never see again. I hope that I am never put to the test, in case my moral courage is not a match for his.

The small torch, which I had kept when we dumped everything else, now became very useful and allowed us to see our way to the farthest part of the bunker. On reaching the bulkhead, we began the task of digging ourselves in. Before we started, Jimmy said that he had something to tell us. It was extremely likely that the Germans would search the ship before it sailed by one of two methods. One was using dogs to sniff out any human scent in cargo holds and the second, a real charmer, was using gas instead of the dogs. This, of course, cheered us up no end.

It was the bad-following-the-good syndrome again. Here we were, having surmounted all sorts of obstacles to get this far, to be told we would either have our throats torn out by Alsatian dogs or be asphyxiated instead. I suggested that possibly our only way out was by prayer, but Joe said that it was hardly fair to ask for help now, considering the situation we had put ourselves in. Jimmy said we should leave it in the hands of Lady Luck, who had looked after us inordinately well up till now, and since we hadn't offended her in any way, maybe she would see us through.

Short of crying and screaming that we didn't want to die, there was nothing else for it but to dig ourselves into the coal. Jimmy explained we were doing this to cover our scent from the dogs, and I was glad there was a reason because it wasn't an easy task with bare hands. We had only been resting for about ten minutes after our exertions when there was a bump and the coal moved under us. Jimmy told us we would have to move as we were obviously lying right above the hopper that fed the ship's furnaces. When you're in trouble there is no greater therapy than keeping yourself occupied, so we moved and did our digging-in chore all over again.

Half an hour later, while I was daydreaming about walking to birdsong along one of our beautiful lochsides in the warm sunshine, Jimmy suddenly said that the ship was moving, which brought me back to reality. I hadn't even heard the engines starting but was told that they had been ticking over for some time and we were now definitely under way. Jimmy explained that it was quite some distance before we would sail clear of the estuary and that the ship's search would be carried out while we were on the move. The ship's pilot, the guards and any stowaways that were found would be taken off the ship when they dropped the pilot. His predictions were spot on: ten minutes later we heard a dog, first whining then barking, followed by the angry voice of the guard shouting at the dog to be quiet. The sound must have come to us through a ventilator which we couldn't see. I'm sure the dog had got a whiff of us and was telling its master about us down below. For some reason the guard didn't want to know.

Then I had another thought. Supposing the guard knew the holds were going to be gassed, then of course he wouldn't be interested in the dog's reaction to any smells coming from the ventilators — be it German or Swedish rats, or even, as in this case, three Britons. This supposition would make a dramatic and final end to our relationship with the little guard from the train. Having exchanged thoughts and fears in whispers, we decided to wait and see what would happen next. We once again settled down to contemplating our filthy navels.

My nerves must have stopped jumping long enough to allow me to doze off. I was awakened by Jimmy and Joe talking quite freely together, and when they saw I was back in the land of the living they told me that we were well clear of the estuary and heading safely for

Sweden and the port of Malmö. The sense of elation that swept through me almost knocked me out. All the planning and dreaming we had done together had finally ended in success. Then, as we hugged each other, waves of fear started to run up and down my spine. Jimmy felt the sudden tension in my body and asked me what was wrong. I felt almost sick as I reminded him of the pattern of events: very soon Fate was going to throw that rotten sucker punch which had followed every time we thought we were winning. Both boys laughed and told me to forget it; nothing could interfere with a safe landing in Malmö. I agreed to set aside my pessimism and behave myself, but deep down in the pit of my stomach the fear remained. Maybe it was just hunger.

CHAPTER
THIRTY-THREE

A couple of hours later, we thought it was about time to make our presence on board known to the Captain, as Jimmy reckoned we had passed the point of no return. At the same time, the bulk-head door swung open and the lights were switched on. There stood one of the ship's officers, presumably checking all was well in the coal-hole. Being naturally polite, we called out a hearty "Good morning" to him. His look of shocked surprise was understandable: we must have looked dreadful in our filthy state. When we explained to him that we were British stowaways, he smiled and said that he could understand English and that he would take us to the Captain. He also explained that the "Old Man" was a real seagoing terror and that he would be furious with us for our audacity in stowing away on his ship.

He took us up on deck and told us to wait. His prediction was spot on. The Captain appeared at the double, hoping that what he had been told wasn't true, but when he saw us he realised that the worst had happened and that he would now be in trouble with the Germans. He was no beauty to start with, and as his tough wrinkled face got redder by the minute, he became more ugly. First he tongue-lashed us in

Swedish, then he switched to English, the main theme being that if ever there was anyone in the world he didn't want to meet, it was definitely us. Our reaction to all this was mutual. We said nothing because, after all, it was his ship and he was entitled to his say — not that any of us felt like interrupting him in the mood he was in.

When he finally ran out of breath, he had a good look around and then he asked the ship's officer (who had been standing by during this tirade) if it was possible to chart him a course for Denmark, which was German-occupied. If he dropped us there, he would be in the clear again and we would be recaptured. Leaving us standing there on deck, the two of them retired to the bridge, whereupon Jimmy had a good look around at the direction we were heading. He told us that the land we could see straight ahead was Sweden and the dimmer bit to the left Denmark, so if the present course altered to the left we were to jump overboard and take our chances on swimming for Sweden. We both nodded in agreement. I think Jimmy might have made it; Joe might not have, but for me it would have been a watery grave for sure.

We were left standing on deck for about fifteen minutes before the friendly officer returned and, with a wink, told us to follow him. He showed us where to wash up and then we could have a meal. Our course as we left the deck was still straight and true, so we smiled at each other and felt a lot better about life. We washed and scrubbed but five minutes later we were dirty again. I thought I would probably spend the rest of my life trying to get rid of the coal dust, but in fact it took only about a week. A friendly cook in the seamen's mess served us with a lovely meaty-smelling soup, which was absolutely delicious. The nice man couldn't understand when he tried to serve us with a heaped main course that we were full and couldn't eat another bite. He looked so disappointed that we went to a lot of trouble to explain to him that after four years on strict rations, our stomachs wouldn't hold a lot, no matter how good and tasty the food was. Finally he accepted that it wasn't his cooking that was the problem and grudgingly cleared the table.

We were left in the mess-room to sit and chat and wonder what was going to happen next. What happened was that practically the whole crew appeared in ones and twos at various times to give us encouraging smiles and the thumbs-up sign. They were probably surprised that the Captain hadn't had us put in irons and thrown in the brig. A regular check on our course showed that we were still heading straight and true for Sweden and the coastline was becoming quite distinct now. It was a beautiful sunny day and we could make out features on land. The officer who had been dealing with us visited us about an hour later and said he would have to have some details from us. There were forms to be filled in for the ship's log. These proved to be just generalities, like names and addresses and a statement that no-one had helped us to stow away on this particular ship. He informed us that the Swedish police had been notified by radio of our presence on board and would be waiting at the dockside to pick us up when we landed at Malmö.

Two hours later, that is exactly what happened. Two well-dressed civilians came on board as soon as the ship was tied up and the one in charge advised us to say nothing until after we had accompanied them to their office in town. The Captain didn't show up to wave goodbye to us, though we would have liked to thank him for his hospitality and our safe delivery to Sweden.

The two CID men were most charming, producing cups of tea for us when we arrived at their office. Then the most amazing interview took place; we were told that we must think very carefully before answering any of the questions we were about to be asked, as our fate for the rest of the war would depend on our answers. They explained that if we declared ourselves to be members of the armed forces, the authorities would have to place us in an internment camp in Sweden until the cessation of hostilities. If, and if was a very big if, on the other hand we were to declare ourselves as civilians, then we would be handed over to the British Consul in Malmö and the Swedish authorities would wash their hands of us.

Here was an interesting choice: to see out the rest of the war in a neutral country, nice and safe, or get back home and risk the possibility of getting killed or maimed properly this time. Were we going to trade one camp for another, or complete the task we had set out to achieve and get home? It might take some people a day, a week, maybe longer to weigh up the pros and cons, but it took the three of us about thirty seconds.

Jimmy looked at us and said "Mister" and Joe and I nodded in agreement. We were registered as civilians, and gave our names and addresses, whereupon the British Consul was immediately notified and we were picked up within the hour.

The three of us gleefully hugged each other and found it hard to believe that it was finally over. All the future planning was out of our hands and had become someone else's problem. Our part of the escape was now successfully completed.

CHAPTER
THIRTY-FOUR

The Consul was a young-old man, very civil service, who gave us the impression that we had interrupted him, and that he would deal with us only because it was his duty. Our first stop was at his office, where he did a very intensive report on our personal details and then a less thorough summary of our escape. When this was completed, he arranged for a light snack to be delivered to the office. After this we were told that we were going shopping. The car drove us to a gents' outfitters which looked very genteel and upmarket. Only when we got inside did we realise just how posh it really was.

The next hour was a fairytale come true and a dream I would love to relive. We were told to choose a whole new wardrobe without giving any thought to expense and that the costs of our three outfits would be borne by the King of Sweden, God bless him.

We must have made a ludicrous sight, still dressed in our filthy old clothes. We started by picking our suits. I chose a brownish two-piece sports suit, then a smart pair of brown shoes to go with it. Coats and hats followed, then two shirts each to match our individual outfits, two pair of socks, a tie and a belt, then two sets of underwear and two sets of pyjamas. Then we had to choose a suitcase to put everything in. Slightly breathless, we reckoned that nothing had been forgotten but we were reminded that we had to choose a full toilet set with nothing left out. This done, we were told there was still something missing and were taken to another department to choose a wristwatch and a pair of cufflinks each. I hope His Majesty received our "Thank you" cards — the Consul assured us that he would.

Next stop was a quiet hotel overlooking the water. I couldn't believe they would let us in looking as we did, but they were waiting for us and we were shown to our rooms and informed that our baths were already drawn. All we had to do was soak in them. After what we had been through in the last few weeks, not to mention the last few years, it was sheer unadulterated luxury. It also felt extremely strange: for the first time in almost five years I was completely alone.

I took full advantage of it now by bathing, shaving and dressing slowly and alone. Finally I went through to Jimmy's room just as Joe was also arriving. We all looked at each other in amazement — three strangers in civilian clothes — then we all howled with laughter and the spell was broken. We had opted for a quiet dinner in the hotel by ourselves. Next day we were going north to Stockholm by train. There we would be taken to the home of the British Military Attaché, where we would stay until further notice — whatever that meant. Dinner was a gastronomic dream and we actually managed to eat three of the five courses, though we insisted on very small portions. After a cup of tea in the lounge, we chatted a bit, but the comfortable-looking beds upstairs were acting like big magnets, so we decided on an early night — which turned out to be a mistake.

Next morning when we met for breakfast, we found that not one of us had had the pleasure of a good night's sleep. Like myself, Jimmy and Joe had tossed and turned all night, going over the last stages of our journey and trying to figure out where the German system had gone wrong and why we had succeeded against the odds. Why were we not picked up in Sagan station? Why didn't the little guard spot our phoney documents on the train? How could we have entered a guarded dock area and then board a guarded ship without being caught? Round and round it went, then a desperate effort to shut it all out, then a few seconds later round and round it would go again — and so it went on through the restless night.

We all felt much better and cheerier after a sumptuous breakfast, and shortly afterwards we were told that a car was waiting to take us to the station. Our cases had already been brought down so, having been given pocket money, we tipped the porter and joined the Consul in the car. He was very sympathetic about our sleepless night but agreed that this phase would surely pass. Our minds just needed to adjust to our new lifestyle. He gave us our tickets for the journey and some more money, which he said we would need for the buffet car on the train. We thought this was very thoughtful of him. He told us that we would be picked up on arrival at Stockholm. After an uneventful train journey a driver came forward and checked we were the correct trio before driving us through this remarkably clean and beautiful city to the Attaché's house, where we were greeted by three lovely ladies and the man himself.

Mr Wright was a middle-aged, handsome man's man. I'm sure if he hadn't been in the job he was in, he would have fitted into the Diplomatic Corps nicely. A few minutes after meeting him you felt that he would be able to solve any problems that you had and that you could confide in him safely. His wife complemented him beautifully. Over the period that we stayed with them she was charming, motherly and quite flawless. The two daughters, one brunette and one blonde, were in their early twenties and both quite capable of turning any man's head. Considering the number of years we had been deprived of any type of female company (apart from my forays to Traudl), this was indeed an excess of feminine beauty to place before us, but what with Jimmy and Joe being happily married and faithful husbands and me being more or less spoken for, we just tried to regard the ladies as ordinary people, which was very difficult.

After we were shown to our rooms in this large but comfortable old house, our host called us to his office where, for the next couple of hours, we underwent a most thorough interrogation, firstly about our home lives, then our army careers, and the time we spent in prison camp, culminating finally in our escape. It all seemed excessive, but then slowly I realised that he was

137

trying to establish whether we were who we claimed to be. In short, it was possible we were plants.

Suddenly, I almost went off the nice gentleman. He asked if we still had the identity cards that I had made, and when we produced them he gave them a cursory glance and said that we were fortunate not to have had them examined as they were pretty poor copies. When we told him that they had been checked by a Control on the train, he laughed and said that we must be joking. When we insisted that it was true, he was astounded. I felt awful at his ridicule, after all the work I had done on the damn things, but on second thoughts I felt better, because without them we wouldn't have been there.

When Jimmy told his story of his visit to the pub in Stettin, our host broke out in hilarious laughter. He then explained that the barmaid who had tried to chat him up was a British agent called Mary, and that if he had given her a chance she would have taken over and arranged our passage to Sweden the easy way.

He then went on to say that we had coincidentally taken an official route for our escape and, though we were Civil Service personnel and therefore covered by the Official Secrets Act, under no circumstances could we disclose the route we had taken to anyone without government permission. It could jeopardise lives if it became common knowledge.

The next piece of news that he gave us was quite shocking and meant that our sleepless nights might go on for some time yet. Unconfirmed news had come through to him that fifty of the airmen who had escaped from Sagan had been caught and, unbelievably, they had all been shot on direct orders from Hitler passed through Heinrich Himmler. He told us that the total number of men involved in the escape had been in excess of sixty. My first thought was, what kind of so-called Escape Committee sends so many men out into a hostile environment with very little hope of success? To my mind it was a wanton and completely irresponsible action and one that had no hope of achieving anything. Jimmy and Joe never agreed with me on this.

After the bad news came the good. We would be issued next day with covering letters of identity, which we could produce on request, and we could write to our next-of-kin informing them that we had arrived safely in Sweden and, with any luck, would be home in the near future. We couldn't tell them exactly where we were in Sweden. Joe then sent a postcard to Danny back in the Jagerndorf camp to say that we were safely through. Incidentally, apparently the guards never found out how we managed to get out of that barrack-room, and a special squad was sent in to investigate — but they had no success either, so it remained a mystery. Danny did such a good job on those bars that he should have got a medal too. I sent a postcard to one of our friends in Lamsdorf asking him to thank the Escape Committee in Stalag VIIIB for their non-co-operation. I never found out if they received the message.

We were told we would eventually be airlifted back to the UK and must be on standby, ready to move out at any moment. During the course of our stay the family was visited by two RAF officers wearing BOAC uniforms. Apparently they flew in and out of Stockholm to collect the diplomatic mail. Their aircraft were unmarked Mosquito bombers, unarmed so that they didn't break the Geneva Convention rules. Not to be outdone, the Germans used the same system but they used Messerschmidts, which were also unmarked and unarmed to fly between Stockholm and Berlin. All very nice and proper, but both sides had a little game of guessing when these particular aircraft would be in the air, and real fighter planes would stooge around and try to shoot them down, with a fair rate of success on both sides.

The next few weeks were spent on a social round of invitations to both British and Swedish homes. We had often heard of the higher standard of living in Sweden but it had to be seen to be believed. Time flew pleasantly by and we slowly recuperated and became fairly normal people again, though we all still had difficulty in sleeping properly. Time was the only cure for this.

One beautiful summer morning John Wright told us that the Invasion had begun and this was the news the whole world was waiting for. We were now on Red Alert to fly home, so we had to be packed and ready to go at any moment. Twenty-four hours later Joe was the first to be taken to the airport and sent home. Jimmy and I were to go on the following day but in separate aircraft. When our turn came I was highly excited as we dressed up in flying suits and then donned a parachute harness.

Jimmy and I then parted to go on our separate bombers. I was given quick instructions on how to plug in the oxygen mask and transmitter and told not to talk over the intercom as the pilot and navigator wanted no interference on this channel while flying. There was a wire mesh cage fitted in the bomb-bay and this could be raised and lowered to carry the mail. Now came the crunch. I was told not to put my parachute pack on to the harness, as I wouldn't be able to get into the bomb-bay if I was wearing it. There wasn't enough space. I was to push my pack in first and then climb in.

After I was in and had located my plug-in point, the horrible truth dawned on me — I didn't need a parachute because there was no way I could possibly wear it if anything happened. This actually wasn't quite true; I could wear it as long as I stayed in the plane. The bomb-bay doors closed and the pilot came on the intercom to check that I was OK and reminded me that I was on radio silence until we arrived home.

In the dark I thought over our sudden parting from the Wright family and how hospitable and friendly they had been. We had become extremely fond of them and would miss them. These thoughts were soon inter-rupted by the roar of twin engines warming up. A few minutes later we were airborne. Listening to what was going on between the pilot and the navigator was a revelation. Everything was being done at top speed. The idea was to get up as high as possible in the shortest time, and when this point was reached, it was a high-speed dive straight down to Scotland. The intercom was alive with staccato bursts of talk — was that something? How about over there? Above? Something caught my eye . . . no, not there, over to the left. All the time I was hoping that the Luftwaffe would be too busy on the new front to worry about us.

CHAPTER
THIRTY-FIVE

It didn't seem to be very long before the pitch of the engines changed to a less menacing tone and, as if in harmony with this, the voices of the crew became less tense. Subconsciously, it also had an effect on me, as I was now able to stop my fingernails biting into the palms of my hands, though I had been completely unaware of this until I relaxed.

Although I could see nothing outside, my stomach told me quite clearly that we had started to dive towards Scotland. Now, for the first time, I started to wonder how Jimmy was doing in his Mosquito and if he had worked out how much good his parachute would be in the case of accidents. This train of thought was soon ended as the crew began to radio in for landing instructions. We were soon bumping along the runway at Leuchars. When we finally came to a standstill, the bomb-bay doors were silently opened and the infernal wire basket was lowered and I was able to throw out my parachute pack before clambering out onto the runway. A truck was waiting to collect the diplomatic mail but I was told to stand by and within a few minutes the plane carrying my big brother landed and finally rolled to a stop near ours.

Jimmy scrambled out and after a big congratulatory success hug we made our way together to the flight office. Here, after getting out of all the flying paraphernalia, we heartily and profusely thanked our respective crews and wished them luck for the future. Unfortunately, this didn't do them much good; we heard later from Sweden that my crew were shot down and killed about six weeks later. Naturalists wonder what drives the lemmings to their suicidal rush to their deaths over cliffs into the sea, but what about the men who enter a war where the odds are stacked against them? Many times in prison camp I thought about what I would do if we ever got home safely, and the recurring answer was that never again would they get me into a situation that didn't correspond with the job I had signed up to do.

Why should a signalman like myself end up lying behind a bren gun on a road block, when his commander-in-chief and all his elite troops were on a ship heading for home? How was it that some people had done so much better? For example, a friend of mine, also a signalman in our line section, was on the same assignment with Joe and me when we ended up in Bolougne and were diverted to the road block. He worked it out and decided that this wasn't why he was in France, and so he slung his hook and headed for home where he was, of course, welcomed as a Dunkirk hero. Believe it or not, by the time we arrived home in 1944 he was a major in the Royal Signals and the three of us were still signalmen. So much for desertion in the face of the enemy and getting your just deserts.

An officer from Military Intelligence came forward and introduced himself. He told us that we would have to go through the whole rigmarole of how, where and when again, but it seemed to get easier each time and he kept the information he required to a minimum. I have to admit that I couldn't tell you his name or what he looked like, and when he stopped me several weeks later in the Intelligence Depot in Wentworth to ask how I was, I had no recollection of having met him before. He said this was understandable as Jimmy and I were quite overwrought on our arrival from Sweden.

When our debriefing session was finally over, we were passed to the Duty Officer for his attention. What we fervently hoped for was a rail warrant to Glasgow but this hope was quickly dashed. We were told to proceed under escort to the War Office in London for some real interrogation by the experts who were waiting for us. Apparently only about a dozen British POWs had reached Sweden since the beginning of the war, so we made up twenty-five percent of this figure, which wasn't bad going for three lads from Glasgow.

Jimmy and I had been in touch with big brother William, who was the only one in the family with a telephone in his home. Only now could we tell him where we were and where we were going next. The family couldn't understand why we weren't allowed to return to Glasgow rather than travel south to London. We couldn't answer this question, and personally I was beginning to think in terms of another escape. All we wanted was to go home, see our family and sleep in our own beds, but for the moment this was impossible.

Instead, after a meal and early bed we had to catch the first train in the morning to Edinburgh and travel with our escort to London. We were promised that after the London debriefing we would finally be allowed to go home. This still seemed awfully remote, and not at all as we had pictured our homecoming.

CHAPTER
THIRTY-SIX

Luckily for us, we had seats reserved on the train, otherwise we would have had to join the crowd of service and civilian travellers who had to sit on their suitcases and various other forms of luggage in the crowded corridors of the Edinburgh-London express. We were being escorted in the nicest possible way to our debriefing session with the Intelligence personnel of the three services about our successful escape from the POW camp.

The three of us were beginning to feel tired and edgy. When you consider that in the morning we had been in Sweden, then flown to Scotland in Mosquito bombers, and were now heading for London in an overcrowded train, this was perhaps understandable. Jimmy O'Neill, my brother, Joe Harkin, my friend, and John McCallum, myself, were hitting a very low ebb after the euphoria of our big success. If we hadn't been so spoiled in Sweden, maybe it wouldn't have been so bad, but coming down to earth with such a big bang was difficult.

If all politicians had to suffer hardship and deprivation after a war was declared, then there would be no more war; talking is easy and cheap, but you still need the silly sods who will go out and do the dirty work for the professional talkers. If the cabinet ministers who declare a state of war were forced to operate from the front line then, as they promised in the two world wars, we would indeed all be home for Christmas. It's strange the thoughts that run through your head when you're suffering from a major anticlimax.

Halfway into England we managed to get a cup of tea and some sandwiches from a trolley at one of the stations we stopped at, and although we complained about the quality, we were grateful to be able to get them at all. As we moved further south, we were shocked at what we saw on the roads. An interminable array of all sorts of tanks and other armoured vehicles were parked along sections of the main roads along with thousands of trucks of all kinds and weights.

My mind went back to the day the efficient German army had rolled past me on the road block outside Bolougne; I had felt sorry for our troops behind me, knowing what they had to face. Now the boot was on the other foot and I could almost sympathise with the enemy, knowing the scale of the equipment that was ready to engage them. Strange pictures and thoughts were racing through my mind. They were brought to an abrupt end as Jimmy shook me awake and told me we were in London.

By the time we had consumed a greasy breakfast in the dingy station restaurant, I was once again fully awake. I was expecting to see the horrific damage that London had suffered at the hands of the Luftwaffe, but the crafty cab driver took a devious route that showed none of this. London looked like a normal bustling metropolitan city as we passed through. Our strictly anonymous escort quickly arranged our security passes at the reception desk in the War Office and handed us over to another escort. We were taken through a maze of corridors and finally arrived at a door which mysteriously opened. Our escort ushered us in and closed the door behind us. Here, we were suddenly greeted by real people again.

Representatives of the three Armed Services interviewed us, each being interested in different things, and extracted information from us that we had no idea we had. The RAF intelligence officer made notes of the fact that the lovely big red Post Office building still stood untouched in the middle of Stettin. By the look on his face this would not be the case for very long. The Navy were naturally interested in what we had seen in the dock area. Military intelligence had the hardest job as their interest stretched from 1939 until now, the middle of 1944. Eventually we were squeezed dry and they handed us over to an officer who would arrange our proper documentation, plus pay, plus leave, plus rail warrants for our journey home and back to a reporting camp on the termination of our leave.

When the smug captain stated that we would be granted twenty-eight days' leave and would then return to the army selection unit designated on our leave passes, it all started to go wrong. I politely interrupted and asked him to repeat the number of days of leave.

149

This he promptly did, whereupon I informed him that as far as I was concerned this was completely unacceptable and nowhere near the amount of accrued leave we were due for the last five years. Can you imagine — the Dunkirk fiasco, four years in POW, you make your own way home — and you're told you can have five and a half days' leave for every year that you were away. I asked the good captain if he could tell me exactly how many days' leave he had had in the last five years, at which point he threatened to bring in the sergeant-major and have me arrested for insubordination.

Jimmy realised I had gone too far and told me to be quiet and give the officer a chance to clarify the situation, which he did. He told us that if at the end of twenty-eight days we felt we needed more time to adjust, then we should ring him and he would make the necessary arrangements. Why he couldn't have said that in the first place I don't know, though it is possible that I didn't give him a chance. The paperwork was duly completed and, after a few nasty looks, we parted company. Now our target was home.

We finally settled down in the northbound train from Euston which, like the last train we were on, was overcrowded. I now had time to think some loving thoughts about Traudl and try to come up with some way of letting her know what had happened since we had parted company. The three of us discussed the problem and always came up with the same answer. Any attempt to get in touch with her would compromise her safety and wellbeing. It seemed ironic that we could inform Stalag VIIIB of our success but couldn't tell Traudl. I felt if we had discussed it with her before we left, she would probably have come up with a solution to the problem. Perhaps the reason we had never discussed it was that, in my heart, I had never really believed we would succeed. I did ask advice from the Foreign Office later. They said there was nothing anyone could do at this stage of the war. So, for the present, it was a case of putting it out of my mind, which I didn't find easy.

CHAPTER
THIRTY-SEVEN

After another rude awakening I was told that we were approaching Glasgow. I began to wonder if I was going to spend the rest of my life dropping off to sleep. Strangely enough, to this day I only have to close my eyes and I can doze off, even standing up. It may have some connection to the severe nervous attacks I had developed, even though these were occurring less and less — thank God, as they were still terrifying when they happened.

Outside the station we said goodbye to Joe for the present and arranged when we would meet again. Then Jimmy and I shared a taxi as we lived quite close to each other. Glasgow didn't look any different after years of war, and soon we were in Maryhill and I was kissing my sister-in-law Clara "hello and goodbye". A few minutes later the taxi was turning into the street where my mother lived. Flags and bunting and "Welcome Home John" banners were strung all over the place and surprised me because I had never been very familiar with any of the neighbours. Most of them would never have recognised me under normal circumstances, but now they knew what I looked like because of the newspaper stories and photographs.

The family re-union doesn't have to be described, but was certainly memorable. No-one seemed to think it strange, though, that in twenty-eight days we would be expected to enter the fray again. With what results next time, I wondered? I thought of asking them to alter the banners to read "Welcome Home John — for twenty-eight days".

During the four years we had been in POW camp we had all assumed that if or when we returned to the UK the war would be over for us. But here we were, faced with the possibility of doing another five years, perhaps even longer. What we had heard in London was that the army was delighted we were back because tradesmen of our calibre were at a premium and that we would be back in service with as little delay as possible. What they didn't know was that at least one tradesman had no intention of going back to the Royal Signals to start all over again. In 1937 I had enlisted in the Reservists in this rank and now in 1944 my rank was still the same. My gut feeling was that there must be something else that I could do in the army that would give me promotion virtually immediately, and when I returned to duty this would be my top priority.

On the surface everything looked the same in Glasgow but things were very different when you moved around. I went into a tobacconist's in Maryhill Road two days later and, without thinking, casually asked the nice old grey-haired man behind the counter for twenty Players. First he looked at me as if I had come from another planet, then he thought over what I had asked for and finally he burst into hilarious laughter. While he was still laughing I went outside the shop and checked the sign above the door to make sure I was in the right establishment. Then I re-entered and repeated my request for twenty Players. When he calmed down, he asked me where I had been hiding for the last few years. After hearing my story, he realised I was one of the three he had read about in the papers, and went on to explain that good cigarettes were at a premium and hard to come by unless you were in the good books of your friendly tobacconist. Then the kind old gentleman produced the said cigarettes from behind the counter and promised that while I was on leave I could have twenty Players every day. Needless to say, we became good friends.

CHAPTER
THIRTY-EIGHT

Suddenly I had fan mail. But when mother said that I would have to answer it all, the fun of being famous evaporated. I compromised by placing a "thank you" ad in the newspapers. Then the neighbours organised a presentation dance in the church hall. The presentation that they made was a leather wallet containing money which had been collected for me. I was supposed to make a speech, but I was completely incapable of doing so. As far as I remember I muttered something about "thanks a million" and sat down. Reporters came and went and one of them even tried to buy the snap-brim soft hat that I had got in Sweden — with no success, I may add.

I had three weeks of going to bed when I felt like it and, even more important, not getting up in the morning until I wanted to, staying in or going out just as I pleased, and all this without armed guards controlling my movements. It seemed too good to be true. We had just spent almost five years in uniform, at all times under the command of someone else in uniform, never having any say in what we were going to do next, nor when we were going to do it.

We had often dreamed and fantasised about how wonderful it would be to be back in the way of life we were now leading, but that was when we thought it would never happen. But it had, and now after three weeks of inactivity, I realised I was bored and unhappy. Mother did her best by suggesting people I should go and visit. This unfortunately didn't solve my problem and it was almost with relief that I realised that in a few days we would be heading south again to start all over again.

Within myself, I knew it was a very different person starting out this time. I may not have been a better person, but I was much harder and definitely more ambitious. After the usual tearful and sad farewells to the family, the three of us met and set out on the next phase of our adventures, wondering how and when this part would end.

CHAPTER
THIRTY-NINE

The Army Selection Training Unit (ASTU) that we had to report to was new and foreign to our previous experience of army discipline. As telephone engineers we were skilled tradesmen, and had been treated with a certain respect, to the extent of being allowed a great deal of laxity in matters of drill and square-bashing and even dress. In this new establishment we were lumped together with rejects from other units, misfits and new recruits. The idea was to classify and put a qualification tag on the finished article. Individually, we might have come to grief in this place, but as a team we managed to stay out of trouble and kept ourselves to ourselves as far as possible. This wasn't always easy, as a lot of the troublemakers were trying to get out of the army altogether.

I came to grief very quickly and it happened very simply. We had just finished eating our main meal in the mess-hall on the second day there and I was about to scrape my plate clean in the swill-bin when the duty sergeant-major screamed at me, asking what I thought I was doing. Politely I explained that I couldn't eat any more. Presumably the bins would be collected and the contents used as pig-swill, so it wouldn't go to waste. I thought this would mollify him but it seemed to have the opposite effect. He became livid and I thought he was going to burst. He began to scream again, asking if I realised that thousands of merchant seamen had died to get that food to us and here was an unworthy sod scraping it into the swill-bin as if it grew on trees. I tried to explain that there had only been a tiny bit left on the plate and that I was very sorry about the seamen, but his rage continued. He took my name, rank and number and put me on a charge for wasting food. Since signing on in 1937 I had never been on a charge, and here I was in 1944 being put on one by a big ugly bastard who had never been out of the country and for five years had been eating and drinking at the expense of the army.

The following morning I was marched into the duty officer and the charge read out. When I explained that my stomach had shrunk and under what circumstances, the charge was dropped and I was marched out again. So I still had a clean sheet. My priority for the remainder of the time spent in this camp was to keep as far away as possible from the sergeant-major. Fortunately I managed this and no further incidents occurred.

After we had been whipped into shape physically, we were assessed on our individual ability to use our brainpower. The result was a mass of very quick postings. The Mensa tests and the Morse code recognition tests created havoc and the assessments were soon made.

Jimmy and Joe were posted to the Royal Signals Depot at Catterick. This was to be our final parting in the army and it turned out to be quite emotional, which was not at all surprising after all we had been through in the past five years. Before they left we received official word that we had been awarded Military Medals for our recent achievement. We had been told that this would probably happen but when it did it was a nice highlight to the last few gruelling months and years! Our battledress tunics were taken to the regimental tailor and were soon returned with three lovely medal ribbons stitched on the chest. They were the ribbons of the MM, the 1939–43 Star as it then was, and the Territorial Medal for twelve years' service (which we wouldn't have been entitled to except that the war years counted double). I had an extra embellishment in the form of a gold vertical stripe on my left forearm, showing that I had been wounded in action. I always kept my hand over the ribbons if the sergeant-major was anywhere in sight so that I wouldn't antagonise him.

I was pretty lonely after the boys left, but as a counter to this the rest of the course became quite intensive. We always knew when the training was going to get rough or dirty because then we had to parade in denims. If anyone had told me then that they would become a pet hatred, I would never have believed them. I hated them then, and still do.

CHAPTER
FORTY

In the middle of the course I was called in to the major's office and asked if I would consider foregoing the trip to Buckingham Palace for the medal presentation. If I would, then he would arrange to have the presentation made by the CO on the barrack square. I readily agreed to this as it suited my retiring nature better.

Eventually the whole course was completed and I was informed that my new category in the army included a note indicating I was a PO3. Just in case this was something nasty and could be held against me, I asked what it meant. It was explained that it was the code for Potential Officer Grade Three. I wonder what I had done wrong to fail Grades One and Two?

Next was the visit to the officer who decided where you went from here. My guardian angel arranged for it to be the nice major I had become fairly friendly with. Earlier in the course he had arranged a trip together on some pretext and had stopped at a restaurant for a very tasty lunch. It dawned on me later that this was partly to see if I knew how to eat properly and wouldn't be an embarrassment in the Mess.

We chatted a little and then he pointed out that there would be no difficulty in disposing of me. I would automatically be returned to the Royal Signals, where it wouldn't take too long to bring me up to date. Quietly I asked if I could tell him a little of what had been going on in my mind over the past few months. He agreed to listen.

In the next few minutes I tried to explain to him how it felt to have signed on as a signalman and be starting all over again five long years later, my rank still the same. My younger brother had volunteered after the war started and was now a corporal in the Signals, and one of the signalmen who had skipped the job on the road-block on which I was wounded and captured was now a full-blown major. Surely he must understand that if this new army and I were going to be compatible there had to be some sort of instant promotion, otherwise I would most likely be returning to No. 1 ASTU as a problem soldier.

When I stopped talking he sat looking at me for some time. Finally he shrugged his shoulders and gave me a rueful smile. He then admitted that if he were to carry out his duty properly, it would be back to the Signals and no arguments. On the other hand it would be intriguing to see if anything could be conjured up to make my dreams come true. He suggested that we should begin by looking at the military manual and seeing what that might produce. I asked if the Military Police would be an option and this was promptly turned down, but it did trigger something in his mind and he remembered that he had a pal in the

Intelligence Corps. He began to check the manual for the required qualifications for the IC and the next few minutes would have made a wonderful script for the music halls.

First question — what university or college did you attend? I told him he could stop right there, but the major was in full flight and wanted details. I told him the best we could do was St George's Road AC (Advanced Central), a school I had left aged 14. He said that if we left out the Road and put AC together it would look like Academy, and St George's Academy sounded like a very good school to him.

The next question was — how many languages do you have and with what degree of fluency? I explained to him that although I had been one year in France, I couldn't speak French, but he insisted that I must know a lot of French words. This I couldn't deny, so he summed it up as "French — fair". Then he insisted that if I had been four years in Germany I must be fluent. I was honest and said that I wasn't capable of carrying on an intelligent conversation in German. His summing up was "German — colloquial".

His next step was to telephone his chum in Wentworth Woodhouse, which was the Intelligence Corps Depot, and after a cosy little chat it was arranged that I would appear there as soon as possible for an interview with their recruiting officer. I thanked this very kind man for his attempt to solve my problem and promised to do my utmost not to let him down.

The interview was a success and I was accepted for training with the new intake. The course turned out to

162

be both rigorous and demanding, physically and mentally, with quite a number of drop-outs, and you emerged as a rather different person. I was posted out to Northern Command to complete my ground training and, operating from Sheffield, part of my security duties included visits to two German POW camps, namely Lodge Moor and Doncaster Racecourse. This was a real turn-up for the book after having done four years in captivity myself. I must say, they were better fed than we were.

CHAPTER
FORTY-ONE

Our section officer was Captain Philip Haigh, who earlier in the war had been unfortunate enough to encounter a hand grenade, but time had healed the damage. Like my own, his nightmares probably went on for a long time, though increasingly spaced out.

He was a lean, dapper, handsome and well-educated man, naturally cheerful, and he always made you feel you were lucky to be working for him. I asked him one day if it would be on the cards for me to be included in his section if he were ever given a posting to Germany. Without hesitation, he said that if it were at all possible, he would keep me in mind; he was as keen to go there as I was. I didn't tell him about Traudl as it didn't seem relevant yet. The way the war was going, it looked as if I wouldn't get the chance. Monty had been told to stand fast and engage the main resistance of the German army while the Americans were racing in their tanks all over the rest of the country. However, the day came and I was recalled to the Intelligence Depot to be told by Captain Haigh that he had finally been detailed to take a section to Brussels, our Field HQ for Germany.

I was one up on the rest of the section as I had already worked with the boss, but it didn't take long to get acquainted during our kitting-up period. Two of the team were Scots. One was Bob Hunter from Larkhall and the other was Andy Thomson from Glasgow. Bob and I became good friends and later I had the pleasure of being best man at his wedding. He was seconded to Intelligence from the Royal Scots Greys, a very proud horse regiment. To me, Bob always looked and walked like a cowboy. To crown it all, if we were ever out on an assignment, he would fold the cover of his revolver holster in, so that the butt stood out — very effective. Andy was different altogether. Where Bob was dark in complexion, Andy was blonde, and it took a bit longer to get to know him, though we became quite friendly later on.

Our sergeant-major was a taciturn little man and much more mature than the rest of us. I never really got to know him as his main job was administration and, of course, most of the time we were out and about and had little contact with each other. My other friend in the new section was "Benny" Goodman, who was a little rounder than the rest of us, which perhaps acounted for his very good nature. His proper name was Victor but everyone preferred to call him Benny. On the whole, I felt that the section was fairly well balanced, with a mixture of what I would call hard men and intellectuals. Whether this had been deliberately achieved or not I wouldn't know, but what I did know was that a very great number of security sections would be required for the occupation of Germany when the capitulation came.

We had been allocated to the MI8 side of the business, which covered port and frontier security. I was hoping for some remote frontier where I could maybe have a chance to contact Traudl.

The section was finally kitted out and we had only to collect our vehicles. As everyone had to be mobile you were either allocated a 30-hundredweight truck or a motorbike. Andy and I were on the bike squad. Along with some others we went off to collect our machines, which turned out to be beautiful gleaming new BSA 500s. My joy at seeing them was short-lived as they were immediately spray painted with horrible camouflage green. There was an almost conciliatory bonus when I learned that Andy was an expert mechanic and specialised in motorbikes. He proved this many times over in the period that we were together. Any tuning or adjustments that he made on his bike were duplicated on mine. The captain, of course, got the ubiquitous Jeep with a driver called Paddy thrown in for good measure. As his name implied, he hailed from the Emerald Isle and was indeed gifted with the gab, which he was willing to demonstrate at all times.

We were all set to go and had started our convoy to the coast when the German High Command decided to call it a day. It is just possible that they heard we were coming but I doubt it. They must have had enough when Hitler opted out in his Berlin bunker.

The VE celebrations stopped us in our tracks and it took us about two days to get to the landing ship tank which was to take us over to Belgium, then about another two days to reach a jubilant HQ which was still celebrating. When we got our marching orders, my heart sank, and I wondered if it had all been in vain — our posting turned out to be Hamburg, in the north-west of Germany — it couldn't have been further away from where I wanted to be. My mind went back over the unbelievable training course — riding through the woods with the motorbike, then up and down old shale bings, through the water and the mud of the tank testing grounds, until I thought I would never be able to walk normally again.

On top of this there was the gruelling physical side: everything had to be done in a set time, followed by intensive map reading and orienteering day-and-night schemes. This was interspersed with square-bashing under a guard drill sergeant instructor and weapon training ranging from the revolver to the bazooka. After all that, I had ended up in Hamburg. It was the old story of Fate kidding you along and then kicking you in the teeth. Then again, the options had been quite clear. A return to the Signals at Catterick, a posting to Scottish Command, or the one I had been offered at Intelligence Corps. Even now I have to admit that this was still the one that would be my first choice, although it was definitely in the wrong direction.

HQ sent us on our way with a sharp reminder to pay close attention to our map reading. Just before the capitulation one of our sections had gone off and when they arrived at their destination they found themselves in a town still occupied by the German army.

The 500-mile run up to the north-east was a real slog. All sorts of convoys were on the move, including heavy and light armour, troops and provisions. Our bikes were red-hot trying to keep our little lot together and eventually we reached the outskirts of Hamburg. Then the picture of the devastation caused by our Air Force began to unfold.

You could see it and you could smell it, but you couldn't comprehend it. It was like a canvas painted by some manic depressive artist who had lost control of his theme and ended up painting a lot of rubbish without being able to stop and carried on and on painting this nightmarish landscape. When we crossed the Elbe bridge into Hamburg the nightmare continued for mile after mile and the smell got worse. Hundreds of thousands of women and children and old people had either been blown to pieces or burned to death in this area. Before the war the residents here had regarded the British as their cousins because of their close relationship in the shipping business. They found it incomprehensible that we could even think of bombing them, but unfortunately, geographically, they were about the nearest German target that was worth bombing.

I still hadn't got used to all the empty shells of buildings as we passed through the main square where the Rathaus was situated and carried on northwards until we reached the dome of the Hauptbahnhof and then turned into the first street after this on the left. We stopped at a small hotel which was to be our home until we were demobbed. There were two fairly similar hotels adjacent to ours, and all three were occupied by security sections. The staff in these establishments had been retained, including cooks, cleaners and chambermaids, so we would eat, sleep and drink here in comparative comfort.

CHAPTER
FORTY-TWO

Early next morning after breakfast, we went down town to the Priengebaude on the corner of the Alster, a little lake in the centre of Hamburg, and occupied our new offices on the top of the building. Here we would do all our interrogations and paper work.

Our next trip was down to the dock area in St Pauli and to our dock offices on the Landungsbrugge. From here we would operate with our fleet of launches and cover the arrival and departure of all shipping on the river. This was one of the world's main ports. Our job included checking crews and passengers, and issuing shore-leave passes where authorised. With all this in mind, it wasn't surprising that our good captain was soon promoted to the rank of major, which suited him and us much better, and with it went the nice Mercedes he had acquired from somewhere. Paddy loved the Merc too.

It took time to get used to the black market that operated in the street outside our hotel. Our trucks and motorbikes parked outside made no difference to the people who traded there. We had to take it in our stride, and in one instance it was quite handy. When I was asked to do a report on the black market, I would go out and arrest someone, bring them in and get the information that I wanted, then give them a drink and turn them loose. I would carry on like this until I had all the information that I needed.

Meantime people were taking rubble out of the houses and carrying bricks and wood back in; glass was being replaced in the windows. It was like watching a colony of ants. Very quickly things were beginning to take some sort of shape and order. I noticed from my bedroom window that two girls occupied a bedroom on the ground floor of the house opposite. One was a very pretty blonde and the other a not-so-pretty brunette, presumably sisters. They certainly showed a healthy interest in what was going on in our rooms, and I made a note to look into the situation when we were a bit more settled. In the first month we were in Hamburg we were tied down with interrogations and arrestable categories till we couldn't think clearly. What really amazed me was the number of people who wanted to denounce someone. It quickly became apparent that the majority of these cases were attempts to settle grudges, and most of them were time-wasters we could do without.

The major called Bob and me into his office one morning to ask if we would do one of the town sections a favour. They had been trying to arrest one of the shipping magnates for some time, but with no success. Our boss had been having a drink with this section officer and asked if maybe a couple of his boys could have a go at picking up the magnate, to which the section officer readily agreed, probably thinking we

171

would have no more success than them. When we were told it was Herr Essberger, I was really surprised, as his shipping line was extremely well known and he would most certainly be very well protected from unwelcome callers. His office building was on the other side of the Alster lake, almost opposite our town office. We were told that his personal office was on the first floor, and on the days he didn't stay in the office, he almost invariably made it a morning visit. The other section's surveillance team claimed that he was never seen entering or leaving the building, so he had to have another way in. Bob and I opted for the direct approach and hoped for the best.

The next morning, at about ten-thirty, we pulled up in front of the building next to Herr Essberger's. Bob parked the truck and I slung over my shoulder the sten-gun that I had decided to bring along for effect. True to form, Bob tucked in the holster cover of his .38 so that the gun butt stuck out. This, along with his black beret, made him look very intimidating. Then we walked along to the Essberger front door.

When we reached the front steps, the action became fast and decisive. We were through the front door like a couple of greyhounds at White City, and I passed through the receptionist's office before she could blink or press any buttons. I pulled the plug on the switchboard. Our next move was to usher the confused young lady out of her office and lock the door, putting the key in my pocket. The three of us then entered the lift and went up to the first floor where there was no mistaking the door that led to the boss's office. We signalled the girl to be quiet and knocked gently on the door. A polite voiced asked us to enter.

I didn't know what to expect but I certainly was surprised at the reception we received. The nice-looking gentleman behind the large desk looked only momentarily surprised at the sight of such unlikely visitors, but breeding tells, and with a charming smile he asked us in beautiful English how he could help us. I explained to him that we were from Intelligence and that he was now under arrest because of his rank in the Party. Personally, I thought he looked quite relieved, as though he was glad it was finally over. We got him to empty the contents of his safe and all the papers on his desk into a couple of boxes and, after returning the key of the office to the young lady, we left quietly. We returned to our office and handed over the boxes and Herr Essberger to our very surprised major, who thanked us and gave us an approving nod.

CHAPTER
FORTY-THREE

The Germans were working like beavers in the rubble of the city, clearing roads, tidying up and digging out the remains of their shattered homes, slowly making places to live in. Brickies, joiners and plumbers were working all the hours God sent to make the ruined buildings habitable again. Money was useless, although almost anything could be procured on the black market. The shops were empty and only the strictest supply of rations could be bought on coupons and, as non-fraternisation was in vogue, help from the troops was not yet a possibility. This is where we were a thorn in the side of the Military Police. We carried a card that authorised us to carry civilians in our vehicles and to consort with them in the line of duty. We often had to produce this and leave a very disgruntled MP behind, especially when our passenger happened to be a pretty girl. Something else that got up their noses was our permits to carry automatics instead of the regulation .38s. We were even issued with Mauser semi-automatics in their strange wooden holsters, which could be clipped on the butt, although the only time I ever used this weapon was for hunting in the forest outside the city.

We eventually conquered the huge pile of routine interrogations which, in turn, led us on to the more interesting work of individual investigations. This required a list of contacts and informants who had to be carefully vetted, so that as little time as possible would be wasted. I had a great stroke of luck when Eric da Silva, one of our section sergeants, asked me if I would take one of his contacts off his hands as he just could not get on with the guy. In all fairness to the German, Eric felt that he had a lot to offer. This led me into a friendship which lasted for many years and was very productive.

Jack Rothschenk was born a Hamburger. He was a little smaller than myself, stockily built, and he spoke fluent English with a broad Brooklyn accent, which he had acquired in the States. He was a broken-down German version of Edward G. Robinson with the voice to match and, to crown it all, he was a seamen's union boss. This was, of course, ideal for the type of information we were looking for and paid off handsomely in the long run. His mode of transport was an old American Studebaker and it suited him and his extravert personality perfectly. Jack was happily married to both his wife and his secretary, who was completely indispensable to him and lived in his office most of the time, though her home was in a little town called Gluckstadt ("Happy Town"), situated near the mouth of the River Elbe.

Benny and I made a racing visit to Gluckstadt one day after a phone call from Jack informed us that Deputy Führer Martin Bormann would be smuggled out in a freighter from there. After our enquiries were complete, we realised that we were a little too late, which was a great pity as it would have put us into the history books. One of our sections did pick up Von Ribbentrop, who had been the German Foreign Minister, so presumably he was in Hamburg trying to find a way out. This was, of course, why we had so many sections and such a strong presence in the port.

Lunchbreak was my favourite time of the day. We would head for the Sergeants' Mess, which was in the Ratsweinkeller in the basement of the Town Hall. The town councillors certainly knew how to live off the ratepayers, as the restaurant and bars below the town hall were opulent. Here we would dine and drink in a manner that had no resemblence to the world outside. These were definitely the best two hours of the day, and set me up for the rigours of the afternoon's work.

Most of the evenings turned out to be serious drinking sessions, though this slowly changed as we began to sort out some kind of love life, which after all was inevitable. I still thought about Traudl but couldn't come up with a solution. I didn't dare risk writing in case the letter was intercepted, which would have led to her arrest and possible death. I decided that patience was required for a while longer. My hormones were not listening again, which was not surprising considering the amount of talent parading around us advertising its availability.

I had craftily solved the problem of how to get at the promiscuous young blonde across the road, who kept giving me the green light from her bedroom window at the front of the house. The section trucks were parked on the other side of the road, so I asked Benny if he would reverse his vehicle up on to the pavement so that the rear end would be right outside blondie's bedroom window, with just enough space for me to climb into the truck. The next step was to tell the young lady of this strategy and arrange a time for our first meeting. This worked out nicely and the meeting duly took place with me sitting on her window sill and her kneeling on a chair inside her bedroom.

Things progressed from then on and Ingeborg and I had a lot of fun together. I was amazed at how little knowledge I had about sex and how to enjoy it, but a spell in Hamburg was a revelation. The Reeperbahn is world-renowned, but I recommend a guided tour with someone well-connected with the area, otherwise it could turn out to be most alarming, and has been known to be fatal.

Jack Rothschenk knew the Reeperbahn and the St Pauli area intimately and was well liked and accepted by the Red Light fraternity. Naturally, I got to know a lot of people in this area as it was adjacent to the Landungsbrucke where our dock offices were. It took me some time to notice that Jack never paid for anything when we were having a night out in St Pauli; there was so much of the old boy network in operation that I was quite amazed. We could go to places where they served T-bone steaks and eggs, and yet some people had difficulty in obtaining the rations shown on their books. Hard liquor was almost unobtainable, but this is where I was a godsend, as our rations were quite generous and of very high quality. We received invitations from people who wouldn't normally have given us the time of day.

One such person was a friend of Jack's called Cesar. He was the oldest son of a patrician Hamburg family with a huge business interest in the dock area. Cesar was a graduate of Oxford, which became apparent when he spoke English; under normal circumstances he wouldn't have consorted with the likes of Jack or myself but, as they say, war makes strange bedfellows. One of his main weaknesses was alcohol, and why shouldn't he befriend a good provider of the hard stuff when it was in extremely short supply? He was great company, and the three of us had some memorable parties, some in very high-class company.

This worked out wonderfully well for me, as Americans in Stuttgart had asked for co-operation from Hamburg on some underground activities which affected them. The boss asked me if there was any possibility of getting close to the source. I talked to Jack about it and he said that the old Anti-Nazi Committee might be able to help. They had a meeting arranged for a couple of weeks later and, as Jack was a member, he would be there; I asked him if it would be possible for me to be present. His answer was an emphatic "No", as the mere sight of a uniform anywhere near the meeting place would cause an automatic cancellation. I then asked him if I would be admitted with him if I was in civvy clothes and he agreed that this would be allowed. Intelligence Corps personnel were allowed to wear civvy clothes in the UK but not abroad, so I had a problem. There was no point in asking the boss because he was duty-bound to say "No", but what he didn't know wouldn't do him any harm. So, Jack and I visited the Merchant Navy tailor and he made me a double-breasted dark suit. The reason I wanted to be at the meeting in person was that I wanted to hear Jack ask the right questions and to hear the answers personally.

We duly attended the meeting and got what sounded like the information we were looking for, though only further investigation would show if this was of any consequence. By a horrible coincidence it led us into the middle of the social group we had been partying with. We had been seeing quite a lot of one charming couple who lived in a big flat in town. It was fairly obvious that Cesar was in love with the wife, whose name was Jacquie, though he was always circumspect when husband Heinz was about. Jack and I were shocked when we were told that the key figure in the equation was indeed our friend Heinz. I passed the information on to the boss, and when he asked me to give him a detailed report, I told him that I could give him an abridged version. Immediately he asked if I had been naughty and broken some rules, and when I admitted that this was indeed the case, he smiled his most charming smile and told me to make it as plausible as possible.

One month later Heinz was dead. He was apparently killed in a freak accident where his head was crushed between his car and a caravan he was using. The funeral was very private.

CHAPTER
FORTY-FOUR

This type of hard work and hard drinking went on until I was finally demobbed in January 1946. After collecting my civvy clothes at Redford Barracks in Edinburgh, I went home to Mum to enjoy about five months' accumulated leave. All the know-alls said that after about a month of inactivity I would be raring to go back to work, but this didn't happen. First, I arranged to get a passport. This didn't take too long, and while I was waiting for it to come through, I applied for an entry visa to Czechoslovakia, but the authorities said this wouldn't be forthcoming for a long time. Coincidentally, the passport arrived at the same time as a letter from the Control Commission for Germany (CCG) asking if I was interested in returning to Germany in the post of a British Passport Officer.

This new and unexpected development required a lot of thought; I was still a Civil Servant and would be required to return to my parent department. The old me would naturally have done exactly what was expected of me but the new me had no qualms about answering the letter and saying that I would indeed be interested in the proposition, thinking that probably nothing would come of it. I decided to say nothing about the offer to the Engineering Department; I still had a few months' leave left, so it wasn't really relevant.

The first surprise came a few weeks later when I was invited to attend an interview in London. When I saw the competition in the waiting room, I gave up any hopes of a post. There were Group Captains, Lt. Colonels, Naval Officers and Uncle Tom Cobley and all — all out to carry on from where they had left off in the war but, please, not back to civvy street. The only laugh I had was when the security man in the entry hall checked my name against his list and said I would be the gentleman from MI, which flummoxed me until I worked it out — he had me down as Military Intelligence.

The board were very nice and very impressive and I would have given all of them a job. After the interview I was thanked politely and ushered out. I thought that would be the end of it, but a few weeks later another letter arrived from this distinguished panel inviting me for a further inquisition. This time I knew who I was before the doorman told me. In the office, to my surprise, there was an old friend working as chief clerk. He had been one of our section sergeants in Hamburg. Taffy, as he was known to us, told me in confidence that I had finished high in the ratings of the last interview and I was definitely on the short-list for one of the posts. When I asked him why he wasn't on it, he said that he had tried and this was the best that he could do.

The board went over much the same ground as the last time, but with a little more emphasis here and there. Again I was thanked but this time they said I would probably hear from them. Sure enough, a couple of weeks later the final demand arrived, but now there was one discordant note from a member of the panel, who apparently was a senior Civil Servant. He very properly pointed out that I was not in a position to accept the post as I was duty-bound to return to my parent department when my leave was finished — so what did I have in mind? My reply was that if the post was offered to me and the Civil Service didn't release me, then I would offer my resignation and take their job, since I considered it important enough to warrant such action.

There was a flurry of whispers and the result was that I would be allowed to take the job, if I agreed to return to the department when the post became redundant. I was advised to apply for a passport immediately, and there were a few knowing smiles when I said that I already held a current passport. How wrong they were in their thinking.

Details of salary, uniform and rank were worked out, and I was to start as a Control Officer, Grade 3, which was the equivalent rank of captain. I then notified my department of what was happening and reported to my new HQ in Germany, where I was informed that I should have taken over Major Haigh's command in Hamburg, but would I please go to Cuxhaven instead and set up the controls for the arrival of the British Forces married families.

CHAPTER
FORTY-FIVE

After we had escaped, I had asked for promotion and responsibility and it was given to me. The post of BPO was certainly a full-time job, requiring lots of memory work on policy and regulations, with no set hours, but with the usual complete freedom to commandeer staff and accommodation. In Cuxhaven I took over the Yacht Club as our Passport Office and employed the best civilian staff available, though my main help came from the Frontier Control Service personnel.

When the Cuxhaven Control was running smoothly, I was transferred to Hamburg and, after changing the three officers who had been employed there for three new ones who could be trained properly, I settled into Major Haigh's old position with a feeling of justifiable pride. To crown it all I was also promoted to the grade of Control Officer 2, equivalent to the rank of major. So, as far as I was concerned, the wheel had come full circle. It was shortly after this that a letter from Traudl got redirected to me with the good news that she was well — and the bad news that she had got tired of waiting to hear from me and had married a Czech army officer!

CHAPTER
FORTY-SIX

A rest period was long overdue, and it finally came in the form of a posting to Lübeck, a town which straddles the River Trave, which in turn runs into the Baltic Sea. This reminded me of our POW posting to Bad Karlsbrunn in Sudetenland, as it was a real holiday area and the workload was almost non-existent. I still kept in touch with Hamburg, and it was on one of these trips that fate decided that for me the war was over.

Normally, my driver Hans would have been at the wheel of the Mercedes on our way back from Hamburg, but on this particular beautiful spring day I had decided to drive myself, or perhaps the gods who control these things had decided for us. In any case we passed a young lady smiling by the roadside, with her thumb in the classic hitchhiking position. It has never been my policy to give people lifts but, to my great surprise, my foot went onto the brake pedal and we came to a stop.

When the beautiful face with the lovely tan asked for a lift into Lübeck, who could have refused? By the time we had reached town I had asked her to have dinner with me, but she accepted only after a lot of persuasion. Her name was Franziska, or Frankie for short, and you know the song about Frankie and Johnnie being lovers. Eventually we were, and still are to this day. We were together from then on and in November 1949 we decided to come home and get married.

Knowing Frankie brought me a great inner peace and a stability that had been sadly lacking. Various people remarked on the more estimable character that I became after meeting her. I was offered another promotion but we both decided that enough was enough, and when you think about it, ten years out of your life is surely all that can be expected from you.

So we kissed Germany goodbye and came home.

Also available in ISIS Large Print:

In Action with the SAS

Roy Close

Already a member of the Territorial Army, Roy was mobilised in 1939 and joined the British Expeditionary Force in France. After three days and two nights on the Dunkirk beaches he was evacuated back to England.

He was then sent to North Africa and a chance meeting resulted in his transferring to the newly formed Parachute Regiment and, from there, the elite Special Air Service.

In 1944 he was infiltrated into German-occupied France where he operated with the Maquis resistance organisation. During the closing stages of the War the scene shifts to Holland and the advance through Germany. The author describes life in newly liberated Paris and Berlin in the early post-war years.

ISBN 0-7531-9364-7 (hb)
ISBN 0-7531-9365-5 (pb)

Lost Souls of the River Kwai

Bill Reed with Mitch Peeke

This is the moving story of a young man who found himself, along with thousands of his comrades, in the nightmare of Japanese captivity. Before long he was a slave labourer on the notorious Burma Railway, living under the most atrocious conditions and subject to barbarous treatment by his captors. Unlike so many (it is said that one Commonwealth POW died for every sleeper laid) Bill Reed somehow managed to survive to tell the tale. Along with his graphic memories of the horrors and hardships of the Railway of Death, Bill also describes how his experiences have affected his life since.

This is a moving and well-written account of war at its darkest and the strength of the human spirit at its strongest.

ISBN 0-7531-9354-X (hb)
ISBN 0-7531-9355-8 (pb)

Friends and Romans

John Miller

With a single daring leap from an Italian train carrying prisoners of war, John Miller jumped out of the war of soldiers and into the war as lived by Italian civilians — many of whom risked their lives to help him.

The year was 1943 and Captain Miller had been in captivity for over a year. Italian anti-fascists harboured and fed him, first in a remote mountain village, then in Rome itself. For months he posed as a deaf-mute and member of the Fascist Youth in order to dodge German patrols and the Italian secret police — until the Allied liberation of Rome brought GIs flooding onto the streets.

This is a war memoir with a difference, in which the heroics are those of ordinary people and everyday life, in which a fugitive forms an intimate bond with people from another culture — and comes to realise the ironies of national conflict.

ISBN 0-7531-9342-6 (hb)
ISBN 0-7531-9343-4 (pb)

They Also Serve

Dorothy Baden-Powell

At the Scandinavian Section of the SOE, Dorothy Baden-Powell was engaged in sending saboteurs into occupied Norway and debriefing them on their return to London. After spending a year and a half with the SOE, she was given an assignment in the WRNS to try to break a ring of enemy spies. They were based on HMS Raleigh, a naval training camp at Plymouth and were sending information to Germany about the movements of British warships from nearly every port in the United Kingdom. She endured the privations of life on the lower deck, the unwelcome scrutiny of a particularly unpleasant WRNS Superintendent, and a trumped-up charge and subsequent court-martial.

Finally, she uncovered an enemy agent trying to be taken on as a sailor, and by a combination of bravery, sheer determination and luck, succeeded in having him captured. With her assignment successfully completed she gladly returned to her job with the SOE.

ISBN 0-7531-9336-1 (hb)
ISBN 0-7531-9337-X (pb)

Undercover Operator

Sydney Hudson

Memoirs of SOE agents have always been rare — many
were either killed in action or executed — and today
they are almost unheard of. But Sydney Hudson's story
is just about as dramatic and thrilling as any to have
ever appeared. After volunteering for guerilla operations
should the Germans occupy Britain, he transferred to
SOE. He spent most of the Second World War in
France, remarkably surviving 15 months captivity and
interrogation before making a daring and thrilling escape
through the Pyrenees into Spain. Shortly after, he was
back in France, again by parachute, to organize resistance
operations until the arrival of the US 3rd Army. More
secret missions followed behind enemy lines with a
female agent. Thereafter he volunteered for further SOE
work in the Far East where he served in India and
Thailand. He was twice decorated with the Distinguished
Service Order for his efforts and also awarded the Croix
de Guerre.

ISBN 0-7531-9340-X (hb)
ISBN 0-7531-9341-8 (pb)

Tracing Your Irish Ancestors
The Complete Guide

JOHN GRENHAM

GILL AND MACMILLAN

Published in Ireland by
Gill and Macmillan Ltd
Goldenbridge
Dublin 8
with associated companies in
Auckland, Budapest, Gaborone, Harare, Hong Kong,
Kampala, Kuala Lumpur, Lagos, London, Madras,
Manzini, Melbourne, Mexico City, Nairobi,
New York, Singapore, Sydney, Tokyo, Windhoek
© John Grenham 1992
0 7171 1898 3
Print origination by
Seton Music Graphics Ltd, Bantry, Co. Cork
Printed by Colour Books Ltd, Dublin

A catalogue record is available for this book from
the British Library.

For Doireann and Eoin

Contents

Part 1 Major Sources

Part 2 Other Sources

Part 3 A Reference Guide

List of Illustrations

Acknowledgments

My greatest debt is to Mr Donal Begley, Chief Herald of Ireland; without his encouragement and endless patience this work would never have been started. I also owe a great deal to the other members of staff at the Genealogical Office, in particular Colette O'Flaherty and Willie Buckley of the Consultation Service, and the Assistant Chief Herald, Fergus Gillespie. My former colleagues in Hibernian Research, Tom Lindert, Anne Brennan, Eileen O'Byrne and Éilis Ellis have all generously shared their knowledge and experience, and contributed very welcome advice and suggestions. I am also grateful to the staff of the National Library, the General Register Office, the Public Record Office of Northern Ireland and the National Archives for all their help to me over the years; I am particularly indebted to Jim O'Shea of the National Library for his help with Chapter 13. The member centres of the Irish Family History Foundation were also of great assistance, especially Dr Chris O'Mahony of Limerick Archives, Seán O Súileabháin of Leitrim County Library, Brian Mitchell of Derry Inner City Trust, and Theo McMahon of Monaghan Ancestral Research, as was Noel Reid of the Irish Family History Society. I owe special thanks to my father, Seán Grenham, who drew the parish maps, and to Jonathan Hession, who took the photographs and helped out with rest and recreation. Needless to say, none of those who helped me have any responsibility for the errors and omissions: these are all my own. Finally, I thank my wife Breda Kearney for all her tolerance and encouragement.

Abbreviations

AH	*Analecta Hibernica*
C. of I.	Church of Ireland
DKPRI	Deputy Keeper of Public Records in Ireland
GRO	General Register Office
GO	The Genealogical Office
IA	*The Irish Ancestor*
IG	*The Irish Genealogist*
IGRS	Irish Genealogical Research Society
ILB	Irish Large Book (National Library)
IMA	*Journal of the Association for the Preservation of the Memorials of the Dead in Ireland*
IMC	Irish Manuscripts Commission
Ir.	Irish (National Library prefix)
IUP	Irish University Press
J	Joly Collection pamphlet (National Library)
JCHAS	*Journal of the Cork Historical and Archaeological Society*
JCLAS	*Journal of the Co. Louth Archaeological and Historical Society*
JGHAS	*Journal of the Galway Historical and Archaeological Society*
JKAHS	*Journal of the Kerry Archaeological and Historical Society*
JKAS	*Journal of the Co. Kildare Archaeological Society*
JLB	Joly Large Book (National Library)
JNMAS	*Journal of the North Munster Antiquarian Society*
JRSAI	*Journal of the Royal Society of Antiquaries of Ireland*
LC	Local Custody
LO	Library Office (National Library)
mf	Microfilm
MS.	Manuscript
MSS.	Manuscripts
MFCI	Microfilm of Church of Ireland records (National Archives)
MP	Member of Parliament

n.d.	no date
NA	National Archives
NL	National Library
O'K	*O'Kief, Coshe Mang etc.* (ed. Albert Casey)
P.	Pamphlet (National Library)
Ph.	Phillimore publication
Pos.	Positive (microfilm)
pr. pr.	privately printed
PRONI	Public Record Office of Northern Ireland
PRS	Parish Register Society Publication
RCBL	Representative Church Body Library
RDKPRI	Report of the Deputy Keeper of Public Records of Ireland
RIA	Royal Irish Academy
TCD	Trinity College Dublin
Unpub.	Unpublished

DOWN & CONNOR DIOCESE

1	Aghagallon & Ballinderry	1828
2	Ahoghill	1833
3	Antrim	1874
4	Armoy	1848
5	Ballintoy	1872
6	Ballyclare	1869
7	Ballymoney	1853
8	Belfast city:	
	Belfast	1798
	Holycross	1868
	St Joseph	1872
	St Malachy	1858
	St Mary	1867
	St Patrick	1875
	St Peter	1866
9	Blaris	1845*
10	Braid & Glenravel	1825
11	Carnlough	1869
12	Carrickfergus	1821
13	Culfeightrin	1825
14	Cushendall	1837
15	Cushendun	1834
16	Derryaghy	1877
17	Duneane	1835
18	Dunloy	1860
19	Glenavy	1848
20	Glenarm	1825
21	Greencastle	1854
22	Kirkinriola	1847
23	Larne	1821
24	Loughguile	1845
25	Portglenone	1864
26	Portrush & Bushmills	1844
27	Ramoan	1838
28	Randalstown	1825
29	Rasharkin	1848

*Local custody

ARMAGH DIOCESE

1	Armagh	1796
2	Ballymacnab	1820
3	Ballymore & Mullaghbhrac	1798
4	Clonfeacle (Moy)	1814
5	Creggan Lr	1845
6	Creggan Upr	1796
7	Derrynoose	1814
8	Drumcree	1844
9	Dungannon	1782
10	Eglish	1862
11	Faughart	1851
12	Forkhill	1844
13	Killeavy Lr	1835
14	Killeavy Upr	1832
15	Kilmore	1845
16	Loughgall	1833
18	Loughgilly	1825
19	Tynan	1822

DROMORE DIOCESE

20	Magheralin	1815
21	Newry	1818
22	Seagoe	1830
23	Shankill (Lurgan)	1822

*Earliest records in Armagh Diocesan Archives

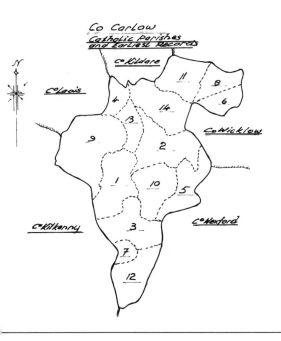

Co Carlow Catholic Parishes and Earliest Records

KILDARE & LEIGHLIN DIOCESE

1	Bagenalstown	1820
2	Ballon & Rathoe	1782
3	Borris	1782
4	Carlow	1787
5	Clonegall	1833
6	Clonmore	1813
7	Graiguenamanagh	1818
8	Hacketstown	1820
9	Leighlinbridge	1783
10	Myshall	1822
11	Rathvilly	1797
12	St Mullin's	1813
13	Tinryland	1813
14	Tullow	1763

]AGH & CLONMACNOISE)CESE

›rumlumman North	1859
›rumlumman South	1837
.crabby	1833

ATH DIOCESE

.arnaross	1805
.ilbride	1832
.ingscourt	1838

.MORE DIOCESE

.nnagh	1845
›allintemple	1862
.astlerahan	1752
.astleterra	1763
.orlough	1877
.rosserlough	1843
)enn	1856
)rumgoon (Cootehill)	1829
)rumlane (Staghall)	1836
)rung (see Kilsherdony)	—
)rumreilly	1867
;langevlin	1867
.ildallon (Ballyconnell)	1867
.illan (Bailieboro)	1835
.illeshandra	1835
.illinagh	1860*
.illinkere	1766
.ilmainhamwood &	
Moybologue	1867
.ilmore	1859
.inawley (Swanlinbar)	1835
.nockbride	1835

Co Cavan Catholic Parishes and Earliest Records

28 Kilsherdony	1803
29 Laragh	1876
30 Lavey	1867
31 Lurgan (Virginia)	1755
32 Mullagh	1842
33 Templeport	1827
34 Urney & Annegeliff	1812

*Earliest records in Cavan Heritage Centre

GALWAY DIOCESE

1 Beagh	1849
2 Ennistymon (Kilmanaheen & Cloony)	1823*
3 Glanaragh (Ballyvaughan)	1854
4 Kilcronin & Kilcorny	1853
5 Kilfenora	1836
6 Kilshanny	1870
7 Liscannor (Kilmacrehy & Killaspuglonane)	1843
8 Lisdoonvarna	1854
9 New Quay (Glanamanagh)	1836*

KILLALOE DIOCESE

10 Broadford	1844
11 Carrigaholt	1852
12 Clarecastle	1834*
13 Clondegad	1846
14 Clonrush (Mountshannon)	1846
15 Corofin	1818
16 Crusheen	1860
17 Doonass & Truagh	1851
18 Doora & Kilraghtis	1821
19 Dysart	1845
20 Ennis	1837
21 Feakle	1860
22 Inagh	1850
23 Inch & Kilmaley	1828
24 Kilballyowen	1878
25 Kildysart	1829
26 Kilfarboy (Milltownmalbay)	1831
27 Kilfidane	1868
28 Kilkee	1836*
29 Kilkeedy	1833
30 Killaloe	1828
31 Killanena (Flagmount)	1842
32 Killard	1855
33 Killimer	1859

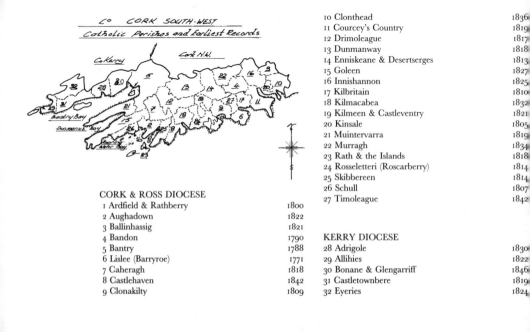

Co Clare
Catholic Parishes and Earliest Records

34 Kilmacduane	1853
35 Kilmihil	1849
36 Kilmurry-Ibrickane	1839
37 Kilmurry-McMahon	1837
38 Kilnoe & Tuamgraney	1832
39 Kilrush (St Senan's)	1827
40 Newmarket	1828
41 O'Callaghan's Mills	1835
42 Ogonnelloe	1832
43 Quin & Clooney	1816
44 Scarriff & Moynoe	1852
45 Sixmilebridge	1828
46 Tulla	1819

LIMERICK DIOCESE

47 Cratloe	1802
48 Parteen & Meelick	1814

*Earliest records in Clare Heritage Centre

Co CORK SOUTH-WEST
Catholic Parishes and Earliest Records

Co Kerry · Cork N.W.
Bantry Bay · Dunmanus Bay

CORK & ROSS DIOCESE

1 Ardfield & Rathberry	1800
2 Aughadown	1822
3 Ballinhassig	1821
4 Bandon	1790
5 Bantry	1788
6 Lislee (Barryroe)	1771
7 Caheragh	1818
8 Castlehaven	1842
9 Clonakilty	1809
10 Clonthead	1836
11 Courcey's Country	1819
12 Drimoleague	1817
13 Dunmanway	1818
14 Enniskeane & Desertserges	1813
15 Goleen	1827
16 Innishannon	1825
17 Kilbritain	1810
18 Kilmacabea	1832
19 Kilmeen & Castleventry	1821
20 Kinsale	1805
21 Muintervarra	1819
22 Murragh	1834
23 Rath & the Islands	1818
24 Rosseletteri (Roscarberry)	1814
25 Skibbereen	1814
26 Schull	1807
27 Timoleague	1842

KERRY DIOCESE

28 Adrigole	1830
29 Allihies	1822
30 Bonane & Glengarriff	1846
31 Castletownbere	1819
32 Eyeries	1824

10	Conna	1834
11	Doneraile	1815
12	Fermoy	1828
13	Glanworth & Ballindangan	1836
14	Glountane	1829
15	Imogeela	1833
16	Kildorrerry	1803
17	Killeagh	1822
18	Kilworth	1829
19	Lisgoold	1807
20	Mallow	1757
21	Midleton	1819
22	Mitchelstown	1792
23	Rathcormac	1792
24	Youghal	1801

CORK & ROSS DIOCESE

25	Carrigaline	1826
26	Cork city:	
	Blackrock	1810
	St Finbarr (South)	1756
	St Mary	1748
	St Patrick	1831
	SS Peter & Paul	1766
27	Douglas	1812
28	Glanmire	1803
29	Glounthaune	1864
30	Monkstown	1875
31	Passage West	1795
32	Tracton Abbey	1802
33	Watergrasshill	1836

WATERFORD & LISMORE DIOCESE

34	Lismore	1820

*Earliest records in Mallow Heritage Centre

CLOYNE DIOCESE

1	Aghada	1785*
2	Annakissy	1805
3	Ballymacoda	1835
4	Blarney	1778
5	Carrigtohill	1817
6	Castlelyons	1791
7	Castletownroche	1811
8	Cloyne	1786
9	Cobh	1812

CLOYNE DIOCESE

1	Aghabulloge	1820
2	Aghinagh	1848
3	Ballyclough	1805
4	Ballyhea	1809
5	Ballyvourney	1825
6	Banteer (Clonmeen)	1847
7	Buttevant	1814
8	Castlemagner	1832
9	Charleville	1774
10	Clondrohid	1807
11	Donaghmore	1790
12	Freemount (Milford)	1827
13	Glountane	1829
14	Grenagh	1840
15	Inniscarra	1814
16	Kanturk	1822
17	Kilnamartyra	1803
18	Liscarroll	1812
19	Macroom	1780
20	Mourneabbey	1829
21	Newmarket	1821
22	Rock & Meelin	1866
23	Shandrum	1829

CORK & ROSS DIOCESE

24	Ballincollig	1820
25	Iveleary	1816
26	Kilmichael	1819
27	Kilmurry	1786
28	Ovens	1816

KERRY DIOCESE

29	Ballydesmond	1868*
30	Boherbue	1833
31	Dromtariffe	1832
32	Millstreet	1853
33	Rathmore	1837

LIMERICK DIOCESE

34	Ballyagran	1841
35	Kilmallock	1837

*Local custody

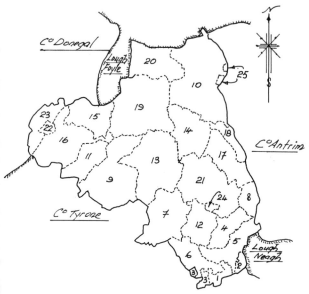

Cᵒ Derry
Catholic Parishes
and Earliest Records

ARMAGH DIOCESE

1	Arboe	1827
2	Ballinderry	1826
3	Cookstown (Desertcreight)	1827
4	Magherafelt	1834
5	Moneymore	1832
6	Lissan	1839

DERRY DIOCESE

7	Ballinascreen	1825
8	Ballyscullion (Bellaghy)	1844
9	Banagher	1848
10	Coleraine (Killowen)	1843
11	Cumber Upr	1863
12	Desertmartin	1848
13	Dungiven	1847
14	Errigal (Garvagh)	1846
15	Faughanvale	1860
16	Glendermot	1864
17	Greenlough	1846
18	Kilrea	1846
19	Limavady	1855
20	Magilligan	1863
21	Maghera	1841
22	St Eugene's (Derry city)	1873
23	Templemore (Derry city)	1823
24	Termoneeny	1837

DOWN & CONNOR DIOCESE

25	Ballymoney	1853
10	Coleraine	1848

CLOGHER DIOCESE

1	Carn (Pettigo)	1836
2	Inishmacsaint	1847

DERRY DIOCESE

3	Burt	1856
4	Clonca	1856
5	Clonleigh	1773
6	Clonmany	1852
7	Culdaff	1838
8	Desertegney	1864
9	Donagh	1847
10	Donaghmore	1840
11	Iskaheen (Moville Upr)	1858
12	Moville Lr	1847
13	Urney	1829

RAPHOE DIOCESE

14	All Saints	1843
15	Annagry	1868
16	Ardara	1867
17	Aughnish	1873
18	Clondahorky	1877
19	Clondavaddog	1847
20	Conwal & Leck	1853
21	Drumholm	1866
22	Glencolumbkille	1880
23	Gortahork (Raymunterdoney)	1849
24	Gweedore	1868
25	Inishkeel (Glenties)	1866
26	Inver	1861
27	Kilbarron	1854
28	Kilcar	1848
29	Killaghtee	1845
30	Killybegs	1850
31	Killygarvan	1868

Cᵒ Donegal
Catholic Parishes
and Earliest Records

32	Killymard	1874
33	Kilmacrennan	1862
34	Kilteevogue	1855
35	Lettermacaward (Dungloe)	1876
36	Mevagh	1871
37	Raphoe	1876
38	Stranorlar	1860
39	Tawnawilly	1872
40	Termon & Gartan	1862

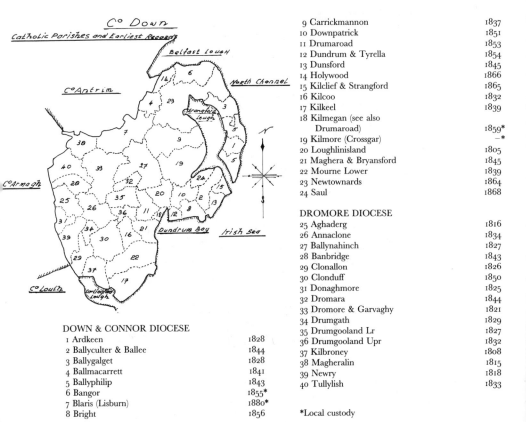

Co Down
Catholic Parishes and Earliest Records

9 Carrickmannon	1837
10 Downpatrick	1851
11 Drumaroad	1853
12 Dundrum & Tyrella	1854
13 Dunsford	1845
14 Holywood	1866
15 Kilclief & Strangford	1865
16 Kilcoo	1832
17 Kilkeel	1839
18 Kilmegan (see also Drumaroad)	1859*
19 Kilmore (Crossgar)	—*
20 Loughlinisland	1805
21 Maghera & Bryansford	1845
22 Mourne Lower	1839
23 Newtownards	1864
24 Saul	1868

DROMORE DIOCESE

25 Aghaderg	1816
26 Annaclone	1834
27 Ballynahinch	1827
28 Banbridge	1843
29 Clonallon	1826
30 Clonduff	1850
31 Donaghmore	1825
32 Dromara	1844
33 Dromore & Garvaghy	1821
34 Drumgath	1829
35 Drumgooland Lr	1827
36 Drumgooland Upr	1832
37 Kilbroney	1808
38 Magheralin	1815
39 Newry	1818
40 Tullylish	1833

DOWN & CONNOR DIOCESE

1 Ardkeen	1828
2 Ballyculter & Ballee	1844
3 Ballygalget	1828
4 Ballmacarrett	1841
5 Ballyphilip	1843
6 Bangor	1855*
7 Blaris (Lisburn)	1880*
8 Bright	1856

*Local custody

CLOGHER DIOCESE

1 Aghavea	1862
2 Aughalurcher (Lisnaskea)	1835
3 Carn (Pettigo)	1836
4 Cleenish	1835
5 Clones	1821
6 Derrygonnelly	1853
7 Drumully	1845
8 Enniskillen	1818
9 Galloon	1847
10 Garrison	1860
11 Inishmacsaint	1847
12 Irvinestown	1846
13 Magheraculmany	1836
14 Roslea	1862
15 Tempo	1845

KILMORE DIOCESE

16 Drumlane	1836
17 Kildallan	1867
18 Killesher	1855
19 Kinawley	1835
20 Knockninny	1855

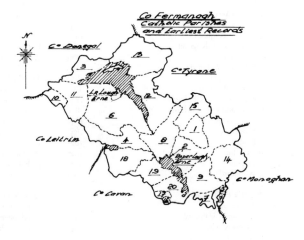

Co Fermanagh
Catholic Parishes and Earliest Records

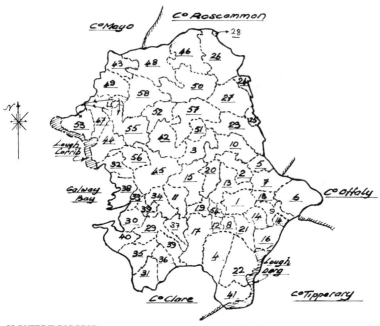

East Galway
Catholic Parishes and Earliest Records

CLONFERT DIOCESE

1	Abbeygormican & Killoran	1846
2	Aughrim & Kilconnell	1828
3	Ballymacaward & Cloonkeenkerrill	1841
4	Ballinakill	1839
5	Ballinasloe (Creagh & Kilcloony)	1820
6	Clonfert	1829
7	Clontuskert	1827
8	Duniry & Ballinakill	1839
9	Fahy & Kilquain	1836*
10	Fohenagh & Kilgerill	1827
11	Kilconickney	1831
12	Kilcooley & Leitrim	1815
13	Killallaghten	1809
14	Killimorbologue	1831
15	Killimordaly (Kiltullagh)	1830
16	Kilmallinogue (Portumna)	1830
17	Killeenadeema	1836
18	Kiltormer	1834
19	Loughrea	1827
20	New Inn	1827
21	Tynagh	1809
22	Woodford	1821

ELPHIN DIOCESE

23	Ahascragh	1840
24	Athleague & Fuerty	1807
25	Dysart & Tisrara	1850
26	Glinsk & Kilbegnet	1836
27	Killian & Killeroran	1804
28	Oran (Cloverhill)	1845*

GALWAY DIOCESE

29	Ardrahan	1839
30	Ballindereen (Kilcolgan)	1854

31	Beagh	1856
32	Claregalway	1849
33	Clarenbridge (Kilcornan)	1837
34	Craughwell	1847
35	Gort (Kilmacduagh)	1848
36	Kilbeacanty	1854
37	Kilchreest	1855
38	Oranmore (Kilcameen & Ballynacourty)	1833
39	Peterswell (Kilthomas)	1854
40	Kinvarra	1831

KILLALOE DIOCESE

41	Mountshannon (Clonrush)	1846

TUAM DIOCESE

42	Abbeyknockmoy	–
43	Addergoole & Liskeevy	1858
44	Annaghdown	1834
45	Athenry	1858
46	Boyounagh	1838
47	Donaghpatrick & Kilcloona	1844
48	Dunmore	1833
49	Kilconly & Kilbannon	1872
50	Kilkerrin & Clonberne	1855*
51	Killascobe	1807
52	Killererin	1851
53	Killursa & Killower	–
54	Kilmeen	–
55	Kilmoylan & Cummer	1813
56	Lackagh	1841
57	Mountbellew (Moylough)	1848
58	Tuam	1790

*Local custody only

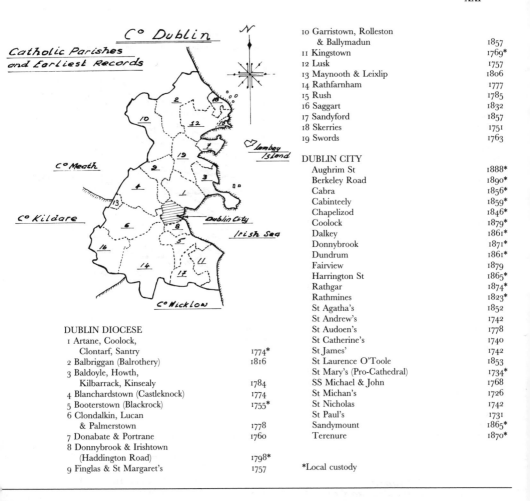

Co Dublin

Catholic Parishes
and Earliest Records

Co Meath

Co Kildare

Lambay Island

Dublin City

Irish Sea

Co Wicklow

10 Garristown, Rolleston	
& Ballymadun	1857
11 Kingstown	1769*
12 Lusk	1757
13 Maynooth & Leixlip	1806
14 Rathfarnham	1777
15 Rush	1785
16 Saggart	1832
17 Sandyford	1857
18 Skerries	1751
19 Swords	1763

DUBLIN CITY

Aughrim St	1888*
Berkeley Road	1890*
Cabra	1856*
Cabinteely	1859*
Chapelizod	1846*
Coolock	1879*
Dalkey	1861*
Donnybrook	1871*
Dundrum	1861*
Fairview	1879
Harrington St	1865*
Rathgar	1874*
Rathmines	1823*
St Agatha's	1852
St Andrew's	1742
St Audoen's	1778
St Catherine's	1740
St James'	1742
St Laurence O'Toole	1853
St Mary's (Pro-Cathedral)	1734*
SS Michael & John	1768
St Michan's	1726
St Nicholas	1742
St Paul's	1731
Sandymount	1865*
Terenure	1870*

DUBLIN DIOCESE

1 Artane, Coolock,	
Clontarf, Santry	1774*
2 Balbriggan (Balrothery)	1816
3 Baldoyle, Howth,	
Kilbarrack, Kinsealy	1784
4 Blanchardstown (Castleknock)	1774
5 Booterstown (Blackrock)	1755*
6 Clondalkin, Lucan	
& Palmerstown	1778
7 Donabate & Portrane	1760
8 Donnybrook & Irishtown	
(Haddington Road)	1798*
9 Finglas & St Margaret's	1757

*Local custody

GALWAY DIOCESE

1 Castlegar	1827
2 Galway (St Nicholas')	1690
3 Killanin (see also Oughterard)	1875
4 Moycullen	1786
5 Oranmore (Kilcameen	
& Ballynacourty)	1833
6 Oughterard (Kilcummin)	1809
7 Rahoon	1819
8 Rosmuck (see also Oughterard)	1840
9 Salthill	1840
10 Spiddal	1861

TUAM DIOCESE

11 Aran Islands	1872
12 Ballinakill	1875
13 Clifden (Omey & Ballindoon)	1838
14 Cong	1872
15 Clonbur (Ross) (see also	
Leenane)	1853
16 Killeen (Lettermullen	
& Carraroe)	1853
17 Leenane (Kilbride)	1853
18 Moyrus	1852
19 Roundstone (see also Moyrus)	1872

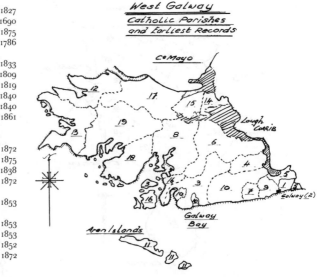

West Galway

Catholic Parishes
and Earliest Records

Co Mayo

Lough Corrib

Galway (2)

Aran Islands

Galway Bay

KERRY DIOCESE

1	Abbeydorney	1835
2	Annascaul (Ballinvoher)	1829
3	Ardfert	1819
4	Ballybunion & Ballydonohoe	1831
5	Ballyferriter	1807
6	Ballyheigue	1857
7	Ballylongford	1823
8	Ballymacelligot	1868
9	Boherbue	1833
10	Bonane	1846
11	Brosna	1868
12	Cahirciveen	1846
13	Cahirdaniel	1831
14	Castlegregory	1828
15	Castleisland	1822
16	Castlemaine	1804
17	Causeway	1782
18	Dingle	1821
19	Dromod (Waterville)	1850
20	Duagh	1819
21	Firies	1830
22	Fossa	1857
23	Glenbeigh	1830
24	Glenflesk	1821
25	Kenmare	1819
26	Kilcummin	1821
27	Kilgarvan	1818
28	Killarney	1792
29	Killeentierna	1801
30	Killorglin	1800*
31	Knocknagoshel	1850*
32	Listowel	1802
33	Lixnaw	1810
34	Milltown	1821
35	Moyvane	1830*
36	Prior (Ballinskelligs)	1832*
37	Rathmore	1837
38	Sneem	1845

39	Spa	1866
40	Tarbert	1859
41	Tralee	1772
42	Tuogh	1843
43	Tuosist	1844
44	Valentia	1825

*Earliest records in local custody

KILDARE & LEIGHLIN DIOCESE

1	Allen & Milltown	1820
2	Baltinglass	1807
3	Balyna (Johnstown)	1785
4	Caragh (Downings)	1849
5	Carbury	1821
6	Carlow	1787
7	Clane	1785
8	Clonbulloge	1808
9	Curragh Camp	1855
10	Kilcock	1770
11	Kildare & Rathangan	1815
12	Kill	1840
13	Monasterevin	1819
14	Naas & Eadestown	1813
15	Newbridge	1786
16	Robertstown	1852*
17	Suncroft (Curragh)	1805

DUBLIN DIOCESE

18	Athy	1753*
19	Ballymore Eustace	1779
20	Blessington	1852
21	Castledermot	1789
22	Celbridge	1768*
23	Kilcullen	1777
24	Maynooth & Leixlip	1806
25	Narraghmore	1827

*Local custody
**Earliest records in Kildare Heritage Centre

Co Kilkenny
Catholic Parishes and Earliest Records

6 Clara (see Gowran)	1809
7 Clough	1858
8 Conahy	1832
9 Danesfort	1819
10 Dunamaggan	1821*
11 Freshford	1773
12 Galmoy	1805
13 Glanmore	1831
14 Gowran	1809
15 Inistioge	1810
16 Johnstown	1814
17 Kilkenny city:	
St Canice's	1768
St John's	1809
St Mary's	1754
St Patrick's	1800
18 Kilmacow	1786*
19 Kilmanagh	1845
20 Lisdowney	1771
21 Mooncoin	1772
22 Muckalee	1801
23 Mullinavat	1843
24 Rosbercon	1817
25 Slieverue	1766
26 Templeorum	1803
27 Thomastown	1782
28 Tullaherin	1732*
29 Tullaroan	1843
30 Urlingford	1805
31 Windgap	1822

KILDARE & LEIGHLIN DIOCESE

| 32 Graiguenamanagh | 1818 |
| 33 Paulstown | 1824 |

*Earliest records in Kilkenny
Archaeological Society

OSSORY DIOCESE

1 Agahviller	1847
2 Ballyhale	1823
3 Ballyragget	1856
4 Callan	1821
5 Castlecomer	1812

DUBLIN DIOCESE

| 1 Athy | 1779 |

KILDARE & LEIGHLIN DIOCESE

2 Abbeyleix	1824
3 Arles	1821
4 Ballinakill	1794
5 Ballyadams	1820
6 Ballyfin (Cappinrush)	1819
7 Clonaslee	1849
8 Doonane	1843
9 Emo	1875
10 Graigue (Killeshin)	1819
11 Leighlinbridge	1783
12 Mountmellick	1814
13 Mountrath	1823
14 Portarlington	1820
15 Portlaoise	1826
16 Raheen	1819
17 Rosenallis	1765
18 Stradbally	1820

KILLALOE DIOCESE

| 19 Roscrea | 1810 |

OSSORY DIOCESE

20 Aghaboe	1794
21 Ballyragget	1856
22 Borris-in-Ossory	1840
23 Camross	1816

Co Laois
Catholic Parishes
and Earliest Records

24 Castletown	1794
25 Durrow	1789
26 Galmoy	1805
27 Lisdowney	1771
28 Rathdowney	1763

ARDAGH & CLONMACNOISE DIOCESE

1	Aughavas	1845
2	Annaduff	1849
3	Bornacoola	1824*
4	Cloone-Conmaicne	1820
5	Drumshanbo (Murhan)	1861
6	Fenagh	1825
7	Gortleteragh	1826
8	Killenummery & Killery	1827
9	Kiltoghert	1826
10	Kiltubbrid	1841
11	Mohill-Manachain	1836

KILMORE DIOCESE

12	Ballinaglera	1883*
13	Ballymeehan	1844
14	Carrigallen	1829
15	Clooneclare	1841
16	Drumlease (Dromahair)	1859
17	Drumreilly Lr	1867
18	Drumreilly Upr (Corlough)	1870
19	Glenade	1867
20	Inishmagrath	1830
21	Killargue	1852
22	Killasnet	1852
23	Kinlough	1835
24	Oughteragh (Ballinamore)	1841*

*Earliest records in Leitrim Heritage Centre

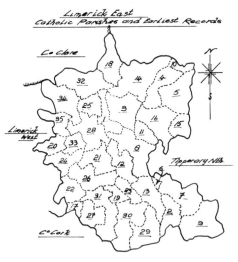

13	Knocklong	1809
14	Murroe & Boher	1814
15	Oola	1809
16	Pallasgreen	1811

CLOYNE DIOCESE

17	Charleville	1774

KILLALOE DIOCESE

18	Castleconnell	1850

LIMERICK DIOCESE

19	Ardpatrick (see Kilfinane)	1861
20	Banogue (see Croom)	1861
21	Bruff	1781*
22	Bruree & Rockhill	1826*
23	Bulgaden	1812
24	Croom	1770
25	Donaghmore	1827
26	Dromin & Athlacca	1817
27	Effin	1843
28	Fedamore	1806
29	Glenroe & Ballyorgan	1853
30	Kilfinane	1832
31	Kilmallock	1837
32	Limerick city:	
	St John's	1788
	St Mary's	1745
	St Michael's	1772
	St Munchin's	1764
	St Patrick's	1805
33	Manister (see Fedamore)	–
34	Mungret & Crecora	1844
35	Patrickswell & Ballybrown	1801

CASHEL & EMLY DIOCESE

1	Ballybricken	1800
2	Ballylanders	1849
3	Caherconlish	1841
4	Cappamore	1843
5	Doon	1824
6	Emly	1809
7	Galbally	1809
8	Hospital	1810
9	Kilbehenny	1824
10	Kilcommon	1813
11	Kilteely	1815
12	Knockaney	1808

*Earliest registers in Limerick Archives

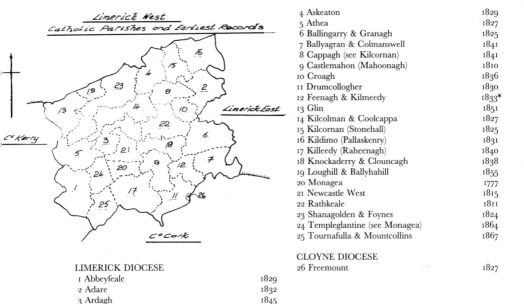

Limerick West
Catholic Parishes and Earliest Records

Co Kerry

Limerick East

Co Cork

4 Askeaton	1829
5 Athea	1827
6 Ballingarry & Granagh	1825
7 Ballyagran & Colmanswell	1841
8 Cappagh (see Kilcornan)	1841
9 Castlemahon (Mahoonagh)	1810
10 Croagh	1836
11 Drumcollogher	1830
12 Feenagh & Kilmeedy	1833*
13 Glin	1851
14 Kilcolman & Coolcappa	1827
15 Kilcornan (Stonehall)	1825
16 Kildimo (Pallaskenry)	1831
17 Killeedy (Raheenagh)	1840
18 Knockaderry & Clouncagh	1838
19 Loughill & Ballyhahill	1855
20 Monagea	1777
21 Newcastle West	1815
22 Rathkeale	1811
23 Shanagolden & Foynes	1824
24 Templeglantine (see Monagea)	1864
25 Tournafulla & Mountcollins	1867

CLOYNE DIOCESE

| 26 Freemount | 1827 |

LIMERICK DIOCESE

1 Abbeyfeale	1829
2 Adare	1832
3 Ardagh	1845

RDAGH & CLONMACNOISE
DIOCESE

Abbeylara	1854
2 Ardagh & Moydow	1793
3 Cashel	1850
4 Clonbroney	1849
5 Clonguish	1829
6 Columcille	1845
7 Dromard	1835
8 Drumlish	1834
9 Granard	1779
10 Kilcommuck	1859
11 Kilglass (Legan)	1855
12 Killashee	1826
13 Killoe	1826
14 Mostrim	1838
15 Mohill-Manachain	1836
16 Rathcline (Lanesboro)	1850
17 Scrabby	1833
18 Shrule (Ballymahon)	1820
19 Streete	1820
20 Templemichael	
& Ballymacormick	1802
21 Taghshiney, Taghsinod	
& Abbeyshrule	1835

MEATH DIOCESE

| 22 Drumraney | 1834 |
| 23 Moyvore | 1831 |

N

Co Longford
Catholic Parishes
and Earliest Records

Co Leitrim
Co Cavan
Co Roscommon
Co Westmeath

ARMAGH DIOCESE

1	Ardee	1763
2	Carlingford	1835
3	Clogherhead	1742
4	Collon	1772*
5	Cooley	1811
6	Creggan Upr	1796
7	Darver	1787
8	Dunleer	1772
9	Dundalk	1790
10	Faughart	1851
11	Kilkerley	1752
12	Kilsaran	1809
13	Lordship	1833*
14	Louth	1833
15	Mellifont	1821
16	Monasterboice	1814
17	St Peter's (Drogheda)	1744
18	Tallanstown	1804
19	Termonfeckin	1823
20	Togher	1791

CLOGHER DIOCESE

21	Carrickmacross	1837
22	Inniskeen	1837

MEATH DIOCESE

23	St Mary's (Drogheda)	1835

Earliest records in Armagh Diocesan Archives

Co Louth
Catholic Parishes and Earliest Records
Co Armagh

Catholic Parishes and Earliest Records
Co Mayo

ACHONRY DIOCESE

1	Attymass	1874
2	Bohola	1857
3	Carracastle	1847
4	Castlemore & Kilcolman	1830
5	Foxford (Toomore)	1833
6	Kilbeagh (Charlestown)	1845
7	Kilconduff & Meelick	1808
8	Kilgarvan	1844
9	Killasser	1847
10	Killedan (Kiltimagh)	1834
11	Kilmovee	1824
12	Kilshalvey, Kilturra, Cloonoghill	1833
13	Templemore	1872

GALWAY DIOCESE

14	Shrule	1831

KILLALA DIOCESE

15	Addergoole	1840
16	Ardagh	1846*
17	Backs	1815*
18	Ballycastle	1859
19	Ballycroy	1860
20	Ballysakeery	1843
21	Belmullet	1836
22	Crossmolina	1831
23	Kilcommon-Erris	1843
24	Kilfian	1826
25	Killala	1852
26	Kilmore-Erris	1816
27	Kilmoremoy	1823
28	Kiltane (Bangor)	1860
29	Lackan	1852
30	Moygownagh	1881

TUAM DIOCESE

31	Achill	1867
32	Aghagower	1828
33	Aghamore	1864
34	Aglish (Castlebar)	1824
35	Annagh	1851
36	Aughaval	1823
37	Balla & Manulla	1837
38	Ballinrobe	1843
39	Ballyovey (Tourmakeady)	1869
40	Bekan	1832
41	Burriscarra & Ballintubber	1839
42	Burrishoole (Newport)	1872
43	Clare Island	1851
44	Cong & The Neale	1870
45	Crossboyne & Tagheen	1862
46	Inishbofin	1867
47	Islandeady	1839
48	Keelogues	1847
49	Kilcolman (Claremorris)	1806
50	Kilcommon & Robeen	1857
51	Kilgeever	1850
52	Kilmaine	1854
53	Kilmeena	1858
54	Kilvine	—
55	Knock	1869
56	Mayo Abbey	1837
57	Turlough	1847

Earliest records in Mayo North Family History Research Centre

Co Meath
Catholic Parishes
and Earliest Records

8 Beauparc (Blacklion)	1815
9 Bohermeen	1831
10 Carnaross	1805
11 Carolanstown	1810
12 Castletown	1805
13 Clonmellon	1757
14 Curraha	1802
15 Drumconrath	1811
16 Duleek	1852
17 Dunboyne	1787
18 Dunderry	1837
19 Dunshaughlin	1789
20 Enniskeen	1838
21 Johnstown	1839
22 Kells	1791
23 Kilbride	1832
24 Kilmessan & Dunsany	1742
25 Kilskyre	1784
26 Lobinstown	1823
27 Longwood	1829
28 Moynalty	1829
29 Moynalvy	1783
30 Navan	1782
31 Nobber	1754
32 Oldcastle	1789
33 Oristown	1757
34 Rathcore & Rathmolyon	1878*
35 Rathkenny	1784
36 Ratoath	1780
37 Rosnaree & Donore	1840
38 St Mary's (Drogheda)	1835
39 Skryne	1841
40 Slane	1851
41 Stamullen	1830
42 Summerhill	1812
43 Trim	1829

*Earliest records in Meath Heritage
Centre, Trim

ARMAGH DIOCESE
1 Collon	1789

KILMORE DIOCESE
2 Kilmainham & Moybologue	1867

MEATH DIOCESE
3 Ardcath	1795
4 Athboy	1794
5 Ballinabracky	1826
6 Ballivor & Kildalkey	1759*
7 Batterstown	1836

ARDAGH & CLONMACNOISE DIOCESE
1 Banagher (Gallen & Reynagh)	1797
2 Clonmacnoise	1826
3 Lemanaghan & Balnahown	1821
4 Ferbane (Tisaran)	1819

CLONFERT DIOCESE
5 Lusmagh	1824

KILDARE & LEIGHLIN DIOCESE
6 Clonbulloge	1808
7 Daingean	1850
8 Edenderry	1820
9 Killeigh	1844
10 Portarlington	1820
11 Rhode	1829

KILLALOE DIOCESE
12 Birr	1838
13 Bournea (Couraganeen)	1836
14 Dunkerrin	1820
15 Kilcolman	1830
16 Kinnitty	1833
17 Roscrea	1810
18 Shinrone	1842

MEATH DIOCESE
19 Ballinabrackey	1826
20 Clara & Horseleap	1821
21 Eglish	1807
22 Kilcormac	1821

Co Offaly

Catholic Parishes
and Earliest Records

23 Rahan	1810
24 Tubber	1821
25 Tullamore	1801

OSSORY DIOCESE
26 Seirkeiran	1830

CLOGHER DIOCESE

1 Aghabog 1871
2 Aughnamullan East 1857
3 Aughnamullan West 1841
4 Ballybay (Tullycorbet) 1862
5 Carrickmacross (see also
  Magheracloone) 1838
6 Castleblayney (Muckno) 1835
7 Clones 1821
8 Clontibret 1861
9 Donagh (Glasslough) 1836
10 Donaghmoyne 1863
11 Drumully 1845
12 Drumsnat & Kilmore 1836
13 Ematris (Rockcorry) 1848
14 Errigal Truagh 1835
15 Killany 1857
16 Killeevan (Newbliss) 1871
17 Mahgeracloone 1826
18 Monaghan & Rockwallis 1827
19 Tydavnet 1825
20 Tyholland 1827

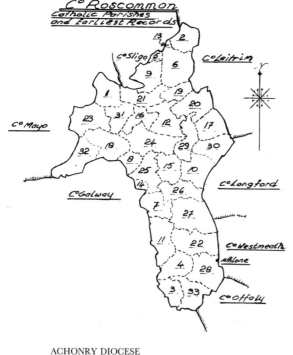

CLONFERT DIOCESE

3 Creagh 1820
4 Taghmaconnell 1842

ELPHIN DIOCESE

5 Aghanagh 1800
6 Ardcarne & Tumna (Cootehall) 1843
7 Athleague & Fuerty 1807
8 Ballintober & Ballymoe 1830
9 Boyle & Kilbryan 1792
10 Cloontuskert 1865
11 Dysart & Tisrara 1850
12 Elphin & Creeve 1808
13 Geevagh 1851
14 Kilbegnet & Glinsk 1836
15 Kilbride (Fourmilehouse) 1835
16 Kilcorkery & Frenchpark 1865
17 Kilglass & Rooskey 1865
18 Kilkeevan (Castlerea) 1804
19 Killukin & Killumod (Croghan) 1811
20 Kilmore & Aughrim 1816
21 Kilnamanagh & Estersnow 1859
22 Kiltoom (Ballybay) 1835
23 Loughglynn (Lisacul) 1817
24 Ogulla & Baslick 1864
25 Oran (Cloverhill) 1845*
26 Roscommon & Kilteevan 1820
27 St John's (Knockcroghery) 1841
28 St Peter's & Drum (Athlone) 1789
29 Strokestown 1830
30 Tarmonbarry 1865
31 Tibohine (Fairymount) 1833

ACHONRY DIOCESE

1 Castlemore & Kilcolman 1830

ARDAGH & CLONMACNOISE DIOCESE

2 Kilronan (Arigna) 1823

TUAM DIOCESE

32 Kiltullagh 1860
33 Moore 1876

*Local custody only

Co Sligo
Catholic Parishes
and Earliest Records

Atlantic Ocean

Sligo Bay

Co Leitrim

Co Mayo

Co Roscommon

8	Kilfree & Killaraght	1844
9	Killoran	1846
10	Kilmacteigue	1845
11	Kilshalvey, Kilturra, Cloonoghill	1840

ARDAGH & CLONMACNOISE DIOCESE

12	Killenummery & Killery	1827

ELPHIN DIOCESE

13	Aghanagh (Ballinafad)	1800
14	Ahamlish	1796
15	Drumcliffe	1841
16	Geevagh	1851
17	Riverstown	1803
18	Sligo	1831*

KILLALA DIOCESE

19	Castleconnor	1835*
20	Easkey	1864
21	Kilglass	1825
22	Kilmacshalgan	1868
23	Kilmoremoy	1823
24	Skreen & Dromard	1817
25	Templeboy	1815

ACHONRY DIOCESE

1	Achonry	1865
2	Ballysadare & Kilvarnet	1842
3	Castlemore & Kilcolman	1830
4	Cloonacool	1859
5	Curry	1867
6	Drumrat	1842
7	Emlafad & Kilmorgan	1824

KILMORE DIOCESE

26	Glenade	1867
27	Kinlough	1835

*Earliest records in Sligo Heritage Centre

ASHEL & EMLY DIOCESE

1	Anacarty (Donohill)	1821
2	Ballingarry	1814
3	Bansha & Kilmoyler	1820
4	Boherlahan & Dualla	1810
5	Cashel	1793
6	Clerihan	1852
7	Clonoulty	1798*
8	Drangan	1811
9	Emly	1809
10	Fethard & Killusty	1806
11	Galbally & Aherlow	1809
12	Golden	1833
13	Killenaule	1742
14	Knockavilla	1834
15	Lattin & Cullen	1846
16	Mullinahone	1809
17	New Inn	1798
18	Oola & Solohead	1809
19	Tipperary	1793

WATERFORD & LISMORE DIOCESE

20	Ardfinnan	1809
21	Ballylooby	1828
22	Ballyneale	1839
23	Ballyporeen	1817
24	Cahir	1776
25	Carrick-on-Suir	1784
26	Clogheen	1778
27	Kilsheelan (Gambonsfield)	1840
28	Newcastle	1814
29	Powerstown	1808

Co Tipperary Sth Riding
Catholic Parishes and Earliest Records

Co Limerick

Co Kilkenny

Co Limerick

Co Cork

Co Waterford

30	St Mary's, Clonmel	1790
31	SS Peter & Paul, Clonmel	1836

*Earliest records in local custody

CASHEL & EMLY DIOCESE

1	Ballina	1832
2	Ballinahinch	1839
3	Borrisoleigh	1814
4	Cappawhite	1804
5	Doon	1824
6	Drom & Inch	1809*
7	Gortnahoe	1805
8	Holycross (Ballycahill)	1835
9	Kilcommon	1813
10	Loughmore	1798
11	Moycarkey	1793
12	Newport	1795
13	Templemore	1807
14	Templetouhy & Moyne	1804
15	Thurles	1795
16	Upperchurch	1829

KILLALOE DIOCESE

17	Birr	1838
18	Borrisokane	1821
19	Castleconnell	1850
20	Castletownarra	1849
21	Cloughprior & Monsea	1834
22	Cloughjordan	1833
23	Couraganeen (Bournea)	1836
24	Dunkerrin (Moneygall)	1820
25	Kilbarron (Terryglass)	1827
26	Kilnaneave & Templederry	1839
27	Kyle & Knock	1845
28	Lorrha & Dorrha	1829
29	Nenagh	1792
30	Shinrone	1842

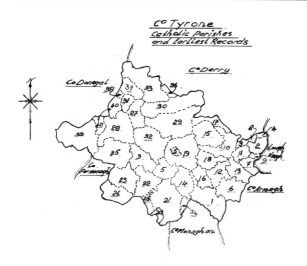

31	Silvermines (Kilmore)	1840
32	Toomevara	1830
33	Youghalarra	1820
34	Roscrea	1817

*Earliest records in local custody

ARMAGH DIOCESE

1	Aghaloo	1832
2	Ardboe	1827
3	Artrea (Magherafelt)	1830
4	Ballinderry	1826
5	Ballintacker	1832
6	Clonfeacle (Moy)	1814
7	Clonoe	1806
8	Coagh	1865
9	Coalisland (see also Donaghenry)	1861
10	Cookstown (Desertcreat & Derryloran)	182
11	Donaghenry (Coalisland)	182
12	Donaghmore (see Killeeshil)	18
13	Dungannon	178
14	Errigal Kieran	18
15	Kildress	18
16	Killeeshil	18
17	Lissan	182
18	Pomeroy	18
19	Termonmaguirk	18

*Earliest records in Armagh Diocesan Archives

CLOGHER DIOCESE

20	Aghalurcher	18
21	Clogher	18
22	Donaghcavey	18
23	Dromore	18
24	Errigal Truagh	18
25	Fivemiletown	18
26	Kilskeery	18

DERRY DIOCESE

27	Ardstraw East	18
28	Ardstraw West	18
29	Bodoney Lr	18
30	Badoney Upr	18
31	Camus (Strabane)	17
32	Cappagh	18
33	Donaghedy (Dunamanagh)	18
34	Drumragh	18
35	Langfield	18
36	Learmount	18
37	Leckpatrick (Strabane)	18
38	Mourne (see also Camus)	18
39	Termonamongan	18
40	Urney	

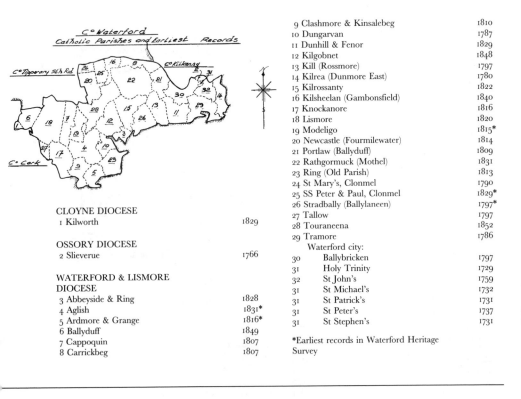

Co Waterford
Catholic Parishes and Earliest Records

9 Clashmore & Kinsalebeg		1810
10 Dungarvan		1787
11 Dunhill & Fenor		1829
12 Kilgobnet		1848
13 Kill (Rossmore)		1797
14 Kilrea (Dunmore East)		1780
15 Kilrossanty		1822
16 Kilsheelan (Gambonsfield)		1840
17 Knockanore		1816
18 Lismore		1820
19 Modeligo		1815*
20 Newcastle (Fourmilewater)		1814
21 Portlaw (Ballyduff)		1809
22 Rathgormuck (Mothel)		1831
23 Ring (Old Parish)		1813
24 St Mary's, Clonmel		1790
25 SS Peter & Paul, Clonmel		1829*
26 Stradbally (Ballylaneen)		1797*
27 Tallow		1797
28 Touraneena		1852
29 Tramore		1786

Waterford city:

30	Ballybricken	1797
31	Holy Trinity	1729
32	St John's	1759
31	St Michael's	1732
31	St Patrick's	1731
31	St Peter's	1737
31	St Stephen's	1731

*Earliest records in Waterford Heritage Survey

CLOYNE DIOCESE
1 Kilworth	1829

OSSORY DIOCESE
2 Slieverue	1766

WATERFORD & LISMORE DIOCESE
3 Abbeyside & Ring	1828
4 Aglish	1831*
5 Ardmore & Grange	1816*
6 Ballyduff	1849
7 Cappoquin	1807
8 Carrickbeg	1807

MEATH DIOCESE
1 Ballinacargy	1837
2 Ballymore	1824
3 Castlepollard (Lickblea)	1763
4 Castletown-Geoghegan	1829
5 Churchtown (Dysart)	1825
6 Clara & Horseleap	1821
7 Clonmellon	1757
8 Collinstown	1784
9 Delvin	1785
10 Drumraney	1834
11 Kilbeggan	1818
12 Kilkenny West	1829
13 Killucan	1821
14 Kinnegad	1827
15 Milltown	1781
16 Moyvore	1831
17 Mullingar	1737
18 Multyfarnham	1824
19 Rochfortbridge	1816
20 Taghmon	1781
21 Tubber	1821
22 Tullamore	1801
23 Turbotstown	1777

ARDAGH & CLONMACNOISE DIOCESE
24 Lenmanaghan & Ballynahown	1821
25 Moate (Kilcleagh & Ballyloughloe)	1824*

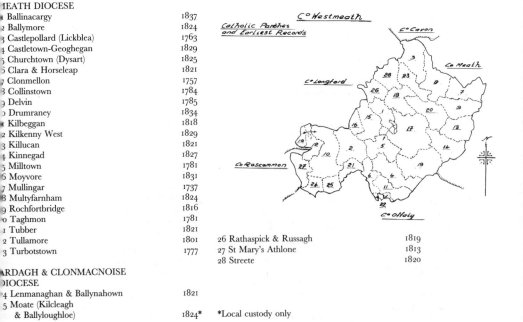

Co Westmeath
Catholic Parishes and Earliest Records

26 Rathaspick & Russagh	1819
27 St Mary's Athlone	1813
28 Streete	1820

*Local custody only

DUBLIN DIOCESE
1 Arklow   1809

FERNS DIOCESE
2 Adamstown   1807
3 Ballagh (Oulart)   1825*
4 Ballycullane (Tintern)   1827
5 Ballindaggin   1871
6 Ballygarrett   1828
7 Ballymore (Mayglass)   1840
8 Ballyoughter   1810
9 Blackwater (Killilla)   1815
10 Bree   1837
11 Bunclody (Newtownbarry)   1834
12 Camolin   1853
13 Carrick-on-Bannow   1830
14 Castlebridge (Screen)   1832
15 Clongeen   1847
16 Cloughbawn   1816
17 Craanford & Ballymurrin   1856
18 Crossabeg   1856
19 Davidstown   1805
20 Enniscorthy   1794
21 Ferns   1819
22 Glinn   1817
23 Gorey   1845
24 Kilanerin   1852
25 Kilaveny & Annacorra   1800
26 Kilmore   1752
27 Kilrush & Askamore   1841
28 Lady's Island   1737
29 Litter   1789
30 Marshalstown   1854
31 Monageer (Boolavogue)   1838
32 Monamolin   1834
33 New Ross   1789
34 Old Ross (Cushinstown)   1759
35 Oylegate & Glenbrien   1803
36 Piercetown & Murrinstown   1811
37 Ramsgrange   1835

Co Wexford
Catholic Parishes and Earliest Records

38 Rathangan (Duncormuck)   1803
39 Rathnure & Templeludigan   1846
40 Suttons (Ballykelly)   1824
41 Taghmon   1801
42 Tagoat & Kilrane   1853
43 Templetown   1792
44 Tomacork (Carnew)   1785
45 Wexford   1671

KILDARE & LEIGHLIN DIOCESE
46 Borris   1782
47 Clonegal   1833
48 St Mullin's   1796

*Earliest records in local custody

Co Wicklow
Catholic Parishes and Earliest Records

DUBLIN DIOCESE
1 Arklow   18
2 Ashford   18
3 Avoca   17
4 Ballymore Eustace   17
5 Blessington   18
6 Boystown (Valleymount)   18
7 Bray   18
8 Dunlavin   18
9 Enniskerry   18
10 Glendalough   18
11 Kilbride & Barnderrig   18
12 Kilquade & Kilmurry   18
13 Rathdrum   17
14 Wicklow   17

FERNS DIOCESE
15 Kilaveny & Annacorra   18
16 Tomacork (Carnew)   17

KILDARE & LEIGHLIN DIOCESE
17 Baltinglass   18
18 Clonmore   18
19 Clonegal   18
20 Hacketstown   18
21 Rathvilly   17

Introduction

The aim of this book is to provide a comprehensive guide for those who wish to trace their ancestors in Ireland. Because the individual circumstances of each family can be so different, the areas of research which may be relevant vary widely from case to case. None the less there are some areas which are important for the vast majority of people, and some which, though less widely relevant, can be extremely important in particular cases. This work is structured to reflect that division, with Part 1 examining the most basic sources, and Part 2 detailing those which have a narrower application. Part 3 then consists of a reference guide to permit quick access to a range of research materials, including county-by-county source lists, printed family histories, occupations and Church of Ireland records.

How the book is to be used depends very much on individual circumstances. For someone with no experience of genealogical research in Ireland, it would be best to start from this Introduction and work through Part 1, leaving Parts 2 and 3 until the basic materials have been exhausted. Someone who has already covered parish registers, land records, census returns and the state records of births, marriages and deaths may wish to start from Part 2. Others may simply want to use the reference guide. As anyone who regularly uses Irish records will know, however, one of the pleasures of research is the constant discovery of new sources of information, and new aspects of sources long thought to be familiar. The information in this book is the product of more than ten years of such discovery in the course of full-time professional research, and it is quite possible that even a hardbitten veteran will find something new in the account of the basic records given in Part 1.

WHERE TO START

The first question to ask before embarking on ancestral research is, 'What do I need to know before I start?' The answer, unhelpfully, is 'As much as possible'. Although, in the long term, the painstaking examination of original documents can provide much pleasure, in genealogy it is usually better to arrive than to travel hopefully. Theoretically it is of course possible to start from your own birth and work back through records of births, marriages and deaths, parish records and census records. In practical terms, however, the more that can be gleaned from older family members or from family documents the better; there is no point in combing through decades of parish records to uncover your great-grandmother's maiden name if you can find it out simply by asking Aunt Agatha. Nor does the information need to be absolutely precise. At this point quantity is more important than quality. Later on in the research, something that seemed relatively insignificant— the name of a local parish priest, a story of a contested will, someone's unusual occupation, even a postmark—may be a vital clue enabling you to follow the family further back. In any case, whether or not such information eventually turns out to be useful, it will certainly be of interest, helping to flesh out the picture of earlier generations. For most people, the spur to starting research is curiosity about their own family, and the kind of anecdotal information provided by the family itself rarely emerges from the documents.

To enable you to use the records to their fullest, three kinds of information are vital: *dates*, *names* and *places*. Dates of emigration, births, marriages and deaths; the names of parents, siblings, cousins, aunts, in-laws; addresses, townland names, parishes, towns, counties . . . Needless to say, not all of this is essential, and absolute accuracy is not vital to start out with. A general location and siblings' names can be used to uncover parents' names and addresses, and their parents' names. A precise name and a date can be used to unlock all the other records. Even the name alone, if it is sufficiently unusual, can sometimes be enough. In general, though, the single most useful piece of information is the precise locality of origin of the family. The county of origin would normally be the minimum information necessary, though in the case of a common surname (of which there are only too many), even this may not be enough. For the descendants of Irish emigrants, the locality is often one of the most difficult things to discover. There are ways of doing this, however, and the best time to do it is generally before starting research in Ireland. The Australian and American sources which are most useful for uncovering the locality of origin of Irish emigrants are detailed at the end of this Introduction.

The only cast-iron rule in carrying out research is that you should start from what you know and use that to find out more. Every family's circumstances are different, and where your research will lead you depends very much on where you start from. Thus, for example, knowing where a family lived around the turn of the century will allow you to uncover a census return with the ages of the individuals, leading to birth or baptismal records giving parent's names and residence, leading on in turn to early land records which may permit the identification of generations before the start of parish

records. At each stage of such research, what the next step should be is
determined by what you have found out. Each discovery is a stepping-stone
to the next. Because of this it is simply not possible to lay down a route
which will serve everyone. It is possible, however, to say that there is no
point in taking, for example, a seventeenth-century pedigree and trying to
extend it forward to connect with your family. Although there may very well
be a connection, the only way to prove it is in expanding your own family
information, working backwards.

WHAT YOU CAN EXPECT TO FIND

What you will uncover depends on the quality of the surviving records for
the area and, again, on what you start out with. In the majority of cases, that
is, for the descendants of Catholic tenant-farmers, the limit is generally the
starting date of the local Catholic parish records, which varies widely from
place to place. It would be unusual, however, for records of such a family to
go back much earlier than the 1780s, and for most people the early 1800s is
more likely to be the limit. In Gaelic culture, genealogy was of crucial
importance, but the collapse of that culture in the seventeenth century and
the subsequent impoverishment and oppression of the eighteenth century have
left a gulf which is almost unbridgeable. This much said, exceptions immediately spring to mind. One Australian family, starting with only the name of
their great-grandfather, his occupation and the date of his departure from
Ireland, uncovered enough information through parish registers and state
records of deaths, marriages and births to link him incontestably to the
Garveys of Mayo, for whom an established pedigree is registered in the
Genealogical Office stretching back to the twelfth century. Another family,
American, knowing only a general location in Ireland and a marriage that
took place before emigration, discovered that marriage in the pedigree of the
McDermotts of Coolavin, which is factually verified as far back as the
eleventh century. Discoveries like this are rare, however, and much likelier in
the case of the Anglo-Irish than for those of Gaelic or Scots Presbyterian
extraction.

Whatever the outcome, genealogical research offers pleasures and insights
which are unique. The desire which drives it is simple and undeniable: it is
the curiosity of the child who asks, 'Where did I come from?' All history
starts from here, and genealogy is the most basic form of history, tracing the
continual cycle of family growth and decay, uncovering the individual strands
of relationship and experience which weave together to form the great pat-
terns of historical change. Reconstructing the details of our own family
history is a way of understanding, immediately and personally, the connection
of the present with the past.

US SOURCES TO IDENTIFY IRISH PLACE OF ORIGIN

NATURALISATION RECORDS

These may contain the date and place of birth, occupation, place of residence, and the name of the ship on which the immigrant arrived. The records are still for the most part in the courts where the naturalisation proceedings took place. Some records are now in Federal Record Centres. Indexes for the states of Maine, Massachusetts, New Hampshire and Rhode Island before 1906, are available at the National Archives, Washington.

CEMETERY AND BURIAL RECORDS

There are two kinds of potentially valuable records: gravestone inscriptions and sextons' records. These vary enormously in usefulness, but may sometimes specify the exact place of origin.

IMMIGRATION RECORDS AND PASSENGER LISTS

The largest single collection is in the National Archives in Washington. The Customs Passenger Lists, dating from 1820, usually give only the country of origin. The Immigration Passenger Lists, from 1883, include details of the last place of residence.

PRINTED OBITUARIES

Around the turn of the century it became common practice to have an obituary printed in a local newspaper, particularly if a senior member of the family died. These are often useful for the information they give regarding the place of origin of the deceased.

MILITARY RECORDS

There are two kinds of records of possible value: service records and veterans' records. Depending on the date and branch of service, these may specify the place or country of origin. See *Guide to Genealogical Records in the National Archives* by Meredith S. Colket, Jnr and Frank E. Bridges (1964).

CHURCH RECORDS

Depending on the date, these can provide a great deal of information on baptisms, marriages and deaths. In particular, the marriages of newly arrived immigrants may specify precise places of origin. Most Catholic records are still in the parishes and, in most cases, only the priest may search them. For other denominations, records may be in local custody or deposited with a variety of record-holding institutions, including public libraries, universities and diocesan archives.

OTHER SOURCES
Vital records and census records are of great genealogical interest, but only rarely give the Irish place of origin. See Val. D. Greenwood's *The Researcher's Guide to American Genealogy* (Baltimore, 1973). Directories and local histories published by subscription sometimes give full information about the subscribers' families. See Clarence S. Peterson's *Consolidated Bibliography of County Histories in Fifty States in 1961* (Baltimore, 1963). Land records are held both federally and locally, and wills are mostly registered in the counties where they are probated.

CANADIAN SOURCES TO IDENTIFY IRISH PLACE OF ORIGIN

NATIONAL AND PROVINCIAL ARCHIVES
The vast bulk of information of genealogical interest can be found in the National and Provincial Archives of Canada, which are familiar with the needs of genealogical research and very helpful. The National Archives, 395 Wellington Street, Ottawa ON K1A ON3 (Tel. 613-995-5138) publishes a useful twenty-page booklet, *Tracing Your Ancestors in Canada*, which is available by post. Some of the information held in the Provincial Archives, in particular the census records, is also to be found in Ottawa, but in general the Provincial Archives have a broader range of information relating to their particular areas.

CIVIL RECORDS
In general the original registers of births, marriages and deaths, which have widely varying starting dates, are to be found in the offices of the Provincial Registrars General, although microfilm copies of some may also be found in Provincial Archives.

CENSUS RECORDS
Country-wide censuses are available for 1851, 1861, 1871, 1881 and 1891. There are, however, many local returns available for earlier years which record a wide variety of information. The largest collection is in the Ottawa National Archives.

OTHER SOURCES
Cemetery and burial records, passenger lists, Church registers and land records may all be of value. The best comprehensive guide is in Angus Baxter's *In search of your Canadian roots* (Baltimore, 1989), which gives details of a wide range of records to be found in the National and Provincial Archives.

AUSTRALIAN SOURCES TO IDENTIFY IRISH PLACE OF ORIGIN

CONVICT TRANSPORTATION RECORDS

There are very comprehensive records relating to convict transportees, originals in possession of Australian archives, microfilm copies of the British Public Record Office records, and Dublin Castle records of those transported from Ireland to Australia, which were computerised and presented to Australia as part of the Bicentennial celebrations of 1988. These last often include details of the conviction and place of residence, and are widely available, with copies in the National Library in Canberra and the genealogical library of Kiama, New South Wales, to name only two repositories.

IMMIGRATION RECORDS

Records of free and assisted immigration are less extensive than convict records, but are substantial. Material dealing with the period before 1901 is held in the State Archives Offices in the various state capitals, with the principal repositories being the New South Wales Archives Office, the Archives Section of the State Library of Victoria, and the J. S. Battye Library of Western Australia. See the NSW State Archives' *Guide to Shipping and Free Passenger Lists*.

CIVIL RECORDS

Civil registration of all births, deaths and marriages became compulsory at different times in the different colonies, as they then were. The information supplied is variable, in the early years in particular, but can include a great deal of secondary material that is very useful, including very often precise places of origin. The original registers and indexes are to be found in the Registrar-General's Offices of the states. These Offices sometimes also have copies of earlier Church registers.

CENSUS RECORDS

The earliest true census took place in 1828, in New South Wales, and has now been published in full. Earlier convict musters also exist. Because of the history of the creation of the various states, the best single records repository for early census returns remains the New South Wales Archives Office.

PART 1

Major Sources

1

Civil Records

State registration of non-Catholic marriages began in Ireland in 1845. All births, deaths and marriages have been registered in Ireland since 1864. In order to appreciate what precisely these records consist of, it is necessary to have some idea at least of how registration began. It was, in fact, an offshoot of the Victorian public health system, in turn based on the Poor Law, an attempt to provide some measure of relief for the most destitute. Between 1838 and 1852, 163 workhouses were built throughout the country, each at the centre of an area known as a Poor Law Union. The workhouses were normally situated in a large market town, and the Poor Law Union comprised the town and its catchment area, with the result that the Unions in many cases ignored the existing boundaries of parishes and counties. This had consequences for research which we shall see later. In the 1850s a large-scale public health system was created, based on the areas covered by the Poor Law Unions. Each Union was divided into Dispensary Districts, with an average of six to seven Districts per Union, and a Medical Officer, normally a doctor, was given responsibility for public health in each District. When the registration of all births, deaths and marriages then began in 1864, these Dispensary Districts also became Registrars' Districts, with a Registrar responsible for collecting the registrations within each District. In most cases the Medical Officer for the Dispensary District now also acted as the Registrar for the same area, but not in every case. The superior of this local Registrar was the Superintendent Registrar responsible for all the Registers within the old Poor Law Union. The return for the entire Poor Law Union (also known both as the Superintendent Registrar's District and, simply, the Registration District) were indexed and collated centrally, and master indexes for the entire country were produced at the General Register Office in Dublin. These are the indexes which are now used for public research.

Because of the history of the system, responsibility for registration still rests with the Department of Health. The arrangement at present is that the local Health Boards hold the original registers, with the General Register Office, at 8–11 Lombard St, Dublin 2, holding the master indexes to all thirty-two counties up to 1921, and to the twenty-six counties of the Republic of Ireland after that date. For Northern Ireland, from 1921, the indexes and registers are held at Oxford House, Chichester St, Belfast.

As well as the master indexes for the entire country, the General Register Office also contains microfilm copies of all the original registers, and is the only part of the registration system which permits public research. The indexes are available to the public on the first floor of 8 Lombard St, at a fee of £1.50 per five years searched, or £12 for a general search. It is important to note that only the indexes are open to the public; to obtain the full information contained in the original register entry, it is necessary to purchase a printout from the microfilm, at £1.50 per entry. These printouts are supplied for information only, and have no legal standing. Full certificates, for use in obtaining passports or in testamentary transactions, cost £5.50. Limited research, covering five years of the indexes, is carried out by the staff in response to postal queries only, for the same fee, £5.50.

INFORMATION GIVEN

One of the peculiarities of the system of registration is that, although the local Registrars were responsible for the Registers themselves, the legal obligation to register births, deaths and marriages actually rested with the public, and was enforced with hefty fines. The classes of people required to carry out registration in each of the three categories is given in what follows, along with a detailed account of the information they were required to supply. It should be remembered that not all of this information is relevant to genealogical research.

Births

Persons required to register births were:
1. the parent or parents, or in the case of death or inability of the parent or parents:
2. the occupier of the house or tenement in which the child was born; or
3. the Nurse; or
4. any person present at the birth of the child.

The information they were required to supply was:
1.   the date and place of birth;
2.   the name (if any);
3.   the sex;
4.   the name, surname and dwelling place of the father;
5.   the name, surname, maiden surname and dwelling place of the mother;
6.   the rank, profession or occupation of the father.

The informant and the Registrar were both required to sign each entry, which was also to include the date of registration, the residence of the informant and his or her 'qualification' (for example, 'present at birth'). Notice to the Registrar of the birth was to be given within twenty-one days, and full details within three months. It should be noted that it was not obligatory to register a first name for the child. The very small proportion for which no first name was supplied appear in the index as, for example, 'Kelly (male)' or 'Murphy (female)'.

Deaths

Persons required to register deaths were:
1.   some person present at death; or
2.   some person in attendance during the last illness of the deceased; or
3.   the occupier of the house or tenement where the death took place; or
4.   someone else residing in the house or tenement where the death took place; or
5.   any person present at, or having knowledge of the circumstances of, the death.

The information they were required to supply was:
1.   the date and place of death;
2.   the name and surname of the deceased;
3.   the sex of the deceased;
4.   the condition of the deceased as to marriage;
5.   the age of the deceased at last birthday;
6.   the rank, profession or occupation of the deceased;
7.   the certified cause of death and the duration of the final illness.

Again, the informant and the Registrar were both required to sign each entry, which was also to include the date of registration, the residence of the informant and his or her 'qualification' (for example, 'present at death'). Notice to the Registrar of the death was to be given within seven days, and full details within fourteen days.

INDEX to BIRTHS REGISTERED in IRELAND in 1866.

District.	Vol.	Page	Name and Registration District.	Vol.	Page	Name and Reg
e	7	411	PELL, John Joseph. Dublin, North	12	584	PERCY, Robert Henry
....	13	326	PELLETT, Anna Maria. Dublin, South	12	656	—— William. Antrin
......	20	266	PELLICAN, John. Listowel	10	500	PERDUE, John. Callar
....	6	991	PELLY, Catherine. Ballinasloe	19	37	—— Mary Anne. Tip
aelin. Lisburn .	1	659	—— Catherine Evangiline. Dublin, South ...	2	745	PERIL, Patrick. Gort
....	17	715	—— John Joseph. Dublin, South	2	737	PERKINS, Cornelius. T
....	11	893	—— Mary. Portumna	14	946	—— Joseph John. D
rth	7	572	PEMBERTON, Marian Sydney. Dublin, North .	17	527	—— Patrick. Naas .
....	5	140	—— (female). Dublin, South	7	811	—— Robert Henry. I
....	11	222	PEMBROKE, Ellen. Tralee.....................	20	627	—— Thomas. Oughte
....	20	104	—— Ellen. Tralee........................	15	596	—— (female). Ballina
....	11	782	—— Margaret. Kilkenny..	8	603	PERKINSON, Barkly. A
....	7	937	—— Mary. Dingle	15	207	PERKISSON, Briget. T
....	7	732	—— Mary Eliza. Kilkenny..............	3	609	PERRILL, Patrick. Cli
....	3	447	—— Patrick. Listowel	10	501	PERRIN Ellen. Dublin.
erick	20	432	PENDER, Anne. Enniscorthy	14	725	—— Henrietta. Ratb
....	19	500	—— Bernard. Carrick-on-Shannon	18	65	—— William Alexande
....	14	82	—— Bridget. Enniscorthy	4	814	—— (female). Cavan
....	14	476	—— Bridget. Enniscorthy	9	753	PERROT, Catherine. D
....	10	128	—— Daniel. Gorey	7	876	—— Sarah. Clonakilt
....	6	178	—— Daniel. Gorey	7	877	PERROTT, Margaret. I
North	7	549	—— Elizabeth. Nenagh	3	651	—— Robert. Cork ..
....	15	394	—— Elizabeth. Carlow	13	447	—— William Cooke C
....	20	154	—— Ellen. Ballymoney	6	194	—— William Thomas.
....	10	735	—— Ellen. Rathdown	12	920	PERRY, Agnes. Belfas
....	2	728	—— Ellen. Enniscorthy	19	764	—— Agnes. Lisburn
....	11	112	—— James. Waterford	9	951	—— Angelina Margare
....	6	613	—— John. Carlow	8	507	—— Ann. Downpatri
....	14	376	—— John. Enniscorthy	14	722	—— Ann Jane. Bally
....	1	173	—— John. Mullingar	13	317	—— Anthony. Ennis
....	3	701	—— Joseph. Athy	13	406	—— Catherine. Balti
thdown	17	889	—— Laurance. Carlow	13	436	—— Eliza. Ballymah
....	5	232	—— Mary. Wexford	14	911	—— Eliza. Naas ....
....	1	264	—— Mary Anne. Carlow	3	505	—— Eliza. Belfast .
H. Parsonstown	18	599	—— Mary Catherine. Carlow...........	18	427	—— Elizabeth. Bally
atrick	11	531	—— Mathew. Wexford	14	910	—— Elizabeth. Larn
....	11	834	—— Michael. Carlow	3	494	—— Ellen. Ballymen
....	2	463	—— Peter. Rathdrum .,...............	2	1061	—— Etheld Letitia. M
e	17	386	—— Thomas. Ballinasloe	19	31	—— Hannah. Larne.
....	7	653	—— William. Waterford	19	925	—— Helena Jane. Le
blin, South	17	622	—— (female). Limerick	10	454	—— Henry. Newry .
....	10	665	PENDERGAST, Anne. Roscommon	18	333	—— James. Dundalk
South	7	672	—— Bridget. Tulla	19	606	—— James. Dublin,
....	16	281	—— Catherine. Swineford	4	579	—— James. Baltingl
....	12	892	—— Ellen. Castlereagh	19	161	—— Jane. Banbridg
....	2	750	—— Margaret. Castlereagh	19	162	—— Jane Eleanor. I
....	15	244	—— Margaret. Killarney..............	5	400	—— John. Lisburn .
k	20	179	—— Mary. Bawnboy	3	51	—— John. Naas ....
....	14	905	—— Mary. Castlebar	19	133	—— Joseph. Ballyn
....	9	950	—— Myles. Wexford	19	955	—— Letitia Anne. D
ir	19	655	—— Pat. Ballinrobe..................	4	51	—— Martin. Newtow
....	9	379	—— Patrick. Rathdown	17	891	—— Mary. Ballymah
rth	7	571	—— Patrick. Monaghan	8	330	—— Mary Anne. Ba
....	11	82	PENDERGRAST, Anne. New Ross	4	969	—— Rebecca. Ballyn
South	7	813	—— Ellen. Killarney	15	315	—— Robinson Gale.
....	1	757	—— Michael. Killarney	15	316	—— Sarah. Downpat
in, North	2	690	PENDERS, Mary. Nenagh	15	584	—— Sarah. Newtow
agh	11	82	PENDLETON, Essie. Lurgan	16	673	—— Sarah. Ballymes
....	8	503	PENGELLY, Michael James. Cork............	20	193	—— Susanna. Down
....	17	38	PENNAFATHER, (male). Rathkeale	10	621	—— Thomas. Trim .
in, North......	2	630	PENNAMEN, Mary Jane Fraser. Belfast	11	277	—— Thomas. Belfast
North	12	547	PENNEFATHER, John Thomas. Dublin, North .	7	608	—— Thomas Shanklin
....	1	838	—— Richard Dymock. Cashel	3	531	—— William. Tippe
....	18	788	PENNELL, (male). Cork	15	101	—— William Gardiner
....	11	43	PENNINGTON, Charles. Banbridge	16	229	—— William Richard
oss	9	871	PENNY, John. Ballymena	11	113	—— William Robinso
....	5	175	—— (male). Wexford	11	922	—— (male). Clonme

Marriages

From 1864 any person whose marriage was to be celebrated by a Catholic clergyman was required to have the clergyman fill out a certificate containing the information detailed below, and forward it within three days of the marriage to the Registrar. In practice, as had already been the case for non-Catholic marriages from 1845, the clergyman simply kept blank copies of these certificates, filled them in after the ceremony and forwarded them to the registrar. It is still important to remember, though, that legal responsibility for the registration actually rested with the parties marrying, not the clergyman.

The information to be supplied was:
1. the date when married;
2. the names and surnames of each of the parties marrying;
3. their respective ages;
4. their condition (i.e. bachelor, spinster, widow, widower);
5. their rank, profession or occupation;
6. their residences at the time of marriage;
7. the name and surname of the fathers of each of the parties;
8. the rank, profession or occupation of the fathers of each of the parties.

The certificate was to state where the ceremony had been performed, and to be signed by the clergyman, the parties marrying, and two witnesses.

GENEALOGICAL RELEVANCE

From a genealogical point of view, only the following information is of genuine interest:

BIRTHS
The name, the date of birth, the place of birth; the name, surname and dwelling place of the father; the name, surname and dwelling place of the mother; and, occasionally, the name, residence and qualification of the informant.

MARRIAGES
Parish in which the marriage took place; names, ages, residences and occupations of the persons marrying; names and occupations of their fathers.

DEATHS
Place of death, age at death and, occasionally, the name, residence and qualification of the informant.

Of the three categories, the most useful is probably the marriage entry, both because it provides fathers' names, thus giving a direct link to the preceding generation, and because it is the easiest to identify from the indexes, as we shall see later. Birth entries are much more difficult to identify correctly from the indexes without precise information about date and place, and even with such information, the high concentrations of people of the same surname within particular localities of the country can make it difficult to be sure that a particular birth registration is the relevant one. Unlike many other countries, death records in Ireland are not very useful for genealogical purposes; there was no obligation to record family information, and the 'age at death' is often very imprecise. This much said, these records can sometimes be of value. The 'person present at death' was often a family member, and the relationship is sometimes specified in the register entry. Even the age recorded may be useful, since it at least gives an idea of how old the person was thought to be by family or neighbours.

A general word of warning about civil registration is necessary: a certain proportion of all three categories simply went unregistered. It is impossible to be sure how much is not there, since the thoroughness of local registration depended very much on local conditions and on the individuals responsible, but experience in cross-checking from other sources such as parish and census records suggests that as much as 10 to 15 per cent of marriages and births simply do not appear in the registers.

RESEARCH IN THE INDEXES

In carrying out research in all three areas, a large measure of scepticism is necessary with regard to the dates of births, marriages and deaths reported by family members before 1900. This is especially true for births: the ages given in census returns, for example, are almost always inaccurate, and round figures—50, 60, 70—should be treated with particular caution. The true date of birth is almost always well before the one reported, sometimes by as much as fifteen years. Why this should be so is a matter for speculation, but it seems unlikely that vanity or mendacity were to blame. It would appear more probable that, up to the start of this century, very few people actually knew their precise date of birth. Since, at least after middle age, almost no one feels as old as they actually are, a guess will usually produce an under-estimate. Whatever the explanation, charitable or otherwise, it is always wiser to search a range of the indexes before the reported date, rather than after.

From 1864 to 1877 the indexes consist of a single yearly volume in each category—births, marriages and deaths—covering the entire country and recording all names in a straightforward alphabetical arrangement. The same arrangement also applies to the non-Catholic marriages registered from 1845. From 1878 the yearly volume is divided into four quarters, with each quarter covering three months and indexed separately. This mean that a search for a name in, for example, the 1877 births index means looking in one place in the index, while it is necessary to check four different places in the 1878 index, one in each of the four quarters. From 1903, in the case of births only, the indexes once again cover the entire year, and only from this year also supply the mother's maiden surname. In all three categories each index entry gives surname, first name, registration district, volume and page number. The deaths indexes also give the reported age at death. The 'volume and page number' simply make up the reference for the original register entry, necessary in order to obtain a photocopy of the full information given in that entry. The remaining three items, surname, first name and registration district, are dealt with in detail below.

SURNAME

The order followed in the indexes is strictly alphabetical, but it is always necessary to keep possible variants of the surname in mind. In the late nineteenth century, when a large majority of the population was illiterate, the precise spelling of their surname was a matter of indifference to most people. Thus members of the same family may be registered as, for example, Kilfoyle, Gilfoyle or Guilfoile. The question of variants is particularly important for names beginning with 'O' or 'Mac'. Until the start of the Gaelic Revival at the end of the last century, these prefixes were treated as entirely optional and, in the case of the 'O's particularly, more often omitted than included. Until well into the twentieth century, for instance, almost all of the O'Briens are recorded under 'Brien' or 'Bryan'. Before starting a search in the indexes, therefore, it is essential to have as clear an idea as possible of the variants to be checked. Otherwise it may be necessary to cover the same period as many as three or four times.

FIRST NAME

Among the vast majority of the population, the range of first names in use in the nineteenth century was severely limited. Apart from some localised names—'Cornelius' in south Munster, 'Crohan' in the Caherdaniel area of the Iveragh Peninsula, 'Sabina' in the east Galway/north Roscommon area— the anglicisation of the earlier Gaelic names was restrictive and unimaginative. John, Patrick, Michael, Mary and Bridget occur with almost unbelievable frequency in all parts of the country. Combined with the intensely local nature of surnames, reflecting the earlier tribal areas of the country, this can present intense difficulties when using the indexes. For example, a single quarter of 1881, from January to March, might contain twenty or more John (O')Reilly (or Riley) registrations, all in the same registration district of Co. Cavan. A further obstacle is the fact that it is very rare for more than one first name to be registered. Thus someone known to the family as John James (O')Reilly

will almost certainly appear in the index as a simple John. It is of course
possible to purchase photocopies of all the original register entries, but unless
some other piece of information such as the parents' names or the townland
address can be used to cross-check, it will almost certainly not be possible to
identify which, if any, of the original register entries is the relevant one. This
uncertainty is compounded still further by the persistent imprecision regarding
ages and dates of birth, which means that over the seven- or eight-year
period when the relevant birth could have taken place, there might be fifty
or sixty births of the same name in the one county. One way to surmount
the problem, if the precise district is known, is to examine the original
registers themselves to build a picture of all families in which the relevant
name occurs. As already mentioned, the originals are still kept in the local
registrars' offices. Although the situation varies from district to district, people
visiting the offices in person are usually allowed to examine the original
books. The relevant addresses can be found in local telephone directories,
under the Health Board. Even in the country-wide indexes, however, despite
all of these problems, there are a number of ways in which the births indexes
can be used successfully, by narrowing the area and period to be searched
with information obtained from other sources, as we shall see.

REGISTRATION DISTRICT
As a result of the original arrangements for administering the system, the
registration districts used were, and still are, largely identical with the old
Poor Law Unions. Since these were based on natural catchment areas,
normally consisting of a large market town and its rural hinterland, rather
than on the already existing administrative divisions of townland, parish and
county, registration districts for births, marriages and deaths cut right across
these earlier boundaries, a fact which can be very significant for research.
Thus, for example, Waterford registration district, centred in the town of
Waterford, also takes in a large part of rural south Co. Kilkenny. The only
comprehensive guide to which towns and townlands are contained in each
registration district is to be found in a series of pamphlets produced in the
nineteenth century by the Registrar-General's Office for the use of each of
the local registrars. These are collected as *Townlands in Poor-law Unions*, copies
of which can be found in the National Library (reference: Ir. 9141 b 35) or in
the reading room of the National Archives. This is particularly useful when
a problem arises identifying a variant version of a townland name given in
the original register entry for a marriage, birth or death. By scanning the lists
of townlands in the relevant district in which the entry is recorded, it is
almost always possible to identify the standard version of the name and, from
this, go on to census, parish and land records. To go in the other direction,
to find out what registration district a particular town or townland is in, the
standard source is the *Alphabetical Index to the Towns, Townlands and Parishes of*

Ireland. Three editions of this were published, based on the census returns for 1851, 1871 and 1901. In the first two, the registration district is recorded as the Poor Law Union; in the 1901 Index it does not appear in the body of the work, but may be found as an appendix. Copies of these can be found on open access in the National Library, the National Archives, the General Register Office itself or in any library. If the original townland or address of the family being researched is known, and the search narrowed to a single registration district, then some at least of the problems picking out the relevant entry, in the births indexes particularly, can be significantly reduced.

RESEARCH TECHNIQUES

BIRTHS

As pointed out above, it is important to approach the birth indexes with as much information as possible from other sources. If the birth took place between 1864 and 1880, the family was Catholic and the relevant area known, it may be best to try to identify a baptism from parish records first, and in many cases, if information rather than a certificate is the aim of the research, the parish record itself will be enough. If the area is known, but not the date, it may be useful to search the 1901 and 1911 census returns to obtain at least an approximate age and, hence, date of birth. If the names of siblings and the order of their birth are known, but the area and date are not, it may be necessary to search a wide range of years in the indexes, noting all births of the names which occur in the family, and then try to work out which births of the relevant names occur in the right order in the same registration district. If the name is unusual enough, of course, none of this may be necessary. In Ireland, however, few of us are lucky enough to have an ancestor called Horace Freke-Blood or Euphemia Thackaberry.

MARRIAGES

As long as care is taken over the question of surname variants, and the names of both parties are known, research in the marriage indexes is straight-forward. If two people married each other, then obviously the registration district, volume and page number references for them in the indexes have to be the same. It is simply necessary to cross-check the two names in the indexes, working back from the approximate date of birth of the eldest child if this is known, until two entries are found in which all three references correspond. Marriage records are especially important in the early years of civil registration, since they record the names of the fathers of people born *c.*1820 to *c.*1840, as well as their approximate ages, thus providing evidence which can be used to establish earlier generations in parish records. For non-Catholic families, the value of these records is even greater, since the records of non-Catholic marriages start in 1845.

DEATHS

As in the case of births, it is essential to uncover as much information as possible from other sources before starting a search of the death indexes. Thus, if a date of birth is known from parish or other records, the 'age at death' given in the index along with the registration district provides at least a rough guide as to whether or not the death recorded is the relevant one. If the location of a family farm is known, the approximate date of death can often be worked out from the changes in occupier recorded in the Valuation Books of the Land Valuation Office (see Chapter 4). Similarly, if the family possessed property, the Will Calendars of the National Archives after 1858 (see Chapter 5) can be the easiest way to pin-point the precise date of death. With such information, it is then usually a simple matter to pick out the relevant entry from the indexes. Information from a marriage entry may also sometimes be useful: along with the names of the fathers of the parties marrying, the register entry sometimes also specifies that one or both of the fathers is deceased. There is no rule about this, however. The fact that a father is recorded as, say, 'John Murphy, labourer', does not necessarily mean that he was alive at the time of the marriage. If an individual is recorded as deceased, this does at least provide an end-point for any search for his death entry. As already pointed out, however, death records give no information on preceding generations, and only occasionally name a surviving family member.

LIVING RELATIVES

It is very difficult to use the records of the General Register Office to trace descendants, rather than forebears, of a particular family. As pointed out above, the birth indexes after 1902 do record the mother's maiden name as well as the name and surname of the child, so that it may be possible to trace all the births of a particular family from that date forward. Uncovering the subsequent marriages of those children without knowing the names of their spouses is a much harder proposition, however. To take one example, the likely range of years of marriage for a Michael O'Brien born in 1905 would be 1925 to 1940; there are certainly hundreds of marriages recorded in the indexes under that name. One could, of course, purchase copies of all the original register entries in the hope that one entry might show the relevant address and father's name, and then investigate births of that marriage, but in most cases the work involved makes the task impracticable. There are, however, other ways of tracking descendants through land, census, voters' and, sometimes, parish records (Chapters 2, 3 and 4).

LATE REGISTRATIONS, ARMY RECORDS, ETC.

LATE REGISTRATIONS

A significant proportion of all births, marriages and deaths were simply not registered, as mentioned above. When the individuals concerned or their relatives later needed a certificate for official purposes, it became necessary to register the event. The index references for these late registrations are included in the volume for the year in which the event took place. Thus, for example, the index reference for someone born in 1880, but whose birth was not registered until 1900, is to be found in the index for 1880. In the case of births and deaths, these references are indexed separately from the main body of the index, at the back of the volume. For marriages, late registrations are written in by hand at the relevant point in the main body of the index. Although the chances of finding a missing registration among these is quite slim, it is still necessary to include them in any thorough search of the indexes.

MARITIME RECORDS

From 1864 up to the present, the General Register Office has kept a separate 'Marine Register' of births and deaths of Irish subjects which took place at sea. From 1886 only, a printed index to this register is bound into the back of the births and death index for each year. For earlier registers, the indexes have to be requested from the staff in the Office. No separate register was kept for marriages at sea.

ARMY RECORDS

The Births, Deaths and Marriages (Army) Act of 1879 required these events to be registered with the Office of the Registrar-General in Dublin, where they affected Irish subjects serving in the British Army abroad. Separate indexes bound into the back of the main yearly indexes start from 1888 and continue until 1930 for births, and 1931 for marriages and deaths. The deaths index for 1902 also contains an index to 'Deaths of Irish Subjects pertaining to the South African War (1898–1902)'.

THE FOREIGN REGISTER

From 1864 the General Register Office was required to keep a separate register of births of Irish subjects abroad, where such birth were notified to the relevant British consul. There is no index to this register, which is small, and is not available in the public research room. It may be requested from the staff of the Office.

THE SCHULZE REGISTER

The General Register Office also holds the 'General Index to Baptisms and Marriages purported to have been celebrated by the Rev. J. G. F. Schulze,

1806–1837'. This records 55 baptisms and *c*.8,000 marriages celebrated in Dublin by this clergyman, without a licence. When some of the marriages were later challenged in court, they were held to be legal, and the volume was acquired by the Register Office. The bulk of the marriages, celebrated at the German Lutheran Church in Poolbeg St, Dublin, are for the years 1825 to 1837, and record only the names of the contracting parties.

USING CIVIL RECORDS WITH OTHER SOURCES

Some of the areas in which information from other sources may be used to simplify research in civil records have already been outlined. What follows is an expanded guide to the ways in which civil records can supplement or be supplemented by those other sources.

BIRTHS
Ages recorded in 1901 and 1911 census returns (see Chapter 2) can be used to narrow the range of years to be searched. If the birth registration is uncovered first, it records the precise residence of the parents, which can then lead to the relevant census returns, providing fuller information on other members of the family.

MARRIAGES
The 1911 census records the number of years a couple have been married, the number of children born and the number of those children still living. This information is obviously very useful in narrowing the range of years to be searched for a particular marriage. In the case of names which are common in a particular area, the fathers' names supplied in the marriage record are often the only firm evidence with which to identify the relevant baptismal record in the parish registers. Once a marriage has been located in civil records, thus showing the relevant parish, it is always worthwhile to check the church record of the same marriage. As church marriage registers were standardised from the 1860s on, they became more informative, in many cases supplying the names, addresses and occupations of both the mother and father of the parties marrying. In the case of most Dublin Catholic parishes, this information is recorded from around 1856.

DEATHS
The records of the Land Valuation Office (Chapter 4), or the testamentary records of the National Archives (Chapter 5) can be used to pin-point the year of death, thus making a successful search more likely. The place of death given, if it is not the home of the deceased person, may be the home of a relative. This can be investigated firstly through land records (Chapter 4), and then through parish and census records, and may provide further information on other branches of the family.

2

Census Records

1. COUNTRY-WIDE

Full government censuses were taken of the whole island in 1821, 1831, 1841, 1851, 1861, 1871, 1901 and 1911. The first four, for 1821, 1831, 1841 and 1851 were largely destroyed in 1922 in the fire at the Public Record Office; surviving fragments are detailed below. Those for 1861 and 1871 were completely destroyed earlier by order of the government. This means that the earliest surviving comprehensive returns are for 1901 and 1911. Because of this the normal rule that census returns should not be available to the public for 100 years has been suspended in the Republic of Ireland, and the original returns can be consulted in the National Archives. (Absurdly, although the original returns for the six northern counties of Antrim, Armagh, Derry, Down, Fermanagh and Tyrone are freely available in the south, copies of these returns held in the Public Record Office of Northern Ireland will not be open to the public until 2001 and 2011.)

1901 and 1911

A. INFORMATION GIVEN
Although these returns are obviously very late for most purposes, the information they contain can still be extremely useful. The 1901 returns record the following:
➢ name;
➢ relationship to the head of the household;
➢ religion;
➢ literacy;
➢ occupation;
➢ age;
➢ marital status;
➢ county of birth;
➢ ability to speak English or Irish.

The returns also record details of the houses, giving the number of rooms, outhouses and windows, and the type of roof. Members of the family not present when the census was taken are not given. The same information was collected in 1911, with one important addition: married women were required to state the number of years they had been married, the number of children born alive and the number of children still living. Unfortunately widows were not required to give this information, although a good number obliged in any case. Only the initials, not the full names, of policemen and inmates of mental hospitals are recorded.

B. USES

(i) *Age.* The most obviously useful information given in 1901 and 1911 is age. Unfortunately this is also the information which needs to be treated with the most caution. Very few of the ages given in the two sets of returns actually match precisely. In the decade between the two censuses, most people appear to have aged significantly more than ten years. Of the two, 1901 seems to be the less accurate, with widespread underestimation of age. None the less, if used with caution the returns do provide a rough guide to age which can help to narrow the range of years to be searched in earlier civil records of births, marriages and deaths, or in parish records.

(ii) *Location.* When the names of all or most of the family are known, along with the general area, but not the precise locality, it is possible to search all the returns for that area to identify the relevant family and thus pinpoint them. This can be particularly useful when the surname is very common; the likelihood of two families of Murphys in the same area repeating all of the children's names is slight.

(iii) *Cross-checking.* At times, again when a name is common, it is impossible to be sure from information uncovered in civil or parish records that a particular family is the relevant one. In such cases, when details of the subsequent history of the family are known—dates of death or emigration, or siblings' names, for instance—a check of the 1901 or 1911 census for the family can provide useful circumstantial evidence. More often than not, any certainties produced will be negative, but the elimination of fake trails is a vital part of any research. An illustration will show why: Peter Barry, born Co. Cork *c.*1880, parents unknown, emigrated to the US in 1897. A search of civil birth records shows four Peter Barrys recorded in the county between 1876 and 1882, with no way of distinguishing which, if any, is the relevant one. A search of the 1901 census returns for the addresses given in the four birth entries shows two of the four still living there. These can now be safely eliminated, and research concentrated on the other two families.

CENSUS OF IRELAND, 1901.

(Two Examples of the mode of filling up this Table are given on the other side.)

FORM A.

RETURN of the MEMBERS of this FAMILY and their VISITORS, BOARDERS, SERVANTS, &c., who slept or abode in this House on the night of SUNDAY, the 31st of MARCH, 1901.

No. on Form B. 3

No.	NAME and SURNAME.	RELATION to Head of Family.	RELIGIOUS PROFESSION.	EDUCATION.	AGE.		SEX.	RANK, PROFESSION, OR OCCUPATION.	MARRIAGE.	WHERE BORN.	IRISH LANGUAGE.	If Deaf and Dumb; Dumb only; Blind; Imbecile or Idiot; or Lunatic.
					Years	Months						
1	Bernard McEnen	Head of Family	Roman Catholic	Read & Write	50		M	Farmer	Married	Co. Cavan	Irish & English	1
2	Mary McEnen	Wife	Roman Catholic	Read & Write	48		F	Farmer's Wife	Married	Co. Cavan	Irish & English	1
3	Maria McEnen	Daughter	Roman Catholic	Read & Write	23		F	Farmer's Daughter	Not Married	Co. Cavan	English	1
4	Ellen McEnen	Daughter	Roman Catholic	Read & Write	19		F	Farmer's Daughter	Not Married	Co. Cavan	English	1
5	John McEnen	Nephew	Roman Catholic	Read & Write	6		M	Scholar	Not Married	Co. Cavan	English	1
6												
7												
8												
9												
10												
11												
12												
13												
14												
15												

I hereby certify, as required by the Act 63 Vic. cap. 6, s. 6 (1), that the foregoing Return is correct, according to the best of my knowledge and belief.

Michael Killen (Signature of Enumerator.)

I believe the foregoing to be a true Return.

Bernard McEnen (Signature of Head of Family.)

CENSUS OF IRELAND, 1911.

Two Examples of the mode of filling up this Table are given on the other side.

FORM A.

No. on Form B.

RETURN of the MEMBERS of this FAMILY and their VISITORS, BOARDERS, SERVANTS, &c., who slept or abode in this House on the night of SUNDAY, the 2nd of APRIL, 1911.

No.	NAME AND SURNAME		RELATION to Head of Family	RELIGIOUS PROFESSION	EDUCATION	AGE (last Birthday) and SEX		RANK, PROFESSION, OR OCCUPATION	PARTICULARS AS TO MARRIAGE				WHERE BORN	IRISH LANGUAGE	If Deaf and Dumb; Dumb only; Blind; Imbecile or Idiot; or Lunatic
	Christian Name	Surname				Age of Males	Age of Females		Whether "Married," "Widower," "Widow," or "Single."	Completed years the present Marriage has lasted.	Total Children born alive.	Children still living.			
1	Patrick	Herd	Head of Family	Roman Catholic	Read and Write	68		Farmer	Widower				County Cavan	Irish and English	
2	Patrick	Herd	Son	Roman Catholic	Read and Write	23		Farmer's Son	Single				County Cavan	English	
3	Alice	Herd	Daughter	Roman Catholic	Read and Write		21		Single				County Cavan	English	
4	Margaret	Herd	Daughter	Roman Catholic	Read and Write		18		Single				County Cavan	English	
5	John	Herd	Son	Roman Catholic	Read and Write	12		Scholar	Single				County Cavan	English	
6	James	Herd	Son	Roman Catholic	Read and Write	10		Scholar					Co Cavan	English	
7															
8															
9															
10															
11															
12															
13															
14															
15															
16															

I hereby certify, as required by the Act 10 Edw. VII., and 1 Geo. V., cap. 11, that the foregoing Return is correct, according to the best of my knowledge and belief.

Patrick Herd　　　Signature of Enumerator.

I believe the foregoing to be a true Return.

Patrick Herd　　　Signature of Head of Family.

(iv) *Marriages.* The requirement in the 1911 census for married women to supply the number of years of marriage is obviously a very useful aid when subsequently searching civil records for a marriage entry. Even in 1901 the age of the eldest child recorded can give a rough guide to the latest date at which a marriage is likely to have taken place.

(v) *Living Relatives.* Children recorded in 1901 and 1911 are the parents or grandparents of people now alive. The ages—generally much more accurate than those given for older members of the family—can be useful in trying to uncover later marriages in civil records. When used together with Land Valuation Office records (see Chapter 4), or the voters' lists of the National Archives, they can provide an accurate picture of the passing of property from one generation to another. Luckily the Irish attitude to land means that it is quite unusual for rural property to pass out of a family altogether.

C. RESEARCH TECHNIQUES

The basic geographical unit used in carrying out both the 1901 and 1911 censuses is the District Electoral Division, a subdivision of the county used, as the name implies, for electoral purposes. To use the returns, ideally the relevant street or townland should be known. The *1901 Townland Index*, based on the census returns, supplies the name and number of the DED in which the townland is situated. County-by-county volumes, on open shelves in the National Archives Reading Room, go through the DEDs in numerical order for both 1901 and 1911, giving the name and number of each of the townlands they contain. To order the returns for a specific townland, it is necessary to supply the name of the county, the number of the DED and the number of the townland, as given in these volumes. For the cities of Belfast, Cork, Dublin and Limerick, separate street indices have been compiled, and are also on open shelves in the Reading Room. Again, each street or part of a street is numbered, and these numbers are necessary to order specific returns. Between 1901 and 1911 some changes took place in the District Electoral Divisions, and their numbering is different in some cases. There is no separate townlands index for 1911, but the changes are minor, so that a DED numbered 100 in 1901 may be 103 in 1911, and can be found simply by checking the Divisions above and below 100 in the 1911 volume for the county.

The returns for 1901 have been bound into large volumes, while those for 1911 are still loose and in boxes. In each case all the returns for a townland or street are grouped together and preceded by an enumerator's abstract which gives the details of the houses and lists the names of the heads of households. These lists can be very useful if the precise townland or street is not known, and it is necessary to search a large area, checking all households of a particular surname, though such a procedure is of course less precise than a check on each of the returns themselves. One problem which can arise in searching a large area is the difficulty of translating from the earlier geographical division of a parish, for instance, to the relevant District Electoral Divisions, since these latter cut across the earlier boundaries. The most straightforward, though cumbersome, way to cover a large area is to take all the townlands in particular civil parishes and check their District Electoral Divisions in the *1901 Townlands Index*. The *1841 Townlands Index*, also known as *Addenda to the 1841 Census*, and available on request from the National Archives Reading Room staff or in the National Library (Ir. 310 c 1), organises townlands alphabetically within civil parishes

2. NINETEENTH-CENTURY CENSUS FRAGMENTS

1821

This census, organised by townland, civil parish, barony and county, took place on 28 May 1821, and aimed to cover the entire population. It recorded the following information :

➤ name;
➤ age;
➤ occupation;
➤ relationship to the head of the household;
➤ acreage of landholding;
➤ number of storeys of house.

Almost all the original returns were destroyed in 1922, with only a few volumes surviving for parts of Counties Cavan, Fermanagh, Galway, Meath and Offaly (King's County). These are now in the National Archives, and full details of call-numbers and areas covered will be found in Chapter 12 under the relevant county. The overall reliability of the population figures produced by the 1821 census has been questioned recently, but there is no doubt as to the genealogical value of the returns. Once again, however, the ages given need to be treated with scepticism.

1831

Again organised by townland, civil parish, barony and county, this census recorded the following:

➤ name;
➤ age;
➤ occupation;
➤ relationship to the head of the household;
➤ acreage of landholding;
➤ religion.

Very little of this survives, with most of the remaining fragments relating to Co. Derry. Details of locations and call-numbers are in Chapter 12 under the relevant county.

No. 38	Townland of *Duffallon*		in the Parish of *Castlerahan*	Ba

N. B.—In Counties where Plowlands or other denominations or sub-denominations are in use, the word " Townland" is to be

Col. 1. No. of House.	Col. 2. No. of Stories	Column 3. NAMES OF INHABITANTS.	Col. 4. AGE.	Column 5. OCCUPATION.	Col. 6. No. of Acres.
		Eliza Fitzsimmons Daughter	15	Spinner	
8	1	Garrett Fitzsimmons	60	Farmer	12
		Cath Fitzsimmons his Wife	57	Spinner	
		Patrick Fitzsimmons his Son	32	Labourer	
		Thos Fitzsimmons Do	27	Labourer	
		John Fitzsimmons Do	23	Labourer	
		Mary Smyth	20	House Servt	
9	1	John Gilroy	39	Farmer	16
		Mary Gilroy his Wife	33	Spinner	
		Patrick Gilroy his Son	10		
		Owen Gilroy his Son	1		
		Mary Gilroy Daughter	15	Spinner	
		Mary Gilroy Do	13	Same	
		Bridget Gilroy Do	7		
		Anne Gilroy Do	5		
10	1	Peter Lynch	64	Farmer	15
		Eliza Lynch his Wife	61	Spinner	
		Hugh Lynch his Son	32	Labourer	
		James Lynch his Son	16	Labourer	
		Anne Lynch Daughter	25	Spinner	
		Mary Lynch Daughter	23	Spinner	
		John Lynch his Nephew	1		
11	1	John Flood	33	Farmer	4½
		Anne Flood his Wife	30	Spinner	
		John Flood his Son	8		
		Mary Flood Daughter	10		
		Cath Flood Do	6		
		Anne Flood Do	3		
12	1	John Smyth	55	Mason	
		Peter Smyth his Son	25	Labourer	
		James Smyth his Son	22	Labourer	
		Patk Smyth Do	15	Labourer	

1841

Unlike the two earlier censuses, the returns in 1841 were filled out by the householders themselves, rather than government enumerators. The information supplied was:

➢ name;
➢ age;
➢ occupation;
➢ relationship to the head of the household;
➢ date of marriage;
➢ literacy;
➢ absent family members;
➢ family members who died since 1831.

Only one set of original returns survived 1922, that for the parish of Killeshandra in Co. Cavan. There are, however, a number of transcripts of the original returns. The 1841 census was the earliest to be of use when state Old Age Pensions were introduced in the early twentieth century, and copies of the household returns from 1841 and 1851 were sometimes used as proof of age. The forms detailing the results of searches in the original returns to establish age have survived and are found in the National Archives for areas in the Republic of Ireland, and the Public Record Office of Northern Ireland for areas now in its jurisdiction. County-by-county indexes to the areas covered, giving the names of the individuals concerned, are found on open shelves in the Reading Room. A number of other miscellaneous copies, some also related to the Old Age Pension, and mostly relating to Northern counties, are detailed (though not indexed) in the pre-1901 census catalogue of the National Archives, on open shelves in the Reading Room. For the counties with significant numbers of these copies, details will be found under the relevant county in Chapter 12. As well as these copies, there are also a number of researchers' transcripts and abstracts compiled from the original returns before their destruction, and donated to public institutions after 1922 in an attempt to replace some of the lost records. Since the researchers were usually interested in particular families rather than whole areas, these are generally of limited value. The most significant collections are the Walsh-Kelly notebooks, which also abstract parts of the 1821, 1831 and 1851 returns, and relate particularly to south Kilkenny, and the Thrift Abstracts in the National Archives. Details of dates, areas covered and locations for the Walsh-Kelly notebooks will be found under Co. Kilkenny in Chapter 12. The Thrift Abstracts are listed in detail in the National Archives pre-1901 census catalogue under 'miscellaneous copies'. Counties for which significant numbers exist are given under the relevant county in Chapter 12.

1851

This recorded the following:

➢ name;
➢ age;
➢ occupation;
➢ relationship to the head of the household;
➢ date of marriage;
➢ literacy;
➢ absent family members;
➢ family members who died since 1841;
➢ religion.

Most of the surviving returns relate to parishes in Co. Antrim, and details will be found in Chapter 12. The comments above on transcripts and abstracts of the 1841 census also apply to 1851.

1861 and 1871

The official destruction of the returns for these two years was commendably thorough. Virtually nothing survives. The only transcripts are contained in the Catholic registers of Enniscorthy (1861), and Drumcondra and Lough-braclen, Co. Meath (1871). Details appear in Chapter 12.

3. CENSUS SUBSTITUTES

Almost anything recording more than a single name can be called a census substitute, at least for genealogical purposes. What follows is a listing, chrono-logical where possible, of the principal such substitutes. It is intended as a gloss on some of the sources given county by county under 'Census Returns and Substitutes' in Chapter 12, and as a supplement covering sources which do not fit the county-by-county format. Any material given in the source-lists of Chapter 12 which is self-explanatory is not dealt with here.

SEVENTEENTH CENTURY

1612–13

Undertakers: The *Historical Manuscripts Commission Report*, 4 (Hastings MSS.) gives lists of English and Scottish large landlords granted land in the northern counties of Cavan, Donegal and Fermanagh.

1630

Muster Rolls: These are lists of large landlords in Ulster, and the names of the able-bodied men they could assemble to fight if the need arose They are arranged by county, and by district within the county. The Armagh County Museum copy is available in the National Library (Pos. 206). Published lists are noted under the relevant county in Chapter 12, along with later lists in the Public Record Office of Northern Ireland

1641

Books of Survey and Distribution: After the wars of the mid-seventeenth century, the English government needed solid information on land ownership throughout

Ireland to carry out its policy of land redistribution. The Books of Survey and Distribution record ownership before the Cromwellian and Williamite confiscations, c.1641, and after, c.1703–4. The Books for Clare, Galway, Mayo and Roscommon have been published by the Irish Manuscripts Commission. For other counties manuscript copies are available at the National Library. Details will be found under the relevant counties in Chapter 12.

1654–56
The Civil Survey: This too was a record of land ownership in 1640, compiled between 1655 and 1667, and fuller than the Books of Survey and Distribution. It contains a great deal of topographical and descriptive information, as well as details of wills and deeds relating to land title. It has survived for twelve counties only: Cork, Derry, Donegal, Dublin, Kildare, Kilkenny, Limerick, Meath, Tipperary, Tyrone, Waterford and Wexford. All these have been published by the Irish Manuscripts Commission. Details will be found under the relevant counties in Chapter 12.

1659
'Pender's Census': This was compiled by Sir William Petty, also responsible for the Civil Survey, and records the names of persons with title to land ('tituladoes'), the total numbers of English and Irish living in each townland, and the principal Irish names in each barony. Five counties, Cavan, Galway, Mayo, Tyrone and Wicklow, are not covered. The work was edited by Seamus Pender and published in 1939. (NL I 6551 Dublin)

1662–66
Subsidy Rolls: These list the nobility, clergy and laity who paid a grant in aid to the King. They supply name and parish, and sometimes, amount paid and occupation.They relate principally to counties in Ulster.

1664–66
Hearth Money Rolls: The Hearth Tax was levied on the basis of the number of hearths in each house; these Rolls list the householders' names, as well as this number. They seem to be quite comprehensive. Details of surviving lists will be found under the relevant counties in Chapter 12. For copies of the Hearth Money Rolls listed in the Public Record Office of Northern Ireland under 'T.307', an index is available on the Public Search Room shelves.

VARIOUS DATES, SEVENTEENTH CENTURY
Cess Tax Accounts: 'Cess' (from an abbreviation of 'assessment') was a very elastic term which could be applied to taxes levied for a variety of reasons. In Ireland it was very often to support a military garrison. The accounts generally consist of lists of householders' names, along with amounts due.

EIGHTEENTH AND NINETEENTH CENTURIES
1703–1838
The Convert Rolls, ed. Eileen O'Byrne, Irish Manuscripts Commission, 1981 (NL Ir.). A list of those converting from Catholicism to the Church of Ireland. The bulk of the entries dates from 1760 to 1790.

1740
Protestant householders are listed for parts of Counties Antrim, Armagh, Derry, Donegal and Tyrone. Arranged by barony and parish, it gives names only. Parts are at the Public Record Office of Northern Ireland, the Genealogical Office, the National Library and the Representative Church Body Library. Details will be found under the relevant counties in Chapter 12.

1749
Elphin Diocesan Census, arranged by townland and parish, and listing householders, their religion, the numbers, sex and religion of their children, and the numbers, sex and religion of their servants. Details of the parishes covered will be found under the relevant counties in Chapter 12.

1766
In March and April of this year, on the instructions of the government, Church of Ireland rectors were to compile complete returns of all house-holders in their parishes, showing their religion, and giving an account of any Catholic clergy active in their area. The result was extraordinarily incon-sistent, with some rectors producing only numerical totals of population, some drawing up partial lists, and the most conscientious detailing all householders and their addresses individually. All the original returns were lost in 1922, but extensive transcripts survive for some areas and are deposited with various institutions. The only full listing of all surviving transcripts and abstracts is in the National Archives Reading Room on the open shelves. However, this does not differentiate between those returns which supply names and those which merely give numerical totals. The details given under the relevant counties in Chapter 12 refer only to those parishes for which names are given.

1795–1862
Charlton Trust Fund marriage certificates. As an encouragement to Protestant population growth, the Charlton Trust Fund offered a small marriage gratuity to members of the Protestant labouring classes. To qualify, a marriage certifi-cate recording occupations and fathers' names and signed by the local Church of Ireland clergyman had to be submitted, and these are now in the National Archives. They are particularly useful for the years before the start of regis-tration of non-Catholic marriages in 1845. The areas covered by the Fund were mainly in Counties Meath and Longford, but a few certificates exist for parts of Counties Cavan, King's (Offaly), Louth and Westmeath, as well as Dublin City. They are indexed in NA Accessions Vol. 37.

1796

Spinning-wheel Premium Entitlement Lists. As part of a government scheme to encourage the linen trade, free spinning-wheels or looms were granted to individuals planting a certain area of land with flax. The lists of those entitled to the awards, covering almost 60,000 individuals, were published in 1796, and record only the name of the individual and the civil parish in which he lived. As might be expected, the majority, over 64 per cent of the total, were in Ulster, but some names appear from every county except Dublin and Wicklow. In the county-by-county source-lists only those counties with significant numbers (more than 3,000 names) include a reference. A microfiche index to the lists is available in the National Archives, and the Public Record Office of Northern Ireland.

1798

Persons who suffered losses in the 1798 Rebellion. A list of claims for compensation from the government for property destroyed by the rebels during the insurrection of 1798. Particularly useful for the property-owning classes of Counties Wexford, Carlow, Dublin, Kildare and Wicklow. (NL I 94107)

1824–38

Tithe Applotment Books. See Chapter 4.

1831–1921

National School Records. In 1831 a country-wide system of primary education was established under the control of the Board of Commissioners for National Education. The most useful records produced by the system are the school registers themselves, which record the age of the pupil, religion, father's address and occupation, and general observations. Unfortunately, in the Republic of Ireland no attempt has been made to centralise these records; they remain in the custody of local schools or churches. The Public Record Office of Northern Ireland has a collection of over 1,500 registers for schools in the six counties of Northern Ireland. The administrative records of the Board of Commissioners itself are now held by the National Archives in Dublin. These include teachers' salary books, which can be very useful if an ancestor was a teacher.

1848–64

Griffith's Valuation. See Chapter 4.

1876

Landowners in Ireland: Return of owners of land of one acre and upwards . . ., London: Her Majesty's Stationery Office, 1876 [reissued by the Genealogical Publishing Company, Baltimore, 1988]. This records 32,614 owners of land in Ireland in 1876, identifying them by province and county; the entries record the address of the owner, along with the extent and valuation of the property. Only a minority of the population actually owned the land they occupied, but the work is invaluable for those who did.

VARIOUS DATES, EIGHTEENTH AND NINETEENTH CENTURIES

➤ **Freeholders**: Freehold property is held either by fee simple, with absolute freedom to dispose of it, by fee tail, in which the disposition is restricted to a particular line of heirs, or simply by life tenure. From the early eighteenth century freeholders' lists were drawn up regularly, usually because of the right to vote which went with freehold of property over a certain value. It follows that such lists are of genealogical interest only for a small minority of the population. Details of surviving lists will be found under the relevant counties in Chapter 12.

➤ **Voters' Lists and Poll Books**: Voters' lists cover a slightly larger proportion of the population than Freeholders' lists, since freehold property was not the only determinant of the franchise. In particular, freemen of the various corporation towns and cities had a right to vote in some elections at least. Since membership of a trade guild carried with it admission as a freeman, and this right was hereditary, a wider range of social classes is covered. Details of surviving lists will be found under the relevant counties in Chapter 12. Poll books are the records of votes actually cast in elections.

➤ **Electoral Records**: No complete collection of the electoral lists used in the elections of this century exists. This is unfortunate, since they can be of great value in tracing living relatives, listing as they do all eligible voters by townland and household. The largest single collection of surviving electoral registers is to be found in the National Archives, but even here the coverage of many areas is quite skimpy.

➤ **Valuations**: Local valuations and revaluations of property were carried out with increasing frequency from the end of the eighteenth century, usually for electoral reasons. The best of these record all householders. Again, details are given under the relevant counties in Chapter 12.

3

Church Records

THE PARISH SYSTEM

After the coming of the Reformation to Ireland in the sixteenth century, the parish structures of the Catholic Church and the Church of Ireland diverged. In general the Church of Ireland retained the older medieval parochial divisions and, as the administrative units of the state Church these were also used for administrative purposes by the secular authorities. Thus civil parishes, the basic geographical units in early censuses, tax records and land surveys, are almost identical to Church of Ireland parishes. The Catholic Church on the other hand, weakened by the confiscation of its assets and the restrictions on its clergy, had to create larger and less convenient parishes. In some ways, however, this weakness produced more flexibility, allowing parishes to be centred on new growing population centres, and, in the nineteenth century, permitting the creation of new parishes to accommodate this growth in population. The differences in the parish structures of the two Churches are reflected in their records. Even allowing for the fact that members of the Church of Ireland were almost always a small minority of the total population, the records of each parish are proportionally less extensive than Catholic records, covering a smaller area, and are thus relatively easy to search in detail. Catholic records, by contrast, cover the majority of the population and a much larger geographical area, and as a result can be very time consuming to search in detail. The creation of new Catholic parishes in the nineteenth century can also mean that the registers relevant to a particular area may be split between two parishes. Both Catholic and Church of Ireland parishes are organised on the diocesan basis first laid out in the Synod of Kells in the Middle Ages, and remain almost identical, although the Catholic system has amalgamated some of the small medieval dioceses.

(1) CATHOLIC RECORDS

Dates

Before the start of civil registration for all in 1864, virtually the only direct sources of family information for the vast majority of the population are the local parish records. However, because of the disadvantages suffered by the Catholic Church from the sixteenth to the nineteenth centuries, record-keeping was understandably difficult, and very few registers survive from before the latter half of the eighteenth century. The earliest Catholic parish records in the country appear to be the fragments for Waterford and Galway Cities dating from the 1680s. Generally speaking, early records tend to come from the more prosperous and anglicised areas, in particular the towns and cities of the eastern half of the island. In the poorest and most densely populated rural parishes of the West and North, those which saw most emigration, the parish registers very often do not start until the mid- or late nineteenth century. However the majority of Catholic registers begin in the first decades of the nineteenth century, and even in poor areas, if a local tradition of Gaelic scholarship survived, records were often kept from an earlier date.

The only way to be sure of the extent of surviving records is to check the individual parish. The National Library catalogue, available at the counter in the main reading room, is the only comprehensive county-wide account of Catholic registers, and records in detail the period covered by each set of registers, including gaps, up to 1880. The catalogue is not entirely accurate—some of the omissions are given below—but it remains the only detailed survey available.

Nature of the records

Catholic registers consist almost exclusively of baptismal and marriage records. Unlike the Church of Ireland, very few parishes kept a register of burials, and in the case of those that did, it is almost always intermittent and patchy. Baptisms and marriages are recorded in either Latin or English, never in Irish. Generally parishes in the more prosperous areas, where English was more common, tended to use English, while in Irish-speaking parishes Latin was used; there is no absolute consistency, however. The Latin presents very few problems, since only first names were translated, not surnames or placenames, and the English equivalents are almost always self-evident. The only difficulties or ambiguities are the following: *Carolus* (Charles); *Demetrius* (Jeremiah or Dermot); *Hugones* (Hugh); *Ioannes* (John or Owen). Apart from names, the only other Latin needing explanation is that used in recording marriage dispensations. These were necessary when the two people marrying were related, *consanguinati*, and the relationship was given in terms of degrees, with siblings first degree, first cousins second degree, and second cousins third degree. Thus a couple recorded as *consanguinati in tertio grado* are second cousins, information which can be of value in disentangling earlier generations. A less frequent Latin comment, *affinitatus*, records an earlier relationship by marriage between the families of the two parties.

BAPTISMS

Catholic baptismal registers almost invariably contain the following information:
➤ date;
➤ child's name;
➤ father's name;
➤ mother's maiden name;
➤ names of sponsors (godparents).

In addition most registers also record the residence of the parents. A typical Latin entry in its full form would read: *Baptisavi Johannem, filium legitimum Michaeli Sheehan et Mariae Sullivan de Lisquill. Sponsoribus, Danielus Quirk, Johanna Donoghue.*

Much more often the entry is abbreviated to: *Bapt. Johannem, f.l. Michaeli Sheehan et Mariae Sullivan, Lisquill, Sp: Daniel Quirk, Johanna Donoghue.* Translated, this is simply 'I baptised John, legitimate son of Michael Sheehan and Mary Sullivan of Lisquill, with godparents Daniel Quirk and Johanna Donoghue.' In many cases even the abbreviations are omitted, and the entries simply consist of dates, names and places.

MARRIAGES

The information given in marriage records is more variable, but always includes at least the following:
➤ date;
➤ names of persons marrying;
➤ names of witnesses.

Other information which may be supplied includes: residences (of all four people); ages; occupations; fathers' names. In some rare cases the relationships of the witnesses to the people marrying are also specified. A typical Latin entry would read: *In matrimonium coniunxi sunt Danielum McCarthy et Brigidam Kelliher, de Ballyboher. Testimonii: Cornelius Buckley, Margarita Hennessy.* Abbreviated, the entry reads: *Mat. con. Danielum McCarthy et Brigidam Kelliher, Ballyboher. Test. Cornelius Buckley, Margarita Hennessy.* 'Daniel McCarthy and Brigid Kelliher, of Ballyboher, are joined in matrimony; witnesses, Cornelius Buckley, Margaret Hennessy.'

Locations

In the 1950s and early 1960s, the National Library carried out a project to microfilm the surviving Catholic parish registers of the entire island. Out of more than 1,000 sets of registers, this project missed only a tiny percentage. Parishes whose records it does not include are: Crossgar (Co. Down); Kilmeen, Clonfert, Fahy, Clonbern (Co. Galway); Killorglin (Co. Kerry); Lanesboro (Co. Longford); Kilmeena (Co. Mayo); Rathcore and Rathmolyon (Co. Meath); Moate (Co. Westmeath); Bray (Co. Wicklow); and the Dublin City and county parishes of Booterstown, Clontarf, Donnybrook, Dun Laoghaire (Kingstown), Naul, St Mary's (Pro-Cathedral), Sandyford and Santry. Almost all these appear to have registers earlier than 1880 in local custody. In addition, the parishes of St John's (Sligo town), Cappawhite (Co. Tipperary) and Waterford City have registers held locally which are fuller than those microfilmed by the Library. Not all of the microfilmed registers in the Library are available to the public; permission for public research has not been granted by the bishops of Ardagh and Clonmacnoise, Cloyne, Down and Connor, Galway, Kerry, and Limerick. In the case of parishes in these dioceses, it is necessary to obtain written permission from the local parish priest before the Library can allow access to the records, although full details of the extent of the surviving registers can be found in the reading room catalogue.

Apart from research in the original records or microfilm copies, one other access route exists to the information recorded in parish registers. This is through the network of local heritage centres which has come into being throughout the country since *c.*1980. These are engaged, as part of the Irish Genealogical Project, in indexing and computerising all the surviving parish records for the country. At the moment of writing, June 1991, about 40 per cent of all Catholic records have been indexed manually, and about 15 per cent are on computer. These records are not directly accessible to the public, but the centres do carry out commissioned research. Full details of the Project and the centres will be found in Chapter 15.

Research in Catholic records

Because the records are so extensive, and there are so many parishes, the first step in any research must be to try to identify the relevant parish. In the ideal case, where a precise town or townland is known, this is relatively simple. Any of the Townland Indices, from 1851, 1871 or 1901 will show the relevant civil parish. There are then a number of ways to uncover the corresponding Catholic parish. Lewis' *Topographical Dictionary of Ireland* (1837), available on open access at most libraries, gives an account, in alphabetical order, of all the civil parishes of Ireland, and specifies the corresponding Catholic parish.

Brian Mitchell's *Guide to Irish Parish Records* (Genealogical Publishing Co., Baltimore, 1987), contains a county-by-county alphabetical reference guide to the civil parishes of Ireland and the Catholic parishes of which they are part. The National Library 'Index of Surnames' (or 'Householders Index') includes a map of the civil parishes in each county, and a key, loosely based on Lewis, to the corresponding Catholic parishes. A guide which is less reliable, though useful if the exact position of the church is required, is *Locations of Churches in the Irish Provinces*, produced by the Society of Latter-day Saints (NL Ir. 7265 i 8). For Dublin City the procedure is slightly different. Where the address is known, the relevant civil parish can be found in the street-by-street listings of the Dublin directories, Pettigrew and Oulton's *Dublin Almanac and General Register of Ireland* (yearly from 1834 to 1849), and Thom's *Irish Almanac and Official Directory* (yearly from 1844). More details of these will be found in Chapter 10. The corresponding Catholic parishes can then be found in Mitchell's *Guide* or in James Ryan's *Tracing your Dublin Ancestors* (Flyleaf Press, 1988).

Unfortunately, in most cases a precise address is not known. How this is to be overcome depends, obviously, on what other information is known. Where a birth, death or marriage took place in the family in Ireland after the start of civil registration in 1864, state records are the first place to look. When the occupation is known, records relating to this may supply the vital link (see Chapter 11). For emigrants, the clue to the relevant area might be provided by passenger and immigration lists, naturalisation papers, burial or death records, or even the postmarks on old family letters. In general, unless the surname is quite rare, the minimum information needed to start research on parish records with any prospect of success is the county of origin. Knowing the county, the areas to be searched in the registers can then be narrowed with the help of the early and mid-nineteenth-century land records, the Tithe Books (*c.*1830), and Griffith's Valuation (*c.*1855) (see Chapter 4). The National Library 'Index of Surnames' provides a guide, on a county basis, to the surnames occurring in these records in the different civil parishes, giving at least an indication of the areas in which a particular surname was most common. For some counties, indexes are now available which give the full names of the householders appearing in Griffith's, and these can be invaluable in narrowing still further the areas of potential relevance. Where such indexes exist, this is noted under the county in Chapter 12.

Because of the creation of new Catholic parishes in the nineteenth century, the apparent starting dates of many Catholic registers can be deceptive. Quite often, earlier records for the same area can be found in the registers of what is now an adjoining parish. To take an example, the Catholic parish of Abbeyleix, Co. Laois (Queen's), has records listed in the National Library catalogue as starting in 1824. In fact the parish was only created in that year, and before then its records will be found in Ballinakill which has records from 1794. Where surviving records appear too late to be of interest, therefore, it is always advisable to check the surrounding parishes for earlier registers. The maps of Catholic parishes accompanying this chapter are intended to simplify this task. It cannot be emphasised too strongly that these maps are not intended to be geographically precise; their aim is merely to show the positions of Catholic parishes relative to each other. Along with the county lists of parishes, they are based on the National Library catalogue which stops at 1880, and thus reflect the position in that year. Since the only published source of information on nineteenth-century Catholic parishes is Lewis' *Topographical Dictionary of Ireland*, which was published in 1837, and the power and public presence of the Church expanded greatly after Catholic Emancipation in 1836, many of the currently available parish lists have serious omissions and need to be used cautiously.

At first sight, parish registers, particularly on microfilm, can appear quite daunting. A mass of spidery abbreviated Latin, complete with blots and alterations, and cross-hatched with the scratches of a well-worn microfilm can strike terror into the heart of even the most seasoned researcher. Some registers are a pleasure to use, with decade after decade of carefully laid out copperplate handwriting; many more, unfortunately, appear to have been intended by local clergymen as their revenge on posterity. The thing to remember is that it is neither possible nor desirable to read every word on every page. The aim is to extract efficiently any relevant information, and the way to do this is by scanning the pages rather than reading them. In general, each parish takes a particular format and sticks to it. The important point is to identify this format, and where in it the relevant information is given. For most purposes, the family surname is the crucial item, so that in the baptismal example given above, the best procedure would be to scan fathers' surnames, stopping to read fully, or note, only those recording the relevant surname. For other formats, such as: 'John Maguire of Patrick and Mary Reilly; Sp. Thos McKiernan, Rose Smith', in which the family surname is given with the child's name rather than with the father's, it is the child's surname which must be scanned. Even with very efficient scanning, however, there are registers which can only be deciphered line by line, which change format every page or two, or which are simply so huge that nothing but hours of eye strain can extract any information. The most notorious are the registers for Cork City, Clonmel, and Clifden, Co. Galway.

In searching parish records, as for census returns and state records of births, marriages and deaths, a large measure of scepticism must be applied to all reported ages. In general, a five-year span around the reported date is the minimum that can be expected to yield results, and ten years is better if time allows, with emphasis on the years before the reported date. An open mind should also be kept on surname variants—widespread illiteracy made consistency and spelling accuracy extremely rare. It is essential, especially if searching more than one parish, to keep a written note of the precise period searched; even the best memory blurs after a few hours in front of a microfilm screen, and it is perfectly, horribly possible to have to search the same records twice. Duplication of research such as this is an endemic hazard of genealogy, since the nature of the research is such that the relevance of particular pieces of evidence often only emerges with hindsight; this is especially true of research in parish records. Take an example: a search in parish records for Ellen, daughter of John O'Brien, born *c.*1840. The search starts in 1842 and moves back through the baptismal registers. There are many baptisms recording different John O'Briens as father, but no Ellen recorded until 1834. If it is then necessary to check the names of her siblings, much of what has already been researched will have to be covered again. The only way to guard against having to duplicate work like this is to note all the baptisms recording John O'Brien as father, even though there is a possibility (and in many cases a probability) that none of them will ultimately turn out to have been relevant.

Apart from the obvious family information they record, Catholic parish registers may also include a wide variety of incidental information: details of famine relief, parish building accounts, marriage dispensations, local censuses, even personal letters. Anything of immediate genealogical interest is noted under the relevant county in Chapter 12.

(2) CHURCH OF IRELAND RECORDS

Dates

Records of the Established Church, the Church of Ireland, generally start much earlier than those of the Catholic Church. From as early as 1634 local parishes were required to keep records of christenings and burials in registers supplied by the Church authorities. As a result, a significant number, especially of urban parishes, have registers dating from the mid-seventeenth century. The majority, however, start in the years between 1770 and 1820; the only country-wide listing of all Church of Ireland parish records which gives full details of dates is the National Archives catalogue, copies of which are also to be found at the National Library and the Genealogical Office.

The nature of the records

BURIALS
Unlike their Catholic counterparts, the majority of Church of Ireland clergymen recorded burials as well as baptisms and marriages. These burial registers are

often also of interest for families of other denominations; the sectarian divide appears to have narrowed a little after death. The information given for burials was rarely more than the name, age and townland, making definite family connections difficult to establish in most cases. However, since early burials generally record the deaths of those born well before the start of the register, they can often be the only evidence on which to base a picture of preceding generations, and are particularly valuable because of this.

BAPTISMS

Church of Ireland baptismal records almost always supply only:
➤ the child's name;
➤ the father's name;
➤ the mother's christian name; and
➤ the name of the officiating clergyman.

Quite often, the address is also given, but this is by no means as frequent as in the case of Catholic registers. The omission of the mother's maiden name can be an obstacle to further research. From about 1820, the father's occupation is supplied in many cases.

MARRIAGES

Since the Church of Ireland was the Established Church, the only legally valid marriages, in theory at least, were those performed under its aegis. In practice, of course, *de facto* recognition was given to marriages of other denominations. None the less, the legal standing of the Church of Ireland meant that many marriages, of members of other Protestant Churches in particular, are recorded in Church of Ireland registers. The information given is not extensive, however, consisting usually of the names of the parties marrying and the name of the officiating clergyman. Even addresses are not usual, unless one of the people is from another parish. After 1845, when non-Catholic marriages were registered by the state, the marriage registers record all the information contained in state records, including occupations, addresses and fathers' names.

As well as straightforward information on baptisms, marriages and burials, Church of Ireland parish records very often include vestry books. These contain the minutes of the vestry meetings of the local parish, which can supply detailed information on the part played by individuals in the life of the parish. These are not generally with the parish registers in the National Archives, but the Public Record Office of Northern Ireland and the Representative Church Body Library in Dublin have extensive collections.

Locations

After the Church of Ireland ceased to be the Established Church in 1869, its marriage records before 1845 and baptismal and burial records before 1870

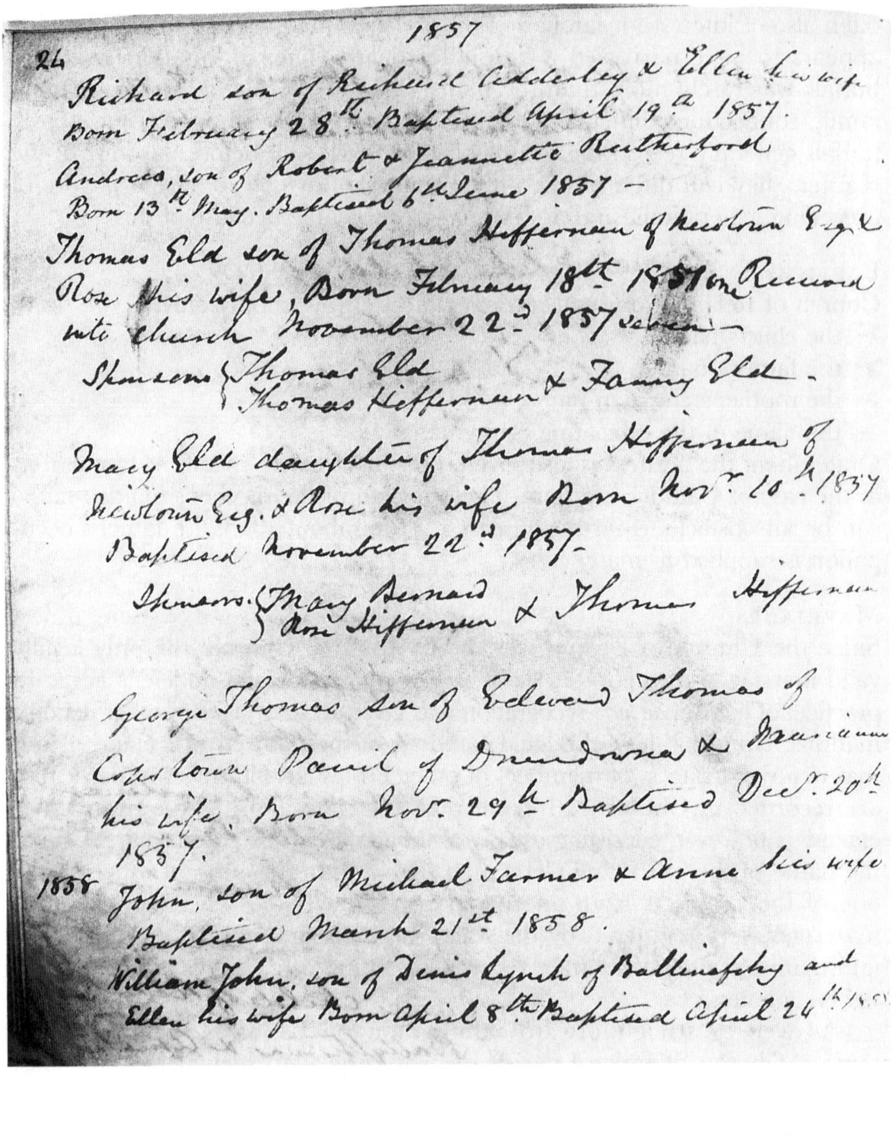

were declared to be the property of the state, public records. Unless the local clergyman was in a position to demonstrate that he could house these records safely, he was required to deposit them in the Public Record Office. By 1922 the original registers of nearly 1,000 parishes, more than half the total for the country, were stored at the Public Record Office, and these were all destroyed in the fire at the Office on 28 June of that year.

Fortunately a large number of registers had not found their way into the Office; local rectors had, in many cases, made a transcript before surrendering the originals, and local historians and genealogists using the Office before 1922 had also amassed collections of extracts from the registers. All these factors mitigated, to some extent, the loss of such a valuable collection. However, it has also meant that surviving registers, transcripts and extracts are now held in a variety of locations. The Appendix to *The Twenty-eighth Report of the Deputy Keeper of Public Records in Ireland* lists the Church of Ireland parish records for the entire island, giving full details of the years covered, and specifying those which were in the Public Office at the time of its destruction. No information on locations is included. A more comprehensive account is supplied by the National Archives catalogue of Church of Ireland records, available in the National Archives reading room at the National Library and in the Genealogical Office. Only the copy in the Archives is fully up to date. As well as the dates of the registers, this catalogue also gives some details of locations, but only when the Archives hold the originals, a microfilm copy, a transcript or abstracts on open access, when the Representative Church Body Library in Dublin holds original registers for dates which make them public records, or when they are still held in the parish. The catalogue does not indicate when microfilm copies are held by the Representative Church Body Library, the Public Record Office of Northern Ireland or the National Library, simply specifying 'local custody'. This is accurate in that the originals are indeed held locally, but unhelpful to researchers. Chapter 14 gives a county-by-county listing of Church of Ireland registers, microfilm and published copies, transcripts and extracts to be found in Dublin, with locations and reference numbers.

In general, for the northern counties of Antrim, Armagh, Cavan, Derry, Donegal, Down, Fermanagh, Leitrim, Louth, Monaghan and Tyrone, surviving registers have been microfilmed by the Public Record Office of Northern Ireland, and are available to the public in Belfast. For those counties which are now in the Republic of Ireland, Cavan, Donegal, Leitrim, Louth and Monaghan, copies of the Public Record Office of Northern Ireland microfilms are available to the public at the Representative Church Body Library in Dublin. For parishes further away from the border, 'local custody' is generally accurate, and it is necessary to commission the local clergyman to search his registers. The current *Church of Ireland Directory* will supply the relevant name and address.

The experience of 1922 has left the Church of Ireland understandably protective of its records, although the legal position remains that its early registers are state property. The National Archives have started a micro-filming programme to cover the surviving registers in the Republic, which has covered the dioceses of Glendalough and Meath to date. However, for the moment, these records are not available to the public on request. It is necessary to obtain written permission from the local clergyman before the Archives can allow access.

(3) PRESBYTERIAN RECORDS

Dates

In general, Presbyterian registers start much later than those of the Church of Ireland, and early records of Presbyterian baptisms, marriages and deaths are often to be found in the registers of the local Church of Ireland parish. There are exceptions, however; in areas which had a strong Presbyterian population from an early date, particularly in the north-east, some registers date from the late seventeenth and early eighteenth centuries. The only published listing remains that included in Margaret Falley's *Irish and Scotch-Irish Ancestral Research* (repr. Genealogical Publishing Co., 1988). This, however, gives a very incomplete and out of date picture of the extent and location of the records. For the six counties of Northern Ireland and many of the adjoining counties, the Public Record Office of Northern Ireland Parish Register Index and appended list of Presbyterian Registers in Local Custody provides a good guide to the dates of surviving registers. The Local Custody list covers all of Ireland, but is much less comprehensive for the south than for the north.

Nature of the records

Presbyterian registers record the same information as that given in the registers of the Church of Ireland (see above). It should be remembered that after 1845 all non-Catholic marriages, including those of Presbyterians, were registered by the state. From that year, therefore, Presbyterian marriage registers contain all the invaluable information given in state records.

Locations

Presbyterian registers are in three main locations: in local custody, in the Public Record Office of Northern Ireland, and at the Presbyterian Historical Society in Belfast. The Public Record Office also has microfilm copies of almost all registers in Northern Ireland which have remained in local custody, and also lists those records held by the Presbyterian Historical Society. For the rest of Ireland, almost all of the records are in local custody. It can be very difficult to locate these since many congregations in the south have moved, amalgamated or simply disappeared over the last sixty years. The very congregational basis of Presbyterianism further complicates matters, since it means that Presbyterian records do not cover a definite geographical area; the same town often had two or more Presbyterian churches drawing worshippers from the same community and keeping distinct records. In the early nineteenth century especially, controversy within the Church fractured the records, with seceding and non-seceding congregations in the same area often in violent opposition to each other. Apart from the PRONI listing, the only guide is *History of Congregations* (NL Ir. 285 h 8) which gives a brief historical outline of the history of each congregation. Lewis' *Topographical Dictionary of Ireland* (1837) records the existence of Presbyterian congregations within each civil parish, and Pettigrew and Oulton's *Dublin Almanac and General Register of Ireland* of 1835 includes a list of all Presbyterian ministers in the country, along with the names and locations of their congregations. *Locations of Churches in the Irish Provinces*, produced by the Society of Latter-day Saints (NL Ir. 7265 i 8), flawed as it is in many respects, can be useful in trying to identify the congregations in a particular area. A brief bibliography of histories of Presbyterianism is given under 'clergymen' in Chapter 11.

(4) METHODIST RECORDS

Despite the hostility of many of the Church of Ireland clergy, the Methodist movement remained unequivocally a part of the Established Church from the date of its beginnings in 1747, when John Wesley first came to Ireland, until 1816, when the movement split. Between 1747 and 1816, therefore, records of Methodist baptisms, marriages and burials will be found in the registers of the Church of Ireland. The split in 1816 took place over the question of the authority of Methodist ministers to administer sacraments, and resulted in the 'Primitive Methodists' remaining within the Church of Ireland, and the 'Wesleyan Methodists' authorising their ministers to perform baptisms and communions. (In theory, at least up to 1844, only marriages carried out by a minister of the Church of Ireland were legally valid.) The split continued until 1878 when the Primitive Methodists united with the Wesleyan Methodists outside the Church of Ireland. What this means is that the earliest surviving registers which are specifically Methodist date from 1815/16, and relate only to the Wesleyan Methodists. The information recorded in these is identical to that given in the Church of Ireland registers.

There are a number of problems in locating Methodist records which are specific to that Church. First, the origins of Methodism, as a movement rather than a Church, gave its members a great deal of latitude in their attitude to Church membership, so that records of the baptisms, marriages and burials of Methodists may also be found in Quaker and Presbyterian registers, as well as the registers of the Church of Ireland. In addition, the ministers of the Church were preachers on a circuit, rather than administrators of a particular area, and were moved frequently from one circuit to another. Quite often the records moved with them. For the nine historic counties of Ulster, the Public Record Office of Northern Ireland has produced a county-by-county listing of the surviving registers, their dates and locations, appended to their Parish Register Index. No such listing exists for the rest of the country. Again, Pettigrew and Oulton's *Dublin Almanac and General Register of Ireland* of 1835 and subsequent years provides a list of Methodist preachers and their stations, which will give an indication of the relevant localities. The next step is then to identify the closest surviving Methodist centre, and enquire of them as to surviving records. Many of the local county heritage centres also hold indexed copies of surviving Methodist records (see Chapter 15).

(5) QUAKER RECORDS

From the time of their first arrival in Ireland in the seventeenth century, the Society of Friends, or Quakers, kept rational and systematic records of the births, marriages and deaths of all their members, and in most cases these continue without a break up to the present. Parish registers as such were not kept. Each of the local weekly meetings reported any births, marriages or deaths to a larger Monthly Meeting, which then entered them in a register. Monthly Meetings were held in the following areas: Antrim, Ballyhagan, Carlow, Cootehill, Cork, Dublin, Edenderry, Grange, Lisburn, Limerick, Lurgan, Moate, Mountmellick, Richhill, Tipperary, Waterford, Wexford and Wicklow. For all but Antrim and Cootehill registers have survived from an early date, and are detailed below.

The entries for births, marriages and deaths do not themselves contain information other than the names and addresses of the immediate parties involved, but the centralisation of the records and the self-contained nature of the Quaker community make it a relatively simple matter to establish family connections; many of the local records are given in the form of family lists in any case.

There are two main repositories for records, the libraries of the Society of Friends in Dublin and Lisburn. As well as the records outlined below, these also hold considerable collections of letters, wills, family papers, as well as detailed accounts of the discrimination suffered by the Quakers in their early years.

Births, marriages and burials

Ballyhagan Marriages. Library of the Society of Friends, Lisburn, also NL
   Pos. 4127

Bandon, 1672–1713, in Casey A. (ed.), *O'Kief, Coshe Mang*, Vol. 11, Ir. 94145 c 12

Carlow births, marriages and deaths up to 1859, Library of the Society of
   Friends, Dublin, also NL Pos. 1021

Cork, births, marriages and deaths up to 1859, Library of the Society of
   Friends, Dublin (NL Pos. 1021), see also Cork (seventeenth to nineteenth
   centuries) NL Pos. 5530

Dublin, births, marriages and deaths up to 1859, Library of the Society of
   Friends, Dublin, also NL Pos. 1021 (births and marriages) and 1022
   (burials)

Edenderry, births, marriages and deaths up to 1859, Library of the Society of
   Friends, Dublin, also NL Pos. 1022; 1612–1814 (in the form of family
   lists), NL Pos. 5531

Grange, births, marriages and deaths up to 1859, Library of the Society of
   Friends, Dublin, also NL Pos. 1022

Lisburn, births, marriages and deaths up to 1859, Library of the Society of
   Friends, Dublin, also NL Pos. 1022

Limerick, births, marriages and deaths up to 1859, Library of the Society of
   Friends, Dublin, also NL Pos. 1022

Lurgan, births, marriages and deaths up to 1859, Library of the Society of
   Friends, Dublin (NL Pos. 1022), see also Lurgan Marriage Certificates,
   Library of the Society of Friends, Lisburn (NL Pos. 4126)

Moate, births, marriages and deaths up to 1859, Library of the Society of
   Friends, Dublin, also NL Pos. 1022

Mountmellick, births, marriages and deaths up to 1859, Library of the
   Society of Friends, Dublin, also NL Pos. 1023, NL Pos. 5530

Mountrath, Library of the Society of Friends, Dublin, also NL Pos. 5530

Richhill, births, marriages and deaths up to 1859, Library of the Society of
   Friends, Dublin, also NL Pos. 1023

Tipperary, births, marriages and deaths up to 1859, Library of the Society of
   Friends, Dublin, also NL Pos. 1024

Waterford, births, marriages and deaths up to 1859, Library of the Society of
   Friends, Dublin, also NL Pos. 1024

Wexford, births, marriages and deaths up to 1859, Library of the Society of
   Friends, Dublin, also NL Pos. 1024

Wicklow, births, marriages and deaths up to 1859, Library of the Society of
   Friends, Dublin, also NL Pos. 1024

Youghal, births, marriages and deaths up to 1859, Library of the Society of
   Friends, Dublin, also NL Pos. 1024

Births, Marriages and Deaths throughout Ireland 1859–1949, Library of the
   Society of Friends, Dublin, also NL Pos. 1024

Leinster Province, births, marriages and deaths, seventeenth century, Library of the Society of Friends, Dublin (NL Pos. 5530)

Munster Province, births, marriages and deaths 1650–1839, Library of the Society of Friends, Dublin (NL Pos. 5531)

Ulster Province Meeting Books, 1673–1691, Library of the Society of Friends, Lisburn (NL Pos. 3747)

Ulster Province Meetings Minute Books to 1782, Library of the Society of Friends, Lisburn (NL Pos. 4124 and 4125)

Other records

(1) PUBLISHED

Eustace, P. B. and Goodbody, O., *Quaker Records, Dublin, Abstracts of Wills* (2 vols, 1704–1785) Irish Manuscripts Commission, 1954–58

Goodbody, Olive, *Guide to Irish Quaker Records 1654–1860*, IMC, 1967, Ir. 2896 g 4

Grubb, Isabel, *Quakers in Ireland*, London, 1927

Leadbetter, *Biographical Notices of the Society of Friends*, NL J 2896

Myers, A. C., *Immigration of Irish Quakers into Pennsylvania*, Ir. 2896 m 2 and 4

Wright and Petty, *History of the Quakers 1654–1700*, Ir. 2896 w 1

(2) MANUSCRIPT

Quaker Pedigrees, Library of the Society of Friends, Dublin, also NL Pos. 5382, 5383, 5384, 5385

Quaker Wills and Inventories, Library of the Society of Friends, Lisburn, also NL Pos. 4127

Manuscript records of the Quaker Library (see *Guide* above), Swanbrook House, Bloomfield Avenue, Donnybrook, Dublin 4.
Tel. 687157, Thurs. 11 a.m. to 1 p.m.

CATHOLIC PARISH MAPS

The most important point to be kept in mind about the maps (see pages xiv to xxxii) is that they are intended as research aids, *not* as precisely accurate depictions of the details of parish boundaries. They aim to show the relative positions of the Catholic parishes which existed up to *c.*1800, and are based largely on the information contained in Lewis' *Topographical Dictionary of Ireland* (1837), and the National Library of Ireland catalogue of Catholic parish registers, which details the records up to 1880. Since this forty-three-year period saw great changes in the Catholic Church in Ireland, many compromises have had to be made; I have erred, consistently I hope, on the side of inclusiveness. Neither of the two major sources used is free of mistakes. As far as possible, where other sources existed I have attempted to cross-check with these. None the less, some mistakes undoubtedly remain.

The starting dates given for the parish registers are the dates of the earliest known surviving record. In some cases, where for example only a few pages of an early register survive, this can be misleading. A full account of the extent of all the surviving records is simply beyond the scope of this book, however. Unless otherwise stated, the dates given are those in the National Library catalogue. Where earlier records are known to have survived locally, or are available in a local heritage centre (see Chapter 15), this is noted. It is very possible that other examples of registers not filmed by the Library exist.

4

Land Records

Because of the destruction of nineteenth-century census returns, surviving land and property records from the period have acquired a somewhat unnatural importance. Two surveys cover the entire country, the Tithe Applotment Books of *c.*1823–38, and Griffith's Valuation dating from 1848 to 1864. Both of these employ administrative divisions which are no longer in widespread use and need some explanation. The smallest division, the *townland*, is the one which has proved most enduring. Loosely related to the ancient Gaelic 'Bally betagh', and to other medieval land divisions such as ploughlands and 'quarters', townlands can vary enormously in size, from a single acre or less to several thousand acres. There are more than 64,000 townlands in the country. They were used as the smallest geographical unit in both Tithe Survey and Griffith's, as well as census returns, and are still in use today. Anything from five to thirty townlands may be grouped together to form a *civil parish*. These are a legacy of the middle ages, pre-dating the formation of counties and generally coextensive with the parishes of the Established Church, the Church of Ireland. They are not to be confused with Catholic parishes which are usually much larger. In turn, civil parishes are collected together in *baronies*. Originally related to the tribal divisions, the *tuatha*, of Celtic Ireland, these were multiplied and subdivided over the centuries up to their standardisation in the 1500s, so that the current names represent a mixture of Gaelic, Anglo-Norman and English influences. A number of baronies, from five in Co. Leitrim to twenty-two in Co. Cork, then go to make up the modern county. Baronies and civil parishes are no longer in use as administrative units.

TITHE APPLOTMENT BOOKS

The Composition Act of 1823 specified that tithes due to the Established Church, the Church of Ireland, which had hitherto been payable in kind, should now be paid in money. As a result, it was necessary to carry out a

41 PARISH OF *Castlerahan*

TOWNLANDS AND LAND-LORDS.	OCCUPIERS.	1st Quality			2nd			3rd			4th		
		A.	R.	P.	A.	R.	P.	A.	R.	P.	A.	R.	P.
Aghlion	Forwarded	52	1	20	73	2	25	10	0	05	4	0	00
"	Peter Lynch He	4	2	~	5	~	~	2	2	~	~	~	~
"	J. B. & I. Lynch	10	~	~	17	~	~	5	~	~	~	~	~
"	J. & P. Keogans	3	~	~	24	1	~	4	~	~	~	~	~
"	J. Kilroy & Brady	4	~	~	12	~	~	3	~	~	7	2	~
"	Garret Fitzsimons	3	~	~	7	~	~	1	1	15	~	~	~
"	Jno. Fitzsimons	4	~	~	7	~	~	~	2	15	~	~	~
"	John Brady	~	~	1	~	~	~	~	~	~	~	~	~
"	Luke Maginis	1	0	30	4	~	~	~	~	~	1	~	~
"	Richd. Glannon	1	~	~	1	~	~	~	~	~	~	~	~
		03	1	10	150	3	25	26	1	35	12	2	~

valuation of the entire country, civil parish by civil parish, to determine how much would be payable by each landholder. This was done over the ensuing fifteen years up to the abolition of tithes in 1838. Not surprisingly, tithes were fiercely resented by those who were not members of the Church of Ireland, and all the more because the tax was not payable on all land; the exemptions produced spectacular inequalities. In Munster, for instance, tithes were payable on potato patches, but not on grassland, with the result that the poorest had to pay most. The exemptions also mean that the Tithe Books are not comprehensive. Apart from the fact that they omit entirely anyone not in occupation of land, certain categories of land varying from area to area are simply passed over in silence. They are *not* a full list of householders. None the less they do constitute the only country-wide survey for the period and are valuable precisely because the heaviest burden of tithes fell on the poorest, for whom few other records survive.

From a genealogical point of view the information recorded in the Tithe Books is quite basic, consisting typically of townland name, landholder's name, area of land, and tithes payable. In addition many Books also record the landlord's name and an assessment of the economic productivity of the land; the tax was based on the average price of wheat and oats over the seven years up to 1823, and was levied at a different rate depending on the quality of the land.

The original Tithe Books for the twenty-six counties of the Republic of Ireland are available in the National Archives. Those for the six counties of Northern Ireland were transferred to the Public Record Office of Northern Ireland in 1924. Photostat copies of these are available at the National Archives, and microfilm copies in the National Library.

The usefulness of the Tithe Books can vary enormously depending on the nature of the research. Since only a name is given, with no indication of family relationships, any conclusions drawn are, inevitably, somewhat speculative. However, for parishes where registers do not begin until after 1850, they are often the only early records surviving. They can provide valuable circumstantial evidence, especially where a holding passed from father to son in the period between the Tithe survey and Griffith's Valuation. The surnames in the Books have been roughly indexed, in the National Library 'Index of Surnames', described more fully below.

GRIFFITH'S VALUATION

In order to produce the accurate information necessary for local taxation the Tenement Act, 1842 provided for a uniform valuation of all property in Ireland to be based on the productive capacity of land and the potential rent of buildings. The man appointed Commissioner of Valuation was Richard Griffith, a Dublin geologist, and the results of his great survey, the *Primary*

Valuation of Tenements.

ACTS 15 & 16 VIC., CAP. 63, & 17 VIC., CAP. 8.

COUNTY OF CAVAN.

BARONY OF CASTLERAHAN.

UNION OF OLDCASTLE.

PARISH OF CASTLERAHAN.

No. and Letters of Reference to Map.		Names. Townlands and Occupiers.	Immediate Lessors.	Description of Tenement.	Area. A. R. P.	Rateable Annual Valuation. Land. £ s. d.	Buildings. £ s. d.	Total Annual Valuation of Rateable Property. £ s. d.
		AGHALION. (Ord. S. 39.)						
1	a	John Lynch,	C. T. Nesbit,	House, offices, and land,	14 2 28	6 5 0	0 10 0	6 15 0
–	b	C. T. Nesbit,	In fee,	Land,	0 3 30	0 5 0	—	0 5 0
2	{a	Bryan M'Donald, }	C. T. Nesbit,	Herd's house & land, }	19 3 22	{ 4 0 0	1 5 0	5 5 0
	{–	John Fitzsimon, }		Land,		{ 4 0 0	—	4 0 0
3		John Fitzsimon,	Same,	House, offices, and land,	5 1 34	2 0 0	1 0 0	3 0 0
4		John Fitzsimon,	Same,	Land,	4 1 34	2 0 0	—	2 0 0
–	a	Rose Fitzsimon,	Same,	House,	—	—	0 10 0	0 10 0
5	a	John Fitzsimon, jun.,	Same,	House, offices, and land,	8 1 35	4 0 0	1 0 0	5 0 0
–	b	John Fitzsimon,	Same,	Land,	0 2 15	0 5 0	—	0 5 0
–	c	John Flood,	Same,	Land (gardens),	0 1 24	0 5 0	—	0 5 0
6			Same,	House, offices, and land,	17 2 8	8 0 0	1 15 0	9 15 0
7		Michael Cogan,	Same,	House, offices, and land,	31 0 12	10 0 0	1 5 0	} 14 0 0
8			Same,	Land,	7 2 16	2 15 0	—	
9	a	Peter Lynch,	Same,	House, offices, and land,	5 0 22	1 18 0	0 10 0	} 2 15 0
				Bog,	7 0 17	0 7 0	—	
–	b	Joseph Brady,	Same,	Ho., off., & sm. garden,	—	—	0 10 0	0 10 0
10				Land,	1 1 33	0 10 0	—	0 10 0
11		Catherine Fitzsimon,	Same,	House and land,	2 0 4	0 10 0	0 5 0	0 15 0
12		Matthew Cogan,	Same,	House, office, and land,	13 0 9	4 10 0	0 10 0	5 0 0
13				Land,	11 0 24	4 0 0	—	
14		Patrick Cogan,	Same,	House, offices, and land,	23 3 18	12 0 0	1 5 0	} 22 5 0
15				Land,	8 2 21	4 0 0	—	
16				Land,	1 2 2	1 0 0	—	
				Land,	0 1 24	0 4 0	—	0 4 0
–	a	John Lynch,	Same,	House, offices, and land,	38 0 30	15 0 0	1 0 0	16 0 0
17	a	Terence & Patk. Cogan,	Same,	House,	—	—	0 5 0	0 5 0
–	b	Vacant,	Terence & Patk. Cogan,	House,	—	—	0 10 0	0 10 0
–	c	Vacant,	Same,	House,	—	—	0 15 0	0 15 0
18		Michael Brady,	C. T. Nesbit,	House, office, and land,	8 2 20	4 0 0	0 15 0	4 15 0
19	a	James Bennett,	Same,	House, offices, and land,	34 2 18	17 10 0	1 5 0	18 15 0
–	b	Margaret Gilroy,	James Bennett,	House,	—	—	0 10 0	0 10 0
–	c	Anne Timmon,	Same,	House,	—	—	0 5 0	0 5 0
–	d	Peter Lynch,	C. T. Nesbit,	Land,	0 0 20	0 1 0	—	0 1 0
–	e	Joseph Brady,	Same,	Land,	0 0 20	0 1 0	—	0 1 0
20		Anthony Brady,	Same,	House, offices, and land,	12 0 14	5 15 0	1 0 0	6 15 0
21		John Lynch,	Same,	House, offices, and land,	12 1 18	6 5 0	1 0 0	7 5 0
22		Edward Fitzsimons,	Same,	House, office, and land,	6 2 16	3 0 0	0 10 0	3 10 0
23	a	Michael Brady,	Same,	Herd's house and land,	14 3 13	7 10 0	0 10 0	8 0 0
–	b	Terence & Patk. Cogan,	Same,	Land,	0 1 24	0 5 0	—	0 5 0
24		Peter Lynch,	Same,	Land,	7 0 31	3 0 0	—	3 0 0
25		John Brady,	Same,	Herd's house and land,	34 3 2	16 0 0	0 5 0	16 5 0
26		Patrick Brady,	Same,	House, offices, and land,	18 1 17	8 15 0	1 15 0	10 10 0
27		C. T. Nesbit,	In fee,	Land,	14 0 13	0 15 0	—	0 15 0

B

Valuation of Ireland, were published between 1848 and 1864. The Valuation is arranged by county, barony, poor law union, civil parish and townland, and lists every landholder and every householder in Ireland. Apart from townland address and householder's name, the particulars given are:

➢ name of the person from whom the property was leased ('immediate lessor');
➢ description of the property;
➢ acreage;
➢ valuation.

The only directly useful family information supplied is in areas where a surname was particularly common; the surveyors often adopted the Gaelic practice of using the father's first name to distinguish between individuals of the same name, so that 'John Reilly (James)' is the son of James, while 'John Reilly (Michael)' is the son of Michael. Copies of the Valuation are widely available in major libraries and record offices, both on microfiche and in their original published form. The dates of first publication will be found under the individual counties in Chapter 12.

The Valuation was never intended as a census substitute, and if the 1851 census had survived, it would have little genealogical significance. As things stand, however, it gives the only detailed guide to where in Ireland people lived in the mid-nineteenth century, and what property they possessed. In addition, because the Valuation entries were subsequently revised at regular intervals, it is often possible to trace living descendants of those originally listed by Griffith. (See 'Valuation Office Records' below.)

Indexes to Griffith's and Tithe Books

In the early 1960s the National Library undertook a project to index the surnames occurring in Griffith's Valuation and the Tithe Books, which produced the county-by-county series known as the 'Index of Surnames' or 'Householders Index'. This records the occurrence of households of a particular surname in each of the civil parishes of a county, giving the exact number of households in the case of Griffith's, as well as providing a summary of the total numbers in each barony of the county. Since it is not a true index, providing only an indication of the presence or absence of a surname in the Tithe Books, and the numbers of the surname in Griffith's, its usefulness is limited. For names which are relatively uncommon it can be invaluable, but is of little assistance for a county in which a particular surname is plentiful. It is most frequently used as a means of narrowing the number of parish records to be searched in a case where only the county of origin of an ancestor is known. The county volumes include outline maps of the civil parishes covered and a guide to the corresponding Catholic parishes. Full sets of the Index of Surnames can be found at the National Library, the

Surname		T	Barony
Fitzgerald	G2		Loughtee L.
Fitzgerald	G	T	Loughtee U.
Fitzgerald		T	Tullygarvey
Fitzgerald	G2	T	Clankee
Fitzgerald	G2		Clanmahon
Fitzmaurice	G		Tullyhunco
Fitzpatrick	G25	T	Tullyhaw
Fitzpatrick	G114	T	Loughtee L.
Fitzpatrick	G24	T	Tullyhunco
Fitzpatrick	G73	T	Loughtee U.
Fitzpatrick	G30	T	Tullygarvey
Fitzpatrick	G9	T	Clankee
Fitzpatrick	G33	T	Clanmahon
Fitzpatrick	G10	T	Castlerahan
Fitzsimmons		T	Tullyhunco
Fitzsimmons	G	T	Loughtee U.
Fitzsimmons	G	T	Clanmahon
Fitzsimon	G	T	Tullyhunco
Fitzsimon	G2	T	Loughtee U.
Fitzsimon	G7	T	Tullygarvey
Fitzsimon	G	T	Clankee
Fitzsimon	G		Clanmahon
Fitizsimon	G5	T	Castlerahan
Fitzsimon	G39	T	Castlerahan
Fitzsimons	G	T	Tullyhaw
Fitzsimons	G6	T	Loughtee L.
Fitzsimons	G12	T	Loughtee U.
Fitzsimons	G8	T	Tullygarvey
Fitzsimons	G7	T	Clankee
Fitzsimons	G14	T	Clanmahon
Fitzsimons	G6	T	Castlerahan
Flack		T	Tullyhunco
Flack	G2	T	Tullygarvey
Flack	G3	T	Clankee
Flaherty		T	Loughtee L.
Flanagan	G14	T	Tullyhaw
Flanagan	G3	T	Loughtee L.
Flanagan	G		Tullyhunco
Flanagan	G10	T	Loughtee U.
Flanagan	G	T	Tullygarvey
Flanagan	G4	T	Clankee
Flanagan	G3	T	Clanmahon
Flanagan	G14	T	Castlerahan
Flanigan	G2	T	Tullyhaw
Flanigan	G		Loughtee L.
Flanigan		T	Loughtee U.
Flannagan	G		Loughtee L.
Flannery	G		Loughtee U.
Fleming	G		Tullyhaw
Fleming	G	T	Loughtee L.
Fleming	G3	T	Tullyhunco
Fleming	G8	T	Loughtee U.
Fleming	G	T	Tullygarvey
Fleming	G	T	Clankee
Fleming	G9	T	Clanmahon
Fleming	G7	T	Castlerahan
Fletcher	G		Loughtee U.
Fleuker	G	T	Clankee
Flewker	G2	T	Clankee
Flinn		T	Clankee
Flinn	G	T	Clanmahon
Flood	G	T	Tullyhaw

Surname		T	Barony
Flood	G21	T	Loughtee U.
Flood	G18	T	Tullygarvey
Flood	G4	T	Clankee
Flood	G14	T	Clanmahon
Flood	G29	T	Castlerahan
Floody	G3	T	Tullygarvey
Floyd	G2	T	Loughtee U.
Flynn	G13	T	Tullyhaw
Flynn	G6	T	Loughtee L.
Flynn	G		Tullyhunco
Flynn	G3	T	Loughtee U.
Flynn		T	Tullygarvey
Flynn	G		Clankee
Flynn	G9	T	Clanmahon
Flynn	G20	T	Castlerahan
Foghlan	G		Tullyhaw
Folbus		T	Tullyhunco
Foley	G2		Tullygarvey
Follett	G		Loughtee U.
Fonor		T	Castlerahan
Forbes	G	T	Tullyhunco
Forbes	G	T	Clankee
Ford	G		Tullyhaw
Ford	G		Loughtee U.
Ford	G2	T	Tullygarvey
Ford	G		Clankee
Forde	G	T	Tullyhaw
Foreman	G6	T	Clankee
Forest		T	Loughtee U.
Forster		T	Loughtee U.
Forster	G10	T	Clanmahon
Forsyth	G3	T	Castlerahan
Forsythe	G3	T	Clanmahon
Fosqua		T	Tullygarvey
Foster	G	T	Tullyhaw
Foster	G6	T	Loughtee U.
Foster	G5		Tullygarvey
Foster	G9	T	Clanmahon
Foster	G3	T	Castlerahan
Fotton		T	Tullygarvey
Fottrell	G		Clankee
Fox	G2	T	Tullyhaw
Fox	G2	T	Tullyhunco
Fox		T	Loughtee U.
Fox	G4	T	Tullygarvey
Fox	G15	T	Clankee
Fox	G2	T	Clanmahon
Fox	G36	T	Castlerahan
Foy	G3	T	Loughtee L.
Foy	G2	T	Loughtee U.
Foy	G26	T	Tullygarvey
Foy	G5	T	Clankee
Foy	G	T	Clanmahon
Foy		T	Castlerahan
Foyragh		T	Tullygarvey
Frances	G	T	Clankee
Francey	G3		Clankee
Francis		T	Loughtee L.
Fraser	G3	T	Tullyhaw
Frazer	G		Tullyhaw
Frazer	G		Loughtee U.
Frazor		T	Tullyhunco

National Archives, the Public Record Office of Northern Ireland, and the Genealogical Office.

In recent years a number of full-name indexes to Griffith's have been produced on microfiche by All-Ireland Heritage and Andrew Morris, both in the US. These list alphabetically all the householders in the Valuation, and show the townland and civil parish in which the entry is recorded. For the moment, the following areas have been covered: Counties Cork, Fermanagh, Limerick, Tipperary, Waterford; the cities of Belfast, Cork and Dublin (All-Ireland Heritage); and Counties Mayo and Wicklow (Andrew Morris). As aids to locating individual families in these counties at the time of the Valuation, these are invaluable. However, they are not widely available as yet. The National Archives has copies of the indexes for Cork City and county, Dublin City, and Co. Fermanagh, while the National Library has copies of those for Counties Mayo and Wicklow.

VALUATION OFFICE RECORDS

The Valuation Office, set up to carry out the original Primary Valuation, is still in existence and has two related sets of records which are potentially valuable. The first of these are the notebooks used by the original Valuation surveyors, consisting of 'field books', 'house books' and 'tenure books'. All three record a map reference for the holdings they deal with, as in the published Valuation. The field books then record information on the size and quality of the holding, the house books record the occupiers' names and the measurements of any buildings on their holdings, and the tenure books give the annual rent paid and the legal basis on which the holding is occupied, whether by lease or at will. The tenure books also give the year of any lease, useful to know before searching estate papers or the Registry of Deeds. As well as containing information such as this, which does not appear in the published Valuation, the valuers' notebooks can also be useful in documenting any changes in occupation between the initial survey and the published results, for instance if a family emigrated in the years immediately before publication, since they pre-date the final publication itself by several years. Unfortunately, they are not extant for all areas. The National Archives now houses those which survive for the Republic of Ireland. Those covering Northern Ireland are now to be found in the Public Record Office of Northern Ireland.

The Valuation Office itself, at 6 Ely Place, Dublin 2, contains the second set of useful records. These are the 'Cancelled Land Books' and 'Current Land Books', giving details of all changes in the holdings, from the time of the Primary Valuation up to the present day. Any variations in the size or status of the holding, the names of the occupier or lessor, or the valuation itself, are given in the revisions carried out every few years. The Books can be very useful in pin-pointing a possible date of death or emigration, or in

CASTLERAHAN PARISH.   CASTLERAHAN BARONY, OLDCASTLE UNION,
CO. CAVAN 32.

Griffith's Valuation Year 1856 - Tithe Applotment Book
Year 1831.

Anderson	G		Cunningham	G2	T	Hanly	G2	T
Armstrong	G	T	Curran	G		Hanna	G	
			Cusack	G		Hanley		T
Balfe	G					Hartley		T
Barclay		T	Daly	G2	T	Haulton		T
Barry	G		Darcy		T	Hawthorn	G5	T
Bartley	G2	T	Darling	G		Haynes	G	
Bates	G		Dempsey	G		Heeny	G2	T
Bell	G		Dolan	G6	T	Heery	G4	T
Bennett	G3	T	Donnelly	G2	T	Henesy	G	
Blackstock		T	Dowland		T	Henway		T
Booker	G	T	Downs	G		Hourigan	G4	T
Boyd	G		Duffy	G3	T	Hughes	G3	
Boyers		T	Duigan	G		Humphries		T
Boylan	G4	T	Duignan	G2	T	Hunter	G3	T
Brady	G42	T				Hyland		T
Bray	G3	T	Evans	G2	T			
Brennan	G	T				Irwin	G2	
Briody	G		Fagan	G6	T			
Brookes	G		Farelly	G	T	James		T
Brown	G		Farrell	G9	T	Johnston	G	
Browne	G		Farrelly	G15	T			
Buchanan	G	T	Finigan	G	T	Kavanagh	G	
Byres	G6		Finn		T	Keane	G	T
			Finnegan	G2	T	Keelan	G	
Caffrey	G13	T	Fitzpatrick	G3	T	Kellett	G2	
Cahill	G4	T	Fitzsimon	G9	T	Kelly	G2	
Caldwell	G3	T	Fitzsimons	G	T	Kennedy	G3	T
Callaghan	G3		Fleming	G2		Kenny	G	
Carey	G		Flood	G5	T	Keoghan	G	T
Carolin		T	Flynn	G3	T	Kerr	G	
Carr	G		Foster	G2	T	Kiernan	G	
Carroll	G		Fox	G6		Kilrian		T
Cartan	G		Freeland	G	T	Kilroy		T
Clarekin	G2	T				Kimmins		T
Clarke	G5	T	Gaffney	G2	T	King	G3	
Cobey		T	Gaghran		T			
Cochrane	G		Galaher	G		Leeson	G	
Cogan	G12		Galligan		T	Leightel	G3	
Colerigg	G2	T	Gavan	G	T	Little		T
Colgan	G4	T	Gaynor	G6	T	Lord	G	
Colingg	G		Geoghegan	G2		Lougheed	G	
Comerford		T	Gibney	G3	T	Loughlin		T
Conaghty	G		Gibson	G	T	Love	G2	T
Condon		T	Gill	G		Lyddy	G	T
Connell	G4	T	Gillick	G	T	Lynch	G51	T
Connor	G	T	Gilroy	G				
Conway	G3		Glannon		T	M'Cabe	G13	T
Cooke	G	T	Goff		T	M'Cahill	G	T
Cooney	G		Gormley	G		M'Cormack	G	
Coote	G5	T	Grattan		T	M'Cutchion		T
Corrigan	G2	T	Graveny		T	M'Dermott	G	
Cosgrave	G	T	Gray		T	M'Donald	G5	T
Coyle	G	T	Griffin		T	M'Donnell	G	
Crawly	G	T	Griffith	G	T	M'Dowell	G2	
Cronin	G3	T				M'Enerny		T
Cullen	G9	T	Halpin	G3	T	M'Enroe	G14	T
						M'Evoy	G	T

identifying a living relative. A large majority of those who were in occupation of a holding by the 1890s, when the Land Acts began to subsidise the purchase of the land by its tenant-farmers, have descendants or relatives still living in the same area. The Cancelled Land Books for Northern Ireland are now in the Public Record Office of Northern Ireland.

ESTATE RECORDS

In the eighteenth and nineteenth centuries the vast majority of the Irish population lived as small tenant-farmers on large estates owned for the most part by English or Anglo-Irish landlords. The administration of these estates inevitably produced large quantities of records—maps, tenants' lists, rentals, account books, lease books etc. Over the course of the twentieth century, as the estates have been broken up and sold off, many collections of these records have found their way into public repositories, and constitute a largely unexplored source of genealogical information.

There are, however, good reasons for their being unexplored. First, it was quite rare for a large landowner to have individual rental or lease agreements with the huge numbers of small tenants on his land. Instead, he would let a significant area to a middleman, who would then sublet to others, who might in turn rent out parts to the smallest tenants. It is very rare for estate records to document the smallest landholders, since most of these had no right of tenure in any case, being simply tenants 'at will'.

A related problem is the question of access. The estate records in the two major Dublin repositories, the National Archives and the National Library, are not catalogued in detail. The only comprehensive guide is given in Richard Hayes' 'Manuscript Sources for the Study of Irish Civilization' and its supplements, copies of which can be found in the National Library and National Archives. This catalogues the records by landlord's name and by county, with entries such as 'NL MS. 3185. Rent Roll of Lord Cremorne's estate in Co. Armagh, 1797'. Hayes gives no further details of the areas of the county covered, and it can be difficult to ascertain from the Tithe Books or Griffith's just who the landlord was; Griffith's only supplies the name of the immediate lessor. The holdings of the Public Record Office of Northern Ireland present similar problems, with access depending on a knowledge of the landlord's name. In addition, it should be added that many of the collections in the National Library have still not been catalogued at all, and thus remain completely inaccessible.

The largest single collection in the National Archives is the Landed Estate Court records, also known as the Encumbered Estate Courts, which are not catalogued in Hayes. The Court was set up to facilitate the sale of estates whose owners could not invest enough to make them productive, and between 1849 and 1857 oversaw the sale of more than 3,000 Irish estates. Its records contain many rentals and maps drawn up for the sales, but are so close in time to Griffith's as to make them of limited use except in very particular circumstances. Once again the principal problem of access is in identifying the relevant landlord, since they too are catalogued by landlord's name.

There are a number of ways to overcome, or partially overcome, this obstacle. With common sense, it is often possible to identify the landlord by examining Griffith's for the surrounding areas—the largest lessor is the likeliest candidate. If the immediate lessor in Griffith's is not the landlord, but a middleman, then it can be useful to try to find this middleman's own holding or residence and see who he was leasing from. Two publications may also be of value. O. H. Hussey de Burgh's *The Landowners of Ireland* provides a guide to the major landowners, the size of their holdings, and where in the country they were situated. *Landowners in Ireland: Return of owners of land of one acre and upwards . . .,* (London: 1876) is comprehensive to a fault, and is organised more awkwardly, alphabetically within county.

Despite all the problems, research in estate records can be very rewarding, especially for the period before the major nineteenth-century surveys. To take one example, the rent rolls of the estate of Charles O'Hara in Counties Sligo and Leitrim, which date from *c.*1775, record a large number of leases to smaller tenants, and supply the lives named in the leases, often specifying family relationships. It must be emphasised, however, that information of this quality is rare; the majority of the rentals and tenants' lists surviving only give details of major tenants.

A more detailed guide to the dates, areas covered, and class of tenants recorded in the estate papers of the National Library and National Archives is in the process of preparation by the Genealogical Office. To date, Counties Cork, Leitrim, Galway, Mayo, Roscommon and Sligo have been covered, and a brief outline of the results will be found in Chapter 12 under these counties.

PART 2

Other Sources

5

Wills

1. THE NATURE OF THE RECORDS

Wills have always been an extremely important source of genealogical information on the property-owning classes, in Ireland as elsewhere. They provide a clear picture of a family at a particular point in time, and can often supply enough details of a much larger network of relationships—cousins, nephews, in-laws and others—to produce quite a substantial family tree. Apart from their genealogical significance, wills can also evoke vividly the long-vanished way of life of those whose final wishes they record.

INFORMATION SUPPLIED
The minimum information to be found in a will is:
➤ the name, address and occupation of the testator;
➤ the names of the beneficiaries;
➤ the name(s) of the executor(s);
➤ the names of the witnesses;
➤ the date the will was made;
➤ the date of probate of the will.
Specific properties are usually, though not always, mentioned. The two dates, that of the will itself and of its probate, give a period during which the testator died. Up to the nineteenth century most wills were made close to the date of death, and witnesses were normally related to the person making the

will. As well as the minimum information, of course, many wills also contain much more, including at times addresses and occupations of beneficiaries, witnesses and executors, and details of family relationships, quarrels as well as affection.

Testamentary Authority before 1857

Before 1857 the Church of Ireland, as the Established Church, had charge of all testamentary affairs. Consistorial Courts in each diocese were responsible for granting probate, that is, legally authenticating a will and conferring on the executors the power to administer the estate. The Courts also had the power to issue letters of administration to the next of kin or the main creditor on the estates of those who died intestate. Each Court was responsible for wills and administrations in its own diocese. However, when the estate included property worth more than £5 in another diocese, responsibility for the will or administration passed to the Prerogative Court under the authority of the Archbishop of Armagh.

Consistorial Wills and Administrations

The wills and administration records of the Consistorial Courts were held locally in each diocese up to the abolition of the testamentary authority of the Church of Ireland in 1857. After that date the Public Record Office began the slow process of collecting the original records and transcribing them into Will and Grant Books. The Office then indexed the wills and Administration Bonds, the sureties which the administrators had to produce as a guarantee that the estate would be properly administered. None of the Consistorial Courts had records of all the wills or administrations they had dealt with. Very little earlier than the seventeenth century emerged, and the majority of the Courts appear to have had serious gaps before the mid-eighteenth century.

All the original wills and administrations in the Public Record Office were destroyed in 1922, along with almost all the Will and Grant Books into which they had been transcribed. The only exceptions are the Will Books for Down (1850–58) and Connor (1818–20, 1853–58), and the Grant Books for Cashel (1840–45), Derry and Raphoe (1818–21), and Ossory (1848–58).

The indexes to wills and administration bonds were not destroyed, although a number were badly damaged. These are available in the reading room of the National Archives. The wills indexes are alphabetical and normally give the testator's address and the year of probate, as well as occasionally specifying his occupation. The administration bonds indexes are not fully alphabetical, being arranged year by year under the initial letter of the surname of the deceased. They give the year of the bond, the full name and usually the address of the deceased, and sometimes his occupation. Some of the wills indexes have been published and details of these will be found at the end of this chapter.

Prerogative Wills and Administrations

To recap: an estate was dealt with by the Prerogative Court, rather than a Consistorial Court, if it covered property worth more than £5 in a second diocese. In general, then, Prerogative wills and administrations tend to cover the wealthier classes, merchants with dealings in more than one area, and those who lived close to diocesan borders. Up to 1816 the Prerogative Court was not housed in a single place, with hearings generally held in the residence of the presiding judge. From 1816 on, the King's Inns building in Henrietta St provided a permanent home. For this reason the records of the Court before 1816 cannot be taken as complete. After 1857 all these records were transferred to the Public Record Office, where the original wills and grants of administration were transcribed into Prerogative Will and Grant Books, and indexed. The indexes survived 1922, but all the original wills and grants, and almost all the Will and Grant Books were destroyed. Details of those Books which survived will be found at the end of this chapter.

The loss of the original Prerogative wills is mitigated to a large extent by the project carried out in the early decades of the nineteenth century by Sir William Betham, Ulster King of Arms. As well as preparing the first index of testators, up to 1810, he also made abstracts of the family information contained in almost all the wills before 1800. The original notebooks in which he recorded the information are now in the National Archives, and the Genealogical Office has his Sketch Pedigrees based on these abstracts and including later additions and amendments. The Public Record Office of Northern Ireland has a copy of the Genealogical Office series, without the additions and amendments, made by a successor of Betham's, Sir John Burke. Betham also made a large number of abstracts from Prerogative Grants up to 1802, the original notebooks for which are also in the National Archives. The Genealogical Office transcript copy (GO 257–260) is fully alphabetical, unlike the notebooks.

The first index to Prerogative wills, up to 1810, was published in 1897 by Sir Arthur Vicars, Burke's successor as Ulster King of Arms, and can be used as a guide to Betham's abstracts and Sketch Pedigrees with the proviso that wills from the decade 1800–1810 are not covered by Betham. The manuscript index for the period from 1811 to 1857 is in the National Archives reading room. As with the consistorial administration bonds indexes, the Prerogative Grants indexes are not fully alphabetical, being arranged year by year under the initial letter of the surname of the deceased.

Testamentary Authority after 1857

The Probate Act of 1857 did away with the testamentary authority of the Church of Ireland. Instead of the Consistorial Courts and the Prerogative Court, power to grant probate and issue letters of administration was vested in a Principal Registry in Dublin and eleven District Registries. Rules similar to those governing the geographical jurisdiction of the ecclesiastical courts applied, with the Principal Registry taking the place of the Prerogative Court, as well as covering Dublin and a large area around it. Transcripts of the wills proved and administrations granted were made in the District Registries, and the originals forwarded to the Principal Registry. Almost all the records of the Principal Registry were destroyed in 1922. The few surviving Will and Grant Books are detailed below. The Will Book transcripts made by the District Registries survived, however. The records of those Districts covering areas now in the Republic—Ballina, Cavan, Cork, Kilkenny, Limerick, Mullingar, Tuam and Waterford—are in the National Archives. For districts now in Northern Ireland—Armagh, Belfast and Londonderry— the Will Books are in the Public Record Office of Northern Ireland.

Fortunately, from 1858 a new system of indexing and organising wills and administrations had been devised. A printed, alphabetically ordered 'Calendar of Wills and Administrations' was produced for every year, and copies of all these have survived. For each will or administration, these record:

➢ the name, address and occupation of the deceased person;
➢ the place and date of death;
➢ the value of the estate;
➢ the name and address of the person or persons to whom probate or administration was granted.

In many cases the relationship of the executor is also specified. This means that despite the loss of so much original post-1857 testamentary material, some information at least is available on all wills or administrations from this period. Very often much that is of genealogical value can be gleaned from the Calendars, including such information as exact dates of death, places of residence and indications of economic status. A consolidated index covers the period between 1858 and 1877, making it unnecessary to search each yearly Calendar. The Calendars are on open access in the National Archives reading room.

Abstracts and Transcripts

As well as the original Consistorial and Prerogative wills and grants, and the transcripts made of them in the Will and Grant Books, a wide range of other sources exists, particularly for material before 1857. The most important of these is the collection of the National Archives itself, gathered after 1922 in

270   WILLS AND ADMINISTRATIONS. 1871.

HORGAN Daniel.

[191]   Effects under £200.

20 March.   Letters of Administration of the personal estate of Daniel Horgan late of Great George's-street **Cork** Builder deceased who died 21 February 1870 at same place were granted at **Cork** to Michael Joseph Horgan of the South Mall in said City Solicitor the Nephew of said deceased for the benefit of Catherine Horgan Widow John Horgan the Reverend David Horgan Ellen Gillman Mary Daly and Margaret Horgan only next of kin of said deceased.

HORNE Christopher.

[67]   Effects under £100,

7 March.   Letters of Administration of the personal estate of Christopher Horne late of Ballinasloe County **Galway** Gentleman a Widower deceased who died 21 March 1867 at same place were granted at the **Principal Registry** to Patrick Horne of Ballinasloe aforesaid M.D. the only Brother of said deceased.

HORNER Isabella.

[17]   Effects under £100.

29 April.   Letters of Administration of the personal estate of Isabella Horner late of Rahaghy County **Tyrone** Widow deceased who died 13 April 1871 at same place were granted at **Armagh** to James Horner of Rahaghy (Aughnacloy) aforesaid Farmer the Son and one of the next of kin of said deceased.

HORNIDGE John Isaiah.

[79]   Effects under £450.

8 June.   Letters of Administration (with the Will annexed) of the personal estate of John Isaiah Hornidge late of the South Dublin Union Workhouse **Dublin** Master of said Workhouse a Widower deceased who died 22 April 1871 at same place were granted at the **Principal Registry** to James Seymour Longstaff of Stephen's-green Dublin Merchant and William Thomas Orpin of George's-terrace George's-avenue Blackrock County Dublin Accountant the Guardians during minority only of the Daughter and only next of kin of deceased.

HOUSTON Eliza.

[337]   Effects under £200.

22 September.   Letters of Administration of the personal estate of Eliza Houston late of

an attempt to replace some at least of what had been lost. As well as original wills from private legal records and individual families, this ever-expanding collection also includes pre-1922 researchers' abstracts and transcripts. It is covered by a card index in the reading room, which also gives details of those wills and grants in the surviving pre-1857 Will and Grant Books. Separate card indexes cover the Thrift, Jennings and Crossley collections of abstracts, and the records of Charitable Donations and Bequests. The Public Record Office of Northern Ireland has made similar efforts, and the copies it holds are indexed in the Pre-1858 Wills Index, part of the Subject Index in the Public Search Room.

INLAND REVENUE RECORDS
The Inland Revenue in London kept a series of Annual Indexes to Irish Will Registers and Indexes to Irish Administration Registers from 1828 to 1879 which are now in the National Archives. These give the name and address of both the deceased and the executor or administrator. As well as the Indexes, the Archives also holds a set of the actual Inland Revenue Irish Will Registers and Irish Administration Registers for the years 1828–39, complete, apart from the Wills Register covering January to June 1834. The Will Registers are not exact transcripts of the original wills, but supply a good deal of detailed information including the precise date of death, the principal beneficiaries and legacies, and a brief inventory of the estate. The Administration Registers are less informative, but still include details of the date of death, the administrator and the estate.

LAND COMMISSION RECORDS
Under the provisions of the Land Purchase Acts, which subsidised the purchase of smallholdings by the tenants who occupied them, it was necessary for those wishing to sell to produce evidence of their ownership to the Irish Land Commission. As a result, over ten thousand wills were deposited with the Commission, the majority from the nineteenth century, but many earlier. The National Library holds a card index to the testators. The original documents are currently in the process of being transferred to the National Archives.

THE REGISTRY OF DEEDS
The registration of wills was normally carried out because of a legal problem anticipated by the executor(s) in the provisions—almost certainly the exclusion of parties who would feel they had some rights over the estate. Because of this, wills at the Registry cannot be taken as providing a complete picture of the family. Abstracts of all wills registered from 1708, the date of the foundation of the Registry, to 1832, were published in three volumes by the Irish Manuscripts Commission between 1954 and 1986. These are available on open shelves at the National Library and National Archives. Although the

abstracts record and index all the persons named, testators, beneficiaries and witnesses, they do not show the original provisions of the wills. These can be found in the original memorials in the Registry.

THE GENEALOGICAL OFFICE
Most of the will abstracts held by the Genealogical Office are covered by the Office's own index, GO MS. 429, which was published in *Analecta Hibernica*, No. 17, 1949 (NL Ir. 941 a 10). The manuscript index has since been added to, but is still not entirely comprehensive, excluding all the Betham material and many of the collections relating to individual families. A guide to the major collections is included in the reference guide at the end of this chapter.

OTHER SOURCES
There are many other collections of will abstracts and transcripts in such public repositories as the National Library, the Representative Church Body Library, the Royal Irish Academy, the Public Record Office of Northern Ireland and Trinity College Library. There are no separate indexes to these testamentary collections. Where a significant group of abstracts or transcripts exists, this is noted in the reference guide which follows.

2. A REFERENCE GUIDE

What follows is an attempt to provide a series of check-lists and guides to the various testamentary sources. Because of the changes in testamentary jurisdiction in 1858, it is divided into two sections, dealing with records before and after that date. Section 1, Pre-1858, includes (1) a general check-list of surviving indexes; (2) a list of surviving Will and Grant Books; (3) a list of major collections of abstracts and transcripts, divided into (i) general collections, (ii) those relating to particular surnames, and (iii) those relating to particular diocesan jurisdictions; (4) a detailed list of surviving consistorial wills and administrations indexes, both published and in the National Archives. Section 2, Post-1858, covers (1) the yearly calendars; and (2) original wills and transcripts.

Section I. pre-1858

1. GENERAL INDEXES
1. Card Indexes, National Archives search room.
2. Pre-1858 Wills Index, PRONI reading room.
3. Indexes to Consistorial Wills and Administrations, diocese by diocese (see below for details).
4. Indexes to Prerogative Wills.

(a) Sir Arthur Vicars, *Index to the Prerogative Wills of Ireland, 1536–1810* (1897);
(b) MS. Index, 1811–1858, National Archives search room.
5. Index to Prerogative Grants, National Archives search room.
6. Index to Wills in the Records of the Land Commission, National Library.

2. SURVIVING WILL AND GRANT BOOKS
1. Prerogative Will Books: 1664–84, 1706–8 (A–W), 1726–28 (A–W), 1728–29 (A–W), 1777 (A–L), 1813 (K–Z), 1834 (A–E), National Archives, included in card index.
2. Prerogative Administrations: Grants 1684–88, 1748–51, 1839; Day Books, 1784–88, National Archives.
3. Consistorial Will Books: Connor (1818–1820, 1853–1858); Down (1850–1858), National Archives.
4. Consistorial Grant Books: Cashel (1840–1845); Derry and Raphoe (1812–1821); Ossory (1848–1858); National Archives.

3. ABSTRACTS AND TRANSCRIPTS
(i): *General Collections*
    1. Betham abstracts from Prerogative Wills, to *c.*1800, National Archives (notebooks); Genealogical Office and Public Record Office of Northern Ireland (Sketch Pedigrees), (see Vicars above).
    2. Betham abstracts from Prerogative Administrations, to *c.*1800, National Archives (notebooks); Genealogical Office (alphabetical listing).
    3. Indexes to Irish Will Registers, 1828–79 (Inland Revenue), National Archives (see Testamentary Catalogue).
    4. Irish Will Registers, 1828–1839 (Inland Revenue), National Archives (see Testamentary Catalogue).
    5. Indexes to Irish Administration Registers, 1828–79 (Inland Revenue), National Archives (see Testamentary Catalogue).
    6. Irish Administration Registers, 1828–1839 (Inland Revenue), National Archives (see Testamentary Catalogue).
    7. Index to Will Abstracts at the Genealogical Office, *Analecta Hibernica*, 17; GO MS. 429.
    8. P. B. Phair and E. Ellis, *Abstracts of Wills at the Registry of Deeds* (1708–1832), IMC, 1954–88.
    9. Abstracts of wills of Irish testators registered at the Prerogative Court of Canterbury, 1639–98, NL MS. 1397.
    10. Abstracts of miscellaneous eighteenth-century wills made by the Protestant clergy and their families, Representative Church Body Library (for the years 1828–39, see also NL MS. 2599).
    11. Leslie Collection, 981 wills, NL MS. 1774, see also NL Pos. 799.
    12. Ainsley Will Abstracts, GO 535 and 631.

13. Wilson Collection, NL Pos. 1990.
14. Welply Collection: 1,500 wills, 100 administrations, Representative Church Body Library, indexed in *The Irish Genealogist*, 1985/86.
15. Richey Collection, NL MSS. 8315–16.
16. Upton Collection, Royal Irish Academy, also NL Pos. 1997, principally families in Co. Westmeath, with some from Counties Cavan and Longford.
17. MacSwiney Papers, Royal Irish Academy, mainly Counties Cork and Kerry.
18. Westropp Manuscripts, Royal Irish Academy, mainly Counties Clare and Limerick.

(ii) *By Surname*

Burke	GO MS. 707.
Butler	Wallace Clare, *The Testamentary Records of the Butler Family*, 1932, NL Ir. 9292 b 11.
Dawson	Almost all eighteenth-century Dawson wills, NL MS. 5644/5.
Domville	NL MSS. 9384–86.
Drought	Crossley Abstracts, National Archives, also GO 417/8.
Gordon	GO MS. 702, Abstracts of most Irish Gordon wills.
Griffith	NL MS. 8392.
Greene	See National Archives Card Index.
Hamilton	Co. Down, PRONI T.702A.
Hill	GO MS. 691–92.
Kelly	GO MS. 415.
Manley	NL D.7075–86, the Manley family of Dublin and Offaly.
Mathews	Prerogative wills and administrations, PRONI T.681.
O'Loghlen	Co. Clare, NL Pos. 2543.
Skerrett	*The Irish Ancestor*, Vol. 5, No. 2, 1975.
Young	NL Pos. 1276.

(iii) *By Diocese*

A word of warning is necessary: the identification of a collection of abstracts or transcripts under a particular diocese does *not* necessarily mean that all the wills it covers belong to that diocese. In the case of the larger collections especially, it is just not possible to be absolutely precise about the areas covered.

Armagh

Four Wills of old English merchants of Drogheda, 1654–1717, JCLAS Vol. XX, 2, 1982

Alphabetical list of the prerogative wills of residents of Co. Louth up to 1810, NL, MS. 7314.

Index to wills of Dundalk residents, JCLAS, Vol. X, No. 2, 113–15, 1942.

Cashel and Emly

White, J. D., 'Extracts from original wills, formerly in the Consistorial Office, Cashel, later moved to Waterford Probate Court', *Kilkenny and South of Ire. Arch. Soc. Jnl.*, Ser. 2, Vol. 2, Pt 2, 1859; Vol. IV, 1862.

Clogher

Swanzy Collection, National Archives, T.1746 (1C–53–16); copies also at the Genealogical Office (GO 420, indexed in 429), and Representative Church Body Library; abstracts from Clogher and Kilmore Will Books, Marriage License Bonds, Administrations, militia lists; principal names include Beatty, Nixon, Armstrong, Young, Veitch, Jackson, Mee, Noble and Fiddes.

Clonfert

GO 707: Numerous abstracts, mainly relating to wills mentioning Burke families.

Cloyne

Welply Abstracts (4 volumes), Representative Church Body Library, indexed in *The Irish Genealogist*, 1985/1986.

Index to Will Abstracts at the Genealogical Office, *Analecta Hibernica*, 17; GO MS. 429.

Connor

Connor Will Book, 1818–20, 1853–58, National Archives.

Stewart-Kennedy notebooks, Will Abstracts, many from Down and Connor; principal families include Stewart, Clarke, Cunningham, Kennedy and Wade, Trinity College Library and PRONI; see also NL Pos. 4066.

Cork and Ross

Welply Abstracts (4 volumes), Representative Church Body Library, indexed in *The Irish Genealogist*, 1985/1986.

Caulfield transcripts, mainly sixteenth century, Representative Church Body Library; see also *Cork Hist. and Arch. Soc. Jnl*, 1903/1904.

Notes from wills of Cork Diocese, 1660–1700, NA M. 2760.

Derry

Amy Young, *300 Years in Inishowen* (NL Ir. 9292 y 1), contains 46 Donegal wills.

Down

Down Will Book, 1850–58, National Archives.

Stewart-Kennedy notebooks, Will Abstracts, many from Down and Connor; principal families include Stewart, Clarke, Cunningham, Kennedy and Wade, Trinity College Library and PRONI.

Dublin and Glendalough

Lane-Poole papers, NL MS. 5359 (abstracts).

Abstracts of wills proved in Dublin diocesan court, 1560–1710, A–E only, GO MS. 290.

Elphin
Wills and Deeds from Co. Sligo, 1605–32, NL. MS. 2164.

Kildare
Betham Collection, National Archives, Abstracts of almost all Kildare wills
    up to 1827; also NL Pos. 1784–85.

Killaloe and Kilfenora
O' Loghlen wills from Co. Clare, NL Pos. 2543.
Wills and Administrations from Counties Clare and Limerick, Westropp
    manuscript volume, 3A 39, Royal Irish Academy.

Kilmore
Swanzy Collection, National Archives, T.1746 (1C–53–16); copies also at the
    Genealogical Office (GO 420, indexed in 429), and Representative Church
    Body Library; Abstracts from Clogher and Kilmore Will Books, Marriage
    Licence Bonds, Administrations, militia lists; principal names include
    Beatty, Nixon, Armstrong, Young, Veitch, Jackon, Mee, Noble and Fiddes.

Leighlin
Carrigan Collection, NL. Pos. 903 (952 wills, mainly Ossory and Leighlin),
    indexed in *The Irish Genealogist*, 1970.
Abstracts from Ossory and Leighlin Admons, *The Irish Genealogist*, 1972.

Limerick
Hayes, R., 'Some Old Limerick Wills', *North Munster Antiquarian Journal*, Vol.
    I, 163–8, Vol. II, 71–5.
Wills and Administrations from Counties Clare and Limerick; Westropp
    manuscript volume, 3A 39, Royal Irish Academy.

Meath
Alphabetical list of the prerogative wills of residents of Co. Louth up to 1810,
    NL. MS. 7314.
Rice, G., 'Extracts from Meath priests' wills, 1658–1782', *Riocht na Midhe*, Vol.
    IV, No. 1, 68–71, 1967.

Ossory
Carrigan Collection, NL. Pos. 903 (952 wills, mainly Ossory and Leighlin),
    indexed in *The Irish Genealogist*, 1970.
Abstracts from Ossory and Leighlin Admons, *The Irish Genealogist*, 1972.
T. U. Sadleir, Abstracts from Ossory Admons, 1738–1884, NA 1A–37–33.
Calendar of Administrations, Ossory, NA T.7425.
GO 683–6, Walsh-Kelly notebooks. Will abstracts, mainly from Ossory.

Raphoe
Amy Young, *300 Years in Inishowen* (NL Ir. 9292 y 1). Contains 46 Donegal
    wills.

Tuam
GO 707, numerous abstracts, mainly relating to wills mentioning Burke families, 1784–1820.

Waterford and Lismore
Wills relating to Waterford, *Decies* (Journal of the Old Waterford Society), 16, 17, 19, 20, 22, 23 (NL Ir. 9414 d 5).

Jennings Collection, National Archives and *Decies* (above); 166 Waterford Wills and Administrations, NL D.9248–9413.

4. CONSISTORIAL WILLS AND ADMINISTRATION BONDS INDEXES, PUBLISHED AND IN THE NATIONAL ARCHIVES

Abbreviations

IA	*The Irish Ancestor* (NL Ir. 9205 1 3)
JCHAS	*Journal of the Cork Historical and Archaeological Society* (NL Ir. 794105 c 1)
JKAS	*Journal of the Kildare Archaeological Society* (NL Ir. 794106 k 2)
O'K.	Albert Casey (ed.) *O'Kief, Coshe Mang etc.* (NL Ir. 94145 c 12)
Ph.	Phillimore publication, open access, NA and NL
RDKPRI	Report of the Deputy Keeper of Public Records of Ireland

	Wills	*Admon Bonds*
Ardagh		
	1695–1858 (also IA, 1970)	1697–1850
Ardfert and Aghadoe		
	1690–1858 (Ph. 1690–1800; O'K. Vol. 5, 1690–1858)	1782–1858 (O'K. Vol. 5, 1782–1858)
Armagh		
	1666–1837 (A–L), 1677–1858 (M–Y), Drogheda District, 1691–1846	
Cashel and Emly		
	1618–1858 (Ph. 1618–1800)	1644–1858
Clogher		
	1661–1858	1660–1858

Clonfert

1663–1857	1771–1857
(IA, 1970)	(IA, 1970)

Cloyne

1621–1858	1630–1857
(Ph. 1621–1800;	(O'K. Vol. 6)
O'K. Vol. 8,	
1547–1858)	

Connor

1680–1846 (A–L),	1636–1858
1636–1857 (M–Y)	

Cork and Ross

1548–1858	1612–1858
(Ph. & O'K. Vol. 8,	(O.K. Vol. 5)
1584–1800; JCHAS	
1895–8: 1548–1833)	

Derry

1612–1858	1698–1857
(Ph. 1612–1858)	

Down

1646–1858	1635–1858

Dromore

1678–1858, with	1742–1858, with
Newry & Mourne,	Newry & Mourne,
1727–1858 (Ph.)	1811–45 (IA, 1969,
	Newry & Mourne)

Dublin and Glendalough

1536–1858	1636–1858
(RDKPRI Nos	(RDKPRI Nos
26 & 30)	26 & 30)

Elphin

1650–1858 (fragments)	1726–1857

Ferns

1601–1858 (fragments),	1765–1833
1603–1838 (F–V),	
1615–1842 (unproved,	
W only. Ph. 1601–1800)	

Kildare

1661–1858		1770–1848
(Ph. 1661–1800;		(JKAS, 1907,
JKAS 1905: 1661–1858)		1770–1858)

Killala and Achonry

1756–1831 (fragments)   1779–1858
(IA, 1975)

Killaloe and Kilfenora

1653–1858 (fragments)   1779–1858
(Ph. 1653–1800)   (IA, 1975)

Kilmore

1682–1858 (damaged)   1728–1858

Leighlin

1642–1858   1694–1845
(Ph. 1642–1800)   (IA, 1972)

Limerick

1615–1858   1789–1858
(Ph. 1615–1800)

Meath

1572–1858 (fragments),   1663–1857
partial transcript, 1635–1838,
NA 1A 42 167

Ossory

1536–1858 (fragments)   1660–1857
(Ph. 1536–1800)

Raphoe

1684–1858 (damaged)   1684–1858
(Ph.)

Tuam

1648–1858 (damaged)   1692–1857

Waterford and Lismore

1648–1858 (damaged)   1661–1857
(Ph. 1648–1800)

Section II. post-1858

1. Yearly calendars of wills and administrations, 1858 to date
Provide: name, address and occupation of the deceased; place and exact date
of death; names and addresses of grantees of probate or administration, and
relationship; exact date of probate; value of the estate.

These are on open access in the search room of the National Archives
and the Public Record Office of Northern Ireland. The consolidated index,
1858–1877, is only in the National Archives.

2. Original wills or transcripts
(a) Card Index, National Archives search room
(b) Surviving Will and Grant Books in the National Archives, as follows:
    (i) Principal Registry Wills, 1874, G–M
         Principal Registry Wills, 1878, A–Z
         Principal Registry Wills, 1891, G–M
         Principal Registry Wills, 1896, A–F
         Principal Registry Wills, Dublin District, 1869, G–M
         Principal Registry Wills, Dublin District, 1891, M–P
         Principal Registry Wills, Dublin District, 1901, A–F
    (ii) Principal Registry Grants, 1878, 1883, 1891, 1893
    (iii) District Registry Will Books:
         Ballina, 1865 to date
         Cavan, 1858–1909
         Cork, 1858–1932
         Kilkenny, 1858–1911
         Limerick, 1858–1899
         Mullingar, 1858–1901
         Tuam, 1858–1929
         Waterford, 1858–1902.
(c) District Registry Will Books in the Public Record Office of Northern
     Ireland:
         Armagh, 1858–1900 (MIC 15C)
         Belfast, 1858–1900 (MIC 15C)
         Londonderry, 1858–1900 (MIC 15C).

6

The Genealogical Office

The Genealogical Office is the successor to the office of Ulster King of Arms, also known simply as 'The Office of Arms', which was created in 1552 when Edward VI designated Bartholomew Butler, the chief heraldic authority in Ireland, with the title of 'Ulster'. The reasons for the choice of 'Ulster' rather than 'Ireland' remain somewhat unclear; it seems likely that the older title of 'Ireland King of Arms' was already in use amongst the heralds at the College of Arms in London. Whatever the reason, Ulster King of Arms acquired full jurisdiction over arms in Ireland and retained it for almost four hundred years until 1943, when the Office was renamed the Genealogical Office, and Ulster became 'Chief Herald of Ireland', with substantially the same powers as his predecessor.

At the outset, the authority of Ulster was limited to those areas of the country under English authority; heraldry, as a feudal practice, was in any case quite alien to Gaelic culture. Up to the end of the seventeenth century, the functions of the Office remained purely heraldic, ascertaining and recording what arms were in use, and by what right families used them. From the late seventeenth century, Ulster began to acquire other duties, as an officer of the crown intimately linked to the government. These duties were largely ceremonial, deciding and arranging precedence on state occasions, as well as introducing new peers to the Irish House of Lords, and recording peerage successions. In essence these two areas, the heraldic and the ceremonial, remained the principal functions of the Office over the succeeding three centuries, with Ulster becoming registrar of the chivalric Order of St Patrick instituted in 1783, and continuing to have responsibility for the ceremonial aspects of state occasions at the court of the viceroy.

The functioning of the Office depended to an inordinate degree on the personal qualities of Ulster, and an unfortunate number of the holders of the position in the eighteenth century especially appear to have regarded it as a sinecure, paying little attention to the keeping of records and treating the manuscript collection as their personal property. It was only with the arrival of Sir William Betham in the early nineteenth century that the business of the Office was put on a sound footing, and serious attention paid to the collection and care of manuscripts. As a consequence, although a number of the official records are much earlier, the vast majority of the Office's holdings do not pre-date the nineteenth century.

In the course of carrying out its heraldic functions, the Office inevitably acquired a large amount of material of genealogical interest, since the right to bear arms is strictly hereditary. None the less, the new title given to the Office in 1943, 'The Genealogical Office', was somewhat inaccurate. Its principal function continues to be heraldic, the granting and confirmation of official achievements to individuals and corporate bodies. Up to the 1980s the Office also carried out commissioned research into family history. This service has been discontinued. In its place, the Office now has a Consultation Service which supplies detailed guidance on how to carry out research on individual families.

GENEALOGICAL OFFICE RECORDS

Manuscripts

The manuscripts of the Genealogical Office are numbered in a single series from 1 to 822. They are, however, of a very mixed nature, reflections of the Office's changing functions over the centuries, and are best dealt with in categories based on those functions. The following account divides them into (1) Official Records, (2) Administrative Records and Reference Works, and (3) Research Material.

(1) OFFICIAL RECORDS

A number of sets of manuscripts are direct products of the official functions of the Office and may be termed official records. On the heraldic side, the principal records are the Visitations (GO 47–9), the Funeral Entries (GO 64–79), the official grants and confirmations of arms (GO 103–111g), and the Registered Pedigrees (GO 156–182). In addition to these, four other manuscript groups reflect duties which Ulster's Office acquired over the centuries. These are the Lords Entries (GO 183–188), Royal Warrants for Changes of Name (GO 26 and 149–154A), Baronets Records (GO 112–4), and Gaelic Chieftains (GO 610 and 627).

The Visitations were an attempt to carry out in Ireland heraldic visitations along the lines of those which the College of Arms had been using in England for almost a century to control the bearing of arms. The results were meagre, confined to areas close to Dublin, and almost certainly incomplete even for those areas. The following places were covered: Dublin and parts of Co. Louth, 1568–70; Drogheda and Ardee, 1570; Swords, 1572; Cork, 1574; Limerick, 1574; Dublin City, 1607; Dublin county, 1610; and Wexford, 1610. They are indexed in GO 117.

The Funeral Entries, covering the period 1588 to 1691, make up some of the deficiencies of the Visitations. Their aim was to record the name, wife and issue of deceased nobility and gentry, along with their arms. In addition, many of the Entries include very beautiful illustrations of the arms and armorial devices used at the funeral, as well as notes on the ordering of the funeral processions and ceremonies. An index to the Entries is found in GO 386.

One of the later effects of the lack of visitations was to make it difficult for Ulster to verify from his own records that a particular family had a right to its arms. This gave rise to the practice, peculiar to Ireland, of issuing 'confirmations' of arms, which were taken as official registrations, and were dependent on an applicant being able to show that the arms in question had been in use in his family for three generations or one hundred years. The records of these confirmations and of actual grants of arms are found in GO 103–111g, dating from 1698 and still current. Earlier grants and confirmations are scattered through the manuscript collection; a complete index to all arms officially recorded in the Office is to be found in GO 422–3. Hayes' 'Manuscript Sources for the Study of Irish Civilization' reproduces this, and includes a summary of any genealogical information.

Since the right to bear arms is hereditary, the authentication of arms required the collection of a large amount of genealogical material. This is undoubtedly the origin of the Registered Pedigrees, GO 156–182, but the series very quickly acquired a life of its own, and the majority of entries are now purely genealogical. It is particularly important for the collection of eighteenth-century pedigrees of Irish émigrés to France, produced in response to their need to prove membership of the nobility; admission to such a position carried very substantial privileges, and the proofs required included the signature of Ulster. The series continues up to the present and is indexed in GO 469, as well as Hayes' 'Manuscript Sources'.

Partly as a result of difficulties concerning the status of lords who had supported James II, from 1698 one of Ulster's duties became the keeping of an official list of Irish peers, 'Ulster's Roll'. In theory all those entitled to sit in the Irish House of Lords, whether by creation of a new peerage or by succession, were obliged to inform Ulster before they could be officially introduced to the House. In practice the vast bulk of information collected relates to successions, with the heirs supplying the date of death and place of burial, arms, marriages and issue. The series covers the period from 1698 to 1939, and is indexed in GO 470.

In order to regulate the assumption of arms and titles, it became necessary after 1784 to obtain a warrant from the King for a change of name and arms. From 1795 the Irish House of Lords made it obligatory to register such a warrant in Ulster's Office. The result is the manuscript series known officially as 'Royal Warrants for changes of name and licences for changes of name'. Most of the nineteenth-century changes came about as a result of wills, with an inheritance made conditional on a change of name. Hayes' 'Manuscript Sources' indexes the series.

A similar need to regulate the improper assumption of titles produced the Baronet's records, GO 112–14. A royal warrant of 1789 for 'correcting and preventing abuses in the order of baronets' made registration of their arms and pedigrees with Ulster obligatory. The volumes are indexed in GO 470.

The records of Gaelic Chieftains in GO 610 and 627 are the consequence of a revival instituted in the 1940s by Dr Edward MacLysaght, the first Chief Herald of Ireland. He attempted to trace the senior lineal descendants in the male line of the last recorded Gaelic 'Chief of the Name', who was then officially designated as the contemporary holder of the title. The practice has met with mixed success, since the collapse of Gaelic culture in the seventeenth century left an enormous gulf to be bridged, and the chieftainships were not in any case originally passed on by primogeniture, but by election within the extended kin-group. None the less, more than twenty chiefs have been designated, and the records of the research which went into establishing their right to the title are extremely interesting.

(2) ADMINISTRATIVE RECORDS AND REFERENCE WORKS

Many of the documents, now part of the general manuscript series, simply derive from the paperwork necessary to run an office. These include cash books, receipts, Ulster's Diaries, letter books, day books, and records of fees due for the various functions carried out by Ulster. Of these, the most interesting from a genealogical point of view are the letter books (GO 361–78), copies of all letters sent out from the Office between 1789 and 1853, and the Betham letters (GO 580–604), a collection of the letters received by Sir William Betham between c.1810 and 1830, and purchased by the Genealogical Office in 1943. The former are indexed volume by volume. The latter are of more potential value. The only index, however, comes in the original catalogue of the sale of the letters, dated 1936, a copy of which is to be found at the Office, though not numbered among the manuscripts. The catalogue lists the letters alphabetically by addressor, and a supplementary surnames index provides a guide to the families dealt with. Another eight volumes of the series, unindexed, are to be found in the National Archives (M.744–51).

As well as documents produced in the day-to-day running of the Office, a large number of manuscripts also relate to the ceremonial functions performed by Ulster. These include official orders relating to changes of insignia, papers dealing with precedence and protocol, records of official functions at the vice-regal court, and the records of the Order of St Patrick. There is little of genealogical interest in these.

In the course of their heraldic and genealogical work, Ulster and his officers accumulated over the years a large series of manuscripts for use as reference works. These include manuscript armories, ordinaries of arms, treatises on heraldry and precedence, a series of English Visitations, and blazons of arms of English and Scottish peers. The bulk of the material is heraldic, but there is a good deal of incidental genealogical information, particularly in the seventeenth-century ordinaries of arms.

(3) RESEARCH MATERIAL

The most useful manuscripts in the Genealogical Office collection are those acquired and created to provide sources for genealogical research. The policy, begun in the early nineteenth century by Sir William Betham and continued by all his successors, has produced a wide range of material, much of it based on records which were destroyed in the Public Record Office in 1922. It may be divided into three broad categories: (i) Betham's own compilations; (ii) the collections of later genealogists; and (iii) other records. The sheer diversity of these documents makes a complete account impractical here; what follows is a broad outline.

The greatest single work produced by Betham is the collection of abstracts of family information from prerogative wills. These are divided into a number of series: GO 223–226 ('Old Series', Vols I–IV) covers wills before 1700; GO 227–254 ('New Series', Vols 1–31) covers wills from 1700 to c.1800. The series are roughly alphabetical, with each volume containing its own index. Sir Arthur Vicars' *Index to the Prerogative Wills of Ireland 1536–1810* provides a guide to wills covered. Many of the sketch pedigrees include later amendments and additions from other sources. GO 255–6 index all the marriage alliances recorded in the wills. Another series, GO 203–14 ('Will Pedigrees', Vols I–XII) represents an unfinished attempt to rearrange all these sketch pedigrees into strictly alphabetical order. Betham also produced a large number of sketch pedigrees based on other sources, collected as 'Ancient Anglo-Irish Families', Vols I–VI (GO 215–19), 'Milesian Families', Vols I–III (GO 220–22), and the '1st series', Vols I–XVI (GO 261–76) and '2nd series', Vols I–VII (GO 292–8). All these are indexed in GO 470.

As well as the sketch pedigrees and the letters (covered above under 'Administrative Records'), there are two other sources in the collection which owe their origin to Betham. The first of these, genealogical and historical excerpts from the plea rolls and patent rolls from Henry III to Edward VI (GO 189–93), constitute the single most important source of information on Anglo-Norman genealogy in Ireland. Betham's transcript of Roger O'Ferrall's

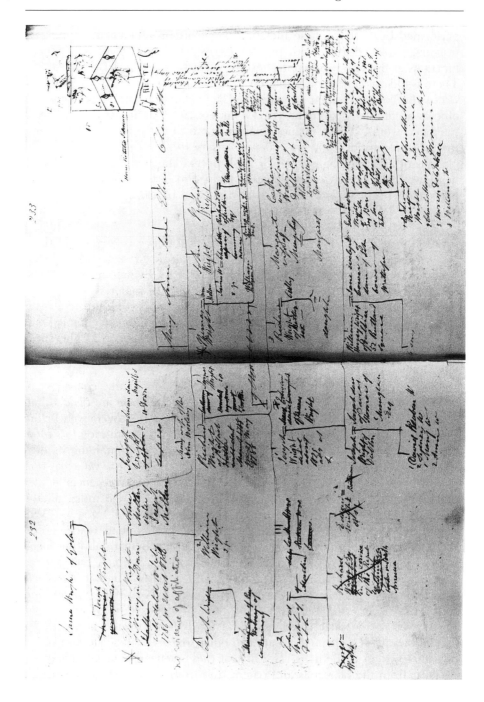

'Linea Antiqua', a collation of earlier genealogies compiled in 1709, is the Office's most extensive work on Gaelic, as opposed to Anglo-Irish genealogy. This copy (in three volumes, GO 145-7, with an index to the complete work in 147) also contains Betham's interpolations and additions, unfortunately unsourced. It records the arms of many of the Gaelic families covered, without giving any authority for them, and is the source of most of the arms illustrated in Dr Edward MacLysaght's *Irish Families*.

Pedigrees and research notes produced by later amateur and professional genealogists make up a large part of the Office's manuscript collection. Among those who have contributed to these are Sir Edmund Bewley, Denis O'Callaghan Fisher, Tenison Groves, Alfred Moloney, T. U. Sadleir, Rev. H. B. Swanzy and many others. For the most part, their records concern either particular groups of families or particular geographical areas. Some of these have their own indexes, some are covered by GO 470 and 117, others have will abstracts only indexed in GO 429. The numerical listing at the end of this chapter provides a guide. As well as these, some of the results of Ulster's Office's own research in the late nineteenth and early twentieth century are classed as manuscripts, GO 800-822. These constitute no more than a fraction of the total research information produced by the Office. They are indexed in Hayes' 'Manuscript Sources'.

A final class of records consists of extremely diverse documents, having only their potential genealogical usefulness in common. It includes such items as freeholders' lists from different counties; extracts from parish registers; transcripts of the Dublin City roll of freemen, of returns from the 1766 census, of city directories from various periods; and much more. More detailed information will be found in the list at the end of this chapter.

Archives

As well as the manuscripts series, now closed, the Genealogical Office also has extremely extensive archive records of the commissioned research it carried out up to the 1980s. For the closing decades of the nineteenth century and the early decades of the twentieth century, these records are still largely concerned with the Anglo-Irish. Manuscripts 800-822 cover perhaps 5 per cent of this material. The remainder is sorted in roughly alphabetical order in boxes along one whole wall of the Genealogical Office strong-room. It is to be hoped that the Office can acquire the resources to sort and index it soon, since it contains a great deal of very valuable information.

After the creation of the Genealogical Office in 1943, the focus of the commissioned research shifted, with most of the work now carried out on behalf of the descendants of emigrants to Australia and North America. There are over 20,000 research files giving details of the results of this research. A continuing project to index the families concerned has so far covered over 6,000 of these; the results are on computer at the Office.

RESEARCH IN GENEALOGICAL OFFICE MANUSCRIPTS

The biggest single obstacle to research in GO manuscripts is the lack of a single, comprehensive index. Many attempts have been made over the centuries of the Office's existence to produce such an index; the result has been a proliferation of partial indexes, each covering some of the collection, none covering it all. These are dealt with below. In addition, the policy used in the creation of manuscripts appears to have become somewhat inconsistent from the 1940s. Before then only the earliest and most heterogeneous manuscripts had been numbered in a single series, with each of the other groups simply having its own volume numbers, 'Lords Entries Vol. II' or 'Registered Pedigrees Vol. 12', for example. The laudable attempt to produce a consistent numbering system, starting at GO 1 and moving through the collection, seems to have given rise to the piecemeal addition of material which was more properly the preserve of the National Library. The subsequent transfers to the Library, and renumbering of remaining material, produced a virtual collapse of the system in the upper numbers. No manuscripts exist for many of the numbers between 600 and 800. The numerical list of manuscripts at the end of this chapter reflects the current situation, with titles no longer in the Office given in brackets.

Indexes

GO 59: This is a detailed calendar of manuscripts 1–58, particularly useful since many of these consist of very early heterogeneous material bound together for preservation.
GO 115: Indexes the following: Arms, A–C; Grants and Confirmations, A and B; Visitations; British Families; Funeral Entries; Registered Pedigrees, Vols 1–10. Only the Visitations (GO 47–9) and British Families (GO 44–6) are not indexed more fully elsewhere.
GO 116: An unfinished index.
GO 117: Duplicates much of the material indexed in GO 422, GO 470 and Hayes' 'Manuscript Sources'. Only the following are not covered elsewhere: Antrim Families (GO 213); Fisher MSS. (GO 280–85); Irish Arms at the College of Heralds (GO 37); Irish Coats of Arms (Fota) (GO 526); Heraldic Sketches (GO 125); Betham Letter Books (GO 362–78); Ecclesiastical Visitations (GO 198–9); Reynell MSS. (GO 445).
GO 148: Index to 'Linea Antiqua'. The version at the end of GO 147, 'Linea Antiqua', Vol. III, is more complete.
GO 255–6: Index to Alliances in Prerogative Wills (Betham).
GO 386: Index to the Funeral Entries.
GO 422–3: Index to arms registered at the Office.

GO 429: Eustace Index to Will Abstracts at the Genealogical Office. The published version in *Analecta Hibernica*, Vol. 17, is less extensive than the manuscript copy.

GO 469: Index to Registered Pedigrees. This appears to be less complete than the version included in Hayes' 'Manuscript Sources'. Attached to it is a typescript copy of the index to the Genealogical Office collection of pedigree rolls.

GO 470: Index to Unregistered Pedigrees. This is the single most useful index in the Office, covering the Lords Entries, the Betham pedigrees and many of the genealogists' pedigree collections. It is divided into three separate parts and gives the descriptive titles in use before the adoption of the single GO numbering system. The flyleaf lists the manuscripts covered.

GO 476: Numerical listing of GO manuscripts, dating from the 1950s, and now inaccurate for the higher numbers.

See also Hayes' 'Manuscript Sources for the Study of Irish Civilization'. This indexes the following: Registered Pedigrees, GO 800–822, Fisher MSS. (GO 280–85).

Access

The question of access to Genealogical Office manuscripts has long been somewhat vexed. The official policy of the Office is that the entire collection is to be microfilmed, and will eventually only be available to the public in that form. For the moment, only the most valuable manuscripts are on National Library microfilm, as follows:

MSS. NL Pos. 8286	GO 47, 48, 49, 64, 65
MSS. NL Pos. 8287	GO 66, 67, 68, 69
MSS. NL Pos. 8288	GO 70, 71, 72, 73
MSS. NL Pos. 8289	GO 74, 75, 76, 77, 78
MSS. NL Pos. 8290	GO 79, 103, 104, 105, 106
MSS. NL Pos. 8290A	GO 93, 94, 95
MSS. NL Pos. 8291	GO 107, 108, 109
MSS. NL Pos. 8292	GO 110, 111, 111A to p. 95
MSS. NL Pos. 8293	GO 111A from p. 96, 111B, 111C
MSS. NL Pos. 8294	GO 111D, 111E, 111F
MS. NL Pos. 8295	GO 112
MS. NL Pos. 8295A	GO 113
MS. NL Pos. 8295B	GO 141
MSS. NL Pos. 8296	GO 145, 146, 147 to p. 42
MSS. NL Pos. 8297	GO 147 from p. 43, 148, 149, 150 to p. 319
MSS. NL Pos. 8298	GO 150 from p. 319, 151, 152
MSS. NL Pos. 8299	GO 153, 154
MSS. NL Pos. 8300	GO 154A, 155, 156, 157, 158, 159 to p. 109

MSS. NL Pos. 8301	GO 159 from p. 110, 160, 161, 162, 163, 164
MSS. NL Pos. 8302	GO 165, 166, 167, 168
MSS. NL Pos. 8303	GO 169, 170
MSS. NL Pos. 8304	GO 171, 172, 173
MSS. NL Pos. 8305	GO 174, 175
MS. NL Pos. 8306	GO 176
MSS. NL Pos. 8307	GO 177, 178
MSS. NL Pos. 8308	GO 179, 180
MSS. NL Pos. 8309	GO 181, 182
MSS. NL Pos. 8310	GO 182A, 183, 184
MSS. NL Pos. 8311	GO 185, 186, 187
MSS. NL Pos. 8312	GO 188

For other manuscripts, access is through the National Library Manuscript reading room at 2 Kildare St, and is at the discretion of the Chief Herald.

GENEALOGICAL OFFICE MANUSCRIPTS

The following is a numerical list of Genealogical Office manuscripts, from 1 to 822. In the upper numbers especially, a significant proportion of the items have been moved. Where this is the case, the title is given in brackets and also, where possible, the destination of the manuscript.

GO MS. Title		Index
1	Case of Precedence, List of Peers, 1634–89	
2	Royal Arms	
3	Letters, Vol. 1, Genealogical Scraps	
4	Exemption from Taxes etc.	
	List of Baronets etc.	
	Authority for Fees	
5	Funeral Arms temp. Preston, Ulster, Commissions for Visitations	
6	Forms of Processions etc.	
7	Treatise on Heraldry, 1347	
8	Fees of Office, Precedence, Royal Pedigrees, Order of Dignities, Irish Parliament	
9	Treatise on Nobility, Pedigrees of Ancient Baronies	
10	Ulster's Diaries, 1698–1800 (numbered 10A)	Own Index
11	Ulster's Diaries, 1800–1837 (numbered 11A)	Own Index
12	Synopsis of Heraldry and Treatise on Funerals	
13	Honours conferred in Ireland	
14	Fees of Office, Vol. 1, History of Ulster's Office	
15	*Monumenta Eblana*	
16	Miscellaneous Pedigrees and Letters	

143	Fisher MSS. Notes, E	
144	Fisher MSS. Notes, F	
145	O'Ferrall's *Linea Antiqua I* (Betham Collection)	147
146	O'Ferrall's *Linea Antiqua II* (Betham Collection)	147
147	O'Ferrall's *Linea Antiqua III* (Betham Collection)	Own Index
148	Index to O'Ferrall	
149	Royal Licences and Warrants, I	
150	King's Letters and other entries II	
151	Royal Warrants, 1820–45, III	
152	Royal Warrants, 1845–68, IV	
153	Royal Warrants, 1868–88, V	
154	Royal Warrants from 1889, VI	
155	Royal Warrants etc.	
156	Royal Warrants etc.	
157	Pedigrees, O'Ferrall's *Linea Antiqua*	see 147
158–82	Pedigrees, Vols I–XXVII	469
183–88	Lords Entries, Vols I–VI	470
189	*Excerpta R. Placit. Com. Banci Hiberniae*, Vol. I, Henry III to Edward I	
190	*Excerpta R. Placit. Com. Banci Hiberniae*, Vol. II, Edward II	
191	*Excerpta R. Placit. Com. Banci Hiberniae*, Vol. III, Edward III	
192	*Excerpta R. Placit. Com. Banci Hiberniae*, Vol. IV, Edward III to Henry VI	
193	*Excerpta Rotulus Patenti Ban. Hiberniae*, Edward I to Edward VI	
194	*Excerpta Rotulus Pipae Hiberniae*, Vol. I, Henry III, Edward II, Edward III	Now NL MS. 760
195	*Excerpta Rotulus Pipae Hiberniae*, Vol. II, Edward II, Edward III	Now NL MS. 761
196	English Genealogy, MSS. TCD, Vol. I	
197	English Genealogy, MSS. TCD, Vol. II	
198	Ecclesiastical Visitations, 1607–93	117
199	Ecclesiastical Visitations, 1607–1781	117
200	High Sheriffs, Constables etc.	
201	(Orders, payments etc.)	AH
	(incl. Cromwellian State Accounts)	Now NL MS. 758
202	Gazette Notices, Changes of Name, 1864–76	
203–14	Will Pedigrees (Prerogative Wills)	see Vicars
215	Ancient Anglo-Irish Families, Vol. I, A–B	470
216	Ancient Anglo-Irish Families, Vol, II, C–F	470
217	Ancient Anglo-Irish Families, Vol. III, G–P	470

315   Order of St Patrick, Installation, 1868
316   Order of St Patrick
317   Order of St Patrick, papers
318   Ulster's Office Forms
319   Official Orders
320   Order of St Patrick, Investiture, Invitations
321   Book of the Vice-Regal Household, 2
322–8 Official Entries and Letters, 1854–1921, Vols 1–7
329   Renumbered 111E
330   Naval Uniforms
331   Uniform Book
332   Schedule of Civil Service Uniforms
333   Coronation of Edward VII
334   Note on Knighthoods of Ireland
335   Ceremonials, Order of St Patrick
336   Ceremonials, Order of St Patrick, 1872–1921
337–9 The Vice-Regal Court, Vols I–III
340   Lists of Knights
340A   Lists of Knights
341   Ulster's Rolls from 1660
342   Peers Pedigrees
343   Official Orders, 1800
344   Order of St Patrick, Certificates of Noblesse
345   Funeral Entries, 1797
346   Dress Regulations
347   Funeral Processions
348–50 Ceremonial Books, Ulster's Office, Vols I–III
351   Index (c.1840)
352   Betham Address Book
353   Day Book, Hawkins and Fortescue, 1777–1809
354   Fortescue, 1788–1809
355   Letter Book, 1814–16
356   Day Book, 1812–18
357   Ledger, 1812–46
358   Ledger, 1809–25
359   Day Book, 1824–39
360   Cash Book, 1839–53
361–78 Letter Books, 1789–1853
379   Coronation of George IV
380   Government Correspondence, 1827–36
381   Government Correspondence, 1828–48
382   The Coronation, 1902
383   Arms, C

488   Kelly of Clare
489   Delafield of Dublin
490–93 Roll of Freemen, Dublin City
494   Concordatum Pedigrees (Sadleir), 1817–21   Not indexed
495   Castleknock Parish Register
496   Crossly's *Peerage*
497   Patent of precedency
498   Montgomery Pedigree
499   Loftus Pedigree
500   Burke–Ryan genealogy
501   Walsh, Kelly and allied families
502   (Betham Draft Book, now NL MS. 496)
503   Donegan family
504   Genealogy of family of Burgo French
505   Pedigrees of Walker and allied families
506   Stafford family history
507   Loss of the Irish Crown Jewels
508   Coachmakers' blazons of arms
509   Alphabet of Irish and English Arms
510   1642 Field Officers
511   Arms of Protestant Bishops of Ireland
512   Bewley Notebooks (Box)   Wills in 429
513   Precedents
514   Ash, Co. Derry, *c.*1736
515   Berkely Peerage, Pedigree, Correspondence and Notes
516   Pedigree of O'Mangan, 1709
517   O'Hanlon of Orior, Co. Armagh
518   Delamere Notes
519   Shaw and Joyce Pedigrees, Gun notes
520–22 Blake and Butler Families of Tipperary and Clare
523   Welply I, Chancery Bills, 1630–1785, mainly Chinnery
          and Phair families
524   Welply II, Exchequer Bills, 1675–1810, mainly Chinnery family
525   Eustace Miscellany   Own Index
526   Fota MS. (photostat), Irish Coats   Own Index
527   MacLysaght Miscellany   Own Index
528–34 Transcripts of Wills from the Society Of   429
          Genealogists, London
535   Ainsworth Wills   Alphabetical
                                                                order

536   Religious Census Returns, 1766, I
537   Religious Census Returns, 1766, II
538   Hearth Money Rolls, Armagh, Donegal, 1664/5

539   Protestant Housekeepers, Antrim, Derry, Donegal, 1740
539a   Index to 539
540   Bibliography of Irish Palatines   Own Index
541   Co. Louth, 17th century miscellany
542   Directories, 1809, Belfast, Cork, Limerick, Waterford
543   Field Officers, 1642; Wolfe and Shaw families; Tipperary
               Attainders, 1688; Index to Book of Postings, 1700; Wives
               Certificates, Benevolent Annuity Co. 1771; Claims Before
               Commissioners, 1662
544   Cook diary, Blair autobiography, Brett, Saunder, Freeman,
               Collis families
545   Guerin
546–51   Irish Obituaries, A–Y
552–3   High Sheriffs of Irish Counties, 1660–1900, I and II
554–5   Students of King's Inns
556   Smith Family History (Nuttall Smith)
557   Sadleir, Marriages and Genealogical Notes   Own Index
558–61   Finucane and O'Brien Pedigrees
562   Blennerhassett
563   (Rental, now NL MS. 5319)
564   Gilles-Kelly notes   Own Index
565   (1) Extracts from the Pole-Hore MSS. catalogue
           (2) Index to pedigrees in Howard and Crisp (ed.),
               Visitation of Ireland, Vols I–VI
           (3) Index to GO MS. 3
           (4) Index to heraldic MSS. in GO 470
           (5) Index to names and places in GO MS. 564
           (6) Index to arms in GO 155–182
           (7) Index to arms in IMA, Vols I–XIII
           (8) Index to arms in GO MSS. 223–298
           (9) Dublin Goldsmiths
           (10) Index to Peers' Pedigrees
566   (Winder Papers, now NL MS. 5229)
567   (Thady O'Halloran's Commonplace Book, now NL
               MS. 5317)
568   (Wolfe Rental, now NL MS. 3908)
569   Directories, Belfast, Cork, Waterford, 1805
570   Magistrates and Grand Jurors in Co. Tipperary from 1658
571   Grantees, Act of Settlement, Counties Tipperary and Offaly
572   1821 Census extracts, Counties Tipperary and Offaly
573–6   Sadleir Pedigree Notebooks 1–4, mainly Tipperary and   470
               Offaly families
577   Dublin Parish Register Extracts

578   Parish Register Extracts

579   Army List, Ireland, 1746

580–604 Betham Letters, Vols 1–25

604a   Sherwood catalogue and Index to Betham letters

605–7   Prerogative Marriage Licences, 1630–1858, A–Z

608   Militia List, 1761

609   Irish Stockholders, 1779

610   Gaelic Chief's Authenticated Pedigrees, I

611   Lodge family

612–17   Index to Ossory, Ferns and Leighlin, Marriage
Licence Bonds, 1691–1845

618   Ossory Administration Bonds, 1660–1857

619   Ware, Bishops

620   Miscellaneous Rentals

621   Photostats, Taylor papers, Hegarty Papers, Inscriptions
from St Bede's R.C. Church, New South Wales

622   Ainsworth Miscellany

623   Limerick Freeholders, 1816–25

624   Frost, Co. Clare families   Own Index

625   *Bozzetti d'arme*   Own Index

626   Directory, Enniskillen, Ballyshannon, Donegal, 1839

627   Register of Gaelic Chiefs

628   Sadleir, Miscellaneous Pedigrees   470

628a   Sadleir, Order of Malta

629   O'Kelly Pedigrees

630   Miscellaneous Pedigrees (1908–1943)   Own Index

631   Ainsworth Wills, II   Not in 429

632   O'Malley

633   Delafield and Butler families

634   (O'Reilly Pedigrees)

635   Warren and allied families

636   Privy Councillors of Ireland

637   Forbes Genealogy

638   Nagle, White, Meekins, Madden, Vereker and
Prendergast Pedigrees

639   Dillon Patents

640   (Betham Pedigrees, now in NL)

641   (Killaloe Catholic Parish Register Listing)

642   Kilkenny College and its masters

643   Material for Names Map

644   (*Stemmata Wyckhamiana*, NL)

645   Nangle (de Angulo) Pedigree

646   (Copies of GO Visitations, GO 46–8)

647   Heard's Irish Pedigrees   470
648   Apothecaries, Dublin
649   (Attainders, 1689)
650   (Burke's *Landed Gentry*)
651   (Burke's *Armory*)
652   Smyly papers, Waller Pedigree
653   Davys family, Co. Roscommon
654   Englefield and Gerrard Pedigrees
655   Phillimore Irish Will Abstracts Index
656   Fitzgerald Funeral Entries
657   Genealogy of Fitzgeralds, Dukes of Leinster
658   Maguire tabular pedigrees
659–61 (Rentals of the Fitzpatrick estates, Co. Laois, now in NL)
662   O'Hea notes
663   (Madden, now in NL)
664   (Changes of Name, now GO 26)
665   Sadleir Miscellany
666   Papers relating to Irish Families in France (Bound
          with GO 667)
667   Co. Wicklow Hearth Money Roll
668–70 Chancery and Exchequer Bills, Marriage Licence Bonds
          and other records, 1629–1747
671   Register of Flags
672   O'Brien Tabular Pedigrees
673   Keating family   Own Index
674–81 (Malachy Moran MSS. now NL MSS. 1543–50)
682   Lascelles Kelly (transcript of 564)
683–4 Walsh-Kelly notebooks
685   Walsh-Kelly notebook, Cork Wills of Galwey, Donovan,
          *c.*1728–1801
686   Walsh-Kelly notebooks
687   Graviana, Nugent, Barons Delvin
688   (Killaloe Marriage Licences)
689   Mackay/McGee Family History
690   Rochfort and Ryland
691–2 Hill, I and II
693   Hill, III (O'Daly, Grey, Gerry, Whitcombe etc.)
694   Hill, IV (Fox)
695–7 Pogue, I–III
698   Coningsby Pedigree
699   O'Malley history
700   Seven wills (Crossle)   Own Index
700a   (Lissan wills and marriage licences)   Own Index

701   C. of I. Parish Register extracts, Ballingarry, Co.
            Limerick; Whitechurch, Co Wexford; Eyrecourt,
            Co. Galway; St Patrick's, Dublin
702   Gordon MS. (Crossle)
702a   Gordon MS. (Crossle), newspaper cuttings
703   (–)
704   Carroll Wills
705   (List of Priests and Sureties, now NL MS. 5318)
706   Glenville Crests
707   Extracts from Tuam, Clonfert and Kilmacduagh, C. of I.
            Diocesan Records
708   Kilkenny Pedigrees (from Burtchaell)
709   (Grants, Q, now 111G)
710   (Parish register listing)
711   Memoir of the Butlers of Ormond
712   (Book of Arms, now NL MS. 472)
713   Irwin, Max, Butler, Crofts, McConnell, Herden
714–38 Loose Pedigrees, A–W   470
739   (Now GO 496)
740   (Johnston)
741   (–)
742   Miscellaneous Pedigrees and Notes, Edwards and
            allied families
743   (Herbert Pedigrees)
744   (Fitzgerald of Derrineel)
745   (Notes for Irish Memorials Association)
746   Kennedy, Scotland and Ireland, 1550–1820
747   (Bewley Miscellany)
748   (–)
749–50 (Knights Dubbed, 1590–1800)
751   (Sketches of Arms)
752   Admissions to freedom of Dublin, 1468
753   (Now GO 517)
754   (Now GO 514)
755   (Verner Family)
756   (Now GO 513)
757   (Now GO 503)
758   (Now GO 499)
759   (Now GO 509)
760   Miscellany, Brownrigg and Ronson
761   (Now GO 519)
762   (Now GO 698)
763   (Now GO 500)

764   (Now GO 511)
765   Grainger and allied families
766   (Now GO 519)
767   (Now GO 504)
768   (Now GO 502)
769   (Now GO 508)
770   (Now GO 505)
771   (Now GO 517)
772   (Now GO 497)
773   (Now GO 506)
774   Royal Warrants in Changes of Name
775   (McWillan Pedigrees)
776   (Now GO 516)
777   Braddyl papers
778   (Montgomery Pedigree)
779–787 (Chevalier O'Gorman papers, now in NL)
788   (Register of Foreign Arms)
789   (Now GO 515)
790   (Photostat and Burgess Books)
791   (Extracts from Registered Pedigrees)
792   Pedigree and notes re Bushe
793   Lt Col O'Hea
794   Lodge Family Histories
795   (−)
796   (−)
797   (Hyde of Co. Cork)
798   History of the Hickeys
799   (−)
800–22 Loose Pedigrees, Searches, Correspondence   Hayes

7

Emigration

For the descendants of emigrants from Ireland wishing to trace their ancestors, it is a natural impulse to try first of all to identify emigration records in Ireland. Unfortunately, no centralised records of emigration exist. For North America in particular, when ships' passenger lists were kept, most appear to have been deposited at the port of arrival rather than departure; in general the authorities were more concerned with recording those entering a country than those leaving. The most comprehensive records for the US, therefore, are the Customs Passenger Lists, dating from 1820, and the Immigration Passenger Lists, from 1883, both in the National Archives in Washington. Unfortunately, the earlier lists are not very informative, giving only the country of origin of the emigrant. They have been collected by the US National Archives for the most important immigrant ports, Boston, New York, Baltimore and Philadelphia, as well as Mobile, New Bedford and New Orleans. Microfilm copies of the lists for New York and Boston are available at the National Library of Ireland. A full reference is given in the lists later in this chapter. No index to these is available in Ireland, making them very difficult to use if a relatively precise date of arrival is not known.

As well as these, however, there are many less comprehensive lists, published and unpublished, which record intending and actual emigrants and ships' passengers to North America. A number of attempts have been made to systematise access to these. The most important are the *Passenger and Immigration Lists Index* (3 vols), ed. P. William Filby and Mary K. Meyer, Gale, Detroit, 1981 (NL: RR 387, p 7), a consolidated index to a wide variety of lists relating to North American immigration from all over the world, and *The Famine Immigrants* (7 vols, indexed), Baltimore, the Genealogical Publishing Company, 1988 (NL Ir. 942 g 12), which records more than half a million Irish arrivals in New York between 1846 and 1851. Even these, however, cover only a fraction of the material of potential value. The listings further on in this chapter organise most of the available materials chronologically, to allow easy reference.

For Australia and New Zealand the situation is somewhat better. Because of the distance, very few emigrants could afford the journey themselves, and most, whether assisted free settlers or transported convicts, are therefore quite well documented. Transportation from Ireland, or for crimes committed in Ireland, lasted from 1791 to 1853, ending some fifteen years earlier than transportation from England. The only mass transportation later than 1853 was of sixty-three Fenians who were sent to Western Australia in 1868, aboard the last convict ship from England to Australia. The records of the Chief Secretary's Office, which had responsibility for the penal system, are the major Irish source of information on transportees. Not all the relevant records have survived, particularly for the period before 1836, but what does exist can provide a wealth of information. The records were formerly housed in the State Paper Office in Dublin Castle, which is now part of the National Archives and is situated at Bishop St, Dublin 8. The principal classes of relevant records are as follows:

1. PRISONERS' PETITIONS AND CASES, 1788–1836
These consist of petitions to the Lord Lieutenant for commutation or remission of sentence, and record the crime, trial, sentence, place of origin and family circumstances.

2. STATE PRISONERS' PETITIONS
These specifically concern those arrested for participation in the 1798 Rebellion, and record the same information as the main series of petitions.

3. CONVICT REFERENCE FILES FROM 1836
These continue the earlier petitions series and may include a wide range of additional material.

4. TRANSPORTATION REGISTERS FROM 1836
These record all the names of those sentenced to death or transportation, giving the name, age, date and county of trial, crime and sentence. Other details, including the name of the transport ship or the place of detention are sometimes also given.

5. MALE CONVICT REGISTER, 1842–47
In addition to the information supplied by the Transportation Registers, this volume also gives physical descriptions.

6. REGISTER OF CONVICTS ON CONVICT SHIPS, 1851–53
This gives the names, dates and counties of trial of those transported to Van Dieman's Land and Western Australia for the period covered.

7. FREE SETTLERS' PAPERS, 1828–52

After serving a minimum of four years, a male convict had the right to request a free passage for his wife and family. The Papers contain lists of those making such a request, along with transportation details and the name and address of the wife. A number of petitions from husbands and wives, and prisoners' letters, are also included.

To celebrate the Australian Bicentenary of 1988, all these records were microfilmed, and a computerised database of the surnames they contain was created. Copies of the microfilms and the database were presented to the Australian Government and can now be found in many state archives. The National Archives in Bishop St also retains copies, and the database in particular can save a great deal of time and effort. It supplies enough details from the originals to identify the relevant record.

For obvious reasons, the records relating to free settlers are more scattered and less easily researched. The single most useful source for early settlers, also invaluable for convicts, is the 1828 census of New South Wales, published by the Library of Australian History in 1980. Although the precise place of origin is not recorded, the details include age, occupation, marital status, and household. For later settlers, the University of Woolongong in Australia has produced on microfiche a complete index and transcript of all information concerning immigrants of Irish origin recorded on ships' passenger lists between 1848 and 1867. The Genealogical Office has a copy of this. The later lists in particular are extremely useful, often recording the exact place of origin as well as parents' names.

Other than these, the principal records likely to be of relevance are in the Colonial Office Papers of the United Kingdom Public Record Office at Kew, class reference CO 201. This class contains a wide variety of records, including petitions for assisted passages, emigrants' lists, records of emigrants on board ship, petitions from settlers for financial assistance, and much else. A number of these have been published in David T. Hawkings' *Bound for Australia* (Sussex: Phillimore and Co. 1987).

The remainder of this chapter is an attempt to present a systematic guide to emigration records of potential genealogical interest. It is divided into (1) passenger and emigrant lists in chronological order, and (2) published works on emigration. The latter is further subdivided into works dealing with (a) North America in general, (b) localities in North America, (c) the 'Scotch-Irish' in North America, (d) Australia and New Zealand, (e) France, (f) South Africa, (g) Argentina, and (h) the West Indies.

1. PASSENGER AND EMIGRANT LISTS
(IN CHRONOLOGICAL ORDER)

From: –   To: North America
Date: 1538–1825
Reference: H. Lancour and Wolfe, *A Bibliography of Ships' Passenger Lists*, London, 1963

From: –   To: America
Date: 17th–19th centuries
Reference: *Passenger and Immigration Lists Index* (3 vols), ed. P. William Filby and Mary K. Meyer, Gale, Detroit, 1981, NL, RR 387, p 7

From: –   To: New England
Date: –
Reference: M. Tepper, *Passengers to America* (a consolidation of ships' passenger lists from the New England Historical and Genealogical Register), Baltimore, 1977, NL 387, p 6

From: Britain   To: North America
Date: 1600–1700
Reference: J. C. Hotten, *Original Lists of Persons emigrating to America, 1600–1700*, London, 1874 [reprint, 1968]

From: Britain and Ireland   To: America and West Indies
Date: 1727–31
Reference: 'Agreements to Serve in America and the West Indies', D. Galenson, *The Genealogist's Magazine*, Vol. 19, No. 2

From: Ireland   To: America
Date: 1735–54
Reference: Lockhart, A., *Emigration Ireland to North America, 1660–1775*, New York, 1976, Ir. 973 1 5 (indentured servants 1749–50, Felons 1735–54)

From: Kilkenny   To: Newfoundland
Date: 1750–1844
Reference: 'Inistiogue emigrants in Newfoundland', in Whelan, K. and Nolan, W. (ed.), *Kilkenny History and Society*, Dublin, 1990, 345–405

From: Larne   To: Charleston, South Carolina
Date: 1773
Reference: Dickson, R. J., *Ulster Emigration to Colonial America, 1718–75*, London, 1976

From: Newry/Warrenpoint   To: New York and Philadelphia
Date: 1791–92
Reference: PRONI T.711/1

From: Ireland   To: Philadelphia
Date: 1800–1819
Reference: M. Tepper, *Passenger Arrivals at Philadelphia Port 1800–1819*, Baltimore, 1986, Ir. 970, p 12

From: Belfast, Dublin, Limerick, Londonderry, Newry, Sligo   To: US
Date: 1803, 1804
Reference: D. F. Begley, *Handbook on Irish Genealogy*, Dublin, 1984 (6th ed.) 101–110, 115

From: Ulster   To: US
Date: June 1804 to March 1806
Reference: PRONI T521/1, indexed in Report of the Deputy Keeper of Public Records (Northern Ireland), 1929

From: Ireland   To: America
Date: 1803–6
Reference: NL Pos. 993, PRONI T.3262

From: Newry   To: US
Date: 1803–31
Reference: Trainor, Brian, 'Sources for the Identification of Emigrants from Ireland to North America in the 19th Century', *Ulster Historical and Genealogical Guild Newsletter*, Vol. 1, Nos 2 and 3 (1979), Ir. 9292 u 3

From: Ireland   To: US
Date: 1811–17
Reference: *Passengers from Ireland*, Baltimore, 1980 (from 'The Shamrock'), see also D. F. Begley, *Handbook on Irish Genealogy*, Dublin, 1984 (6th ed.), 110–117

From: Londonderry   To: US
Date: 1815–16
Reference: PRONI T.2964 (add.)

From: Counties Carlow and Wexford   To: Canada
Date: 1817
Reference: K. Whelan and W. Nolan (ed.), *Wexford: History and Society*, Dublin, Geography Publications, 1987

From: –   To: New York
Date: 1820–65
Reference: Passenger arrivals lists, New York port, unindexed, NL Pos.
3919–4580, see National Library, Hayes Catalogue, for details of dates

From: –   To: Baltimore
Date: 1820–34
Reference: M. Tepper, *Passenger Arrivals at the Port of Baltimore*, Baltimore, 1982

From: Ireland   To: US
Date: 1821
Reference: *Irish Genealogical Helper*, No. 6, Jan. 1976, Ir. 9291 i 3

From: (not given)   To: New York (Arrivals)
Date: 1820–65
Reference: NL Pos. 3919–4520 (see Hayes Catalogue for details)

From: (not given)   To: Boston (Arrivals)
Date: 1820–64
Reference: NL Pos. 5896–959 (see Hayes Catalogue for details)

From: Ireland   To: Boston
Date: 1820–39
Reference: NL Special list, No. 200

From: –   To: US
Date: 1821–23
Reference: *Passengers Arriving in the U.S., 1821–1823*, NL 3251 u 1

From: Ireland   To: US
Date: 1822
Reference: *Irish-American Genealogist*, 1978, Ir. 9291 i 3

From: Londonderry   To: US
Date: 1826–90
Reference: PRONI D.2892

From: Co. Londonderry (parishes of Aghadowey, Balteagh, Bovevagh,
Coleraine, Dunboe, Drumachose, Limavady, Magilligan, Tamlaghfinlagan)
To: US
Date: 1833–34
Reference: See S. Martin, *Historical Gleanings from Co. Derry*, Dublin, 1955, Ir.
94112 m 2, also D. F. Begley, *Handbook on Irish Genealogy*, Dublin, 1984 (6th
ed.), 117–120

From: Counties Antrim and Derry   To: US
Date: 1833–39
Reference: Mitchell, Brian, *Irish Emigration Lists 1833–39*, Baltimore, Genealogical Publishing Company, 1989; PRONI MIC.6

From: Newry   To: St John's, New Brunswick
Date: 7 April 1834
Reference: Murphy, Peter, *Together in Exile*, Nova Scotia, 1991, 272–7

From: Londonderry   To: Philadelphia
Date: 1836–71
Reference: PRONI MF 14

From: Liverpool (Irish passengers)   To: Philadelphia
Date: 1840
Reference: PRONI T.2746

From: Limerick   To: North America
Date: 1841
Reference: *North Munster Antiquarian Journal*, Vol. XXIII, 1981

From: Shillelagh, Co. Wicklow (Coolattin estate)   To: US
Date: 1842–44
Reference: NL MS. 18, 429

From: Ireland   To: US
Date: 1846–51
Reference: *The Famine Immigrants* (7 vols, indexed), Ir. 942 g 12

From: Londonderry   To: America
Date: 1847–71
Reference: Brian Mitchell (ed.), *Irish Passenger Lists 1847–1871*, Baltimore, Genealogical Publishing Co. 1988

From: Coolattin (see above)   To: Quebec
Date: 1848
Reference: N1 MS. 18, 524, see also *West Wicklow Historical Society Journal*, No. 1

From: Ahascragh, Co. Galway, and Castlemaine, Co. Kerry   To: –
Date: 1848–52
Reference: *Analecta Hibernica*, Vol. 22, 1960

From: Ireland   To: Australia
Date: 1848–50
Reference: 'Barefoot and Pregnant? Female Orphans who emigrated from
Irish workhouses to Australia', 'Familia', *Ulster Genealogical Review*, Vol. II, No.
3, 1987

From: Londonderry   To: Philadelphia, St John, Quebec
Date: 1850–65
Reference: PRONI MF 13

From: Co. Galway (parishes of Kilchreest, Killigolen, Killinane, Killora,
Kilthomas and Isserkelly)   To: US and Australia
Date: *c*.1852–59
Reference: GO MS. 622

From: Liverpool (Irish Passengers)   To: US
Date: Oct.–Dec. 1853
Reference: R. ffolliott, *The Irish Ancestor*, 1975, 6–10

From: Queenstown (Cobh)   To: US
Date: May–June 1884
Reference: NL MS. 20616

From: Armagh, Derry, Donegal, Louth, Tyrone   To: (not given)
Date: 1890–1921
Reference: PRONI P.648(9) (Members of Girls' Friendly Society)

2. PUBLISHED WORKS ON EMIGRATION

(A) NORTH AMERICA, GENERAL

Bradley, A. K., *History of the Irish in America*, Chartwell, 1986, Ir. 942 b 19
Coldham, P. W., *The Complete Book of Emigrants, 1607–60* [. . .], Baltimore, 1987
Concannon and Cull, *Irish-American Who's Who*, Ir. 942 i 13
Davin, N. F., *The Irishman in Canada*, Shannon 1968, Ir. 971 d 1
Dickson, R., *Emigration to Colonial America 1775*, Ir. 3252 d 3
Donohoe, H., *The Irish Catholic Benevolent Union*, Ir. 973 d 6
Doyle, D., *Ireland, Irishmen, and Revolutionary America*, Dublin, 1981, Ir. 942 d 12
Doyle and Edwards (ed.), *America and Ireland 1776–1976*, London, 1980, Ir. 973 a 5
Elliott, B. S., *Irish Migrants in the Canadas* (Irish Protestants from Co. Tipperary
    especially), McGill, 1988
Friendly Sons of St Patrick,1771–1892, Ir. 973 c 1
Fromers, V., 'Irish Emigrants to Canada in Sussex Archives, 1839–47', *The
    Irish Ancestor*, 1974, 31–42
Hartigan, J., *The Irish in the American Revolution*, Washington, 1908, Ir. 973 h 8

Holder (ed.), *Emigrants from Britain to American Plantations, 1600–1700*, 9291 w 1

The Irish-American Genealogist, 1973–, Ir. 9291 i 3

Journal of the American-Irish Historical Society, Ir. 973 a 1

Knowles, Charles, *The Petition to Governor Shute in 1718: Scotch-Irish Pioneers in Ulster and America*, Ir. 973614

Leeson, F, 'Irish Emigrants to Canada, 1839–47', from the Wyndham estates in Counties Clare (especially), Limerick and Tipperary

Linden, *Irish Schoolmasters in the American Colonies, 1640–1775*, Ir. 942 r 9

Lockhart, A., *Emigration: Ireland to North America, 1660–1775*, New York, 1976, Ir. 973 l 5

Maguire, *The Irish in America*, New York, 1868, Ir. 973 m 3

Mannion, J. J., *Irish Settlements in Eastern Canada*, Toronto, 1974, Ir. 971 m 11

McGee, *Irish Settlers in North America*, New York, 1852, Ir. 970 m 1

Meagher, T. J., *From Paddy to Studs*, Westport, 1986, Ir. 942 f 8

Meyer (?), Early Irish Emigrants to America, 1803, 1806, *The Recorder*, June 1926, 973 r 1

Miller, K. A., *Exiles and Emigrants*, Oxford, 1985, Ir. 942 m 26

Mitchell, Brian, *Irish Emigration Lists 1833–39*, Baltimore, Genealogical Publishing Company, 1989 (Counties Antrim and Derry)

O'Brien, M. J., *A Hidden Phase of American History*, Baltimore, 1973 (Irishmen in the American Revolution), Ir. 9733 o 25

O'Brien, M. J., *Irish Settlers in America*, a consolidation of articles from the *Journal of the American-Irish Society*, Genealogical Publishing Company, Baltimore, 1979, Ir. 942 o 23

O'Driscoll, R. and Reynolds L. (ed.), *The Untold Story: the Irish in Canada*, Toronto, 1988 (2 vols)

Potter, G., *To the Golden Door*, Boston, 1960, Ir. 973 p 4

Reynolds, F., *Ireland's Important and Heroic Part . . .* (Irish in the American Revolution), Chicago, n.d., Ir. 973 r 3

Ridges, J. T., *Erin's Sons in America* (The AOH), New York, 1986, Ir. 973 r 7

Roberts, E. F., *Ireland in America*, London, 1931, Ir. 973 r 2

Shannon, W. V., *The American Irish*, New York, 1963, Ir. 973 s 3

Trainor, Brian, 'Sources for the Identification of Emigrants from Ireland to North America in the 19th Century', *Ulster Historical and Genealogical Guild Newsletter*, Vol. 1, Nos 2 and 3 (1979), Ir. 9292 u 3

Werkin, E., *Enter the Irish-American*, New York, 1976, Ir. 973 w 9

White, J., *Sketches from America*, London, 1870, Ir. 942 w 7

Wittke, C., *The Irish in America*, Baton Rouge, 1956, Ir. 973 w 2

(B) LOCALITIES IN NORTH AMERICA

Adams, E. and O'Keeffe, B. B., *Catholic Trails West: The Founding Catholic Families of Pennsylvania* (Vol. 1, St Joseph's Church, Philadelphia), Baltimore, Genealogical Publishing Company, 1988

Akenson, D. H., *The Irish in Ontario*, McGill, 1985, Ir. 971 a 8

Bannon, T., *Pioneer Irish in Onondaga*, London, 1911, Ir. 971 b 2

Burchell, R. A., *San Francisco Irish, 1848–1880*, Manchester University Press, 1979, Ir. 973 b 12

Callahan, *Irish-Americans and their Communities of Cleveland*

Clark, D., *The Irish Relations* (Irish-Americans in Philadelphia), New Jersey, 1982, Ir. 973 c 26

Clark, D., *The Irish in Philadelphia*, Philadelphia, 1973, Ir. 973 c 11

Cullen, J. B., *Story of the Irish in Boston*, Boston, 1893, Ir. 973 c 8

Cushing, J., *Irish Emigration to St John, New Brunswick, 1847*, St John, 1979, Ir. 942 c 16

Donovan, G. F., *The Irish in Massachusetts, 1620–1775*, St Louis, 1931, Ir. 9744 d 2

Fanning, C. (ed.), *Mr Dooley and the Chicago Irish*, New York, 1976, Ir. 973 d 10

Flannery, J. B., *The Irish Texans*, San Antonio, 1980, Ir. 973 f 4

Funchion, M. F., *The Irish in Chicago*, Chicago, 1987, Ir. 970 i 15

Funchion, M. F., *Chicago's Irish Nationalists 1881–1890*, New York, 1976, Ir. 973 f 1

Gearon, M. M., *Irish Settlers in Gardner, Massachusetts*, Gardner, 1932, Ir. 9744 g 1

Guerin, T., *The Gael in New France*, Montreal, 1946, Ir. 971 g 4

'Irish Settlers in early Delaware', *Pennsylvania History*, April 1947, Ir. 973 p 2

Kilkenny, J. F., 'The Irish of Morrow County, Oregon', *Historical Quarterly*, June 1968, Ir. 942 p 6

MacDonald, *History of the Irish in Wisconsin in the Nineteenth Century*, Washington, 1954, Ir. 973 m 9

Mackenzie, A. A., *The Irish in Cape Breton*, Cape Breton, 1979, Ir. 942 m 20

Mahony, M. E., *The Irish in Western Pennsylvania*, Pittsburgh, 1977, Ir. 973 m 16

New England Irish Guide 1987, Ir. 973 n 6

Niehaus, E. F., *The Irish in New Orleans 1800–1860*, Baton Rouge, 1965, Ir. 973 n 3

Oberster, W. H., *Texas Irish Empresarios and Their Colonies*, Austin, 1953, Ir. 973 o 10

O'Brien, M. J., *Pioneer Irish in New England*, New York, 1937, Ir. 974 o 6

O'Brien, M. J., *In Old New York: Irish Dead in Trinity and St Paul's Churchyards*, New York, 1928, Ir. 973 o 8

O'Brien, M. J., 'Grantees of Land in Virginia', *Journal of the American Irish Historical Society*, 13, 1913–14, 973 a 1

O'Gallagher, M., *St Patrick's and St Brigid's, Quebec*, Quebec, 1981, Ir. 942 o 29

Prendergast, T. F., *Forgotten Pioneers: Irish Leaders in Early California*, San Francisco, 1942, Ir. 942 p 13

Punch, T. M., *Some Sons of Erin in Nova Scotia*, Halifax, 1980, Ir. 971 p 10

Quigly, H., *The Irish Race in California and on the Pacific Coast*, San Francisco, 1878, Ir. 973 q 1

Redmond, P. M., *Irish Life in Rural Quebec*, Duquesne, 1983, Ir. 942 r 6
Ryan, D. P., *Beyond the Ballot Box: Boston Irish 1845–1917*, London, 1983, Ir. 973
    r 4
Stewart, H. L., *The Irish in Nova Scotia*, Kentville, 1950, Ir. 971 s 2
Toner, P. M., *New Ireland Remembered: historical essays on the Irish in New Brunswick*,
    New Brunswick, 1988
Vinyard, J., *The Irish on the Urban Frontier* (Irish in Detroit 1850–1880), New
    York, 1976, Ir. 973 v 1
Williams, H. A., *History of the Hibernian Society of Baltimore 1803–1951*, Baltimore,
    1951, Ir. 942 w 1

(c) SCOTCH-IRISH IN NORTH AMERICA

Bolton, C. K., *Scotch-Irish Pioneers*, Baltimore, 1967, Ir. 973 b 5
Cummings, H. M., *Scots Breed* (Scotch-Irish in Pennsylvania), Pittsburgh, 1964,
    Ir. 942 c 17
Dickson, R. J., *Ulster Emigration to Colonial America, 1718–75*, London, 1976
Dunaway, W., *Scotch-Irish of Colonial Pennsylvania*, Genealogical Publishing
    Company, Baltimore, 1985, Ir. 974 d 16
Glasgow, M., *Scotch-Irish in Northern Ireland and the American Colonies*, New York,
    1936, Ir. 973 g 16
Marshall, W. F., *Ulster Sails West*, Ir. 973 m 5
Scotch-Irish Heritage Festival, Winthrop, 1981, Ir. 942 s 15
Shaw, J., *The Scotch-Irish in History*, Springfield, 1899, Ir. 942 s 13
Stone, F., *Scots and Scotch-Irish in Connecticut*, Univ. of Connecticut, 1978, Ir.
    929 p 5
The Ulster-American Connection, New University of Ulster, 1976, Ir. 942 u 3
Wood, S. G., *Ulster Scots and Blandford Scouts* (Ulster Irish in Massachusetts),
    Mass, 1928, Ir. 973 w 1

(d) AUSTRALIA AND NEW ZEALAND

Cleary, P. J. S., *Australia's Debt to Ireland's Nation-builders*, Sydney, 1933, Ir. 994 c 6
Coffey and Morgan, *Irish Families in Australia and New Zealand 1788–1979* (4
    vols, biographical dictionary), Melbourne, 1979, Ir. 942 c 14
Curry, C. H., *The Irish at Eureka*, Sydney, 1954, Ir. 993 c 7
Hawkings, David T., *Bound for Australia*, Sussex, Phillimore and Co., 1987
Hogan, J., *The Irish in Australia*, Melbourne, 1888, Ir. 994o
Hughes, Robert, *The Fatal Shore*, London, 1988
Kiernan, C. (ed.), *Australia and Ireland, 1788–1988*, Dublin, 1986, Ir. 942 a 9
Kiernan, T. J., *The Irish in Australia*, Dublin, 1954, Ir. 994 k 1
McDonagh and Mandle, *Ireland and Irish-Australians*, Sydney, 1982, Ir. 942 i 12
O' Farrell, P., *The Irish in Australia*, New South Wales, 1987, Ir. 942 o 29
Robinson, P., *The Hitch and Brood of Time: Australians 1788–1828*, Oxford, 1985,
    Ir. 993 r 5

Robson, L. L., *The Convict Settlers of Australia*, Melbourne, 1965
The Ulster Link (Magazine of the Northern Irish in Australia and New Zealand), Ir. 994 u 1

(E) FRANCE
Griffin, G., *The Wild Geese* (pen portraits), Ir. 920041 g 5
Hayes, R., *Ireland and Irishmen in the French Revolution*, Dublin, Ir. 94404 h 1
Hayes, R., *Irish Swordsmen of France*, Dublin, Ir. 94404 h 3
Hayes, R., *Biographical Dictionary of Irishmen in France*, Dublin 1949, Ir. 9440 h 16
Hayes, R., *Old Irish Links with France*, Dublin, Ir. 944 h 11
Lee, G. A., *Irish Chevaliers in the Service of France*, Ir. 340 l 3
Mathorez, J., 'Les irlandais nobles ou notables à Nantes aux XVIIe et XVIIIe siècles', Ir. 941 p 20
O'Callaghan, J. C., *History of the Irish Brigades*, Ir. 944 o 13
O'Connell, M. J., *The Last Colonel of the Irish Brigade* (Count O'Connell, 1745–1833)
Hennessy, M., *The Wild Geese*, London, 1973, Ir. 942 h 10
Jones, P., *The Irish Brigade*, London, 1981, Ir. 942 j 3
Swords, L., *Irish-French Connections 1578–1978*, Paris, 1978, Ir. 942 i 6
Terry, James, *Pedigrees and Papers*, Ir. 9292 t 7

(F) SOUTH AFRICA
Dickson, G. D., *Irish Settlers to the Cape (1820)*, Cape Town, 1973, Ir. 968 d 7
The Irish in South Africa, 1920–1921, Ir. 968 i 2

(G) ARGENTINA
Coghlan, Eduardo, *Los Irlandeses en la Argentina*, Buenos Aires, 1987
Murray, *The Irish in Argentina*, Ir. 982 m 8

(H) WEST INDIES
'Documents relating to the Irish in the West Indies, with accounts of Irish Settlements, 1612–1752', *Analecta Hibernica*, Vol. 4, 140–286
Oliver, Vere L., *Caribbeana: Miscellaneous Papers Relating to the History, Topography, Genealogy and Antiquities of the British West Indies* (5 vols), London, 1912, NL 9729 o 1
Oliver, Vere L., *The History of the Island of Antigua* (3 vols), London, 1894-9
Oliver, Vere L., *Monumental Inscriptions of the British West Indies*, London, 1904

8

The Registry of Deeds

1. SCOPE OF THE RECORDS

Since research in the Registry of Deeds can be very laborious and time-consuming, it is prudent to be aware of the limitations of its records before starting work there. The Registry was set up by the Irish Parliament in 1708 to assist in regularising the massive transfer of land ownership from the Catholic Anglo-Norman and Gaelic populations to the Protestant Anglo-Irish which had taken place over the preceding century. The registration of deeds was not obligatory; the function of the Registry was simply to provide evidence of legal title in the event of a dispute. These two facts, the voluntary nature of registration and the general aim of copperfastening the Cromwellian and Williamite confiscations, determine the nature of the records held by the Registry. The overwhelming majority deal with property-owning members of the Church of Ireland, and a disproportionate number of these relate to transactions which carried some risk of legal dispute. In other words, the deeds registered are generally of interest only for a minority of the population and constitute only a fraction of the total number of property transactions carried out in the country.

The implications of these facts are worth spelling out in detail. Over the most useful period of the Registry's records, the non-Catholic population of Ireland constituted, at most, 20 per cent of the total. The majority of these were dissenting Presbyterians largely concentrated in the north, and suffering restrictions on their property rights similar to those imposed on Catholics; very few deeds made by dissenting Protestants are registered. Of the remaining non-Catholics, the majority were small farmers, tradesmen or artisans, usually in a position of economic dependence on those with whom they might have property transactions, and thus in no position to dispute the terms of a deed. The records of the Registry therefore cover only a minority of the non-Catholic minority. There are exceptions of course—large land-lords who made and registered great numbers of leases with their smaller tenants, marriage settlements between families of relatively modest means, the business transactions of the small Catholic merchant classes, the registration of the holdings of the few surviving Catholic landowners after the relaxation of the Penal Laws in the 1780s—but these remain very definitely exceptions. And for the vast bulk of the population, the Catholic tenant farmers, the possibility of a deed having been registered can almost certainly be discounted, since they owned nothing and had almost no legal rights to the property they rented.

A further limit to the scope of the records is the scant use made of the Registry before the middle of the eighteenth century. It was only from about the 1750s that registration became even relatively widespread, and its major genealogical usefulness is for the century or so from then until the 1850s, when it is generally superseded by other sources.

With these limitations in mind, it should now be said that, for those who made and registered deeds, the records of the Registry can often provide superb information. The propensity to register deeds appears to have run in families, and a single document can name two or three generations, as well as leading back to a chain of related records which give a picture of the family's evolving fortunes and the network of its collateral relationships.

2. REGISTRATION

Registration worked in the following way. After a deed had been signed and witnessed, one of the parties to it had a copy known as a 'memorial' made, signed it and had it witnessed by two people, at least one of whom had been a witness to the original. The memorial was then sworn before a Justice of the Peace as a faithful copy of the original and sent to the Registry. Here it was transcribed into a large manuscript volume and indexed. The original memorial was retained and stored, and these are all still preserved in the vaults of the Registry. For research purposes, however, the large manuscript volumes containing the transcripts of the memorials are used. Registration of a deed normally took place fairly soon after its execution, within a month or two in most cases, though delays of up to two years are quite common. If the gap between the execution and the registration of a deed is much more, this may be significant; it indicates an impending need for one of the parties to the deed or their heirs to be able to show legal proof of its execution. The most common reason for such a need would have been the death of one of the parties.

3. THE INDEXES

The indexing system used by the Registry is complicated and only partial. There are two sets of indexes, one by grantor's name (i.e. the name of the party disposing of the asset), and one by the name of the townland in which the property was situated. The Grantors' Index is fully alphabetical, and is divided into a number of sets covering different initial letters and periods. Between 1708 and 1833 the Grantors' Index records only the name of the grantor, the surname of the first grantee, along with the volume, and page and deed number. No indication is given of the location of the property concerned, an omission which can make a search for references to a family with a common surname very cumbersome indeed. After 1833 the Index is more comprehensive, showing the county in which the property was situated. In general, the Index is remarkably accurate, but there are some mistakes, particularly in the volume and page references. In such a case, the deed number can be used to trace the transcript; several transcribers worked simultaneously on different volumes, and the volume numbers were sometimes transposed. If, for example, Volume 380 is not the correct reference, Volumes 378–382 may contain the transcript. Within each volume the transcripts are numerically consecutive.

The Lands Index is subdivided by county, and within each county is roughly alphabetical, with townland names grouped together under their initial letter. This means that a search for deeds relating to, say, Ballyboy, Co. Roscommon, involves a search through all the references to Co. Roscommon townlands which start with 'B'. The information given in the Index is brief, recording only the surnames of two of the parties, as well as the volume, page and deed numbers. As with the Grantors' Index, the Index is divided into a number of sets covering different periods. After 1828 the Index further subdivides the townlands into baronies, making research a good deal more efficient. Along with the county volumes, there are separate indexes for corporation towns and cities. The subdivisions within these are somewhat eccentric, particularly in the case of Dublin, making it necessary to search even more widely than in the rural indexes. It should be pointed out that the Registry does not make it possible to trace the history of all the transactions in which a property was involved, since, inevitably, some of the deeds recording the transactions have not been registered.

In general, of the Registry's two sets of indexes, the Grantors' Index is the most genealogically useful, since it is strictly alphabetical and lists transactions by person rather than by property. The single greatest lack in the Registry is of an index to the grantees. The social range covered, given the distribution of wealth in the country, could be enhanced greatly by the production of such an index. Microfilm copies of both the Lands Index and the Grantors' Index, amounting to more than 400 reels, are available at the

National Library. Volume 1 of Margaret Falley's *Irish and Scotch-Irish Ancestral Research*, available on open shelves in the Library reading room, gives a complete breakdown of the locations and microfilm numbers of the indexes up to 1850 (pp 71–90). The Public Record Office of Northern Ireland also has a microfilm copy of the indexes, as well as of the memorial books themselves.

4. NATURE OF THE RECORDS

The archaic and legalistic terminology used in deeds can often make it extremely difficult to work out what precisely the parties to a deed intended it to do. This is particularly true in cases where earlier agreements are referred to but not recited in full. However, from a genealogical point of view, the precise nature of the transaction recorded is not always vital, and with a little practice it becomes relatively easy to pare the document down to the essentials of dates, placenames and personal names. It should be kept in mind that *all* personal names—buyers, sellers, trustees, mortgagees, witnesses—may be important and should be noted. None the less, there are numerous cases in which the nature of the deed is of interest, and in any case some advance knowledge will speed up the process of interpretation. What follows, therefore, is an attempt to clarify some of the less familiar terms, and to describe the most common or useful documents likely to be encountered.

The most important part of most deeds, the opening, follows an almost invariable pattern. After the phrase 'A memorial of', indicating that the transcript is of a copy rather than the original, the following are stated: (1) the nature of the deed; (2) the date on which the original was made; and (3) the names of the parties to the deed. It must be remembered that a number of people could constitute a single party for the purposes of a legal transaction. A typical opening would then be:

> A memorial of an indented deed of agreement dated October 13th 1793 between John O'Hara of Oak Park, Co. Meath, farmer, and George O'Hara of Balltown, Co. Meath, farmer, his eldest son of the first part, William Coakley of Navan, Co. Meath, merchant, of the second part, and Christopher French of Navan, gentleman, of the third part, in which . . .

Very often it is necessary to read no more than this to know that a deed is not relevant; if, for example, the research is on the O'Haras of Sligo, it is clear at a glance that the above document has no direct relevance. As happens so often in genealogy, however, the significance of information in a deed may only become clear retrospectively, in the light of something uncovered later. When carrying out a search for a particular family, therefore, it is a good idea to note briefly the important points in all deeds examined—names, addresses and occupations—whether or not they seem immediately relevant, so that if it subsequently emerges, for example, that the O'Haras of Sligo and Meath are related, the relevant deeds can be readily identified again.

Categorising the kinds of deeds which appear in the Registry can be difficult, since many of them are not what they appear to be. The most common misleading description in the opening of the memorial is the 'deed of lease and release', which may in fact be a conveyance or sale, a mortgage, a marriage settlement or a rent charge. 'Lease and Release' was a legal device whereby the obligation to record a conveyance publicly could be avoided; it was not obligatory to record a transaction to a tenant or lessee already in occupation, and it was not obligatory to record a lease for one year only. Accordingly, a lease for one year was first granted, and then the true transaction, conveyance, mortgage, marriage settlement or other, was carried out. It remained popular as a method of conveyance until 1845, when the *Statute of Uses* which made it possible was repealed.

Despite the difficulties created by such disguises as the 'lease and release', the underlying transactions do fall into a number of broad classes:

1. LEASES

By far the most common of the records in the Registry, leases could run for any term between 1 and 999 years, or could depend on the lives of a number of persons named in the document, or could be a mixture of the two, lasting, for example, three lives or sixty years, whichever was longer. Only leases for more than three years could be registered. The most genealogically useful information in leases is to be found in the lives they mention. The choice of lives generally rested with the lessee or grantee, and in most cases those chosen were related. Often the names and ages of the grantee's children can appear, extremely valuable for families in the eighteenth century. Leases for 900 years, or for lives renewable in perpetuity, which were much more common in Ireland than elsewhere, amounted to a permanent transfer of the property, although the grantor remained the nominal owner. As might be imagined, such leases provided a rich basis for legal disputes.

2. MARRIAGE SETTLEMENTS

Any form of pre-nuptial property agreement between the families of the prospective bride and groom was known as a 'marriage settlement', or 'marriage articles'. A variety of transactions can therefore be classed in this way. What they have in common is their aim to provide security, in particular to the women; since married women could hold no property in their own right, it was common practice for the dowry to be granted to trustees, rather than directly to the future husband, which allowed her some degree of independence. Commonly, also, the family of the prospective husband, or the husband himself, granted an annuity out of the income of his land to the future wife and children if he should pre-decease them. The information given in settlements varies, but in general it should include at a minimum the names, addresses and occupations of the bride, groom and bride's father. In addition, other relatives—brothers, uncles, etc.—also put in an appearance. For obvious reasons, therefore, marriage settlements are among the most useful of the records to be found in the Registry. The period for which they were most commonly registered appears to have been the three decades from 1790 to 1820. In searching the Grantors' Indexes for them, it should be remembered that they are not always indicated as such, and that the formal grantor may be a member of either family, making it necessary to search under both surnames.

3. MORTGAGES

In the eighteenth and nineteenth centuries, these were very commonly used as a form of investment on the one hand, and as a way of raising short-term cash on the other. They do not generally provide a great deal of family information, but since they were an endless source of legal disputes, they form a disproportionate number of the deeds registered. It was quite common for mortgages to be passed on to third or fourth parties, each hoping to make money, and the resulting deeds can be very complicated.

4. BILLS OF DISCOVERY

Under the Penal Laws, Catholics were not allowed to possess more than a very limited amount of land, and a Protestant who discovered a Catholic in possession of more than this amount could file a Bill of Discovery to claim it. In practice, most Bills appear to have been filed by Protestant friends of Catholic landowners to pre-empt hostile Discovery, and as a means of allowing them to remain in effective possession. Registered Bills are not common, but they are extremely interesting, both genealogically and historically.

5. WILLS

Only those wills likely to be contested legally, in other words those which omitted someone, almost certainly a family member who might have a legitimate claim, would have been registered. Abstracts of the personal and geographical information in all the wills registered between 1708 and 1832 have been published in P. B. Phair and E. Ellis (ed.), *Abstracts of Wills at The Registry of Deeds* (3 vols), Irish Manuscripts Commission, 1954–88. The full provisions of the wills are only to be found in the original memorials.

6. RENT CHARGES

These were annual payments of a fixed sum payable out of the revenue from nominated lands. They were used to provide for family members in straitened circumstances, or to pay off debts or mortgages in instalments. Once made, they could be transferred to others, and were valuable assets in their own right. Depending on the terms, they can provide useful insights into family relationships and family fortunes.

Other miscellaneous classes of deed also appear. As outlined above, the only common feature is that they record a property transaction of some description; any family information they may contain is a matter of luck

More than most other repositories, research in the Registry of Deeds provides a very vivid sense of the past. The sack-covered, cumbersome transcript volumes, dusty and yellowing, smell of accumulated time, of lives long finished. It is a place to be approached in a spirit of patient exploration.

9

Newspapers

Newspapers are one of the most enjoyable and most difficult of genealogical sources. Faced with so much of the everyday particularity of the past, it is virtually impossible to confine oneself to biographical data; again and again research is sidetracked by simple curiosity. In addition to this, the endemic imprecision of family information means that it is almost always necessary to search a wide range of dates. A sustained search for genealogical information in original newspapers is, as a result, extremely time-consuming. If the efficient use of research time is a priority, newspapers are certainly not the place to start.

With this proviso in mind, it must be added that the destruction of so many Irish records in 1922 gives a disproportionate importance to Irish newspapers, and that when newspapers do produce information, it can be extremely rich. Event are reported virtually as they happen, within a few weeks at most, and the reports have an authority and accuracy which is hard to match, even making all necessary allowances for journalistic errors. Nor is it now any longer always necessary to search the original papers themselves, as we shall see.

1. INFORMATION GIVEN

There are two principal formats in which useful information appears, biographical notices and, in the early papers, advertisements. Up to the 1850s, the former consist largely of marriage announcements and obituaries; birth announcements tend to be sparse, relate only to the wealthiest classes, and often give no more than the father's name, taking the form, 'on the 12th, the lady of George Gratton Esq., of a son'. After the mid-nineteenth century, the number of birth notices rises sharply, but they remain relatively uninformative.

Marriage announcements contain a much broader range of information, from the bare minimum of the names of the two parties, to comprehensive accounts of the addresses, occupations and fathers' names. In the majority of cases, the name of the bride's father and his address are supplied, in a form such as 'married on Tuesday last Michael Thomson Esq. to Miss Neville eldest daughter of James Neville of Bandon Esq.' For many eighteenth-century marriages, a newspaper announcement may be the only surviving record, particularly where the relevant Church of Ireland register has not survived.

Obituaries are by far the most numerous newspaper announcements, and cover a much broader social spectrum than either births or marriages. Again, the kind of information given can vary widely, from the barest 'died at Tullamore Mr Michael Cusack' to the most elaborate, giving occupation, exact age and family relationships: 'died at the house of her uncle Mr Patrick Swan in George's St in the 35th year of her age Mrs Burgess, relict of Henry Burgess Esq., late of Limerick'. Precision such as this is rare, however; most announcements confine themselves to name, address, occupation and place of death. Because of the paucity of Catholic burial records, newspaper obituaries are the most comprehensive surviving records of the deaths of the majority of the Catholic middle classes. From about the 1840s, the number of both obituaries and marriage announcements rose sharply; unfortunately these events are by then usually more easily traceable in parish or civil records.

Advertisements, in the early newspapers especially, were more often paid announcements than true advertisements in the modern sense, and an extraordinary variety of information can be gleaned from them. The most useful types are as follows:

(I) ELOPEMENTS
A husband would announce that his wife had absconded, and disclaim all responsibility for any debts she might contract. Usually his address and her maiden surname are given.

(II) BUSINESS ANNOUNCEMENTS
The most useful are those which record the place and nature of the business, which announce a change of address or ownership for the business, or which record the succession of a son to a business after his father's death.

(III) BANKRUPTCIES
These generally request creditors to gather at a specified time and place, and can be useful in narrowing the focus of a search for relevant transactions in the Registry of Deeds.

As well as advertisements and biographical notices, of course, newspapers also reported the news of the day, concentrating on the details of court cases with particular relish. For an ancestor who was a convict, these hold great interest, since much of the evidence was reported verbatim, and may provide vital clues for further research. However, uncovering the relevant report depends very much on knowing the date of conviction with some degree of accuracy, as well as the area in which the trial is likely to have taken place.

2. PERSONS COVERED

Apart from reports of trials, genealogical information to be found in news-papers relates to fairly well-defined social groups. First, then as now, the doings of the nobility were of general interest, and their births, marriages and deaths are extensively covered. Next in terms of coverage are the merchant and professional classes of the towns in which the newspapers were published. These would include barristers and solicitors, doctors, masters of schools, military officers and clergy, as well as the more prosperous business people. It should be remembered that, from about the 1770s, this would include the growing Catholic merchant class. Next are the farming gentry from the surrounding areas. After them come the less well-off traders, traceable largely through advertisements. Finally, the provincial papers also cover the inhabitants of neighbouring towns in these same classes, albeit sparsely at times. *No* information is to be found concerning anyone at or below middle-farmer level, the great bulk of the population, in other words. This remains true even from the third and fourth decades of the nineteenth century, when the number of announcements rose markedly and the social classes covered broadened somewhat.

3. DATES AND AREAS

The earliest Irish newspapers were published in Dublin at the end of the seventeenth century. It was not until the mid-eighteenth century, however, that they became widespread and began to carry information of genealogical value. The period of their prime usefulness is from about this time, *c.*1750, to around the mid-nineteenth century, when other sources become more accessible and thorough. Obviously not all areas of the country were equally well served, particularly at the start of this period. Publications tended to be concentrated in particular regions, as follows:

(1) DUBLIN

The most important eighteenth-century publications were the *Dublin Evening Post*, started in 1719, *Faulkner's Dublin Journal*, from 1725, the *Freeman's Journal*, from 1763, and the *Dublin Hibernian Journal*, from 1771. As well as carrying plentiful marriage and obituary notices relating to Dublin and surrounding areas from about the mid-century, these papers also reproduced notices which had first appeared in provincial papers, something which should be kept in mind in cases where the original local newspapers have not survived. From the early nineteenth century a great proliferation of publications began to appear; unfortunately the custom of publishing family notices fell into disuse in the first decades of the century, and did not resume until well into the 1820s.

(II) CORK

After Dublin, Cork was the area of the country best served by newspapers, with many publications following the lead of the *Corke Journal* which began in 1753. As well as publishing notices relating specifically to Cork City and county, these papers also carried much of interest for other Munster counties, notably Kerry, and, like the Dublin papers, republished notices relating to Munster which had originally appeared in other publications. An index exists to newspaper biographical notices relating to Counties Cork and Kerry between 1756 and 1827, details of which will be found below.

(III) LIMERICK/CLARE

There was a great deal of overlap between the earliest Clare newspapers, the *Clare Journal* from 1787, and the *Ennis Chronicle* from 1788, and those of Limerick, where the first publications were the *Munster Journal* (1749) and the *Limerick Chronicle*. As well as Clare and Limerick, both groups of papers had extensive coverage of Co. Tipperary, and in the case of the Limerick publications, this coverage also extended to Kerry and Galway. The Molony series of manuscripts in the Genealogical Office (see Chapter 6) includes extensive abstracts from the Clare papers. Details of a more accessible and far-ranging set of abstracts will be found below.

(IV) CARLOW/KILKENNY

This area was covered by a single publication, *Finn's Leinster Journal*, which began in 1768. Although the advertisements are useful, early biographical notices are sparse. The earliest have been published in *The Irish Genealogist* (1987/88).

(V) WATERFORD

The earliest newspapers here were the *Waterford Chronicle* (1770), the *Waterford Herald* (1791), and the *Waterford Mirror* (1804). Few of the earliest issues appear to have survived. For surviving issues before 1800, *The Irish Genealogist* has published the biographical notices (1974, and 1976–80 incl.). Notices to 1821 are included with the abstracts for Clare/Limerick.

(VI) BELFAST AND ULSTER

The single most important newspaper in this area was the *Belfast Newsletter* which began publication in 1737. It had a wider geographical range than any of the Dublin papers, covering virtually all of east Ulster. Outside Belfast the most significant publications were the *Londonderry Journal*, from 1772, which also covered a good area of Donegal and Tyrone, and the *Newry Journal* and *Strabane Journal*, of which very few, if any, early issues survive.

4. LOCATIONS

The best single repository for Irish newspapers is the British Library. After 1826 the Library was obliged to hold a copy of all Irish publications, and from that date its collection is virtually complete. It also has an extensive, though patchy, collection before that date. Within Ireland the largest collection is held by the National Library, though this is by no means comprehensive. Many unique copies are held in local libraries and other repositories. No complete guide to dates and locations exists as yet. A census of the dates and locations of all surviving early Irish newspapers has recently been carried out jointly by the National Library and the British Library, however, and it is to be hoped that this will be published in the near future. For areas now in Northern Ireland, the Public Record Office of Northern Ireland has published a complete guide, *Northern Ireland Newspapers: Checklist with Locations*.

5. INDEXES

A number of indexes exist to the biographical material found in newspapers, which can greatly lighten the burden of research. Those dealing with single publications are as follows:

(i)   National Library index to the *Freeman's Journal* from 1763 to 1771;
(ii) National Library index to marriages and deaths in *Pue's Occurrences* and the *Dublin Gazette*, 1730–1740, NL MS. 3197;
(iii) Henry Farrar's *Biographical Notices in Walker's Hibernian Magazine 1772–1812* (1889);
(iv) Card indexes to the biographical notices in the *Hibernian Chronicle* (1771–1802), and the *Cork Mercantile Chronicle* (1803–1818), held by the Irish Genealogical Research Society in London;
(v)   Index to biographical material in the *Belfast Newsletter* (1737–1800— unfortunately in chronological rather than alphabetical order), held by the Linen Hall Library in Belfast.

As well as these, Volume 6 of Albert Casey's *O'Kief, Coshe Mang etc.* reprints the biographical notices from the *Kerry Evening Post* from 1828 to 1864, and these are included in the general index at the back of the volume. More useful than any of these, however, are two extraordinary works produced by Rosemary ffolliott, her 'Index to Biographical Notices Collected from Newspapers, Principally Relating to Cork and Kerry, 1756–1827', and 'Index to Biographical Notices in the Newspapers of Limerick, Ennis, Clonmel and Waterford, 1758–1821'. Both are in fact much more than simple indexes, transcribing and ordering alphabetically all the notices they record. Some idea of their scope can be gleaned simply by listing the newspapers they cover.

The former includes biographical notices relating to Cork and Kerry from the surviving issues of the following Cork papers: the *Cork Advertiser*, the *Cork Chronicle*, the *Cork Evening Post*, the *Cork Gazette*, the *Corke Journal*, the *Cork Mercantile Chronicle*, the *Cork Morning Intelligence*, the *Southern Reporter*, *The Constitution*, the *Hibernian Chronicle* and the *Volunteer Journal*. As well as these, it also records all notices relating to Cork and Kerry in *Finn's Leinster Journal*, the *Dublin Gazette*, the *Dublin Hibernian Journal*, *Faulkner's Dublin Journal*, the *Freeman's Journal*, the *Magazine of Magazines*, the *Limerick Chronicle* and the *Waterford Mirror*. The latter index extracts and indexes the biographical notices from the *Clonmel Herald*, the *Clonmel Gazette*, the *Clonmel Advertiser*, the *Ennis Chronicle*, the *Clare Journal*, the *Limerick Evening Post*, the *Limerick Gazette*, the *Limerick Chronicle*, the *Munster Journal*, the *Waterford Chronicle* and the *Waterford Mirror*. In addition, a number of eighteenth-century Dublin newspapers are included: the *Freeman's Journal*, *Faulkners' Dublin Journal*, the *Dublin Hibernian Journal* and the *Hibernian Chronicle*, and all notices for the areas covered by the above publications extracted, as well as notices relating to other Munster counties, and to Counties Galway, Mayo, Roscommon, Leitrim, Longford and King's (Offaly). Between the two works, then, virtually all the surviving eighteenth-century notices for the southern half of the country are extracted, along with a large proportion of notices up to 1821/1827, and most of the entries relating to Connacht, south Leinster and Munster which were picked up and reprinted by the Dublin papers. All in all, the two compilations constitute a magnificent work of scholarship. Unfortunately, neither is as widely available as it should be. The National Library and Cork City Library hold manuscript copies of the Cork and Kerry index (NL MSS. 19172–5). Limerick Archives (see Chapter 15 under 'The Irish Genealogical Project') has a copy of the more extensive Limerick, Ennis, Clonmel and Waterford index. The Genealogical Office has microfiche copies of both. Unfortunately these are not directly accessible to the public.

10

Directories

For those areas and classes which they cover, Irish directories are an excellent source, often supplying information not readily available elsewhere. Their most obvious and practical use is to find out where precisely in the larger towns a family lived, but for members of the gentry, and the professional, merchant and trading classes, they can show much more, providing indirect evidence of reversals of fortune or growing prosperity, of death and emigration. In many cases directory entries are the only precise indication of occupation. The only classes totally excluded from all directories are, once again, the most disadvantaged, small tenant farmers, landless labourers and servants. Virtually all classes other than these are at least partly included, in some of the nineteenth-century directories in particular. One point to be kept in mind when using any directory is that every entry is at least six months out of date by the time of publication. The account which follows divides directories into 1. Dublin Directories, 2. Country-wide Directories, and 3. Provincial Directories, supplying in each case the dates, locations and information included, followed, in the first two categories, by a chronological check-list.

1. DUBLIN DIRECTORIES

The Gentleman's and Citizen's Almanack, produced by John Watson, began publication in Dublin in 1736, and continued until 1844. However, the first true trade directories in Ireland were those published by Peter Wilson for Dublin City, starting in 1751 and continuing until 1837, with a break from 1754 to 1759. From the outset, these were considered as supplements to Watson's *Almanack* and were regularly bound with it. In 1787 the two publications were put together with the *English Court Registry*, and, until it ceased publication in 1837, the whole was known as *The Treble Almanack*.

Initially the information supplied in Wilson's *Directory* consisted purely of alphabetical lists of merchants and traders, supplying name, address and occupation. In the early years these were quite scanty, but grew steadily over the decades from less than a thousand names in the 1752 edition to almost five thousand in 1816. As well as merchants and traders, the last decades of the eighteenth century also saw the inclusion of separate lists of those who might now be termed 'The Establishment'—officers of the city guilds and of Trinity College, state officials, those involved in the administration of medicine and the law, Church of Ireland clergy etc. The range of people covered expanded markedly if a little eccentrically, in the early nineteenth century. The most permanent addition was a new section added in 1815 which covered the nobility and gentry. As well as this, a number of other listings of potential use to readers were added, though some appear only intermittently. Persons covered by these lists include pawnbrokers, bankers, apothecaries, police, dentists, physicians, militia officers and ships' captains.

The most significant difference between the *Treble Almanack* and Pettigrew and Oulton's *Dublin Almanac and General Register of Ireland*, which began annual publication in 1834, is the inclusion in the latter of a street-by-street listing, initially only of the inhabitants of Dublin proper, but enlarged year by year to encompass the suburbs. From 1835 this listing was supplemented by an alphabetical list of the individuals recorded. In theory at least, the combination of the two listings should now make it possible to track the movements of individuals around the city, an important feature since changes of address were much more frequent in the nineteenth century, when the common practice was to rent rather than purchase. Unfortunately, in practice the alphabetical list is much less comprehensive than the street list.

Pettigrew and Oulton also extended even further the range of persons covered. The officers of virtually every Dublin institution, club and society, as well as clergy of all denominations, are included. Another significant difference from the earlier *Treble Almanack* which should be kept in mind is the extension of the coverage outside the Dublin area. Under the rubric 'Official Authorities of Counties and Towns' Pettigrew and Oulton record the names of many of the rural gentry and more prosperous inhabitants of the large towns in their guise as local administrators. This is particularly useful for areas which were not served by a local directory, or for which none has survived. Similarly the officials of many of the better-known institutions and societies in the larger country towns are also recorded, as well as the more important provincial clergy.

The successor to Pettigrew and Oulton was Alexander Thom with his *Irish Almanac and Official Directory* which began in 1844 and has continued publication up to the present. As the name implies, it continued the extension of coverage outside Dublin. To take one year as an example, the 1870 edition includes, as well as the alphabetical and street listings for Dublin, alphabetical lists of the following for the entire country: army officers; attorneys, solicitors and barristers; bankers; Catholic, Church of Ireland and Presbyterian clergy;

coast guard officers; doctors; MPs; magistrates; members of the Irish Privy Council; navy and Marine officers; officers of counties and towns; and peers. Although Thom's is generally regarded as a Dublin directory, its usefulness goes well beyond Dublin.

As well as these annual directories, Dublin was also included in the country-wide publications of Pigot and Slater issued at intervals during the nineteenth century. The only significant difference is the arrangement of the individuals listed under their trades, making it possible to identify all those engaged in the same occupation, important at a time when many occupations were handed down from one generation to the next. These directories are dealt with more fully below.

Check-list

1751–1837   Wilson' *Directory*, from 1787 issued as part of *The Treble Almanack*.

1834–49   Pettigrew and Oulton's *Dublin Almanac and General Register of Ireland*.

from 1844   Thom's *Irish Almanac and Official Directory*, see also Pigot's and Slater's country-wide *Directories* from 1820.

The most comprehensive collections are held by the National Library and the National Archives. Copies can be requested directly at the reading room counter in both repositories without a call number.

2. COUNTRY-WIDE DIRECTORIES

Until the productions of Pigot and Co. in the early nineteenth century, very little exists which covers the entire country. Although not true directories in the sense of the Dublin publications, four works may be used in a similar way, at least as far as the country gentry are concerned. The earliest of these is George Taylor and Andrew Skinner's *Road Maps of Ireland* (1778), which prints maps of the principal routes from Dublin to the country towns, including the major country houses and the surnames of their occupants, with an alphabetical index to these surnames. The aim of William Wilson's *The Post-Chaise Companion* (1786) is similar, providing a discursive description of what might be seen on various journeys through the countryside. These descriptions include the names of the country houses and, again, their owners' surnames. There is no index. The next publications were the two editions, in 1812 and 1814, of Ambrose Leet's *Directory*. This contains an alphabetical listing of placenames—towns, villages, country houses, town-lands, in an arbitrary mix—showing the county, the nearest post town, and, in the case of the houses, the full name of the occupant. These names are then themselves indexed at the back of the volume.

l366

1 N.—Bessborough-avenue.
Of North-strand-road.

1 Boyd, Mrs.	8l.
2 Flanagan, Mr. Thomas	
3 Preest, Mr. Patrick,	9l.
4 M'Carthy, Mr. Patk. J. G.P.O.	7l.
5 Hutchin, Mrs.	7l.
6 Purcell, Mr. Thomas,	10l.
7 Conroy, Mr. John,	10l.
8 Hatchell, Geo. master mariner,	8l.
9 Harbron, Mr. Wm. J.	9l.
10 Bell, Mr. Peter,	9l
11 Keane, Alphons., photographer, and 94 North-strand,	9l.
12 Byrne, Mr. Joseph,	8l.
13 Goulding, Daniel, carpenter,	7l.
14 O'Kelly, Mr. Alexander,	7l.
15 Curtis, Mrs.	8l
16 O'Callaghan, Mrs.	8l.

Link Line

19 Frazer, Mr. James,	7l.
20 Reynolds, Mr. Thomas,	6l.
21 Robinson, Mr. Charles,	6l.
22 Armstrong, Mr. Andrew,	6l.

Link Line.

24 Wren, Mr. James,	6l.
25 Carroll, Mr. Patrick,	7l.
26 Byrne, Mr. Patrick,	7l.
27 M'Cauley, Mr. Peter,	7l.
28 Gregan, Mr. Hugh,	

Drumcondra Link Line Railway

32 Tomlinson, Mr. William,	12l.
33 Halliday, Mr. Thomas,	9l.
34 Grimes, James, engineer,	9l.
35 Wilcocks, Mr. Joseph,	9l.
36 Dillon, Mr. Andrew,	9l.
37 Lacy, Mr. James,	9l.
38 Scott, Mr. William,	9l.
39 Lambert, Mr. Thomas	7l.
40 Mooney, Mr. Mathew,	7l.
41 Hayden, Mr. John,	7l.
42 Smith, Mrs.	7l.
43 Hendry, Mr. William,	7l.
44 Sweny, Mr. Herbert Sidney,	7l.
45 Tuites, Mr. R.	7l.
46 Griffith, John,	7l.
47 Homan, Mr. Thomas,	4l. 10s.
48 Kennedy, Mrs.	4l. 10s.
49 Murphy, Mrs.,	6l.
50 Holmes, Mr. William,	6l.
51 Langan, Mr. John	

Bethesda-place.
Upper Dorset-street.
Three small cottages

3 S.—Bishop-street.

22½ Dunne, J. fishmonger,	7l.
23 Tenements,	16l.
24 Hayden, Mrs. board & lodging,	16l.

here Redmond's-hill & Peter's-row inters.

25 Kelly, James, grocer, wine and spirit dealer, & 13 Peter's-row,	58l.
26, 27, 27A, 28 to 39 Jacob, W. R. & Co. (limited)	
40, 41 & 42 Tonge and Taggart, South City foundry and iron works,	37l., 17l.
43 to 45 Tenements,	14l. to 17l.
46 Jacob, W. R. and Co. (limited) stores,	17l.

...........*here Bishop-court intersects*........

47 to 49 Tenements,	20l. 9l.
50 Jacob, W. R. and Co. stores,	30l.
51 Tenements,	26l.
52 & 53 Tenements,	21l., 24l.
54 & 55 Tenements,	17l., 16l.
56 Leigh, P. provision merchant,	21l.

Black-street.
Infirmary-road.
Twenty small houses — Artizan's Dwellings company.

3 N.—Blackhall-parade.
From Blackhall-street to King-street, Nth.
P. St. Paul.—Arran-quay W.

1 Bourke, Mr. James,	9l.
2 Duffy, Mrs. lodgings,	9l.
3 Murphy, Mrs. M.	13l.
4 & 5 Condron, J. horseshoer and farrier,	8l.
6 & 7 Chew T. C. & Co. wool merchants, with 55 and 56 Queen-street, and 27 Island-street	
8 Dardis, Mr. M.	17l.
9 Clarke, Joseph, watch maker,	14l.
10 Tenements,	14l.
11 Duignan, Mrs.	14l.

3 N.—Blackhall-place.
From Ellis's-quay to Stoneybatter.
P. St. Paul.—Arran-quay W.

KING'S, OR BLUE COAT HOSPITAL—George R. Armstrong, esq. agent and registrar; Rev. T. P. Richards, M.A. chaplain & head master

1 and 2 Menton, Denis, dairy, and 17 King-street, north,	59l.
3 and 4 Losty, Mr. M. J.	30l. 34l.
5 Young, Mr. William	
6 and 7 Paul and Vincent, farming implement manufs. millwrights, and iron founders, chemical ma-	

30 McKeever, Mr. J.	
34 Dixon, Mrs.	
35 King, Mrs. M.	
36 Kirk, Mr. B.	
37 Muldoon, Mr. T.	
38 Behan, Mr. P.	
39 Donovan, Mr. Henry,	
40 Dublin Prison Gate Mission Laundry workroom, and dormitories—J. C. Wilkinson, secretary.	

3 N.—Blackhall-street
From Queen-street to Blackhall pla
P. St. Paul.—Arran-quay W.

1 Gorman, Mrs.	
2 Hopkins, Mr. Robert,	

........*here Blackhall-parade intersects*

3 Gordon, Samuel, wholesale manufacturer,	
4 The National Hotel—John We proprietor,	
5 Baird, Mrs.	
6 Clancy, Mrs. Mary,	
„ Doyle, Mr. T. M.	
„ Montgomery, Mr. James	
7 Dillon, Mr. John,	
8 Lemass, Mr. Joseph,	
9 Nurses' Training Institut Miss Tierney Superintende	
10 Mooney, Mrs.	
11 and 12 Ruins,	
13 Keogh, Mrs. J.	
14 Vacant,	
15 Tenements,	

........*here Blackhall-place interse*

16 to 18 Fitzgerald, P. corn an stores,	10l.
19 & 20 Hickey & Co. stores offic	
21 & 22 Cairn's Memorial Home,	
23 Correll, Mr. J.	
24 Doran, Mr. C. J.	
25 Leahy, Mr. W. J.	
26 Doheney, Mr. Joseph	
27 Eivers & Rispin, cattle salesm	
„ Curtis, T. H. forage contrac	
28 Ralph, Mrs.,	
29 Hickey, Paul, & Co. cattle sa corn, hay, and wool facto	
30 Scott, Mr. John F.	
31 Byrne, Mr. P. J.	
32 Coble, Mrs.	

3 S.—Blackpitts
From New-row, South, to Gree
P. St. Nicholas Without, east sid
Luke, west.—Merchants'-qu
..... LETTER BOX,

The earliest country-wide directory covering more than the gentry was Pigot's *Commercial Directory of Ireland* published in 1820. This goes through the towns of Ireland alphabetically, supplying the names of nobility and gentry living in or close to the town, and arranging the traders of each town according to their trade. Pigot published a subsequent edition in 1824, and his successors, Slater's, issued expanded versions in 1846, 1856, 1870, 1881 and 1894; These followed the same basic format, dividing the country into four provinces, and then dealing with towns and villages alphabetically within each province. With each edition the scope of the directory was steadily enlarged, including ever more towns and villages. 'Guide to Irish Directories', Chapter 4 of *Irish Genealogy: A Record Finder* (Dublin: Heraldic Artists, 1981) includes a detailed county-by-county listing of the towns and villages covered by each edition. Otherwise, the most important differences between the various editions are as follows:

1824. This includes a country-wide alphabetical index to all the clergy, gentry and nobility listed in the entries for individual towns, omitted in subsequent issues.

1846. This includes the names of schoolteachers for the towns treated, a practice continued in following editions.

1881. This supplies the names of the principal farmers near each of the towns treated, giving the relevant parish. This feature was continued in the 1894 edition.

From 1824 separate alphabetical listings are given for the clergy, gentry and nobility of Dublin and most of the larger urban centres.

The best single collection of these directories is in the National Library, where most of the early editions have now been transferred to microfiche.

Check-list

1778	George Taylor and Andrew Skinner, *Road Maps of Ireland* (reprint IUP, 1969) NL Ir. 9141 t 1
1786	William Wilson's *The Post-Chaise Companion*, NL J 9141 w 13
1812	Ambrose Leet, *A List of [. . .] noted places*, NL Ir. 9141 l 10
1814	Ambrose Leet, *A Directory to the Market Towns, Villages, Gentlemen's Seats and other noted places in Ireland*, NL Ir. 9141 l 10
1820	J. Pigot, *Commercial Directory of Ireland*, NL Ir. 9141 c 25.
1824	J. Pigot, *City of Dublin and Hibernian Provincial Directory*, NL Ir. 9141 p 75
1846	Slater's *National Commercial Directory of Ireland*, NL Ir. 9141 s 30
1856	Slater's *Royal National Commercial Directory of Ireland*

1870   Slater's *Royal National Commercial Directory of Ireland*
1881   Slater's *Royal National Commercial Directory of Ireland*
1894   Slater's *Royal National Commercial Directory of Ireland*
        See also Dublin directories from 1834

3. PROVINCIAL DIRECTORIES

John Ferrar's *Directory of Limerick*, published in 1769, was the first directory to deal specifically with a provincial town, and the practice spread throughout Munster in the remaining decades of the eighteenth century, with Cork particularly well covered. In the nineteenth century, local directories were produced in abundance, especially in areas with a strong commercial identity such as Belfast and the north-east, and, again, Munster. The quality and coverage of these varies widely, from the street-by-street listings in Martin's 1839 *Belfast Directory* to the barest of commercial lists. A guide to the principal local directories is included in the county source lists in Chapter 12. These lists cannot, however, be regarded as complete; many small, local publications, especially from the first half of the nineteenth century, are now quite rare, with only one or two surviving copies. Locating these can be extremely difficult. Some guides are:

James Carty, *National Library of Ireland Bibliography of Irish History 1870–1911*, Dublin, 1940.
Edward Evans, *Historical and Bibliographical Account of Almanacks, Directories etc. in Ireland from the Sixteenth Century*, Dublin, 1897.
M. E. Keen, *A Bibliography of Trade Directories of the British Isles in the Victoria and Albert Museum*, London, 1979.

PART 3

A REFERENCE GUIDE

11

Occupations

APOTHECARIES

(a) GO MS. 648, Apothecaries, apprentices, journeymen and prosecutions, 1791–1829
(b) List of Licensed Apothecaries of Ireland 1872, NL Ir. 61501 i 1
(c) Admissions to the guilds of Dublin, 1792–1837, Reports from Committees, *Parliamentary Papers*, 1837, Vol. 11 (ii)
(d) NL Report on Private Collections, No. 208
(e) Records of Apothecaries Hall, Dublin, 1747–1833, NL Pos. 929

ARTISTS

(a) *Artists of Ireland* (1796), Williams, NL Ir. 9275 w 3
(b) *Royal Hibernian Academy Exhibitors, 1826–1875*, NL Ir. 921 r 2
(c) *The Artists of Ireland*, Ann Crookshank and Knight of Glin, NL Ir. 750 c 2

ARMY/MILITIA

(a) GO MS. 608. 1761, Militia Lists for Counties Cork, Derry, Donegal, Down, Dublin, Kerry, Limerick, Louth, Monaghan, Roscommon, Tyrone, Wicklow
(b) GO MS. 579, Army Lists 1746–1772 (Athlone, Bandon, Cork, Drogheda, Dublin, Galway, Gort, Thurles, Tullamore)
(c) *Ireland's Memorial Records* (Biographical notes on soldiers in Irish regiments who died in World War I), NL Ir. 355942 i 3; see also GRO death records, 1914–1918 (separate listing)

(d) British Army records: (i) War Office records at the Public Record Office, Kew; Regimental records; Muster Rolls; Casualties; Widows; Soldiers' Documents (pensioners); Registers of Royal Hospital, Kilmainham, and Chelsea Hospital (Royal Hospital records also on microfilm at National Archives)

(e) Births, Marriages and Deaths of army personnel, 1796–1880; General Register Office, St Catherine's House, London

(f) Some published works:

Officers of the district corps of Ireland, 1797, King, NL Ir. 355 a 10

Officers (. . .) upon the establishment of Ireland, NL P 91

General and Field Officers 1740, Mullan, NL 355942 l 4

General and Field Officers 1755, Mullan, NL LO

General and Field Officers 1759, Mullan, NL LO

The Irish Army under King James, Thorpe, NL P 11 and P 12

English Army Lists, Dalton, NL 355942 d 2

Army Lists, Annual, Quarterly

A Bibliography of Regimental Histories of the British Army, A. S. White, NL 355942 w 13

In Search of Army Ancestry, G. Hamilton Edwards, Phillimore, 1977

ATTORNEYS AND BARRISTERS

(a) *King's Inns Admission Papers 1723–1867*, Phair and Sadlier, IMC, 1986, NL Ir. 340 k 1

(b) Dublin Directories, from the late eighteenth century

BAKERS

(a) Admissions to the guilds of Dublin, 1792–1837, Reports from Committees, *Parliamentary Papers*, 1837, Vol. 11 (ii)

(b) Freemen's Rolls of the City of Dublin, 1468–1485 and 1575–1774 in (i) GO 490–93 (Thrift Abstracts), (ii) Dublin City Archives (Original Registers), (iii) NL MSS. 76–9

BARBERS AND SURGEONS

(a) Admissions to the guilds of Dublin, 1792–1837, Reports from Committees, *Parliamentary Papers*, 1837, Vol. 11 (ii)

(b) Freemen's Rolls of the City of Dublin, 1468–1485 and 1575–1774 in (i) GO 490–93 (Thrift Abstracts), and (ii) Dublin City Archives (Original Registers)

BOOKSELLERS

(a) *Dictionary of Printers and Booksellers, 1668–1775*, E. R. McC. Dix, NL 6551 b 1, 6551 b 4

(b) *Notes On Dublin Printers in the Seventeenth Century*, T. P. C. Kirkpatrick, NL Ir. 65510941 k 1

(c) See also under 'Dix' in NL Author Catalogue for various provincial
     centres
(d) *Irish Booksellers and English Authors*, R. C. Cole, Dublin, 1954

BOARD OF ORDNANCE EMPLOYEES
     (Mainly concerned with the upkeep of fortifications and harbours, with
     some of the principal locations being Buncrana, Enniskillen, Ballincollig,
     Cobh, Spike Island), *The Irish Genealogist*, 1985, NL Ir. 9291 i 2

BRICKLAYERS
     Records of the Bricklayers and Stonemasons Guild from 1830, NA Acc.
     1097

CARPENTERS, MILLERS, MASONS, PLUMBERS
(a) Admissions to the guilds of Dublin, 1792–1837, Reports from Committees,
     Parliamentary Papers, 1837, Vol. 11 (ii)
(b) Freemen's Rolls of the City of Dublin, 1468–1485 and 1575–1774 in (i)
     GO 490–93 (Thrift Abstracts), (ii) Dublin City Archives (Original Registers),
     and (iii) NL MSS. 76–9

CLERGYMEN
(1) Catholic
(a) *Maynooth Students, 1795–1895*, Hamill, NL Ir. 37841 h 15
(b) Priests Lists (by diocese), 1735–1835, NL MS. 1548
(c) List of Priests and Sureties, 1705, NL MS. 5318

(2) Church of Ireland
(a) List of regular clergy in Ireland, by county, with place of birth, order
     and residence, 1824, *Archivium Hibernicum*, Vol. 3, 49–86
(b) Biographical Succession Lists
(i) *By diocese*
     Ardfert and Aghadoe. Canon J. B. Leslie, NL Ir. 274146 l 2
     Armagh. Canon Leslie, NL Ir. 27411 l 4
     Cashel and Emly. John Seymour
     Connor. NL MS. 1773 (Leslie manuscript)
     Cork, Cloyne and Ross. William Meade
     Cork and Ross. W. Maziere Brady, *Records of Cork and Ross*
     Derry. Canon Leslie, NL Ir. 27411 l 7
     Down. Canon Leslie
     Dromore. H. B. Swanzy, NL Ir. 27411 s 2
     Dublin. NL MS. 1771 (Leslie manuscript)
     Clogher. Canon Leslie, NL Ir. 27411 l 3
     Ferns. Canon Leslie, NL Ir. 27413 l 3

Leighlin. NL MS. 1772 (Leslie manuscript)

Ossory. Canon Leslie, NL Ir. 27413 l 5

Raphoe. Canon Leslie, NL Ir. 27413 l 8

Ross. Charles Webster

Waterford and Lismore. William Remison

Fasti Hibernicae (Vols 1–5), Henry Cotton, NL Ir. 2741002 c 5

Fasti of St Patrick's, Dublin, H. J. Lawlor

(ii) Unpublished material on all clergy not covered above in Representative Church Body Library. See also NL MSS. 1775–6 (Leslie manuscript)

(c) NL MS. 2674, Pedigrees and families of Church of Ireland clergymen, from the seventeenth to the nineteenth century

(d) Fothergill, Gerald, *A List of Emigrant Ministers to America, 1690–1811*, London, 1904

(e) Church of Ireland Directories, as follows:

1814   *Ecclesiastical Registry*, Samuel Percy Lea

1817   *Irish Ecclesiastical Register*

1818   *Irish Ecclesiastical Register*

1824   *Irish Ecclesiastical Register*

1827   *Irish Ecclesiastical Register*

1830   *Ecclesiastical Register*, John C. Erck

1841   *The Churchman's Almanack and Irish Ecclesiastical Register*, John Medlicott Burns

1842   *Irish Ecclesiastical Directory*

1843   *The Irish Clergy List*, John Medlicott Burns

1858   *Clerical Directory of Ireland*, Samuel B. Oldham

1862   to date, annually, *Church of Ireland Directory*

(3) Methodist

(a) *Minutes of the Methodist Conference*, 1757 to date, NL Ir. 287 m 4

(b) Published works:

Crookshank, C. H., *History of Methodism in Ireland, 1740–1860* (3 vols), Belfast, 1885–8; [Vol. 4 (1860–1960), H. Lee Cole, Belfast, 1961] NL Ir. 287 c 2

Cole, H. L., *History of Methodism in Dublin*, NL I 287 c 4

Gallagher, W., *Preachers of Methodism*, Belfast, 1965, NL Ir. 287 g 1

Smith, W., *History of Methodism in Ireland*, Dublin, 1830, J 2871, NL Ir. 2871 s 2

(4) Presbyterian

(a) Names of Presbyterian Clergymen and their congregations in Counties Antrim, Armagh, Down, Donegal, Fermanagh, Tyrone, Cork, Dublin, King's, Louth, Westmeath and Mayo, 1837, *New Plan for Education in Ireland 1838*, Part 1 (27, 28) 200–205

(b) Published Works:

Ferguson, Rev. S., *Brief Biographical Notices of some Irish Covenanting Ministers* (1897) [particularly eighteenth century], NL Ir. 285 f 1

History of Congregations, NL Ir. 285 h 8

Irwin, C. H., *A History of Presbyterians in Dublin and the South and West of Ireland*, 1890, NL Ir. 285 i 1

Latimer, W. T., *History of the Irish Presbyterians*, Belfast, 1902, NL Ir. 285 l 1 (early ministers especially)

McComb's Presbyterian Almanack, NL Ir. 285 m 1

Marshall W. F., *Ulster Sails West* (including Ulster Presbyterian ministers in America, 1680–1820), NL Ir. 973 m 5

McConnell, J., *Fasti of the Irish Presbyterian Church*, Belfast, 1938, NL Ir. 285 m 14

Reid, James Seiton, *History of the Presbyterian Church*, London, 1853, NL Ir. 285 r 1

Smith and McIntyre, *Belfast Almanack 1837*

Stewart, Rev. David, *The Seceders in Ireland, With Annals of Their Congregations*, Belfast, 1950

Witherow, Thomas, *Historical and Literary Memorials of Presbyterianism in Ireland*, Belfast, 1879

(c) Belfast Directories, *Martins's*, 1835–42, NL Ir. 9141111 [*sic*] m 4; from 1852, NL Ir. 91411 b 3

CLOCKMAKERS

(a) National Museum MS. List of Watch and Clockmakers in Ireland, 1687–1844, NL Pos. 204

(b) 'A List of Irish Watch- and Clockmakers', Geraldine Fennell, NL Ir. 681 f 10

COAST GUARD
See *Navy*

CONVICTS

(a) *Parliamentary Papers* Vol. 22 (1824): Convictions, 1814–23, Limerick City Assizes and Quarter sessions; All persons committed for trial under the Insurrection Act, 1823–24 in Counties Clare, Cork, Kerry, Kildare, Kilkenny, King's, Limerick and Tipperary

(b) Records of the State Paper Office, Prisoners' Petitions, see Chapter 7, 'Emigration'.

(c) Prosecutions at Spring Assizes, 1842–43, *Parliamentary Papers*, 1843, Vol. 50, (619) 34 ff.

(d) Original Prison Registers from *c.*1845 for individual prisons, in many cases giving details of prisoners' families; unindexed, in chronological order. National Archives

COOKS AND VINTNERS
(a) Admissions to the guilds of Dublin, 1792–1837, Reports from Committees, *Parliamentary Papers*, 1837, Vol. 11 (ii)
(b) Freemen's Rolls of the City of Dublin, 1468–1485 and 1575–1774 in (i) GO 490–93 (Thrift Abstracts), (ii) Dublin City Archives (Original Registers), and (iii) NL MSS. 76–9

DOCTORS
(a) Index to Biographical File of Irish Medics, T. P. C. Kirkpatrick, NL Library Office
(b) See under Kirkpatrick in NL Author Catalogue
(c) Local and Dublin Directories from the late eighteenth century
(d) Medical Directories: 1846, Croly, NL Ir. 6107 c 3; 1852–1860 (intermittent), NL Ir. 6107 i 2; from 1872 annually, NL Ir. 6107 i 2
(e) Addison, *Glasow University Graduates*
(f) Doolin, W., *Dublin's Surgeon Anatomists*, NL Ir. 610 p 4

GOLDSMITHS
(a) GO 665, Dublin Goldsmiths, 1675–1810
(b) *Journal of the Cork Hist. and Arch. Soc.* Ser. 2, Vol. VIII, 1902

LINEN WORKERS/WEAVERS
(a) Workers and Manufacturers in Linen, in *The Stephenson Reports*, 1755–84, NL Ir. 6551, Dublin
(b) 1796 Linen Board premiums for growing flax, NL Ir. 633411 i 7
(c) 1796 Spinning-wheel premium entitlement lists (64 per cent Ulster); All-Ireland Heritage microfiche index, National Archives

MEMBERS OF PARLIAMENT
NL MSS. 184 and 2098. See also local history source-lists under the relevant county

MERCHANTS
(a) Admissions to the guilds of Dublin, 1792–1837, Reports from Committees, *Parliamentary Papers*, 1837, Vol. 11 (ii)
(b) Freemen's Rolls of the City of Dublin, 1468–1485 and 1575–1774 in (i) GO 490–93 (Thrift Abstracts), (ii) Dublin City Archives (Original Registers), and (iii) NL MSS. 76–9
(c) See also local directories under county source lists

NAVY
(a) *The Navy List*, 1814, 1819, 1827–79, 1885 *et seq.*, NL 35905 Top floor [*sic*] (Seniority and disposition lists of all commissioned officers, masters,

pursers, surgeons, chaplains, yard officers, coast guards, revenue cruisers, packets)
(b) Records of the Public Record Office, Kew. See *Naval Records for Genealogists*, N. A. M. Rodger, HMSO, 1984
(c) *A Naval Biographical Dictionary (1849)*, W. R. O'Byrne, NL 9235 0 1

POLICEMEN
(a) RIC records, National Archives (Mf)
(b) Dublin Metropolitan Police records, National Archives and Garda Archives, Phoenix Park
(c) Annual RIC Directories from 1840, NL Ir. 3522 r 8

POST OFFICE EMPLOYEES
Pre-1922 records of the Post Office in the Public Record Office of Northern Ireland, Belfast

PRINTERS
(a) *Dictionary of Printers and Booksellers*, 1668–1775, E. R. McC. Dix, 6551 b 1, 6551 b 4
(b) *Notes on Dublin Printers in the Seventeenth Century*, T. P. C. Kirkpatrick, NL Ir. 65510941 k 1
(c) See also under 'Dix' in NL Author Catalogue for various provincial centres

PRISON WARDERS
Index to Registered Papers, State Paper Office (Original applications available)

PUBLICANS
Excise Licences in premises valued under £10, 1832–1838; Reports from Committees, *Parliamentary Papers*, 1837–38, Vol. 13 (2), 558–601 and 602–607

RAILWAY WORKERS
(a) (1870s to 1950s) Irish Transport Genealogical Archives, Irish Railway Record Society, Heuston Station, Dublin (open Tues. 8–10 p.m., by appointment with archivist)
(b) *Records of the Irish Transport Genealogical Museum*, Joseph Lecky

SEAMEN
(a) 'In Pursuit of Seafaring Ancestors', Frank Murphy, *Decies* 16, NL Ir. 9414 d 5
(b) Agreements and Crew Lists series in Public Record Office, Kew
(c) Cox, N. G., 'The Records of the Registrar-General of Shipping and Seamen', *Maritime History*, Vol. 2, 1972

SILVERSMITHS
(a) Assay Office, registrations of goldsmiths and silversmiths from 1637, see (b) below
(b) NL Pos. 6851 (1637–1702)
    Pos. 6785 (1704–1855, with some gaps)
    Pos. 6782 Freemen, 1637–1779
    Pos. 6784, 6788, 6851, Apprentices
(c) NA M. 465, Notes and pamphlets relating to goldsmiths and silversmiths in Cork, Dublin and Galway

SMITHS
(a) Admissions to the guilds of Dublin, 1792–1837, Reports from Committees, *Parliamentary Papers*, 1837, Vol. II (ii)
(b) Freemen's Rolls of the City of Dublin, 1468–1485 and 1575–1774 in (i) GO 490–93 (Thrift Abstracts), (ii) Dublin City Archives (Original Registers), and (iii) NL MSS. 76–9

STONEMASONS
See *Bricklayers* above

TEACHERS
(a) List of all parochial schools in Ireland, including names of teachers and other details, 1824. Irish Education Enquiry, 1826, 2nd Report. (2 vols), NL Ir. 372 i 6. Indexed in 'Schoolmasters and mistresses in Ireland', Dingfelder, NL Ir. 372 d 38
(b) National School Records, National Archives (National Teachers' salary books from 1831)
(c) Published Works:
Akenson, D. H., *The Irish Education Experiment*, London, 1970
Brenan, *1775–1835: Schools of Kildare and Leighlin*, NL Ir. 37094135 b 4
Corcoran, T. S., 'Some lists of catholic lay teachers and their illegal schools in the later Penal times', NL Ir. 370941 c 12
ffolliott, R., 'Some schoolmasters in the diocese of Killaloe, 1808', *North Munster Antiquarian Journal*, Vol. XI, 1968
Linden, *Irish school-masters in the American colonies*, NL Ir. 942 l 9
Teachers of Cashel and Emly, 1750–60, *Catholic Bulletin*, Vol. XXIX, 784–8

WATCHMAKERS
See *Clockmakers*

WEAVERS
See *Linen-workers*

12

County Source Lists

The source lists included here are intended primarily as working research tools, with references as specific as possible, and very little explanation of the records given. An outline of some of the categories used is thus necessary here.

CENSUS RETURNS AND SUBSTITUTES

Where no indication of the nature of the record is given, a description should be found in Chapter 2, 'Census Returns'. Griffith's Valuation and the Tithe Books are dealt with in Chapter 4, 'Land Records'. Locations are given in the text for all records mentioned, with, if possible, exact reference numbers. National Library call-numbers for published works should be found in the Local History or Local Journal sections.

LOCAL HISTORY

The bibliographies given are by no means exhaustive, and the works cited vary enormously in their usefulness. A large proportion of the entries also give the National Library call-number, but the absence of such a number does not mean that the work in question is not in the library.

LOCAL JOURNALS

The journals noted are those originating in, or covering part of, the particular county. Where possible, National Library call-numbers are given. The absence of the number means that the journal started publication relatively recently and, at the time of writing, had not yet been assigned a number.

GRAVESTONE INSCRIPTIONS

Many of the largest collections of indexed transcripts of gravestone inscriptions are now held by local heritage centres. For counties where this is the case, the name of the relevant centre is supplied. Further details will be found in Chapter 15, 'Services'. This section does not cover the transcripts published in the *Journal of the Association for the Preservation of the Memorials of the Dead*, since the records are not treated in a geographically consistent way. None the less, over the forty-seven years of its existence between 1888 and 1934, the *Journal* published a huge volume of inscriptions, many of which have since been destroyed. A composite index to surnames and places for the first twenty years of publication was published in 1910; the remaining volumes have their own indexes. The references to the IGRS collection in the Genealogical Office give the number of entries recorded in each graveyard. Again, National Library call-numbers for the local history journals or local histories will be found in the sections dealing specifically with the journals and histories.

ESTATE RECORDS

With the exception of Counties Cork, Galway, Leitrim, Mayo, Roscommon and Sligo, which include a summary of relevant catalogued records in the National Archives and National Library, the references given here cover only a fraction of the material of potential genealogical interest. A more detailed account of the nature of these records is given at the end of Chapter 4, 'Land Records'.

PLACENAMES

The only references given here are to works referring specifically to the relevant counties. Material of more general application for the entire island is as follows:

TOWNLANDS INDEXES
Produced on the basis of the returns of the 1851, 1871 and 1901 censuses, these list all the townlands in the country in strict alphabetical order.

ADDENDA TO THE 1841 CENSUS
Also known as the 1841 Townlands Index, this is also based on the census returns, but organises townlands on a different basis. They are grouped alphabetically within civil parishes, which are then grouped alphabetically within baronies, which are grouped by county. The organisation is very

useful in tracking down variant townland spellings; once it is known that a particular townland is to be found in a particular area, but the later Townlands Indexes do not record it, the general area can be searched in the 1841 Addenda for names which are close enough to be possible variants. (NL Ir. 310 c 1)

TOWNLANDS IN POOR-LAW UNIONS
Produced by the Office of the Registrar-General for use by local registration officers, this lists townlands in each Registration District, or Poor-Law Union (see Chapter 1, 'Civil Records'). It is useful in attempting to identify place-names given in civil records. (NL Ir. 9141 b 35)

TOPOGRAPHICAL DICTIONARY OF IRELAND, SAMUEL LEWIS, 1837
This goes through civil parishes in alphabetical order, giving a brief history, an economic and social description, and the names and residences of the 'principal inhabitants'. It also records the corresponding Catholic parish and the locations of Presbyterian congregations. The accompanying *Atlas* is useful in determining the precise relative positions of the parishes.

Other works of general interest include Yann Goblet's *Index to Townlands in the Civil Survey (1654–56)* (Irish Manuscripts Commission, 1954); *Locations of Churches in the Irish Provinces* (Church of Jesus Christ of Latter-day Saints, 1978), NL Ir. 7265 i 8; *The Parliamentary Gazetteer of Ireland* (1846), NL Ir. 9141 p 30.

CO. ANTRIM

Census returns and substitutes

1630	Muster Roll of Ulster. Armagh Co. Library, NL Pos. 206; PRONI D.1759/3C/1
1642	Muster Roll, PRONI T.8726/2
1659	Pender's 'Census', NL I 6551, Dublin
1666	Hearth Money Roll, NL Pos. 207
1666	Subsidy Roll, PRONI T.3022/4/1
1669	Hearth Money Roll, PRONI T.307 and NL MS. 9584
1740	Protestant Householders in the parishes of: Aghoghill, Armoy, Ballintoy, Ballymena, Ballymoney, Bellewillen, Billy, Clogh, Drumaul, Dunkegan, Dunluce, Finvoy, Kilraghtis, Loghall, Manybrooks, Rasharkin, Rathlin, Ramoan, GO 559, PRONI T.808/15258
1766	Aghoghill parish. RCB Library, NL MS. 4173, NA M.2476(1); Ballintoy parish. GO 536, NL MS. 4173; also PRONI T.808/15264
1776	'Deputy Court Cheque Book' (votes cast), PRONI D.1364/L/1
1779	Map of Glenarm, including tenants' names, *The Glynns*, No. 9, 1981
1796	Catholic migrants from Ulster to Mayo. See Mayo
1799–1800	Militia Pay Lists and Muster Rolls, PRONI T.1115/1A and B
1821	Government census, various fragments. Thrift Abstracts, NA
1820s/30s	Tithe Books
1832–37	Belfast Poll Book, PRONI D.2472
1833–39	Emigrants from Co. Antrim. Brian Mitchell, *Irish Emigration Lists 1833–39*, Baltimore, 1989
1837	Valuation of towns returning MPs (occupants and property values). Lisburn. *Parliamentary Papers*, 1837, Reports from Committees, Vol. II (i), Appendix G
1837	Marksmen (illiterate voters) in parliamentary boroughs: Belfast. *Parliamentary Papers*, 1837, Reports from Committees, Vol. II (i), Appendix A
1851	Aghoghill (Craigs townland only), Aghagallon (townlands of Montiaghs to Tiscallon), Agahalee, Ballinderry, Ballymoney (Garryduff townland only), Barnacastle, Drumkeeran, Dunaghy, Grange of Killyglen, Killead (Ardmore to Carnagliss townlands only), Kilwaughter, Larne, Rasharkin (Killydonnelly to Tehorney townland only), Tickmacreevan, NA and PRONI MIC. 5A/11–26
1855	Belfast Register of Electors, PRONI BELF5/1/1/1–2

1856/7	Voters' Lists. NL ILB 324
1861/2	Griffith's Valuation, Belfast—Alphabetical index to householders (All-Ireland Heritage)
1871	Creggan Upper, *Archivium Hibernicum*, Vol. 3
1876	Belfast Register of Electors, PRONI BELF5/1/1/1–2
1901	Census
1911	Census

Local history

Antrim Co. Library: subject catalogue of books and other material relating to Co. Antrim (1969), NL Ir. 941 p 43

Atkinson, E. D., *Dromore, an Ulster Diocese*, Dundalk, 1925

Ballymena: *Old Ballymena: a history of Ballymena during the 1798 Rebellion*, The Ballymena Observer, 1857, repub. 1938

Barr, W. N., *The oldest register of Derryaghy, Co. Antrim 1696–1772*, NL Ir. 9293 b 3

Bassett, G. H., *The Book of Antrim*, 1888

Benn, George, *A History of the Town of Belfast*, London, 1877–80

Bennett, T. J. G., *North Antrim Families*, Scotland, 1974

Boyd, H. A., *A History of the Church of Ireland in Ramoan Parish*, 1930

Carmody, Rev. W. P., *Lisburn Cathedral and its Past Rectors*, 1926

St John Clarke, H. J., *Thirty centuries in south-east Antrim: the Parish of Coole or Carnmoney*, Belfast, 1938, NL Ir. 27411 c 3

Ewart, L. M., *Handbook to the dioceses of Down, Connor and Dromore.*

'Notes on the ancient deeds of Carrickfergus', *R. Soc. Antiq.*, NL Ir. J. 1893

Hill, George, *The MacDonnells of Antrim*, Belfast, 1877

Joy, Henry, *Historical Collections relative to the town of Belfast*, Belfast, 1817

Lee, Rev. W. H. A., *St Colmanell, Aghoghill: A History of its Parish*, 1865

McSkimin, Samuel, *The History and Antiquities of the Town of Carrickfergus 1318–1839*, Belfast, 1909

Marshall, Rev. H. C., *The Parish of Lambeg*, 1933

Millin, S. S., *Sidelights on Belfast History*, 1932

O'Laverty, Rev. James, *An Historical Account of the Dioceses of Down and Connor*, 4 vols, Dublin, 1878–89

Owen, D. J., *History of Belfast*, Belfast, 1921, NL Ir. 94111 o 1

'Presbyterians in Glenarm', *The Glynns*, Vol. 9, 1981

Reeves, William, *Ecclesiastical Antiquities of Down, Connor and Dromore*, 1847

Robinson, Philip, *Irish Historic Towns Atlas: Carrickfergus*, Dublin, Royal Irish Academy, 1988

Shaw, William, *Cullybackey, the Story of an Ulster Village*, 1913

Shearman, H., *Ulster*, London, 1949 (incl. bibliographies), NL Ir. 91422 s 3

Young, Robert M., *Historical Notices of Old Belfast and its Vicinity*, 1896

Young, Robert M., *The Town Book of the Corporation of Belfast, 1613–1816*, 1892

Local journals

The Glynns: Journal of the Glens of Antrim Historical Society, NL Ir. 94111 9 2
Down and Connor Historical Society Magazine, NL Ir. 94115 [*sic*]
Lisburn Historical Society Journal, NL Ir. 94111 l 3
East Belfast Historical Society Journal, NL Ir. 94115 e 3

Directories

1819 Thomas Bradshaw, *General Directory of Newry, Armagh, Dungannon, Portadown, Tandragee, Lurgan, Waringstown, Banbridge, Warrenpoint, Rostrevor, Kilkeel and Rathfryland*
1820 J. Pigot, *Commercial Directory of Ireland* (Antrim, Belfast, Lisburn)
1820 Joseph Smyth, *Directory of Belfast and its Vicinity*
1820 *Belfast Almanack*
1824 Pigot and Co., *City of Dublin and Hibernian Provincial Directory*, NL Ir. 9141 p 75
1835 William Matier, *Belfast Directory*
1839 Matthew Martin, *Belfast Directory*, issued also 1841 and 1842
1846 Slater's *National Commercial Directory of Ireland*
1850 James A. Henderson, *Belfast Directory*
1852 James A. Henderson, *Belfast and Province of Ulster Directory*, issued also in 1854, 1856, 1858, 1861, 1863, 1865, 1868, 1870, 1877, 1880, 1884, 1887, 1890, 1894, 1900
1856 Slater's *Royal National Commercial Directory of Ireland*
1860 Hugh Adair, *Belfast Directory*
1865 R. Wynne, *Business Directory of Belfast*
1870 Slater's *Directory of Ireland*
1881 Slater's *Royal National Commercial Directory of Ireland*
1887 *Derry Almanac* (Portrush only)
1888 G. H. Bassett, *The Book of Antrim*
1894 Slater's *Royal Commercial Directory of Ireland*

Gravestone inscriptions

Ardclinis: *The Glynns*, Vol. IV, 1976
Ballycarley N.S. Presbyterian: *Gravestone Inscriptions, Co. Antrim*, Vol. 2
Ballygarvan R.C.: *Gravestone Inscriptions, Co. Antrim*, Vol. 2
Ballykeel: *Gravestone Inscriptions Co. Down*, Vol. I, George Rutherford, 1977
Ballyvallagh: *Gravestone Inscriptions Co. Antrim*, Vol. 2
Bunamargy: IGRS Collection, GO
Culfeightrin: *The Irish Ancestor*, Vol. II, No. 2, 1970
Glynn: *Gravestone Inscriptions Co. Down*, Vol. II, George Rutherford

Islandmagee: *Gravestone Inscriptions Co. Down*, Vol. II, George Rutherford
Killycrappin: *The Glynns*, Vol. V, 1977
Kilmore: *The Glynns*, Vol. IV, 1976
Kilroot: *Gravestone Inscriptions Co. Down*, Vol. II, George Rutherford
Lambeg: *Inscriptions on Tombstones in Lambeg Churchyard*, William Cassidy
Lisburn Cathedral: *Lisburn Cathedral and its Past Rectors*, W. P. Carmody, 1926
Magheragall: *Family Links*, Vol. 1, Nos 2 and 3, 1981
Raloo C. of I., Pres., N.S. Pres.: *Gravestone Inscriptions Co. Antrim*, Vol. 2
Templecorran: *Gravestone Inscriptions Co. Down*, Vol. II, George Rutherford

Estate records

Hereford estate, nineteenth century, *Lisburn Historical Society Journal*, No. 1,
    1978.

Placenames

Townland maps, Londonderry Inner City Trust
Placenames of Co. Antrim: Tickmacreevan, *The Glynns*, Vol. 10, 1982; Ard-
    clinis, *The Glynns*, Vol. 11, 1983; Parish of Skerry, *The Glynns*, Vol. 12,
    1984; Parish of Lough Guile, *The Glynns*, Vol. 13, 1985; Armoy, *The
    Glynns*, Vol. 14, 1986; Carncastle and Killyglen, *The Glynns*, Vol. 15, 1987

CO. ARMAGH

Census returns and substitutes

1630	Muster Roll of Ulster, Armagh Co. Library, NL Pos. 206
1634	Subsidy roll, NA M.2471, 2475
1654–56	Civil Survey, NL Ir. 31041 c 4
1659	Pender's 'Census', NL I 6551 Dublin
1661	Books of Survey and Distribution, PRONI T.370/A and D.1854/1/8
1664	Hearth Money Roll, *Archivium Hibernicum*, 1936, also NL MS. 9856 (typed and indexed) and PRONI T.604
1689	Protestants attainted by James II, PRONI T.808/14985
1737	Tithe-payers, Drumcree, NL I 920041 p 1
1738	Freeholders, Armagh Co. Library, NL Pos. 206

1740	Protestant householders: Creggan, Mullaghbrack, Loughgall, Derrynoose, Shankill, Lurgan, Tynan parishes. NA 1A 46 100; GO 539; PRONI T.808/15258
c.1750	Volunteers and yeomanry of Markethill and district. See 'Cornascreeb' in NL Author catalogue
1753	Poll Book. GO MS. 443; NA M.4878; PRONI T.808/14936
1766	Creggan parish. GO 537; NA Parl. Ret. 657, PRONI
1770	Armagh City householders, NL MS. 7370 and PRONI T.808/14977
1793–1908	Armagh Militia Records, Armagh Co. Library, NL Pos. 1014
1796	Catholic migrants from Ulster to Mayo. See Mayo. Also 'Petition of Armagh migrants in the Westport area', *Cathair na Mart*, Vol. 2, No. 1 (Appendix)
1796	Spinning-Wheel Premium Lists. Microfiche index in National Archives, comprising, in the case of Co. Armagh, over 4,000 names
1799–1800	Militia Pay Lists and Muster Rolls, PRONI T.1115/2A–C
1813–20	Armagh Freeholders, NL Ir. 94116 a 1, Ir. 352 p 2; PRONI ARM 5/2/1–17
1820s/30s	Tithe Books
1821–31	Freeholders, PRONI T.862
1821	Government census, Kilmore parish, PRONI T.450. Various fragments. Thrift Abstracts, NA
1830–65	Methodist Records, Newry circuit, *Seanchas Ardmhacha*, 1977, Vol. 7, No. 2
1834–37	Valuation of Armagh town (heads of households), *Parliamentary Papers, 1837*, Reports from Committees, Vol. II (1), Appendix G
1837	Marksmen (i.e. illiterate voters), Armagh Borough, *Parliamentary Papers, 1837*, Reports from Committees, Vol. II (1), Appendix A
1839	Valuation of Co. Armagh, Armagh Co. Library, NL Pos. 99
1839	Freeholders, PRONI T.808/14961
1851	Freeholders, PRONI T.808/14927
1851	Government census. Various fragments, Thrift Abstracts, NA
1864	Griffith's Valuation
1864(?)	Tynan parish. See Marshall, NL I 94116
1901	Census
1911	Census

Local history

Armagh Road Presbyterian Church, Portadown (1868–1968), NL Ir. 2741 p 25
Armagh Royal School: Prizes and prizemen, 1854, NL P 439
'Balleer School: Copy-book of letters, 1827–29', NL Ir. 300 p 106

Donaldson, John, *A Historical and Statistical Account of the Barony of Upper Fews*
Ewart, L. M., *Handbook to the dioceses of Down, Connor and Dromore*
Galogly, John, *The History of St Patrick's Parish, Armagh*, 1880
Gwynn, A., *The medieval province of Armagh*, Dundalk, 1946, NL Ir. 27411 g 1
Historical sketches of various parishes, NL Ir. 27411 l 4 and 5
Hogg, Rev. M. B., *Keady Parish: A Short History of its Church and People*, 1928
Hughes, Thomas, *The History of Tynan Parish*, 1910
Marshall, J. J., *The History of Charlemont Fort and Borough . . .*, 1921
Mullaghbrack from the tithe-payers list of 1834, NL I 920041 p 1
Nelsen, S., *History of the Parish of Creggan in Counties Armagh and Louth from 1611 to
    1840*, 1974, NL Ir. 941 p 43
Patterson, T., 'The Armagh Manor Court Rolls, 1625–27 and incidental notes
    on 17th century sources for Irish surnames in Co. Armagh', *Seanchas
    Ardmhacha*, 1957, 295–322
Shearman, H., *Ulster*, London, 1949 (incl. bibliographies), NL Ir. 91422 s 3
Stewart, James, *Historical Memoirs of the City of Armagh*, ed. Ambrose Coleman,
    Dublin, 1900
Swayne, John, *The register of John Swayne, Archbishop of Armagh, and Primate of
    Ireland, 1418–39*

Local journals

Craigavon Historical Society Review (from 1973)
Mullaghbawn Historical and Folk-Lore Society, NL Ir. 800 p 50
Seanchas Ardmhacha (Journal of the Armagh Diocesan Historical Society), NL
    Ir. 27411 s 4
Seanchas Dhroim Mor (Journal of the Dromore Diocesan Historical Society),
    NL Ir. 94115 s 3

Directories

1819   Thomas Bradshaw, *General Directory of Newry, Armagh, Dungannon, Porta-
        down, Tandragee, Lurgan, Waringstown, Banbridge, Warrenpoint, Rostrevor, Kilkeel
        and Rathfryland*
1820   J. Pigot, *Commercial Directory of Ireland* (Antrim, Belfast, Lisburn)
1824   Pigot and Co., *City of Dublin and Hibernian Provincial Directory*, NL Ir.
        9141 p 75
1841   Mathew Martin, *Belfast Directory*, issued also in 1842
1846   Slater's *National Commercial Directory of Ireland*
1852   James A. Henderson, *Belfast and Province of Ulster Directory*, issued also
        in 1854, 1856, 1858, 1861, 1863, 1865, 1868, 1870, 1877, 1880, 1884,
        1887, 1890, 1894, 1900
1856   Slater's *Royal National Commercial Directory of Ireland*

1865   R. Wynne, *Business Directory of Belfast*
1870   Slater's *Directory of Ireland*
1881   Slater's R*oyal National Commercial Directory of Ireland*
1883   S. Farrell, *County Armagh Directory and Almanac*
1888   G. H. Bassett, *The Book of Armagh*
1894   Slater's *Royal Commercial Directory of Ireland*

Gravestone inscriptions

Creggan: *Seanchas Ardmhacha*, Vol. VI, 1976
Sandy Hill, Armagh City: *Seanchas Ardmhacha*, 1985
    Irish World (26 Market Square, Dungannon, Co. Tyrone, BT70 1AB)
have transcribed and computerised the inscriptions of more than 300 graveyards in the six counties of Northern Ireland, principally in the four western
counties of Armagh, Derry, Fermanagh and Tyrone.

Estate records

Brownlow estate rentals, Co. Armagh, 1636, 1659, 1667–77, Armagh Co.
    Library, NL Pos. 207.
Richard Johnstone: rentals, Counties Armagh, Down and Monaghan,
    1731, Armagh Co. Library, NL Pos. 1014.

Placenames

Townland maps, Londonderry Inner City Trust

CO. CARLOW

Census returns and substitutes

1641   Book of Survey and Distribution, NL MS. 971
1659   Pender's 'Census', I 6551, Dublin
1767   'Co. Carlow Freeholders', *The Irish Genealogist*, 1980
1798   Persons who Suffered Losses in the 1798 Rebellion, NL I 94107
1820s/30s Tithe Books
1832–37   Voters registered in Carlow Borough, NL, *Parliamentary Papers*,
           1837, Reports from Committees, Vol. II (2), 193–96

1837   Marksmen (illiterate voters) in parliamentary boroughs: Carlow,
            NL, *Parliamentary Papers*, 1837, Reports from Committees, Vol. II
            (i), Appendix A
1852/3   Griffith's Valuation, microfiche index (All-Ireland Heritage)
1901   Census
1911   Census

Local history

Brennan, M., *Schools of Kildare and Leighlin, 1775–1835*
Brophy, M., *Carlow Past and Present*, NL Ir. 94138 b 1
Carlow Parliamentary Roll, 1872 NL Ir. 94138 m 1
Coleman, James, 'Bibliography of the counties Carlow, Kilkenny and
    Wicklow', *Waterford and S–E of Ire. Arch. Soc. Jnl*, 11, 1907–8, 126–33, NL
    Ir. 794105 w 1
Coyle, James, *The Antiquities of Leighlin*
Hore, H. J., *The Social State of the Southern and Eastern Counties of Ireland in the
    Sixteenth Century*, 1870
O'Toole (ed.), *The Parish of Ballon, Co. Carlow*, 1933, NL Ir. 94138 o 3
Ryan, J., *The history and antiquities of the County Carlow*, Dublin, 1833, NL Ir.
    94138 r 1

Local journals

Carloviana, NL Ir. 94138 c 2
The Carlovian (1958), NL Ir. 92 p 88
Carlow Past and Present

Directories

1788   Richard Lucas, *General Directory of the Kingdom of Ireland*, NL Pos. 3729
1820   J. Pigot, *Commercial Directory of Ireland*
1824   Pigot and Co., *City of Dublin and Hibernian Provincial Directory*, NL Ir.
            9141 p 75
1839   T. Shearman, *New Commercial Directory for the Cities of Waterford and
            Kilkenny, Towns of Clonmel, Carrick-on-Suir, New Ross and Carlow*
1846   Slater's *National Commercial Directory of Ireland*
1856   Slater's *Royal National Commercial Directory of Ireland*
1870   Slater's *Directory of Ireland*
1881   Slater's *Royal National Commercial Directory of Ireland*
1894   Slater's *Royal Commercial Directory of Ireland*

Gravestone inscriptions

Ballycopagan New Cemetery: *Co. Carlow Tombstone Inscriptions*, Vol. 2, Ir. 9295 c 3

Ballymurphy: *Co. Carlow Tombstone Inscriptions*, Vol. 3, Ir. 9295 c 3

Borris: *Co. Carlow Tombstone Inscriptions*, Vol. 2, Ir. 9295 c 3

Cloonegoose: *Co. Carlow Tombstone Inscriptions*, Vol. 2, Ir. 9295 c 3

Dunleckny: Andrew Morris (microfiche)

Kilcullen: *Co. Carlow Tombstone Inscriptions*, Vol. 3, Ir. 9295 c 3

Killedmond: *Co. Carlow Tombstone Inscriptions*, Vol. 3, Ir. 9295 c 3

Kiltennel: *Co. Carlow Tombstone Inscriptions*, Vol. 2

Linkardstown: IGRS Collection, GO

Rathanna: *Co. Carlow Tombstone Inscriptions*, Vol. 3, Ir. 9295 c 3

St Michael's: *Co. Carlow Tombstone Inscriptions*, Vol. 1, Ir. 9295 c 3

St Mullin's: *Co. Carlow Tombstone Inscriptions*, Vol. 1, Ir. 9295 c 3

Placenames

O'Toole, Edward, *The Place-names of Co. Carlow*, Ir. 94138 o 3

CO. CAVAN

Census returns and substitutes

1612–13	'Survey of Undertakers Planted in Co. Cavan', *Historical Manuscripts Commission Report*, 4, (Hastings MSS.) 1947, 159–82
1630	Muster Roll, *Breifny*, 1977/8, also NL Pos. 206
1664	Hearth Money Roll, parishes of Killeshandra, Kildallan, Killenagh, Templeport, Tomregan, PRONI
1703–4	Tenants of Robert Craigies, Co. Cavan (parishes of Kildallon and Killeshandra), *The Irish Ancestor*, 1978
1761	Poll Book, PRONI
1766	Protestants in parishes of Kinawley, Lavey, Lurgan, Munter-connaught, RCB Library, GO MS. 536/7, NA m 2476 (e)
1796	Catholic migrants from Ulster to Mayo. See Mayo
1802	Protestants in Enniskeen parish, *The Irish Ancestor*, 1973
1813–21	Freeholders, Co. Cavan, NL Ir. 94119 c 2
1814	Youthful Protestants in the parishes of Drung and Larah, *The Irish Ancestor*, 1978

1821	Parishes of Annageliffe, Ballymacue, Castlerahan, Castleterra, Crosserlough, Denn, Drumlumman, Drung, Kilbride, Kilmore, Kinawley, Larah, Lavey, Lurgan, Mullagh, Munterconnaught, National Archives
1833	Arms registered with the Clerk of the Peace, April, ILB 04 p 12 (over 1,500 names)
1820s/30s	Tithe Books
1841	Killeshandra parish (part). Also, some certified copies of census returns for use in claims for old age pensions. National Archives
c.1850	'List of inhabitants of Castlerahan barony', with Killinkere parish registers, NL Pos. 5349
1851	Certified copies of census returns for use in claims for old age pensions. National Archives
1856/7	Griffith's Valuation
1901	Census
1911	Census

Local history

Cavan County Library, *Guide to Local Studies Dept.*, NL Ir. 0179 p 6
Cavan Freeholders since 1813, NL Ir. 94119 c 2
Cullen, S., 'Sources for Cavan Local History', in *Breifny*, 1977–78
Cullen, S., *Sources for Cavan Local History*, 1965, NL Ir. 941 p 66
Cunningham, T. P., *The Ecclesiastical History of Larah Parish*, 1984, NL Ir. 27412 c 2
Healy, John, *History of the Diocese of Meath*, 2 vols, Dublin, 1908
MacNamee, James J., *History of the Diocese of Ardagh*, Dublin, 1954
McNiffe, L., 'A Short History of the Barony of Rosclogher, 1840–60', *Breifny*, 1983–84
Monahan, Rev. J., *Records Relating to the Diocese of Armagh and Clonmacnoise*, 1886
O'Connell, Philip, *The Diocese of Kilmore: its History and Antiquities*, Dublin, 1937
Shearman, H., *Ulster*, London, 1949 (incl. bibliographies), NL Ir. 91422 s 3
Smyth, T. S., *A civic history of the town of Cavan*, Cavan, 1934, Ir. 94119 s 1
'Sources of Information on the Antiquities and history of Cavan and Leitrim: Suggestions', *Breifny*, 1920–22

Local journals

Breifne, NL Ir. 94119 b 2
Breifny Antiquarian Society Journal (1920–33), NL Ir. 794106 b 1
Ardagh and Clonmacnoise Historical Society Journal (1926–51), NL Ir. 794105
The Drumlin, a Journal of Cavan, Leitrim and Monaghan, NL Ir. 05 d 345
Heart of Breifny, NL Ir. 94119 h 1

Directories

1820   J. Pigot, *Commercial Directory of Ireland*
1824   Pigot and Co., *City of Dublin and Hibernian Provincial Directory*, NL Ir. 9141 p 75
1852   James A. Henderson, *Belfast and Province of Ulster Directory*, issued also in 1854, 1856, 1858, 1861, 1863, 1865, 1868, 1870, 1877, 1880, 1884, 1887, 1890, 1894, 1900
1856   Slater's *Royal National Commercial Directory of Ireland*
1870   Slater's *Directory of Ireland*
1881   Slater's *Royal National Commercial Directory of Ireland*
1894   Slater's *Royal Commercial Directory of Ireland*

Gravestone inscriptions

Ballanagh (C. of I.): GO MS. 622, 107
Billis: GO MS. 622, 182
Callowhill: *Breifne*, 1982/3
Castlerahan: *Breifne*, 1925/6
Cavan: *Breifne*, 1986
Cloone (St Michael's): *Seanchas Ardmhacha*, Vol. 10, No. 1, 1980/81, 63–84
Crosserlough: *Breifne*, 1976 and IGRS Collection, GO
Denn: *Breifne*, 1924
Darver: *Breifne*, 1922
Drumlane: *Breifne*, 1979
Kildrumfertan: *Breifne*, 1965
Lavey: GO MS. 622, 181
Lurgan: *Breifne*, 1961
Magherintemple: *Breifne*, 1963
Munterconnaught: *Breifne*, 1927/8
Templeport: *Breifne*, 1971

Estate records

1771 survey of the estates of Alexander Sanderson, NL.
Settings of Lord Headford's Cavan estates, 1831 (including a list of tenants' names by townland), NL MS. 25394.

Placenames

Parishes, baronies and denominations in each parish, alphabetical, NL JP 2168
Townland maps, Londonderry Inner City Trust

CO. CLARE

Census returns and substitutes

1641	Book of Survey and Distribution, Irish Manuscripts Commission, 1947. Also NL MS. 963
1659	Pender's 'Census', NL I 6551, Dublin
1745	Voters, TCD MS. 2059
1821	Ennis (part), see pre-1901 census catalogue, National Archives
1820s/30s	Tithe Books
1829	Freeholders, NL P.5556
1837	Marksmen (illiterate voters) in parliamentary boroughs: Ennis. NL, *Parliamentary Papers*, 1837, Reports from Committees, Vol. II (i), Appendix A
1850	Deaths in Kilrush and Ennistymon workhouses, hospitals, infirmaries, 25/3/1850–25/3/1851. NL, Accounts and Papers, *Parliamentary Papers*, 1851, Vol. 49, (484) 1–47
1855	Griffith's Valuation
1866	Kilfenora, NL Pos. 2440
1901	Census
1911	Census

Local history

Clancy, J., *Short History of the Parish of Killanena or Upper Feakle*, NL Ir. 941 p 27

Clancy, J., 'Gleanings in 17th century Kilrush', *North Munster Antiq. Jnl*, No. 3, 1942–43

Coleman, J., 'Limerick and Clare Bibliography', *Limerick Field Club Jnl*, No. 3, 1907

Dwyer, Philip, *The Diocese of Killaloe, from the Reformation to the Close of the Eighteenth Century*, Dublin, 1878

Enright, F., 'Pre-famine Reform and Emigration on the Wyndham Estate in Clare', *The Other Clare*, 1984

Fahey, J., *The History and Antiquities of the Diocese of Kilmacduagh*, Dublin, 1893

Frost, James, *The history and topography of Co. Clare from the earliest times to the beginning of the eighteenth century*, Dublin, 1893, NL Ir. 94143 f 3

Hayes-McCoy, G. A., *Index to 'The Compossicion Booke of Connoght, 1585'*, Irish Manuscripts Commission, Dublin, 1945

O'Mahoney, C., 'Emigration from Kilrush Workhouse, 1848–1859', *The Other Clare*, 1983

Westropp Manuscripts, Royal Irish Academy, Will abstracts mainly from Counties Clare and Limerick

White, Rev. P., *History of Clare and the Dalcassian Clans of Tipperary, Limerick and Galway*, Dublin, 1893

Local journals

The Other Clare (Journal of the Shannon Archaeological and Historical Society). NL Ir.
    9141 p 71
North Munster Antiquarian Society Journal. NL Ir. 794105 n 1 (Index 1897–1919,
    NL Ir. 7941 n 1)
Dál gCais. NL Ir. 94143 d 5

Directories

1788   Richard Lucas, *General Directory of the Kingdom of Ireland*, NL Pos. 3729
1820   J. Pigot, *Commercial Directory of Ireland*
1824   Pigot and Co., *City of Dublin and Hibernian Provincial Directory*, NL Ir.
        9141 p 75
1842   *A Directory of Kilkee*, NL Ir. 61312 h 1
1846   Slater's *National Commercial Directory of Ireland*
1856   Slater's *Royal National Commercial Directory of Ireland*
1866   George H. Bassett, *Directory of the City and County of Limerick and of the
        principal Towns in Counties Tipperary and Clare*, NL Ir. 914144 b 5
1870   Slater's *Directory of Ireland*
1881   Slater's *Royal National Commercial Directory of Ireland*
1886   Francis Guy, *Postal Directory of Munster*, NL Ir. 91414 g 8
1893   Francis Guy, *Postal Directory of Munster*
1894   Slater's *Royal Commercial Directory of Ireland*

Gravestone inscriptions

Ballyalla (Ennis): GO MS. 622, 79/80
Ballyvaughan: IGRS Collection, 5, GO
Cloony South: IGRS Collection, 12, GO
Coad: IGRS Collection, 32, GO
Corofin, St Catherine's: IGRS Collection, 24, GO
Kilcorcoran: IGRS Collection, 41, GO
Kildeema: IGRS Collection, 30, GO
Kilfarboy: IGRS Collection, 56, GO
Kilfenora (ex. Cathedral): IGRS Collection, 48, GO
Killaloe Cathedral: *Year Book of St Flannan's Cathedral*
Killaspuglonane: IGRS Collection, 12, GO
Killenagh: IGRS Collection, 7, GO
Killernan: IGRS Collection, 95, GO
Killinaboy: IGRS Collection, 28, GO
Kilmacrehy: IGRS Collection, 50, GO

Kilmurry Ibrickane: IGRS Collection, 28, GO
Kilrush (C. of I.): IGRS Collection, 27, GO
Kilshanny: IGRS Collection, 30, GO
Kiltenantlea (Dooass): IGRS Collection, 19, GO
Kilvoidane: IGRS Collection, 15, GO
Memorials of the Dead in West Clare (Cantwell), *The Other Clare*, 1983
Milltown Malbay (C. of I.): IGRS Collection, 18, GO
Noughaval: IGRS Collection, 22, GO
Rath: IGRS Collection, 17, GO

Estate records

Note on the Leconfield estate papers at the National Archives, Accession No.
    1074 (Vandeleur leases, Kilrush, 1816–1929, Lord Leconfield rentals,
    1846–1917, including comments on age, health, poverty, etc.), *North
    Munster Antiquarian Journal*, Vol. XXIII, 1981.
Roxton estate rentals, Inchiquin barony, Co. Clare, 1834, NA MS. 5764.
O'Callaghan-Westropp estate rentals, barony of Tulla Upper, NL MS. 867.
19th Century, Inchiquin Papers, NL MSS. 14, 355 ff. (Dromoland especially).

Placenames

Frost, J., 'Townland Names of Co. Clare', *Limerick Field Journal*, Vols 1 and 2,
    1897–1904, NL Ir. 794105 l 1
Townland maps, Londonderry Inner City Trust

CO. CORK

Census returns and substitutes

1641	Survey of Houses in Cork City, listing tenants and possessors, National Archives, Quit Rent Office Papers
1641	Book of Survey and Distribution (proprietors in 1641, grantees in 1666–68), NL MS. 966–7
1654	*Civil Survey*, Vol. VI, Parishes of Aghabulloge, Aghina, Aglish, Ballinaboy, Ballyvourney, Carnaway, Carrigrohanbeg, Clondrohid, Currykippane, Desertmore, Donoughmore, Drishane,

Garrycloyne, Granagh, Inchigeelagh, Inniscarra, Kilbonane, Kilcolman, Kilcorney, Kilmihil, Kilmurry, Kilnamartyra, Knockavilly, Mocloneigh, Macroom, Matehy, Moviddy, Templemichael, Whitechurch

1662–7	Subsidy rolls, Condons and Clangibbons baronies (extracts), NA M.4968. Also NA M.2636 (Grove-White Abstracts)
1700–1752	Freemen, Cork City. National Archives, M.4693
1753	Also later years. Householders St Nicholas parish, Cork City, C. of I. registers
1756–1827	Biographical notices from Cork and Kerry newspapers, arranged alphabetically, NL MSS. 19,172–5
1757	Able-bodied male Protestants, parishes of Brigown, Castletown Roche, Clonmeen, Farrihy, Glanworth, Kilshannig, Marshallstown, Roskeen, *An Anglo-Irish Miscellany*, M. D. Jephson, 1964
1766	Parishes of Aghabullog, Aghada, Ardagh and Clonpriest, Ballyhea, Carrigdownane, Castlelyons, Castlemartyr, Castletown Roche, Churchtown, Clenor, Clondrohid, Clondullane, Clonfert, Clonmee, Clonmult and Kilmahon, Cloyne and Ballintemple, Coole, Farrihy, Garrycloyne, Glanworth, Ightermurragh, Imphrick, Inniscarra and Matehy, Kildorrery, Killogrohanebeg, Kilnamartyra, Kilshannig, Kilworth and Macroney, Knockmourne and Ballynoe, Lisgoold and Ballykeary, Litter, Macroom, Magourney and Kilcolman, Mallow, Marshalstown, Middleton, Mourne Abbey, Nathlash and Carrigdownane, Ruskeen and Kilcummy, Templemolaga, Shandrum, Whitechurch and Grenagh, Youghal, NA 1A 41 67; Rathbarry, Ringrone, NA 1A 46 49; Dunbulloge, JCHAS Vol. 51; Kilmichael, JCHAS Vol. 26
1783	Freemen and freeholders, Cork City, NL P 2054
1793	Householders in the parish of St Anne's, Shandon, 1793, and of additional houses built up to 1853, JCHAS, Vol. 47, 87–111
1814	Jurors, Co. Cork, Grove-White Abstracts, NA M2637
1817	Freemen, Cork City, NL P722
1820s/30s	Tithe Books
1830	Houseowners, St Mary's Shandon. JCHAS Vol. 49
1830–37	Registered householders, Cork City (alphabetical). NL, Reports from Committees, *Parliamentary Papers*, 1837/8, Vol. 13 (2), 554–7
1832–37	Voters, Cork City, NL, Reports from Committees, *Parliamentary Papers*, 1837/8, Vol. 13 (1), 320/1
1834–37	Valuation of Bandonbridge, Kinsale, Youghal towns, Houses valued over £5 (householders), NL, *Parliamentary Papers*, 1837, Reports from Committees, Vol. II (1), Appendix G
1834	Protestant parishioners in the Ballymodan part of Bandon, NL MS. 675

1834	Protestant families in Magourney parish. With C. of I. parish registers, NA M 5118
1837	Marksmen (i.e. illiterate voters), Bandonbridge, Kinsale, Youghal Boroughs. NL, *Parliamentary Papers* 1837, Reports from Committees, Vol. II (1), Appendix A
1837	Lists of waste and poor, Cork City parishes. NL, Reports from Committees, *Parliamentary Papers*, 1837/8, Vol. 13 (1), 324–34
1843–50	Records of Easter and Christmas dues paid in the parish of Ballyclogh, with name of parishioners, including children, NL Pos. 5717
1851	Parishes of Kilcrumper (part), Kilworth, Leitrim (part), Macrony (part), NA m. 4685
1851/3	Griffith's Valuation, Alphabetical index to householders (microfiche), National Archives
1901	Census
1911	Census

Local history

Ballydesmond emigration: see Quit Rent Papers, National Archives, see also *Analecta Hibernica*, Vol. 22

Barry, E., *Barrymore: the records of the Barrys of Co. Cork*, NL Ir. 9292 b 19

Bennett, G., *The history of Bandon and the principal towns of the West Riding of Cork*, Cork, 1869, NL Ir. 94145 b 1

Brady, W. Maziere, *Clerical and Parochial Records of Cork, Cloyne and Ross*, 3 vols, London, 1864

Casey, A. (ed.), *O'Kief Coshe Mang etc.*, NL Ir. 94145 c 12

Caulfield, R., *The register of the parish of Holy Trinity Cork, 1643–1668*, P 1079

Caulfield, R., *The Annals of St Fin Barres Cathedral*, Cork, 1870

Caulfield, R., The Pipe Roll of Cloyne, JCHAS, 1918

Caulfield, R. (ed.), *Council Book of the Corporation of Cork, 1609–43, 1690–1800*, Guildford, 1876

Caulfield, R. (ed.), *Council Book of the Corporation of Kinsale*, Guildford, 1879

Caulfield, R. (ed.), *Council Book of the Corporation of Youghal, 1610–1659, 1666–87, 1690–1800*, Guildford, 1878

Cole, Rev. J. H., *Church and Parish Records of the United Dioceses of Cork, Cloyne and Ross*, Cork, 1903 (Continuation of Brady—see above)

Collins, J. T., 'Co. Cork families 1630–35', JCHAS, No. 204, 1961

Cusack, Mary F., *A History of the City and County of Cork*, Dublin, 1875

Darling, John, *St Multose Church Kinsale*, Cork, 1895

Dennehy, The Ven. Archdeacon, *History of Queenstown*, Cork, 1923

Gibson, C. B., *The history of the county and city of Cork*, London, 1861, J 94145

Grove-White, Col James, *Historical and Topographical Notes etc. on Buttevant, Castletownroche, Doneraile, Mallow and places in their vicinity*, Cork, 1905–16

Grove-White, Col James, *History of Kilbryne Doneraile, Cork*, Cork, 1915

Grove-White Abstracts, National Archives, indexed extracts from the following Church of Ireland parish registers: Ballyclogh (NA M 2601); Ballyhooly (NA M 2602); Bridgetown and Kilcummer (NA M 2603); Buttevant (NA M 2604); Carrigleamleary (NA M 2605); Castlemagner (NA M 2606); Castletownroche (NA M 2607); Churchtown (NA M 2609); Clenor (NA M 2610); Clonfert and Newmarket (NA M 2611); Clonmeen (NA M 2612); Doneraile (NA M 2613); Drishane (NA M 2614); Dromtariffe (NA M 2615); Farahy (NA M 2616); Glanworth (NA M 2617); Kanturk (NA M 2618); Kilbolane (NA M 2619); Kilbrin (NA M 2620); Kilshannig (NA M 2621); Holy Trinity (NA M 2608); Kilworth (NA M 2622); Lisgoold (NA M 2623); Litter (NA M 2624); Mallow (NA M 2625); Marshallstown (NA M 2626); Monanimy (NA M 2628); Mourne Abbey (NA M 2627); Rahan (NA M 2629); St Finbarr and SS Peter and Paul (NA M 2630); St Nathlash (NA M 2631); Shanrahan (NA M 2632); Tullylease (NA M 2633); Wallstown (NA M 2634)

Hartnett, P. J., *Cork City, its History and Antiquities*, 1943

Holland, Rev. W., *History of West Cork and the Diocese of Ross*, Skibbereen, 1949

Hore, H. J., *The Social State of the Southern and Eastern Counties of Ireland in the Sixteenth Century*, 1870

Jephson, M. D., *An Anglo-Irish Miscellany*, NL Ir. 9292 j 2

Maps of Kilmeen and Castleventry parishes, NL Ir. 94145 o 5

McLysaght, E., *The Kenmare Manuscripts*, Dublin, 1942

MacSwiney Papers, Royal Irish Academy. Historical notes and will abstracts, mainly from Counties Cork and Kerry

O'Murchadha, D., *Family Names of Co. Cork*, Dublin, 1985

O'Sullivan, Florence, *The History of Kinsale*, Dublin, 1916

Post Office Directory, 1844–45, J 914145

Quinlan, P., *Old Mitchelstown and the Kingston family*, Ir. 941 p 66

Reedy, Rev. Donal A., *The Diocese of Kerry*, Killarney

Smith, Charles, *The ancient ant present state of the county and city of Cork*, Dublin, 1750 (see also JCHAS, 1893–94)

Tucky, Francis, *The County and City of Cork Remembered*

West, W., *Directory and picture of Cork, 1810*, J 914145

Windele, J., *Cork historical and descriptive notices . . . to the middle of the 19th century*, Cork, 1910, NL Ir. 94145 w 3

Windele MSS.: Information on Cork and Kerry families, including Coppinger, Cotter, Crosbie, O'Donovan, O'Keeffe, McCarthy, Sarsfield and others, NL Pos. 5479

Local journals

Cork Historical and Archaeological Society Journal, NL Ir. 794105 c 1

Bandon Historical Journal, NL Ir. 94145 b 12

Seanchas Chairbre, NL Ir. 94145 s 6
Seanchas Duthala (Duhallow magazine), NL Ir. 94145 s 3

Directories

1787   Richard Lucas, *Cork Directory*, JCHAS, 1967
1788   Richard Lucas, *General Directory of the Kingdom of Ireland*, NL Pos. 3729
1797   John Nixon, *Cork Almanack*
1809   Holden's *Triennal Directory*
1810   William West, *Directory of Cork*
1812   John Connor, *Cork Directory*
1817   John Connor, *Cork Directory*
1820   J. Pigot, *Commercial Directory of Ireland*
1824   Pigot and Co., *City of Dublin and Hibernian Provincial Directory*, NL Ir. 9141 p 75
1826   John Connor, *Cork Directory*
1828   John Connor, *Cork Directory*
1846   Slater's *National Commercial Directory of Ireland*
1856   Slater's *Royal National Commercial Directory of Ireland*
1870   Slater's *Directory of Ireland*
1875   Francis Guy, *Directory of the County and City of Cork*
1881   Slater's *Royal National Commercial Directory of Ireland*
1886   Francis Guy, *Postal Directory of Munster*, NL Ir. 91414 g 8
1889   Francis Guy, *City and County Cork Almanack and Directory*, issued annually from this date
1894   Slater's *Royal Commercial Directory of Ireland*

Gravestone inscriptions

Abbeystrewery (C. of I. interior): IGRS Collection, 30, GO
Adrigole (C. of I.): IGRS Collection, 4, GO
Aghinagh: JCHAS, No. 216, 1967
Aughadown (C. of I. interior): IGRS Collection, 15, GO
Ballyclogh: *O'Kief Coshe Mang etc.*, Vol. 8
Ballycurrany: JCHAS, No. 237, 1978
Ballymodan, St Peter's: Droichead na Banndan Community Cooperative Society Ltd, 1986
Ballyvourney: *O'Kief, Coshe Mang etc.*, Vol. 6
Bantry Abbey: IGRS Collection, 393, GO
Bantry: IGRS Collection, 77, GO
Bantry (St Finbarr's): IGRS Collection, 101, GO
Bere Island: IGRS Collection, 17, GO
Caheragh (C. of I.): IGRS Collection, 13, GO

Caheragh (Catholic): IGRS Collection, 4, GO
Carrigrohanebeg: JCHAS, No. 218, 1968
Catlemagner: *O'Kief, Coshe Mang etc.*, Vol. 6
Castletown Berehaven: IGRS Collection, 37, GO
Clondrohid: *O'Kief, Coshe Mang etc.*, Vol. 6
Clonfert: *O'Kief, Coshe Mang etc.*, Vol. 6
Clonmeen (Lyre and Banteer): *O'Kief, Coshe Mang etc.*, Vol. 7
Clonmult: JCHAS, No. 223/4/5, 1976/7
Cullen: *O'Kief, Coshe Mang etc.*, Vol. 6
Dangandonovan: JCHAS, No. 229, 1974
Desertmore: JCHAS, No. 219, 1969
Drishane: *O'Kief,Coshe Mang etc.*, Vol. 6
Dromagh: *O'Kief, Coshe Mang etc.*, Vol. 8
Dromtariffe: *O'Kief, Coshe Mang etc.*, Vol. 6
Drumlave: IGRS Collection, 1, GO
Dunderrow: JCHAS, No. 224, 1971
Fermoy (Military only): *The Irish Sword*, Nos 51/3, 1977/9
Inchigeela: *O'Kief, Coshe Mang etc.*, Vol. 6
Kilbrin: *O'Kief, Coshe Mang etc.*, Vol. 8
Kilbrogan: (Catholic and C. of I.) Droichead na Banndan Community Co-
    operative Society Ltd, 1986
Kilcaskan: IGRS Collection, 7, GO
Kilcatherine: IGRS Collection, 4, GO
Kilcoe (C. of I.): IGRS Collection, 2, GO,
Kilcoe (old): IGRS Collection, 6, GO
Kilcorney: *O'Kief, Coshe Mang etc.*, Vol. 7
Kilcrea Friary: JCHAS, No. 226, 1972
Kilcummin: *O'Kief, Coshe Mang etc.*, Vol. 6
Killaconenagh: IGRS Collection, 49, GO
Killeagh: JCHAS, No. 226, 1972
Kilnaglory: JCHAS, No. 220, 1969
Kilnamanagh: IGRS Collection, 5, GO
Kilnamartyra: *O'Kief, Coshe Mang etc.*, Vol. 6
Kilmeen: *O'Kief, Coshe Mang etc.*, Vol. 6
Lackeragh: IGRS Collection, 1, GO
Lisgoold: JCHAS, No. 237, 1978
Macloneigh: *O'Kief, Coshe Mang etc.*, Vol. 8
Macroom: *O'Kief, Coshe Mang etc.*, Vol. 8
Mallow: *O'Kief, Coshe Mang etc.*, Vol. 8
Molagga: *The Irish Genealogist*, 1955
Nohovaldaly: *O'Kief, Coshe Mang etc.*, Vol. 8
Rossmacown R.C.: IGRS Collection, 13, GO
St Finbarr's: *St Finbarr's Cathedral*, A. C. Robinson, 1897

Skibbereen R.C. Cathedral interior: IGRS Collection, 13, GO
Thornhill: IGRS Collection, 1, GO
Timoleague: GO MS. 622, 113
Tisxon: JCHAS, No. 222, 1970
Titeskin: JCHAS, No. 221, 1970
Tullylease: *O'Kief, Coshe Mang etc.*, Vol. 8
Youghal (Collegiate Church): *The Handbook for Youghal*, W. G. Field, 1896/
    1973

Estate records

LANDLORD

Lord **Arden**: NL MS. 8652, Rentals 1824–1830, all tenants, covering town-
    lands in the civil parishes of Bregoge, Buttevant, Catlemagner, Clonfert,
    Dromtarriff and Dungourney.

Earl of **Bantry**: NL MS. 3273, Rentals, 1829, all tenants, covering townlands
    in the civil parishes of Kilcaskan, Kilcatherine and Killaconenagh.

(**Barrymore** barony): 'Tenant Farmers on the Barrymore Estate', JCHAS
    Vol. 51, 31–40.

Bennett: Rental of the Bennett estate, 1770 (mainly Cork City and sur-
    rounding areas), NL Pos. 288.

Sir John **Benn-Walsh**: Donnelly, J. S., 'The journals of Sir John Benn-Walsh
    relating to the management of his Irish estates (1823–64)', *Journal of the
    Cork Hist. and Arch. Soc.*, Vol. LXXXI, 1975.

Bishop of Cork: NA M6087. Rentals 1807–1831, major tenants only,
    townlands in the civil parishes of Aghadown, Ardfield, Fanlobbus,
    Kilbrogan, Kilmocomoge, Kilsillagh, Ross, St Finbarr's, Skull.

Boyle/Cavendish: NL MSS. 6136–898. The Lismore Papers. Rentals,
    valuations, lease books, account books for the estates of the Earls of Cork
    and the Dukes of Devonshire, 1570–1870, generally covering only major
    tenants. A detailed listing is given in NL Special List 15, covering
    townlands in the civil parishes of Ahern, Ardagh, Ballymodan, Ballynoe,
    Brinny, Clonmult, Clonpriest, Ightermurragh, Kilbrogan, Killeagh, Kill-
    owen, Kinneigh, Knockmourne, Lismore, Mogeely, Murragh, St Finbarr's,
    Youghal.

Richard **Cox**: NA Gordon Presentation 214. Rentals 1839, major tenants only,
    townlands in the civil parishes of Aghinagh, Clondrohid, Desertserges,
    Fanlobbus, Kilcaskan, Kilmeen, Kilmichael, Kilnamartery, Macloneigh.

Earbery estates: NL MS. 7403, Rentals 1788–1815 (principally major tenants);
    NL MS. 5257, full tenants list, 1800; townlands in the civil parishes of
    Aghabulloge, Clondrohid, Donoghmore, Kilmurry.

Robert Hodges **Eyre**: NL MSS. 3273, 3274, Rentals, 1833 and 1835, of the
    Bere Island estate, all tenants, civil parish of Killaconenagh.

James **Graham**: NA M2329, Rentals *c*.1763, major tenants only, covering townlands in the civil parish of Killathy.

Rev. Edmund **Lombard**: NL MS. 2985, Rentals, 1795, major tenants only, covering townlands in the civil parishes of Kilmacdonagh and Kilshannig.

Newenham?: NL MS. 4123, Rentals *c*.1825, all tenants, covering townlands in the civil parishes of Kilcrumper, Kilworth, Leitrim, Macroney.

Richard **Neville**: NL MS. 3733, Rentals of lands in Counties Cork, Kildare and Waterford, principally major tenants, covering townlands in the civil parishes of Aglishdrinagh and Cooliney.

O'Murchadha, D., 'Diary of Gen. Richard O'Donovan, 1819–23', JCHAS, 1986 (Lands in West Cork).

Perceval, Lord Egmont: Rentals, 1688–1750, major tenants only, NL Pos. 1355 (1688), NL Pos. 4674 (1701–12, 1713–14), NL Pos. 4675 (1714–19), NL Pos. 4676 (1720–24, 1725–27), NL Pos. 4677 (1728–33), NL Pos. 4678 (1734–38), NL Pos. 4679 (1739–41, 1742–46), NL Pos. 4680 (1747–50), covering townlands in the civil parishes of Aglishdrinagh, Ballyclogh, Bregoge, Brigown, Britway, Buttevant, Castlemagner, Churchtown, Clonfert, Cullin, Dromtarriff, Hackmys, Imphrick, Kilbrin, Kilbrogan, Kilbroney, Kilcaskan, Kilgrogan, Kilmichael, Kilroe, Liscarroll, Rathbarry.

George **Putland**: NL MSS., 1814–1827, eleven rentals of land in Counties Cork, Carlow, Kilkenny, Tipperary and Wicklow, principally major tenants, covering townlands in the civil parishes of Garrycloyne, Matehy and Templeusque.

Thomas **Ronayne**: NL MS. 1721, Rentals 1755–1777, major tenants only, covering townlands in the civil parishes of Carrigaline, Clonmel, Killanully, Kilquane, Middleton and Templerobin.

Shuldam: NL MS. 3025, Estate map 1801–1803, with some tenants' names given, covering townlands in the civil parishes of Dreenagh, Fanlobbus, Iveleary and Kilmichael.

(No landlord given): NL MS. 13018, Rental *c*.1835–37, major tenants only, covering townlands in the civil parishes of Castlelyons, Gortroe, Knockmourne and Rathcormack.

(No landlord given): NL MS. 3273, Rentals 1821, covering all tenants, townlands in the civil parish of Kilmocomoge.

Placenames

Townland Maps, Londonderry Inner City Trust
'Placenames in the parish of Kilcaskan', M. MacCarthaigh, JCHAS, 1980

CO. DERRY

Census returns and substitutes

1618	Survey of Derry City and county, TCD MS. 864 (F.I.9.)
1620–22	Muster Roll, PRONI T.510/2
1628	*Houses and Families in Londonderry, 15 May 1628* (ed. R. G. S. King, 1936)
1630	Muster Roll of Ulster. Armagh Co. Museum, NL Pos. 206 and PRONI T.1759/3C/2
1654/6	Civil Survey, Vol. III. NL I 6551, Dublin
1659	Pender's 'Census', NL Ir. 31041 c 4
1661	Books of Survey and Distribution, PRONI D.1854/1/23 and T.370/C
1663	Hearth Money Roll, NL MS. 9584 and PRONI T.307
1740	Protestant Householders: Aghadowey, Anlow, Artrea, Arigall, Ballinderry, Ballynascreen, Ballyscullion, Balten, Banagher, Beleaghron, Belerashane, Belewillen, Boveva, Coleraine, Comber, Desart, Desartloin, Desertmartin, Drumachose, Dunboe, Dungiven, Faughanvale, Glendermot, Killcranaghen, Killowen, Killylagh, Kilrea, Lissan, Creely, Tamlaghtard, Tamlaght, Templemore, Termoneny. GO 539 and PRONI T.808/15258
1766	Artrea, Desertlin, Magherafelt, NA 1A 46 49; Boveagh, Comber, Drumachose, Inch, NA 1A 41 100; Protestants in Ballynascreen, Banagher, Dungiven, Leck; Desertmartin (all); RCB Library. Also PRONI T.808/15264–7
1796	Catholic migrants from Ulster to Mayo. See Mayo
1796	Spinning-Wheel Premium Lists. Microfiche index in National Archives. Names and parishes of those granted spinning-wheels by the government on the basis of areas planted with flax, comprising, in the case of Co. Londonderry, over 8,000 names
1797–1804	Yeomanry muster rolls, PRONI T.1021/3
1808–13	Freeholders lists, NA M.6199
1813	Freeholders (A–L), PRONI T.2123
1820s/30s	Tithe Books
1829	Census of Protestants, Chapel of the Woods parish, PRONI T.308
1832	Voters List, Londonderry City, PRONI T.1048/1–4
1831	Aghadowey, Aghanloo, Agivey, Arboe, Artrea, Ballinderry, Balteagh, Banagher, Ballyaughran, Ballymoney, Ballynascreen, Ballyrashane, Ballyscullion, Ballywillin, Boveagh, Clondermot, Coleraine, Cumber, Desertlyn, Derryloran, Desertmartin,

Desertoghill, Drumachose, Dunboe, Dungiven, Errigal, Faughan-vale, Kilcrea, Kilcunaghan, Killeagh, Killowen, Lissane, Maghera, Magherafelt, Macosquin, Tamlaght, Tamlaght Finlagan, Tamlaght O'Crilly, Tamlaghtard, Templemore, Termoneny, Killdollagh (Glendermot). National Archives and PRONI MIC5A/6–9

1833–39   Emigrants from Co. Londonderry, in Brian Mitchell, *Irish Emigration Lists, 1833–39*, Baltimore, 1989

1833/4   Emigrant lists, various parishes, Martin, *Historical Gleanings from Co. Derry*, NL Ir. 94112 m 5

1837   Aldermen, Burgesses and Freemen of Coleraine. *Parliamentary Papers*, 1837, Reports from Committees, Vol II (2), Appendix B

1837   Valuation of towns returning MPs (occupants and property values). *Parliamentary Papers*, 1837, Reports from Committees, Vol. II (i), Appendix G

1837   Marksmen (illiterate voters) in parliamentary boroughs: Londonderry and Coleraine. *Parliamentary Papers*, 1837, Reports from Committees, Vol. II (i), Appendix A

c.1840:   Freeholders Register, PRONI D.834/1

1858/9   Griffith's Valuation

1868   Voters List, Londonderry City, PRONI D.1935/6

1901   Census

1911   Census

Local history

Bernard, Nicholas (ed.), *The Whole Proceedings of the Siege of Drogheda* [&] *Londonderry*, Dublin, 1736

Boyle, E. M. F–G., *Records of the town of Limavady, 1609–1808*, Londonderry, 1912, NL Ir. 94112 b 2

Carson, W. R. H., *A bibliography of printed material relating to the county and county borough of Londonderry*, 1969, NL Ir. 914112 c 8

Colby, Col, *Ordnance Survey Memoir of the county of Londonderry*, Dublin, 1837

Ferguson, Rev. S., *Some items of Historic Interest about Waterside* (with tables of householders in Glendermot parish, 1663, 1740), Londonderry, 1902

Graham, Rev. John, *Derriana, a History of the Siege of Derry and the Defence of Enniskillen in 1688 and 1689, with Biographical Notes*, 1823, NL J94112

Henry, Samuel, *The Story of St Patrick's Church, Coleraine*, n.d.

Hughes, Sam, *City on the Foyle*, Londonderry, 1984

Innes R., *Natural History of Magilligan Parish in 1725*

Kernohan, J. W., *The County of Londonderry in Three Centuries*, Belfast, 1921

King, R. G. S., *A Particular of the houses and families in Londonderry, 15/5/1628*. NL Ir. 94112 l 1

Londonderry Voters list, 1868, NL JP 733
Martin, S., *Historical gleanings from Co. Derry*, Dublin 1955, NL Ir. 94112 m 5
Moody. T. W., *The Londonderry plantation. 1609–41*, Belfast 1939, NL Ir. 94112
    m 2
Mullen, Julia, *The Presbytery of Limavady*, Limavady, 1989
Mullen, T. H., *Ballyrashane*, 1969, NL Ir. 9292 m 33
Mullen, T H., *Ulster's Historic City, Derry, Londonderry*, Coleraine, 1986
Mullen, T. H., *Aghadowey*, NL Ir. 94112 m 8
Murray, Rev. Lawrence P., *History of the Parish of Creggan in the Seventeenth and
    Eighteenth Centuries*, Dundalk, 1940
O'Laverty, Rev. James, *An Historical Account of the Dioceses of Down and Connor*,
    4 vols, Dublin, 1878–89
Phillips, Sir Thomas, *Londonderry and the London Companies*, PRONI, Belfast,
    1928
Public Record Office of Northern Ireland, *A Register of Trees for Co.
    Londonderry, 1768–1911*, Belfast, 1984 (including names of tenant planters)
Simpson, Robert, *The Annals of Derry*, Londonderry, 1847
Witherow, Thomas, *Derry and Enniskillen, in the year 1689*, 1873, 1885
Witherow, Thomas (ed.), *A True Relation of the Twenty Week Siege . . .*, London,
    1649
Young, William R., *Fighters of Derry, their Deeds and Descendants*, 1932

Local journals

Benbradagh (Dungiven parish magazine)
Down and Connor Historical Society Magazine, NL Ir. 94115 [*sic*]
Clogher Record (Journal of the Clogher Diocesan Historical Society), NL Ir. 94114 c 2
Derriana (Journal of the Derry Diocesan Historical Society), NL Ir. 27411 d 4
South Derry Historical Society Journal, NL Ir. 914112 s 21

Directories

1820	J. Pigot, *Commercial Directory of Ireland*
1824	Pigot and Co., *City of Dublin and Hibernian Provincial Directory*, NL Ir. 9141 p 75
1835	William Matier, *Belfast Directory*
1842	Mathew Martin, *Belfast Directory*
1846	Slater's *National Commercial Directory of Ireland*
1852	James A. Henderson, *Belfast and Province of Ulster Directory*, issued also in 1854, 1856, 1858, 1861, 1863, 1865, 1868, 1870, 1877, 1880, 1884, 1887, 1890, 1894, 1900
1856	Slater's *Royal National Commercial Directory of Ireland*
1865	R. Wynne, *Business Directory of Belfast*

1870   Slater's *Directory of Ireland*
1881   Slater's *Royal National Commercial Directory of Ireland*
1887   *Derry Almanac*
1894   Slater's *Royal Commercial Directory of Ireland*

Estate records

Desertmartin Estate Rentals, *Derriana*, 1981–82.

Gravestone inscriptions

Ballinderry: *South Derry Historical Society Journal*, 1982/3
Derry City: Irish World (see below)
Eglish: *South Derry Historical Society Journal*, 1981/2
Magherafelt (Old): *South Derry Historical Society Journal*, 1980/81
Old Glendermot: (unpub.) National Archives, search room
     Irish World (26 Market Square, Dungannon, Co. Tyrone, BT70 1AB)
have transcribed and computerised the inscriptions of more than 300
graveyards in the six counties of Northern Ireland, principally in the four
western counties of Armagh, Derry, Fermanagh and Tyrone.

Placenames

Munn, A. M., *Note on the placenames (. . .) of Derry*, NL Ir. 92942 m 18
Townland maps, Londonderry Inner City Trust

CO. DONEGAL

Census returns and substitutes

1612–13   'Survey of Undertakers Planted in Co. Donegal', *Historical Manus-
          cripts Commission Report*, 4 (Hastings MSS.), 1947, 159–82
1630   Muster Roll, *Donegal Annual*, Vol. X, No. 2. NL Pos. 206
1641   Book of Survey and Distribution, NL MS. 968
1654   Civil Survey, Vol. III, I 6551 Dublin
1659   Pender's 'Census', NL Ir. 31041 c 4
1665   Hearth Money Roll, GO 538, NL MS. 9583, PRONI T.307/D
1740   Protestant Householders: parishes of Clonmeny, Culdaff, Desert-
          egney, Donagh, Fawne, Movill, Templemore. GO 539

1761–75	Freeholders NL P. 975; GO MS. 442; PRONI T.808/14999
1766	Donoghmore parish, NA m 207/8; Protestants in Leck, NA 1A 41 100
1770	Freeholders entitled to vote, NL MSS. 987–8
1782	Persons in Culdaff, *300 Years in Inishowen*, Amy Young
1796	Spinning-Wheel Premium Lists. Microfiche index in National Archives, comprising, in the case of Co. Donegal, over 14,000 names
1799	Protestant Householders, Templecrone parish, *The Irish Ancestor*, 1984
1802/3	Protestants in part of Culdaff parish, *300 Years in Inishowen*, Amy Young
1820s/30s	Tithe Books
1857	Griffith's Valuation
1901	Census
1911	Census

Local history

Allingham, H., *Ballyshannon: its history and antiquities (with some account of the surrounding neighbourhood)*, Londonderry, 1879, NL Ir. 94113 a 1

Conaghan, Pat, *Bygones: New Horizons on the History of Killybegs*, Killybegs, 1989

Doherty, William J., *Inis-Owen and Tirconnel: being some account of the antiquities . . . of Donegal*, Dublin, 1895, NL Ir. 94113 d 1

Harkin, William, *Scenery and Antiquities of North West Donegal*, 1893

Hill, George, *Facts from Gweedore*, Dublin, 1854

Lucas, Leslie W., *Mevagh Down the Years*, Belfast, 1983

MacDonagh, J. C. T., 'Bibliography of Co. Donegal', *Donegal Hist. Soc. Jnl*, 1947–50, 217–30

Maguire, V. Rev. Canon, *The History of the Diocese of Raphoe*, 2 vols, Dublin

Shearman, H., *Ulster*, London, 1949 (incl. bibliographies), NL Ir. 91422 s 3

Swan, H. P., *The Book of Inishowen*, Buncrana, 1938

Young, Amy, *300 Years in Inishowen*, Belfast, 1929, NL Ir. 9292 y 1

Local journals

Donegal Annual, NL Ir. 94113 d 3

Journal of the Donegal Historical Society (1947–51), as above

Clogher Record (Journal of the Clogher Diocesan Historical Society), NL Ir. 94114 c 2

Derriana (Journal of the Derry Diocesan Historical Society), NL Ir. 27411 d 4

Directories

| 1824 | Pigot and Co., *City of Dublin and Hibernian Provincial Directory*, NL Ir. 9141 P 75 |

1839 *Directory of the Towns of Sligo, Enniskillen, Ballyshannon Donegal, etc.*
1846 Slater's *National Commercial Directory of Ireland*
1854 James A. Henderson, *Belfast and Province of Ulster Directory*, issued also in 1856, 1858, 1861, 1863, 1865, 1868, 1870, 1877, 1880, 1884, 1887, 1890, 1894, 1900
1856 Slater's *Royal National Commercial Directory of Ireland*
1870 Slater's *Directory of Ireland*
1881 Slater's *Royal National Commercial Directory of Ireland*
1887 *Derry Almanac*, annually from this year
1894 Slater's *Royal Commercial Directory of Ireland*

Gravestone inscriptions

Assaroe Abbey: *Donegal Annual*, Vol. III, No. 3, 1957
Ballyshannon: *Donegal Annual*, Vol. XII, No. 2, 1978, see also Allingham (above: 'Local history')
Finner: *Where Erne and Drowes Meet the Sea*, P. O'Gallachair
Inver C. of I.: IGRS Collection, GO
Killaghtee: IGRS Collection, 31, GO
St Catherine's (old) Killybegs: IGRS Collection, GO
SS. Conal and Joseph: IGRS Collection, GO

Estate records

LANDLORD
Thomas **Connolly**, Henry **Bruen**, H. G. **Cooper**, Sarah E. **Connolly**, Sale of estates of with rentals, Parishes of Drumholme, Donegal, Ballyshannon, NL ILB 347 1 15.
William **Connolly**: Lives in leases on the Ballyshannon estate, 1718–58, NL MS. 5751, and *Donegal Annual*, No. 33, 1981 (1718–26).
A. **Murry-Stewart**: Rentals, 1842, 1845, including lands in the parishes of Killymard, Killybegs, Killaughtee, Kilcar, Innisgale, NL MS. 5465, 5466.
H. G. **Murry-Stewart**: Rentals, 1847–1859, including lands in the parishes of Killymard, Killybegs, Killaughtee, Kilcar, Innisgale, NL MSS. 5467–5476.

Placenames

Townland maps, Londonderry Inner City Trust

CO. DOWN

Census returns and substitutes

1630	Muster Roll of Ulster. Armagh Co. Library, NL Pos. 206, PRONI D.1759/3C/1
1642–43	Muster Roll, PRONI T.563/1
1642	Donaghadee Muster Roll, PRONI T.2736/1
1659	Pender's 'Census', NL Ir. 31041, c 4
1661	Books of Survey and Distribution, PRONI T.370/A and D.1854/1/18
1663	Subsidy Roll. NL Pos. 206; NA M.2745; PRONI T.307
1708	Householders in Downpatrick town, *The City of Downe*, R. E. Parkinson, NL Ir. 94115 p 1
1740	Protestant Householders (part), PRONI T.808/15258
1766	Kilbroney, Seapatrick, Inch, Shankill, NL MS. 4173
1777	Freeholders Register (also 1780–95), PRONI DOW 5/3/1 and 2
1789	'Deputy Court Cheque Book' (votes cast), PRONI D.654/A3/1B
*c.*1790	Lecale Barony freeholders, PRONI T.393/1
1796	Catholic migrants from Ulster to Mayo, see Mayo
1796	Spinning-Wheel Premium Lists. Microfiche index in National Archives, comprising, in the case of Co. Down, over 5,000 names
1798	Persons who Suffered Losses in the 1798 Rebellion. NL I 94107
1799–1800	Militia Pay Lists and Muster Rolls, PRONI T.1115/4A–C
1813–21	Freeholders, PRONI T.761/19
1815–46	Downpatrick electors, NL MS. 7235
1821	Various parishes, Thrift Abstracts, National Archives
1824	Freeholders, PRONI T.761/20
1820s/30s	Tithe Books
1832–37	Belfast Poll Book, PRONI D.2472
1837	Valuation of towns returning MPs (occupants and property values): Newry. *Parliamentary Papers*, 1837, Reports from Committees, Vol. II (i), Appendix G
1837	Marksmen (illiterate voters) in parliamentary boroughs: Newry, Downpatrick. *Parliamentary Papers*, 1837, Reports from Committees, Vol. II (i), Appendix A
1841–61	Religious censuses, parish of Scarva, RCBL MS. 65
1851	Various Parishes. Thrift Abstracts, National Archives
1851/61	Census of Presbyterian Parishioners of Loughinisland, *Family Links*, Vol. 1 Nos 5 and 7, 1982/83
1852	Poll Book (votes cast), incomplete, PRONI D.671/02/5–6
1855	Belfast Register of Electors, PRONI BELF5/1/1/1–2
1857	Poll Book (votes cast), incomplete, PRONI D.671/02/7–8

1863/4 Griffith's Valuation, Belfast—Alphabetical index to householders, All-Ireland Heritage microfiche, National Archives

1876 Belfast Register of Electors, PRONI BELF5/1/1/1–2

1901 Census

1911 Census

Local history

The Ards: a local history source list, NL Ir. 914115 p 15

Atkinson, Edward D., *An Ulster Parish: Being a History of Donaghcloney*, 1898 (Waringstown, Co. Down)

Castlereagh: some local sources, NL Ir. 914115 p 15

Clandeboye: a reading guide, NL Ir. 914115 p 15

Cowan, J. Davison, *An Ancient Parish, Past and Present; being the Parish of Donaghmore, County Down*, London, 1914, NL Ir. 94115 c 1

Crossle, Francis, *Local Jottings of Newry Collected and Transcribed* (Vols 1–34), Newry, 1890–1910

Donaghadee: a local history list, NL Ir. 9411 s 12

Ewart, L. M., *Handbook to the dioceses of Down, Connor and Dromore*

Haddock, Josiah, *A Parish Miscellany, Donaghcloney*

Hamilton, William, *The Hamilton Manuscripts* (containing some account of the settlement of the territories of Upper Clandeboye, Great Ares and Dufferin . . . in the reigns of James I and Charles I), (ed. T. K. Lowry), Belfast 1867. NL Ir. 94115 h 1

Harris, Walter, *The Ancient and Present State of the County of Down*, Dublin, 1744, I 94115 h 2

Hill, Rev. George, *Montgomery Manuscripts, 1603–1706*, Belfast, 1869

Keenan, Padraic, *Historical Sketch of the Parish of Clonduff*, Newry, 1941

Killyleagh and Crossegar: a local history list, NL Ir. 914115 p 15

Knox, Alexander, *History of the County Down*, Dublin, 1875

Linn, Capt. Richard, *A history of Banbridge* (ed. W. S. Kerr), Belfast, 1935, (including Tullylish)

O'Laverty, Rev. James, *The History of the Parish of Hollywood*, n.d.

O'Laverty, Rev. James, *An Historical Account of the Dioceses of Down and Connor*, 4 vols, Dublin, 1878–89

Parkinson, Edward, *The City of Down from its earliest days*, Belfast, 1928

Pilson, A., *Downpatrick and its Parish Church* (including lists of clergy and churchwardens), 1852. P 1938

Pooler, L. A., *Down and its Parishes*, 1907

Reside, S. W., *St Mary's Church, Newry: its History*, 1933

Shearman, H., *Ulster*, London, 1949 (incl. bibliographies), NL Ir. 91422 s 3

Smith, Charles, and Harris, Walter, *The ancient and present state of the county of Down*, Dublin, 1744, I 94115 h 2

Smith, K., Bangor Reading List, *Journal of the Bangor H.S.*
Stevenson, John, *Two Centuries of Life in Down, 1600–1800*, Belfast, 1920
Stewart, Rev. D., *Tullylish, Parish of: Historical Notes*

Local journals

Down and Connor Historical Society Magazine, NL Ir. 94115 [*sic*]
East Belfast Historical Society Journal (from 1981)
Journal of the Bangor Historical Society
Lecale Miscellany (from 1983)
Old Newry Journal (from 1977)
Saintfield Heritage
Seanchas Dhroim Mor (Journal of the Dromore Diocesan Historical Society), NL Ir.
    94115 s 3
Upper Ards Historical Society Journal, NL Ir. 94115 u 1

Directories

1819   Thomas Bradshaw, *General Directory of Newry, Armagh, Dungannon, Porta-down, Tandragee, Lurgan, Waringstown, Banbridge, Warrenpoint, Rostrevor, Kilkeel and Rathfryland*
1820   J. Pigot, *Commercial Directory of Ireland*
1820   Joseph Smyth, *Directory of Belfast and its Vicinity*
1824   Pigot and Co., *City of Dublin and Hibernian Provincial Directory*, NL Ir. 9141 p 75
1841   Mathew Martin, *Belfast Directory*, issued also in 1842
1846   Slater's *National Commercial Directory of Ireland*
1852   James A. Henderson, *Belfast and Province of Ulster Directory*, issued also in 1854, 1856, 1858, 1861, 1863, 1865, 1868, 1870, 1877, 1880, 1884, 1887, 1890, 1894, 1900
1856   Slater's *Royal National Commercial Directory of Ireland*
1865   R. Wynne, *Business Directory of Belfast*
1870   Slater's *Directory of Ireland*
1881   Slater's *Royal National Commercial Directory of Ireland*
1883   S. Farrell, *County Armagh Directory and Almanac*
1894   Slater's *Royal Commercial Directory of Ireland*

Gravestone inscriptions

Vols 1–19, R. S. J. Clarke, 1966–81, NL Ir. 9295 c 1

Aghlisnafin, Vol. 9
Annahilt, Vol. 18
Ardkeen, Vol. 13
Ardglass, Vol. 8
Ardquin, Vol. 13
Baileysmill, Vol. 2
Ballee, Vol. 8
Balligan, Vol. 14
Balloo, Vol. 17
Ballyblack, Vol. 12
Ballycarn, Vol. 3
Ballycopeland, Vol. 16
Ballycranbeg, Vol. 13
Ballycruttle, Vol. 8
Ballyculter, Vol. 8
Ballygalget, Vol. 13
Ballygowan, Vol. 5
Ballyhalbert, Vol. 15
Ballyhemlin, Vol. 14
Ballykinler, Vol. 9
Ballymacashin, Vol. 6
Ballymageogh, Vol. 10
Ballymartin, Vol. 10
Ballynahinch,Vol. 9
Ballyphilip, Vol 13
Ballytrastan, Vol. 13
Bangor, Vol. 17
Barr, *An Ancient Irish
    Parish*, J. D. Cowan
Blaris, Vol. 5
Boardmills, Vol. 2
Breda, Vol. 1
Bright, Vol. 8
Cargacreevy, Vol. 18
Carrowdore, Vol 14
Carryduff, Vols 1 and 18
Castlereagh, Vol. 1

Clandeboye, Vol. 17
Cloghy, Vol. 14
Clough, Vol. 9,
Comber, Vol. 5
Copeland Islands, Vol. 16
Donaghadee, Vol. 16
Donaghcloney, *An Ulster Parish*
    E. D. Atkinson
Donaghmore, *An Ancient Irish
    Parish*, J. D. Cowan
Downpatrick, Vol. 7
Dromara, Vol. 19
Dromore, Vol. 19
Drumaroad, Vol. 9
Drumbeg, Vol. 3
Drumbo, Vols 1, 4 and 18
Dundonald, Vol. 2
Dunsfort, Vol. 8
Edenderry, Vol. 3
Eglantine, Vol. 18
Gilnahirk, Vol. 18
Glasdrumman, Vol. 10
Glastry, Vol. 15
Glansha, Vol. 1
Greyabbey, Vol. 12
Groomsport, Vol. 17
Hillhall, Vol. 1
Hillsborough, Vol. 18
Holywood, Vol. 14
Inch, Vol. 7
Inishargy, Vol. 14
Kilcarn, Vol. 5
Kilclief, Vol. 8
Kilhorne, Vol. 10
Kilkeel, Vol. 10
Killarney, Vol. 2
Kilarsey, Vol. 6

Killinakin, Vol. 6

Killinchy, Vols 5 and 6

Killough, Vol. 8

Killybawn, Vol. 1

Killyleagh, Vols 6 and 7

Killysuggan, Vol. 5

Kilmegan, Vol. 9

Kilmood, Vol. 5

Kilmore, Vol. 3

Kilwarlin, Vol. 18

Kircubbin, Vol. 12

Knock, Vol. 4

Knockbreckan, Vols 1 and 18

Knockbreda, Vol. 2

Legacurry, Vol. 2

Lisbane, Vol. 13

Loughaghery, Vol. 18

Loughinisland, Vols 9 and 12

Magheradrool, Vols 9 and 12

Magherahamlet, Vol. 9

Magheralin, Vol. 19

Maze, Vol. 18

Millisle, Vol. 16

Moira, Vol. 18

Moneyrea, Vol. 1

Mourne, Vol. 10

Movilla, Vol. 11

Newtownards, Vol. 11

Old Court, Vol. 8

Portaferry, Vol. 13

Rademan, Vol. 3

Raffrey, Vol. 5

Rathmullen, Vol. 9

Ravara, Vol. 5

Saintfield, Vol. 3

Saul, Vols 7 and 8

Seaforde, Vol. 9

Slanes, Vol. 14

Tamlaght, Vol. 10

Templepatrick, Vol. 14

Tullymacnous, Vol. 6

Tullynakill, Vol. 1

Waringstown, *An Ulster Parish*,
   E. D. Atkinson

Whitechurch, Vol. 15

BELFAST INSCRIPTIONS

Christ Church, Vol. 1

Shankill, Vol. 1

Milltown, Vol. 2

Balmoral Friend's, Vol. 3

St George's, Vol. 1

Friar's Bush, Vol. 2

Balmoral, Vol. 3

Malone Presbyterian, Vol. 3

Placenames

Townland maps, Londonderry Inner City Trust

CO. DUBLIN

Census returns and substitutes

1568	Herald's Visitation of Dublin, GO 46; NL Pos. 957
1607	Herald's Visitation of Dublin City, GO 48; NL Pos. 8286
1610	Herald's Visitation of Dublin county, GO 48; NL Pos. 8286
1621	St John's parish cess lists, also for years 1640 and 1687, Appendix to Vol. 1 of the Parish Register Society, 1906
1634	Subsidy roll, NA M.2469
1641	Book of Survey and Distribution, NL MS. 964
1652	Inhabitants of the baronies of Newcastle and Uppercross, NA 1A 41 100
1654–56	Civil Survey, Vol. VII, Irish Manuscripts Commission
1659	Pender's 'Census'
1663–68	Subsidy roll for Co. Dublin, NA M.2468
1663	Hearth Money Roll for parts of Counties Dublin and Kildare, *Kildare Arch. Soc. Jnl*, Vol. X, 245
1664	Persons with 6 hearths or upwards, Dublin City, RDKPRO 57, 560
1667–1810	Assessments for the parish of St Bride's, TCD M.2063
1680–86	Index to an applotment book for Dublin City, NA M.4979
1680	Pipe water accounts, *The Irish Genealogist*, 1987
1696	Poll tax assessments for 1696 and 1699, NA M.2469
1711–1835	Annual Cess Applotment books of St Michan's parish, RCBL
1730–40	Index to marriages and deaths in *Pue's Occurrences* and *The Dublin Gazette*, NL MS. 3197
1756	Inhabitants of St Michael's parish, *The Irish Builder*, Vol. 33, 701/1
1763–71	Index to *Freeman's Journal*, Dublin, NL reading room counter
1766	Religious census, Parishes of Castleknock, Taney, Donnybrook, Crumlin, RCB Library, Crumlin; also in GO 537
1767	Freeholders, Dublin City, NA M.4910–2
1778–82	Catholic Merchants, Traders and Manufacturers of Dublin, *Reportorium Novum* 2 (2), 1960, 298–323
1791–1831	Register of children at Baggot St school (Incorporated Soc. for Promoting Protestant Schools), NL Pos. 2884
1791–1957	Register of Admissions to Pleasant's Female Orphan Asylum, including places of birth and families, NL MS. 1555. See also NL MSS. 1556 and 1558
1793–1810	Census of Protestants in Castleknock, GO 495
1798	List of persons who suffered loss of property in 1798, NL JLB 94107

1798–1836 Register of children at Santry school (Incorporated Soc. for Promoting Protestant Schools), NL Pos. 2884
1800–1816 Card index to biographical notices in *Faulkner's Dublin Journal*, NL
1805–39   Register of children at Kevin St school (Incorporated Soc. for Promoting Protestant Schools), NL Pos. 2884
1806   Voters Lists, by occupation, Dublin City, Ir. 94133 d 13
1820   Freemen voters, NL P 734
1821   Some extracts. Thrift Abstracts, National Archives
1820s/30s Tithe Books
1830   Freeholders, Dublin City and county, NL MS. 11, 847
1831   Householders in St Bride's parish, NL P. 1994
1834/5   Returns of those liable for paving-tax. Inquiry into the impeachment of Alderman Richard Smith, State Paper Office
1835   Dublin City Parliamentary Election (Alphabetical list of voters with addresses and occupations), Ir. 94133 d 12
1835–37   Dublin county freeholders and leaseholders, NL MS. 9363
1840–1938 Admissions and Discharge registers for Dublin City workhouses (North and South Union), National Archives
1841   Voters Lists, Dublin City, Ir. 94133 d 15
1841   Some extracts. Thrift Abstracts, National Archives
1848/51   Griffith's Valuation. Alphabetical index to householders on microfiche in National Archives
1851   Index to heads of households, by street and parish, National Archives
1864   City of Dublin Voters List, by district and street, Ir. 94133 d 16
1865/6   Voters Lists, Dublin City, Ir. 94133 d 15
1878   Parliamentary Voters, South Dock Ward, NL ILB 324 d
1901   Census
1911   Census

Local history

Adams, B. N., *History and Description of Santry and Cloghran Parishes*, Dublin, 1883
Alphabetical list of the constituency of the University of Dublin, 1865, Ir. 37841 t 2 and 1832; JP 1375; also LO
Appleyard, D. S., *Green Fields Gone Forever*, Ir. 94133 a 5 (Coolock and Artane area)
Ball, F. E., *A history of the county of Dublin*, Dublin, 1902–20, Ir. 94133 b 1:

1. Monkstown, Kill-o'-the Grange, Dalkey, Killiney, Tully, Stillorgan, Kilmacud
2. Donnybrook, Booterstown, St Bartholomew, St Mark, Taney, St Peter, Rathfarnham

3. Tallaght, Cruagh, Whitechurch, Kilgobbin, Kiltiernan, Rathmichael, Old Connaught, Saggart, Rathcoole, Newcastle.
4. Clonsilla, Leixlip, Lucan, Aderrig, Kilmactalway, Kilbride, Kilmahuddrick, Esker, Palmerstown, Ballyfermot, Clondalkin, Drimnagh, Crumlin, St Catherine, St Nicholas Without, St James, St Jude, Chapelizod
5. Howth
6. Castleknock, Mulhuddert, Cloghran, Ward, St Margaret's, Finglas, Glasnevin, Grangegorman, St George, Clonturk

Blacker, Rev. Beaver H., *Sketches of the Parishes of Booterstown and Donnybrook*, 1860–74

Clarke, Mary, 'Sources for Genealogical Research in Dublin Corporation Archives', *The Irish Genealogist*, 1987

Craig, Maurice, *Dublin 1660–1800*, Dublin, 1952

Cullen, L. N., *Princes and Pirates: the Dublin Chamber of Commerce, 1783–1983*, Ir. 94133 c 17

Donnelly, N., Series of short histories of Dublin parishes, Ir. 27413 d 1

Donnelly, N., *State of RC Chapels in Dublin 1749*, I 2820941 p 10

Doolin, W., *Dublin's Surgeon Anatomists*, Ir. 610 p 4

Dublin in Books: A reading list from the stock of Dublin Public Libraries (1982), Ir. 01 p 9

See Dublin under 'Municipal Council' (in NL Author Catalogue) for reports of various corporation meetings, lists of freemen, aldermen, bailiffs etc.

Gilbert, Sir John T., *A History of the City of Dublin*, Dublin, 1854–59

Gilbert Library: Dublin and Irish Collections, Ir. 02 p 50

Harris, Walter, *The History and Antiquities of the City of Dublin*, Dublin, 1776

Harrison, W., *Dublin Houses/or Memorable Dublin Houses, 1890*, Ir. 94133 h 5

Kingston, Rev. John, *The Parish of Fairview*: 'Including the present parishes of Corpus Christi, Glasnevin, Larkhill, Marino, and Donnycarney', Dundalk, 1953

Lawler, Hugh J., *The Fasti of St Patrick's, Dublin*, 1930

Le Fanu, T. P., *The Huguenot Churches of Dublin and their Ministries* (1905), P. 2274

MacGiolla Phadraig, Brian, *History of Terenure*, Dublin, 1954

MacSorley, Catherine M., *The Story of Our parish: St Peter's Dublin*, Dublin, 1917

Maxwell, Constantia, *Dublin under the Georges, 1714–1830*, London, 1956, Ir. 94133 h 5

McCready, C. T., *Dublin street names, dated and explained*, Dublin, 1892 (including bibliography), Ir. 92941 m 1 (and LO)

Monks, W., *Lusk, a Short History*, Ir. 9141 p 85

O'Driscoll, J., *Cnucha: a history of Castleknock and district*, Ir. 94133 o 9

Shepherd, E., *Behind the Scenes: the story of Whitechurch district*, Ir. 94133 s 8

St Peter's Parochial Male and Female Boarding Schools, Sunday, Daily and Infant Schools: Reports 1850–60, P. 439

Stephen's Green Club, list of members, 1882, Ir. 367 s 12

Warburton, John, Whitlow, James, and Walsh, Robert, *History of the City of Dublin*, London, 1818

Local journals

Dublin Historical Record (Journal of the Old Dublin Society), Ir. 94133 d 23
Reportorium Novum: Dublin diocesan historical record, Ir. 27413 r 3

Directories

1751 Peter Wilson, 'An Alphabetical List of the Names and Places of Abode of the Merchants and Traders of the City of Dublin', issued annually as part of *The Treble Almanack*, from 1755 to 1837
1820 J. Pigot, *Commercial Directory of Ireland*
1824 Pigot and Co., *City of Dublin and Hibernian Provincial Directory*, NL Ir. 9141 p 75
1834 Pettigrew and Oulton, *Dublin Almanack and General Register of Ireland*, issued annually from 1834 to 1849
1844 Alexander Thom, *Irish Almanack and Official Directory*, issued annually from 1844
1846 Slater's *National Commercial Directory of Ireland*
1856 Slater's *Royal National Commercial Directory of Ireland*
1870 Slater's *Directory of Ireland*
1881 Slater's *Royal National Commercial Directory of Ireland*
1894 Slater's *Royal Commercial Directory of Ireland*

Gravestone inscriptions

Abbotstown (Castleknock): IGRS Collection, 29, GO. Also GO MS. 622, 89
Baldoyle, old: IGRS Collection, 3, GO
Chapelizod: *The Irish Genealogist*, Vol. V, No. 4, 1977
Cloghran: *History and Description of Santry and Cloghran Parishes*, B. W. Adams, 1883
Clondalkin (Kilmahuddrick): IGRS, Dublin City and County Gravestone Inscriptions, Vol. 2 (unpub.), NA Search Room and GO
Clondalkin (Mount St Joseph): IGRS Dublin City and County Gravestone Inscriptions, Vol. 2 (unpub.), NA Search Room and GO
Cloghran, south: IGRS Collection, 11, GO
Dalkey: *The Irish Genealogist*, Vol. V, No. 2, 1975
Dublin City: Christ Church, *Inscriptions on the monuments (. . .) in Christ Church (. . .)*, John Finlayson, 1878
   Crumlin: *The Irish Genealogist*, Vol. 7, No. 3, 1988
   Goldenbridge: IGRS Dublin City and County Gravestone Inscriptions, Vol. 1 (unpub.), NA Search Room and GO

Huguenot cemetery, Merrion Row, 1693: IGRS Dublin City and County Gravestone Inscriptions, Vol. 2 (unpub.), NA Search Room and GO; Parkinson, Dublin Family History Society, 1988

Jewish Graveyard, Fairview Strand: IGRS Collection, 137, GO

Merrion: IGRS Dublin City and County Gravestone Inscriptions, Vol. 2 (unpub.), NA Search Room and GO

St Andrew's (coffin plates): *The Irish Genealogist*, Vol. V, No. 1, 1974

St Andrew's (interior): IGRS Collection, 50, GO

St Catherine's, S. Murphy, Divelina, 1987

St James' (C. of I.): (unpub.), National Archives Search Room

St Matthew's (C. of I.), Ringsend: IGRS Dublin City and County Gravestone Inscriptions, Vol. 2 (unpub.), NA Search Room and GO

SS. Michael and John (coffin plates): *The Irish Genealogist*, Vol. V, No. 3, 1976

St Paul's (C. of I.): JRSAI, Vol. CIV, 1974

St Paul's (C. of I. graveyard): IGRS Collection, 6,

Kilbarrack: IGRS Collection, 38, GO

Kilbride (Baldonnell): IGRS, Dublin City and County Gravestone Inscriptions, Vol. 2 (unpub.), NA Search Room and GO

Killiney (old churchyard): *The Irish Genealogist*, Vol. IV, No. 6, 1973

Kill o' the Grange: *The Irish Genealogist*, Vol. IV, No. 5, 1972

Kilmactalway (Castle Bagot, Baldonnell): IGRS Dublin City and County Gravestone Inscriptions, Vol. 2 (unpub.), NA Search Room and GO

Kilternan (C. of I. interior): IGRS Collection, 18, GO

Kilternan (old): IGRS Dublin City and County Gravestone Inscriptions, Vol. 2 (unpub.), NA Search Room and GO

Leixlip: *The Irish Genealogist*, Vol. IV, No. 2, 1969

Lucan: *The Irish Genealogist*, Vol. V, No. 6, 1976

Lucan (Esker old): IGRS Dublin City and County Gravestone Inscriptions, Vol. 2 (unpub.), NA Search Room and GO

Lucan (St Mary's): IGRS Dublin City and County Gravestone Inscriptions, Vol. 2 (unpub.), NA Search Room and GO

Monkstown: *The Irish Genealogist*, Vol. IV, Nos 3 and 4, 1970/1

Mulhuddert: GO MS. 622, 96

Newcastle (C. of I.): IGRS Dublin City and County Gravestone Inscriptions, Vol. 2 (unpub.), NA Search Room and GO

Newcastle (Loughtown Lr): IGRS Dublin City and County Gravestone Inscriptions, Vol. 2 (unpub.), NA Search Room and GO

Newcastle (R.C.): IGRS Dublin City and County Gravestone Inscriptions, Vol. 2, (Unpub.), NA Search Room and GO

Old Connaught: IGRS Collection, 54, GO

Palmerstown: *The Irish Genealogist*, Vol. V, No. 8, 1978

Portmarnock old: IGRS Collection, 81, GO

Portmarnock (C. of I.): IGRS Collection, GO
Rathcoole: IGRS Dublin City and County Gravestone Inscriptions, Vol. 2
    (unpub.), NA Search Room and GO
Rathfarnham: *The Irish Genealogist*, 1987
Rathmichael: IGRS Collection, 31, GO
St Doolough's, Balgriffin: IGRS Collection, 48, GO
Santry: *History and Description of Santry and Cloghran Parishes*, B. W. Adams, 1883
Tallaght: *The Irish Genealogist*, Vol. IV, No. 1, 1968
Taney: *The Parish of Taney*, F. E. Ball, 1895
Tully: IGRS Collection, 50, GO
Whitechurch: *The Irish Genealogist*, 1990

Estate records

Claremorris estate rental, Galway, Mayo, Dublin, 1833, NL.

Placenames

Placenames of Dublin, The O'Rahilly, Ir. 92942 o 2
Parish Guide to the Archdiocese of Dublin (1958) Ir. 27413 d 3

CO. FERMANAGH

Census returns and substitutes

1612–13	'Survey of Undertakers Planted in Co. Fermanagh', *Historical Manuscripts Commission Report*, 4 (Hastings MSS.), 1947, 159–82
1630	Muster Roll, PRONI T.808/15164
1631	Muster Roll, *History of Enniskillen*, W. C. Trimble
1659	Pender's 'Census', Ir. 31041 c 4
1661	Books of Survey and Distribution, PRONI T.370/B and D.1854/1/20
1662	Subsidy roll (Enniskillen), NL MS. 9583; PRONI T.808/15068
1665	Hearth Money Roll, NL MS. 9583, *Clogher Record*, 1957; PRONI T.808/15066
1747	Poll Book (votes cast), PRONI T.808/15063
1766	Boho, Derryvullen, Devenish, Kinawley, Rossory, NA m. 2476 (d)

1770	Freeholders, GO 443, NL MS. 787–8
1788	Poll Book (votes cast), PRONI T.808/15075, T.543, T.1385
1794–99	Militia Pay Lists and Muster Rolls, PRONI T.1115/5A–C
1796	Catholic migrants from Ulster to Mayo. See Mayo
1796–1802	Freeholders, PRONI D.1096/90
1797	Yeomanry Muster Rolls, PRONI T.1021/3
1821	Parishes of Aghalurcher (part) and Derryvullen, NA and PRONI
1820s/30s	Tithe Books
1832	Enniskillen registered voters. Reports from Committees, *Parliamentary Papers*, 1837–38, Vol. 13 (2), 554–7
1837	Freeholders. Reports from Committees, *Parliamentary Papers*, 1837–38, Vol. 11 (1), (39) 7–21
1841	Certified copies of census returns for use in claims for old age pensions. National Archives and PRONI
1851	Townland of Clonee, parish of Drumkeeran. Certified copies of census returns for use in claims for old age pensions, National Archives
c.1861	Protestant inhabitants of Boho parish, NA T.3723
1862	Griffith's Valuation. Alphabetical index to householders, on microfiche, National Archives
1901	Census
1911	Census

Local history

Belmore, Earl of, *Parliamentary Memoirs of Fermanagh and Tyrone, 1613–1885*, Dublin, 1887

Bradshaw, W. H., *Enniskillen Long Ago: an Historic Sketch of the Parish . . .*, 1878

Dundas, W. H., *Enniskillen parish and town*, 1913, Dundalk, Ir. 94118 d 2

Graham, Rev. John, *Derriana, a History of the Siege of Derry and the Defence of Enniskillen in 1688 and 1689, with Biographical Notes*, 1823

King, Sir Charles (ed.), *Henry's 'Upper Lough Erne in 1739'*, Dublin, 1892

MacKenna, J. E., *Devenish, its history, antiquities and traditions*, 1897

Martin, S., *Historical gleanings from Co. Derry (and some from Fermanagh)*, Dublin, 1955, Ir. 94112 m 5

O'Connell, Philip, *The Diocese of Kilmore: its History and Antiquities*, Dublin, 1937

Shearman, H., *Ulster*, London, 1949 (incl. bibliographies), Ir. 91422 s 3

Steele, W. B., *The parish of Devenish*, 1937

Trimble, W., *The history of Enniskillen*, Vols I–III, Enniskillen, 1921, Ir. 94118 t 1

Directories

1824	Pigot and Co., *City of Dublin and Hibernian Provincial Directory*, NL Ir. 9141 p 75

1839   *Directory of the Towns of Sligo, Enniskillen, Ballyshannon, Donegal, etc.*
1846   Slater's *National Commercial Directory of Ireland*
1852   James A. Henderson, *Belfast and Province of Ulster Directory*, issued also
        in 1854, 1856, 1858, 1861, 1863, 1865, 1868, 1870, 1877, 1880, 1884,
        1887, 1890, 1894, 1900
1856   Slater's *Royal National Commercial Directory of Ireland*
1870   Slater's *Directory of Ireland*
1881   Slater's *Royal National Commercial Directory of Ireland*
1887   *Derry Almanac*, annually from this year
1894   Slater's *Royal Commercial Directory of Ireland*

Local journals

Clogher Record (Journal of the Clogher Diocesan Historical Society), Ir. 94114 c 2

Gravestone inscriptions

Aghalurcher: *Clogher Record*, Vol. II, No. 2, 1958
Aghavea: *Clogher Record*, Vol. IV, Nos 1 and 2, 1960/1
Devenish: St Molaise's and Devenish Abbey: *Devenish, its History, Antiquities,
    and Traditions,* J. E. MacKenna, F. E. Bigger, 1897
Donagh: *Clogher Record*, Vol. 1, No. 3, 1955
Drumully: *Clogher Record*, Vol. 1, No. 2, 1954
Enniskillen: *Enniskillen Parish and Town*, W. H. Dundas, 1913
Galoon: *Clogher Record*, Vol. X, No. 2, 1980
Holywell: *Clogher Record*, Vol. II, No. 1, 1957
Kinawley: *Clogher Record*, Vol. I, No. 4 1956
Monea: *The Parish of Devenish*, W. B. Steele, 1937
Templenafrin: *Clogher Record*, Vol. II, No. 1, 1957
Tullymageeran: *Clogher Record*, Vol. II, No. 3, 1959

Irish World (26 Market Square, Dungannon, Co. Tyrone, BT70 1AB) have
transcribed and computerised the inscriptions of more than 300 graveyards in
the six counties of Northern Ireland, principally in the four western counties of
Armagh, Derry, Fermanagh and Tyrone.

Placenames

Townland maps, Londonderry Inner City Trust

CO. GALWAY

Census returns and substitutes

1640	Irish Papist Proprietors, Galway Town. In Hardiman (see 'Local History' below), Appendix 7
1641	Book of Survey and Distribution NL MS. 969
1657	English Protestant Proprietors, Galway town. In Hardiman (see 'Local History' below)
1727	A Galway election list, JGHAS 1976
1749	Parishes of Ahascra, Athleague, Ballynakill, Drimatemple, Dunamon, Kilbegnet, Killian, Killosolan. NA 1A 36 1
1791	Survey of Loughrea town (occupiers). JGHAS,Vol. 23 No. 3
1794	Catholic Freemen of Galway town, JGHAS Vol. 9, No. 1
1798	List of those who suffered loss in 1798 Rebellion. NL JLB 94107
1806–10	Catholic householders, Killalaghten. In the Catholic parish registers of Killalaghten. NL Pos. 2431
1820s/30s	Tithe Book
1821	Parishes of Aran, Athenry, Kilcomeen, Kiltallagh, Killimore, Kilconickny, Kilreekill. National Archives. Also Loughrea (fragments) GO Ms 622, 53 ff.
1827	Protestants in Aughrim parish. NA M 5359
1829–58	Rentals of the estate of Sir George Shee, in and around Dunmore; National Archives, M.3105–3120.
1834	List of parishioners, Kinvara and Killina; NL Pos 2442.
1836	Freeholders, Co. Galway; *The Galway Advertiser*, March 1836.
1837	Valuation of towns returning M.P.s (occupants and property values): Galway. *Parliamentary Papers*, 1837, Reports from Committees, Vol II (i), Appendix G
1841	Loughrea census fragments; National Archives. M 1502 & GO MS. 622, 53 ff.
1848–52	Ahascra assisted passages, *Anecta Hibernica*, Vol 22, 1960
1850–59	Emigrants to Australia and the US from the parish of Kilcreast, with some from the parishes of Killigolen, Killinane, Killora, Rilthomas and Isserkelly, GO MS. 622
1851	Loughrea census fragments; National Archives, M 150
1855	Griffith's Valuation
1901	Census
1911	Census

Local history

Berry, J. F. *The Story of St Nicholas' Church, Galway*, 1912. Ir 7265 b 5
Cooney, D. L. *Methodism in Galway*, 1978, Ir. 200 p 14

D'Alton, E. *History of the Arch-diocese of Tuam*, Dublin 1928, Ir. 27412 d 1
Egan, Patrick K. *The parish of Ballinasloe its history from the earliest times to the present day*, Dublin, 1960
Fahey, J., *The History and Antiquities of the Diocese of Kilmacduagh*, Dublin, 1893
Goaley, M., *History of Annaghdown*, Ir. 274 p 31
Hardiman, James, *History of the town county of Galway . . . to 1820*, Galway, 1958, I 94124 h 1
Hayes-McCoy, G. A., *Index to 'The Compossicion Booke of Connoght, 1585'*, Irish Manuscripts Commission, Dublin, 1945
Irish Countrywomen's Association, *Portrait of a Parish: Ballynakill, Connemara*
Kavanagh, M., *A Bibliography of the Co. Galway*, 1965. Ir. RR 01524
Knox, H. T., *Notes on the Early History of the Diocese of Tuam Killala and Achony*, Dublin, 1904
MacLochlainn, T., *A Historical Survey of the Parish of Ahascra, Caltra & Castleblakeney*, 1979. Ir. 9141 p 79
MacLochlainn, T., *The Parish of Aughrim & Kilconnell*, 1980, Ir. 94124 m 4
MacLochlainn, T., *The Parish of Lawrencetown & Kiltormer*, 1981, Ir. 94124 m 5
Naughton, M., *The History of St Francis' Parish, Galway*, 1984, Ir. 27412 n 1
O'Neill, T. P., *The Tribes & Other Galway Families, 1484–1984*, Ir. 927, p 5
O'Sullivan, M. D., *Old Galway: the history of a Norman colony in Ireland*, Cambridge, 1942, Ir 94124 o 4
Robinson, Tim, *Connemara*, Roundstone, 1990.

Local journals

Journal of the Galway Historical and Archaeological Society. Ir. 794105 g 1

Directories

1820   J. Pigot, *Commercial Directory of Ireland*
1824   Pigot & Co., *City of Dublin and Hibernian Provincial Directory*, NL Ir 9141 p 75
1846   Slater's *National Commercial Directory of Ireland*
1856   Slater's *Royal National Commercial Directory of Ireland*
1870   Slater's *Directory of Ireland*
1881   Slater's *Royal National Commercial Directory of Ireland*
1894   Slater's *Royal Commercial Director of Ireland*

Gravestone inscriptions

Claregalway: IGRS Collection, 172, GO
Clontuskert: IGRS Collection, GO
Cregg: IGRS Collection, 70, GO

Drumacoo: IGRS Collection, GO
Kilmacduagh: *The Irish Ancestor*, Vol. VII, No. 1, 1975
Tumnahulla: IGRS Collection, 2, GO

Estate records

LANDLORD
Bellew estate wages book, 1679–1775, NL MS. 9200.
Col John **Browne**: NL Pos. 940, Account of the sales of the estates of Col.
  John Browne in Counties Galway and Mayo, compiled in 1778, giving
  names of major tenants and purchasers 1698–1704, and those occupying
  the estates in 1778, covering townlands in the civil parishes of Ballynakill,
  Cong, Kilcummin, Killannin, Omey, Ross.
Lord **Clanmorris**: NL MS. 3279, Estate rental, 1833, all tenants, covering
  townlands in the civil parish of Claregalway.
Dillon, Barons Clonbrock: NL MS. 19501, tenants' ledger 1801–06, indexed;
  NL MSS. 19585–19608 (24 vols), rentals and accounts, 1827–1840, all
  tenants; NL MSS. 22008, 22009, maps of the Co. Galway estates, with
  full valuation of all tenants' holdings; NL MSS. 19609–19616, rentals and
  accounts, 1840–44, all tenants; covering townlands in the civil parishes of
  Ahascragh, Aughrim, Fohanagh, Kilcoona, Killaan, Killallaghtan,
  Killosolan, Kilteskil.
Francis Blake **Knox**: NL MS. 3077, Rental, 1845–66, covering townlands in
  the civil parishes of Annaghdown, Kilmacduagh, Kilmoylan.
French family: NL MS. 4920, rent ledger, Monivea estate, 1767–77, major
  tenants only; NL MS. 4929, estate accounts and wages book, 1811/12, all
  tenants, with index; NL MS. 4930, accounts and wages book, 1830–33,
  Covering townlands in the civil parishes of Abbeyknockmoy, Athenry,
  Cargin, Claregalway, Monivea, Moylough, Oranmore.
Lieut Edward **Hodson**: NL MS. 2356, Rent rolls and tenants' accounts,
  1797–1824, indexes. Covering townlands in the civil parish of Kiltormer.
Richard **St George** Mansergh St George: NL Pos. 5483, (a) Rental of
  Headford town (all tenants), (b) estate rentals (major tenants only), both
  1775, covering townlands in the civil parishes of Cargin, Donaghpatrick,
  Kilcoona, Kilkilvery, Killursa.
George **Shee**: NA M3105–3120, yearly rentals of the estate in and around
  Dunmore, 1837–1859, all tenants, covering townlands in the civil parishes
  of Addergoole, Boyounagh, Clonbern, Dunmore.
Trench: NL MS. 2577, Estate rental, 1840–50. Covering townlands in the
  civil parishes of Ballymacaward, Kilbeacanty, Killaan, Killimordaly.
Theobold **Wolfe**: NL MS. 3876, estate maps with names of major tenants,
  1760, indexed. Covering townlands in the civil parishes of Kilmallinoge
  and Tiranascragh.

(No Landlord Given): NL 21 g 76 (14) and 21 g 76 (26). Maps of Cloonfane and Carogher townlands in Dunmore parish, with tenants' names, mid-nineteenth century.

(No Landlord Given): NL MS. 4633, survey of occupiers, townlands of Ballinasoora, Streamsfort, Fortlands, Woodlands, parish of Killimordaly. 1851.

(No Landlord Given): NL MSS. 2277–2280, Rentals, 1854–85, townlands of Ballyargadaun, Leitrim More, Kylebrack, Knockash, in the civil parishes of Leitrim and Kilteskil.

Placenames

Townland maps. Londonderry Inner City Trust

CO. KERRY

Census returns and substitutes

1586	Survey of the estates of the Earl of Desmond, recording lease-holders, NA M.5037
1641	Book of Survey and Distribution, NL MS. 970
1654	Civil Survey, Vol. IV, Dysert, Killury, Rathroe, I 6551 Dublin
1659	Pender's 'Census', Ir. 31041 c 4
1756–1827	'Biographical notices from Cork and Kerry newspapers, arranged alphabetically', NL MSS. 19,172–5
1799	Petition of 300 prominent Catholics of Co. Kerry, *The Dublin Evening Post*, 9 June 1799
1821	Some extracts, Tralee and Annagh, Thrift Abstracts, National Archives
1821	Parish of Kilcummin. Royal Irish Academy, McSwiney papers, parcel f, no. 3
1820s/30s	Tithe Books
1834–35	Householders, parishes of Dunquin, Dunurlin, Ferriter, Killemlagh, Kilmalkedar, Kilquane, Marhin, Prior, JKAHS, 1974–75
1835	Tralee Voters, JKAHS, No. 19, 1986
1847–51	Assisted passages, Castlemaine estate, Kiltallagh parish, *Analecta Hibernica*, No. 22, 1960

1852   Griffith's Valuation
1901   Census, indexed in Jeremiah King's *County Kerry, Past and Present*,
          1931, NL I 94146
1911   Census

Local history

Allman, J., *Causeway, location, lore and legend*, Naas, 1983
Harrington, T. J., *Discovering Kerry*, Dublin, 1976
Brady, W. Maziere, *The McGellycuddy Papers*, London, 1867
Casey, A. (ed.), *O'Kief, Coshe Mang etc.* Ir. 94145 c 12
Cusack M. F., *History of the kingdom of Kerry*, London, 1871
Denny, H., *A Handbook of Co. Kerry Family History etc.*, 1923, Ir. 9291 d 1
Donovan, T. M., *A Popular History of East Kerry*, 1931
Finuge Heritage Society, *A span across time: Finuge, a folk history*
Hickson, Mary, *Selections from Old Kerry Records, Historical and Genealogical*,
          London, 1872–74
Keane, L., *Knocknagoshel: then and now*, Kerry County Library, 1985
King, J., *County Kerry, Past and Present*, 1931 I 94146
Lansdowne, H., *Glanarought and the Petty-Fitzmaurices*, 1937, Ir. 94146 l 1
McLysaght, E., *The Kenmare Manuscripts*, Dublin, 1942
McMoran, R., *Tralee, a short history and guide to Tralee and environs*, 1980
MacSwiney Papers, Royal Irish Academy. Historical notes and will abstracts,
          mainly from Counties Cork and Kerry
Mould, D. C. Pochin, *Valentia: portrait of an island*, Dublin, 1978
O'Connor, T., *Ardfert in Times Past*, Tralee, 1990
Reedy, Rev. Donal A., *The Diocese of Kerry*, Killarney
Smith, Charles, *The Ancient and Present State of the County of Kerry*, Dublin, 1756
Windele MSS. Information on Cork and Kerry families, including Cop-
          pinger, Cotter, Crosbie, O'Donovan, O'Keeffe, McCarthy, Sarsfield and
          others. NL Pos. 5479. See also Casey, A. (ed.), *O'Kief, Coshe Mang etc.* (NL
          Ir. 94145 c 12), Vol. 7

Local journals

Journal of the Kerry Archaeological Historical Society, Ir. 794105 k 1
Kerry Archaeological Magazine (1908–20), reference as above
Kenmare Literary and Historical Society Journal

Directories

1824   Pigot and Co., *City of Dublin and Hibernian Provincial Directory*, NL Ir.
          9141 p 75

1846   Slater's *National Commercial Directory of Ireland*
1856   Slater's *Royal National Commercial Directory of Ireland*
1870   Slater's *Directory of Ireland*
1881   Slater's *Royal National Commercial Directory of Ireland*
1886   Francis Guy, *Postal Directory of Munster*, NL Ir. 91414 g 8
1893   Francis Guy, *Directory of Munster*
1894   Slater's *Royal Commercial Directory of Ireland*

Gravestone inscriptions

Aghadoe: *O'Kief Coshe Mang etc.*, Vol. 6
Aghavallin (C. of I.): Kerry Genealogical Society (see below)
Aglish: *O'Kief, Coshe Mang etc.*, Vol. 6
Ardfert: *O'Kief, Coshe Mang etc.*, Vol. 8
Ballymacelligot: *O'Kief, Coshe Mang etc.*, Vol. 8
Caherciveen (Killevanoge): IGRS Collection, 57, GO
Caherciveen (Marian Place): IGRS Collection, 5, GO
Castleisland: *O'Kief, Coshe Mang etc.*, Vol. 6
Clogherbrien: *O'Kief, Coshe Mang etc.*, Vol. 8
Currans: *O'Kief, Coshe Mang etc.*, Vol. 6
Duagh: Finuge Heritage Society (see below)
Dysert: *O'Kief, Coshe Mang etc.*, Vol. 6
Finuge: Finuge Heritage Society (see below)
Galey: Finuge Heritage Society (see below)
Kilcummin: *O'Kief, Coshe Mang etc.*, Vol. 6
Killarney and Muckross Abbey: *O'Kief, Coshe Mang etc.*, Vol. 6
Kilnanare: *O'Kief, Coshe Mang etc.*, Vol. 6
Killeentierna: *O'Kief, Coshe Mang etc.*, Vol. 6
Killorglin: *O'Kief, Coshe Mang etc.*, Vol. 8
Lislaughtin Abbey (Aghavallin): Kerry Genealogical Society (see below)
Murher: Kerry Genealogical Society (see below)
Nohoval: *O'Kief, Coshe Mang etc.*, Vol. 8
O'Brennan: *O'Kief, Coshe Mang etc.*, Vol. 8
Raheenyhooig: (Dingle) IGRS Collection, 49, GO
Rathmore: *O'Kief, Coshe Mang etc.*, Vol. 6
Tralee: *O'Kief, Coshe Mang etc.*, Vol. 8
Finuge Heritage Society: Teach Siamsa, Finuge House, Co. Kerry
Kerry Genealogical Society, 119/120 Rock St, Tralee, Co. Kerry *NOT THERE*

Estate records

LANDLORD
Browne, Earls of Kenmare: assorted rentals, maps and estate accounts for
  areas around Kenmare and in the barony of Dunekerron, from 1620 to

1864 in McLysaght, E., *The Kenmare Manuscripts*, Dublin, 1942. See also *O'Kief, Coshe Mang etc*, Vols 6, 7, 9.

The Orpen estates: G. Lyne, 'Land Tenure in Tuosist and Kenmare', [1696–1775], *Kerry Arch. and Hist. Soc. Jnl*, 1976/78/79.

Thomas Sandes. Rental of the estate, 1792–1828, covering parts of the parishes of Aghavallin, Kinaughtin, Murher, NL MS. 1792.

Placenames

Townland Maps, Londonderry Inner City Trust

CO. KILDARE

Census returns and substitutes

1641	Book of Survey and Distribution. NL MS. 971. Also JKAS, Vol. X, 1922–8
1654	Civil Survey, Vol. VIII. I 6551 Dublin
1659	Pender's 'Census', Ir. 31041 c 4
1663	Hearth Money Roll (partial), JKAS, Vol. 10, No. 5, Vol. 11, No. 1
1775–1835	*Schools of Kildare and Leighlin*, Brennan, Ir. 37094135 b 4
1798	List of those who suffered loss in 1798 Rebellion. NL JLB 94107
1820s/30s	Tithe Books
1831	Kilcullen, Protestant returns. Nineteenth century census returns, National Archives
1837	Registered Voters, NL MS. 1398
1840	Castledermot and Moone, NL Pos. 3511
1851	Griffith's Valuation
1901	Census
1911	Census

Local history

Andrews J. H., *Irish Historic Towns Atlas: Kildare*, Dublin, Royal Irish Academy, 1986

Carville, Geraldine, *Monasterevin, Valley of Roses*, Moore Abbey, 1989

Comerford, Erv. M., *Collections relating to Kildare and Leighlin*, 1883

Costello, Con, *Looking Back, Aspects of History, Co. Kildare*, Naas, 1988
Costello, Con, *Kildare: Saints, Soldiers and Horses*, Naas, 1991
Doohan, Tony, *A History of Cellbridge*, n.d.
Dunlop, Robert, *Waters under the Bridge*, Brannockstown, 1988
Leadbeater, Mary, *The Annals of Ballitore*, London, 1862, Ir. 92 1 8
Kavanagh, M. V., *A Contribution towards a Bibliography of the Co. Kildare*, 1977, Ir. 94135 k 1
Mac Suibhne, Peadar, *Rathangan*, 1975
Mulhall, Mary, *A History of Lucan*, Lucan, 1991
Naas Local History Group, *Nas na Riogh: . . . an illustrated history of Naas*, Naas, 1990
Nelson, Gerald, *A History of Leixlip*, Kildare Co. Library, 1990
O Conchubhair, Seamus, *A History of Kilcock and Newtown*, 1987
O Muineog, Micheal, *Kilcock GAA, A History*, 1989
O'Sullivan, Peter, *Newcastle Lyons, A Parish of the Pale*, Dublin, Geography Publications, 1986
Paterson, J. (ed.), *Diocese of Meath and Kildare: an historical guide*, 1981. Ir. 941 p 75
Raymond, B., *The Story of Kilkenny, Kildare, Offaly and Leix*, 1931 I 9141 p 1
Reid, J. N. S., *Church of St Michael & All Angels, Clane*, 1983
'Some Authorities for Kildare County History', *Kildare Arch. Soc. Jnl*, No. 10, 1922–28, 155–60

Local journals

Journal of the Co. Kildare Archaeological Society, Ir. 794106 k 2

Directories

1788   Richard Lucas, *General Directory of the Kingdom of Ireland*, NL Pos. 3729
1824   Pigot Co., *City of Dublin and Hibernian Provincial Directory*, NL Ir. 9141 p 75
1846   Slater's *National Commercial Directory of Ireland*
1856   Slater's *Royal National Commercial Directory of Ireland*
1870   Slater's *Directory of Ireland*
1881   Slater's *Royal National Commercial Directory of Ireland*
1894   Slater's *Royal Commercial Directory of Ireland*

Gravestone inscriptions

Athy: GO MS. 622, 89
Ballyshannon (Kilcullen): GO MS. 622, 108
Barberstown: *Kildare Arch. Soc. Jnl*, 1977/8
Castledermot (C. of I.): IGRS Collection, 71/2, GO
Castledermot Friary: IGRS Collection, 2, GO

Castledermot (R.C.): IGRS Collection, 5, GO
Dunmanogue: IGRS Collection, 21, GO
Fontstown: GO MS. 622, 148/9
Harristown: GO MS. 622, 126/7
Killeen Cormac: IGRS Collection, 58/55, GO
Kilteel: *Kildare Arch. Soc. Jnl*, 1981/82
Knockbane: IGRS Collection, 2, GO
Knockpatrick: IGRS Collection, 57, GO
Ladychapel: IGRS Collection, 145, GO
Mageny: GO MS. 622, 108
Taghadoe: IGRS Collection, 12, GO
Timolin: IGRS Collection, 33, GO

Placenames

Townland Maps, Londonderry Inner City Trust

CO. KILKENNY

Census returns and substitutes

1641	Book of Survey and Distribution NL MS. 975
1654	Civil Survey, Vol. VI, Kilkenny City I 6551 Dublin
1659	Pender's 'Census'. NL Ir. 31041 c 4
1664	Hearth Money Rolls, parishes of Agherney, Aghavillar, Bellaghtobin, Belline, Burnchurch, Callan, Castleinch, Clone, Coolaghmore, Coolcashin, Danganmore, Derrinahinch, Dunkitt, Earlstown, Eyverk, Fartagh, Inishnagg and Stonecarthy, Jerpoint, Kells, Kilbeacon and Killahy, Kilcolm, Kilferagh, Kilkredy, Killamery, Killaloe, Killree, Kilmoganny, Kiltackaholme, Knocktopher and Kilkerchill, Muckalee and Lismatigue, Outrath, Ratbach, Rathpatrick, Tullaghanbrogue, Tullaghmaine, Urlingford. *The Irish Genealogist*, 1974–75
1684–1769	Registers of Kilkenny College, NL Pos. 4545
1702	Partial lists, St Mary's and St Canice's parishes Kilkenny City. NA 1A 55 83
1715	Protestant males between 16 and 60 in St John's parish, Kilkenny City, NA 1A 55 83

1750–1844	Inistiogue emigrants in Newfoundland, *Kilkenny History and Society*, ed. Whelan and Nolan, 345–405
1775	Landowners, GO 443
1785–1879	Kilkenny city deeds, *Old Kilkenny Review*, Vol. 2, No. 4
1797	Chief Catholic inhabitants, Parishes of Graiguenamanagh and Knocktopher, *The Irish Ancestor*, 1978
1809–19	Freeholders. NL MS. 14181
1811–58	Registers and Accounts of St Kieran's College, NL Pos. 973
1821	Extracts from the 1821 census, parishes of Aglish, Clonmore, Fiddown, Kilmacow, Polerone, Rathkyran, Whitechurch. GO 684 (Walsh-Kelly notebooks), also *The Irish Genealogist*, Vol. 5, 1978
1821	Parishes of Aglish and Portnascully, *The Irish Ancestor*, 1976; Extracts from Pollrone parish, *The Irish Genealogist*, 1977
1820s/30s	Tithe Books
1831	Extracts from the 1831 census, parishes of Aglish, Clonmore, Kilmacow, Polerone, Rathkyran, Tybroghney, GO 684 (Walsh-Kelly notebooks)
1841	Extracts from the 1841 census, parishes of Aglish and Rathkyran, GO 684 (Walsh-Kelly notebooks)
1841	Townlands of Aglish and Portnahully, parish of Aglish, *The Irish Ancestor*, 1977
1849/50	Griffith's Valuation
1851	Parish of Aglish, *The Irish Ancestor*, 1977. Also GO 684 (Walsh-Kelly notebooks)
1850s	Castlecomer assisted passages. See Hayes catalogue.
1901	Census
1911	Census

Local history

Alsworth, W.J., *History of Thomastown and District*, 1953, NL JP, 1996

Brennan, T. A., *A History of the Brennans of Idaugh in Co. Kilkenny*, 1979, NL Ir. 9292 b 45

Burtchaell, G., *MPs for the County and City of Kilkenny 1295–1888*, Dublin, 1888

Carrigan, Rev. William, *The History and Antiquities of the Diocese of Ossory*, 4 vols, Dublin, 1905

Coleman. James, 'Bibliography of the counties Carlow, Kilkenny and Wicklow,' *Waterford and S–E of Ire. Arch. Soc. Jnl*, 11, 1907–8, 126–33

Egan, P. M., *Illustrated Guide to the City and County of Kilkenny*, Ir. 914139 e 2

Fitzmaurice, S. A., 'Castleharris', *Old Kilkenny Review*, 1979

Healy, William, *History and antiquities of Kilkenny county and city*, Kilkenny, 1893, NL Ir. 94139 h 1

Hogan, John, *Kilkenny, the Ancient City of Ossory*, Kilkenny, 1884

Hore, H. J., *The Social State of the Southern and Eastern Counties of Ireland in the Sixteenth Century*, 1870

Kenealy, M., 'The Parish of Aharney and the Marum Family', *Old Kilkenny Review*, 1976

Kilkenny Corporation, *Catalogue of Deeds*, NL Ir. 94139 k 2

Nolan, W., *Fassidinin: Land, Settlement and Society in South-East Ireland, 1600–1850*, 1979, NL Ir. 94139 n 1

Phelan, M., 'Callan Doctors', *Old Kilkenny Review*, 1980

Prim, J. G. A., 'Documents connected with the city of Kilkenny militia in the 17th and 18th centuries', *Kilkenny and S–E Ire. Arch. Soc. Jnl*, 1854–55, 231–74

Raymond, B., *The Story of Kilkenny, Kildare, Offaly and Leix*, 1931 NL I 9141 p 1

Whelan K. and Nolan, W. (ed.), *Kilkenny History and Society*, Dublin, 1990

Local journals

Journal of the Butler Society

Old Kilkenny Review, NL Ir. 94139 o 3

Kilkenny and South-East of Ireland Archaeological Society Journal, J 7914 (to 1890), NL Ir. 794105 r 1 (after 1890), indexed, as *The Journal of the Royal Society of Antiquaries of Ireland*, in three parts, 1849–89, 1881–1910, 1911–1930, Ir. 794105 r 1

Transactions of the Ossory Archaeological Society, NL Ir. 794105 o 1

Deenside

Directories

1788   Richard Lucas, *General Directory of the Kingdom of Ireland*, NL Pos. 3729

1820   J. Pigot, *Commercial Directory of Ireland*

1824   Pigot and Co., *City of Dublin and Hibernian Provincial Directory*, NL Ir. 9141 p 75

1839   T. Shearman, *New Commercial Directory for the Cities of Waterford and Kilkenny, Towns of Clonmel, Carrick-on-Suir, New Ross and Carlow*

1846   Slater's *National Commercial Directory of Ireland*

1856   Slater's *Royal National Commercial Directory of Ireland*

1870   Slater's *Directory of Ireland*

1881   Slater's *Royal National Commercial Directory of Ireland*

1884   George H. Bassett, *Kilkenny City and County Guide and Directory*

1894   Slater's *Royal Commercial Directory of Ireland*

Gravestone inscriptions

Ballygurrim: IGRS Collection, 16, GO
Ballyreddin: IGRS Collection, 7, GO
Ballytarsny: IGRS Collection, 24, GO
Beal Borr (Annamult): IGRS Collection, 7, GO
Ben Fada(Radestown): IGXS Collection, 27, GO
Cappagh (Inistioge): GO MS. 622, 173
Castle Inch: IGRS Collection, 30, GO
Church Clara: IGRS Collection, 56, GO
Clashacrow: IGRS Collection, 10, GO
Clonmore: IGRS Collection, 30, GO
Danesfort: GO MS. 622, 147
Dunkitt: IGRS Collection, 113, GO
Dunmore old (Bleach Rd): IGRS Collection, 33, GO
Dysert (Castlecomer): IGRS Collection, 13, GO
Freynestown (Liscoffin): IGRS Collection, 18, GO
Freshford old: IGRS Collection, 148, GO
Gaulskill old: IGRS Collection, 39, GO
Gaulskill C. of I.: IGRS Collection, 11, GO
Grove (Tullaghanbrogue): IGRS Collection, 119, GO
Johnswell: IGRS Collection, 197, GO
Kells Priory: IGRS Collection, 16, GO
Kells (St Kieran's): IGRS Collection, 76, GO
Kilbeacon: IGRS Collection, 42, GO
Kilbride: IGRS Collection, 13, GO
Kilcolumb: IGRS Collection, 53, GO
Kilcready: IGRS Collection, 35, GO
Kilcurl: IGRS Collection, 5, GO
Kilfera (with Sheestown): IGRS Collection, 3, GO
Kilkenny (St Canice's Cathedral): *The History (. . .) of St Canice, Kilkenny*,
    James Graves and J. G. A. Prim, 1857
St Canice's Graveyard: IGRS Collection, 502, GO
St Canice's R.C.: IGRS Collection, 45, GO
St John's Priory: IGRS Collection, 116, GO
St John's (Dublin Rd): IGRS Collection, 611, GO
St Mary's, Kilkenny: *Old Kilkenny Review*, 1979/80/81
St Maul's, Green Bridge: IGRS Collection, 18, GO
St Patrick's Graveyard: IGRS Collection, 280, GO
Killahy: IGRS Collection, 13, GO
Killaspy: IGRS Collection, 3, GO
Kilmacow: IGRS Collection, 119, GO
Kilmodimoge (Bullock Hill): IGRS Collection, 6, GO

Kilree: IGRS Collection, 73, GO
Kilvinoge: IGRS Collection, 10, GO
Knocktoper: *Kilkenny Gravestone Inscriptions: 1, Knocktopher*, Kilkenny Archaeological
    Society, 1988
Maddoxtown: IGRS Collection, 60, GO
Muckalee: IGRS Collection, 23, GO
Outrath: IGRS Collection, 86, GO
Portnascully: IGRS Collection, 52, GO
Rathcoole: IGRS Collection, 22, GO
Sheepstown: IGRS Collection, 4, GO
Sheestown: See Kilfera
Stonecarty: IGRS Collection, 22, GO
Templemartin: IGRS Collection, 51, GO
Thornback: IGRS Collection, 137, GO
Three Castles: IGRS Collection, 66, GO
Tubrid Old: IGRS Collection, 3, GO
Tullamaine: IGRS Collection, 34, GO
Ullid: IGRS Collection, 15, GO

Placenames

O'Kelly, O., *The Placenames of the Co. Kilkenny*, 1985, Ir. 92942 o 15

CO. LAOIS

Census returns and substitutes

1641	Book of Survey and Distribution, NL MS. 972
1659	Pender's 'Census', NL Ir. 31041 c 4
1664	Hearth Money Roll, parishes of Killenny and Moyanna. National Archives, Thrift Abstracts 3737
1668–69	Hearth Money Roll baronies of Maryborough and Upper Ossory. National Archives, Thrift Abstracts 3738
1758–75	Freeholders, *Co. Kildare Archaeological Society Journal*, Vol VIII, 309–27
1766	Parish of Lea, RCB Library
1821	Mountrath. Nineteenth century census returns, National Archives

1820s/30s	Tithe Books
1832, 1840	Owners and occupiers, Lea parish; NL MS. 4723/4
1844	Register of Arms, Baronies of Upper Ossory, Maryborough, Cullenagh, 433 names
1847	Voters' List, NL ILB 04 P 12
1851/2	Griffith's Valuation
1901	Census
1911	Census

Local history

Abbeyleix, 1953, Ir. 94137 s 1

Carrigan, Rev. William, *The History and Antiquities of the Diocese of Ossory*, 4 vols, Dublin, 1905

Ledwich, Edward A., *A Statistical Account of the Parish of Aghaboe*, 1796

Members of Parliament for Laois and Offaly, 1801–1918, 1983, Ir. 328 m 6

O'Byrne, D., *History of Queen's County*, 1856, Ir. 94137 o 2

O'Hanlon, John and O'Leary, Edward, *History of the Queen's County*, Dublin, 1907–14, Ir. 94137 o 3

O'Shea and Feehan, *Aspects of Local History*, 1977, Ir. 941 p 36

Paterson, J. (ed.), *Diocese of Meath and Kildare: an historical guide*, 1981, Ir. 941 p 75

Raymond, B., *The Story of Kilkenny Kildare, Offaly and Leix*, 1931, I 9141 p 1

Local journals

Laois Heritage: bulletin of the Laois Heritage Society, Ir. 9413705 l 1

Directories

1788	Richard Lucas, *General Directory of the Kingdom of Ireland*, NL Pos. 3729
1824	Pigot and Co., *City of Dublin and Hibernian Provincial Directory*, NL Ir. 9141 p 75
1846	Slater's *National Commercial Directory of Ireland*
1856	Slater's *Royal National Commercial Directory of Ireland*
1870	Slater's *Directory of Ireland*
1881	Slater's *Royal National Commercial Directory of Ireland*
1894	Slater's *Royal Commercial Directory of Ireland*

CO. LEITRIM

Census returns and substitutes

1600–1868	Roll of all the gentlemen . . ., NL P 2179
1659	Pender's 'Census', NL Ir. 31041 c 4
1791	Freeholders, GO 665
1792	Protestants in the barony of Mohill, *The Irish Ancestor*, Vol. 16 No. 1
1807	Freeholders, Mohill barony, NL MS. 9628
1820	Freeholders, NL MS. 3830
1821	Parish of Carrigallen, NL Pos. 4646
1820s/30s	Tithe Books
1851	Catholic Householders, Mohill Parish. Leitrim Heritage Centre, Ballinamore, Co. Leitrim
1852	Voters in Oughteragh, Cloonclare, Cloonlogher, *Breifne*, Vol. 5, No. 20
1856	Griffith's Valuation
1861	Catholic householders, Mohill parish. Leitrim Heritage Centre, Ballinamore, Co. Leitrim
1901	Census
1911	Census

Local history

Clancy and Forde, *Ballinalera Parish, Co. Leitrim: aspects of its history and traditions*, 1980, NL Ir. 94121 c 2

Freeman,T.W., *The Town and District of Carrick-on-Shannon*, 1949, NL P. 1916

Hayes-McCoy, G. A., *Index to 'The Compossicion Books of Connoght, 1585'*, Irish Manuscripts Commission, Dublin, 1945

Kiltubbrid, 1984, NL Ir. 397 k 4

Logan, P. L., *Outeragh, My Native Parish*,1963, NL Ir. 941 p 74

'Sources of Information on the Antiquities and history of Cavan and Leitrim: Suggestions', *Breifny* 1920–22

MacNamee, James J., *History of the Diocese of Ardagh*, Dublin, 1954

Monahan, Rev. J., *Records Relating to the Diocese of Ardagh and Clonmacnoise*, 1886

O'Connell, Philip, *The Diocese of Kilmore: its History and Antiquities*, Dublin, 1937

Local journals

Ardagh and Clonmacnoise Historical Society Journal (1926–51), NL Ir. 794105
Breifne, Ir. 94119 b 2

Breifny Antiquarian Society Journal (1920–33), Ir. 794106 b 1
The Drumlin: a Journal of Cavan, Leitrim and Monaghan, Ir. 05 d 34

Gravestone inscriptions

Leitrim Heritage Centre, Ballinamore, Co. Leitrim, holds indexed transcripts
of gravestone inscriptions covering the entire county, comprising 85 Catholic churches and graveyards, 27 Church of Ireland, and 1 Presbyterian.

Directories

1824   Pigot and Co., *City of Dublin and Hibernian Provincial Directory*, NL Ir.
        9141 p 75
1846   Slater's *National Commercial Directory of Ireland*
1856   Slater's *Royal National Commercial Directory of Ireland*
1870   Slater's *Directory of Ireland*
1881   Slater's *Royal National Commercial Directory of Ireland*
1894   Slater's *Royal Commercial Directory of Ireland*

Estate records

LANDLORD
Earl of **Bessborough**: NA M3374; rental, 1805, major tenants only; NA
    M3370, valuation of estate, 1813, all tenants; NA M3383, tenants with
    leases, 1813; NA M3384, rental, 1813, all tenants; covering townlands in
    the civil parishes of Fenagh and Kiltubbrid.
Clements: NL MSS. 3816–3827, rentals of the Woodford estate, 1812–1828,
    all tenants, covering townlands in the civil parish of Carrigallen; NL
    MSS. 12805–7, 3828, rental, 1812–1824 (with gaps) of Bohey townland in
    Cloone civil parish.
Sir Humphrey **Crofton**: NL MS. 4531. Rental, March 1833, with tenants'
    names in alphabetical order, covering townlands in the civil parishes of
    Cloone, Kiltoghert, Mohill, Oughteragh.
William **Johnson**: NL MS. 9465, rental of the Drumkeeran estate, 1845–56,
    all tenants, covering townlands in the civil parish of Inishmagrath.
King: NL MS. 4170, Rent roll and estate accounts, 1801–1818, major tenants
    only, covering townlands in the civil parishes of Fenagh and Kiltubbrid.
Earl of **Leitrim**: NL MS. 12787; rental and accounts, 1837–42, all tenants;
    NL MSS. 5728–33; rentals 1838–65, all tenants; NL MSS. 5803–5,
    rentals, 1842–55, all tenants; NL MSS. 12810–12; rentals 1844–8, all
    tenants; NL MSS. 179, 180; rentals 1844 and 1854, all tenants; covering
    townlands in the civil parishes of Carrigallen, Cloone, Clooneclare,
    Inishmagrath, Killasnet, Kiltoghert, Mohill.

Viscount **Necomen**: NA M2797, rental, 1822, mainly larger tenants, covering townlands in the civil parish of Drumlease.

Francis **O'Beirne**: NL MS. 8647 (14), rental, 1850, mainly large tenants, covering townlands in the civil parishes of Cloone, Drumlease, Kiltoghert.

Charles Manners **St George**: NL MSS. 4001–22, annual accounts and rentals. Covering townlands in the civil parish of Kiltoghert.

Nicholas Loftus **Tottenham**: NL MS. 9837, 26 maps, with major tenants only, covering townlands in the civil parishes of Clooneclare, Inishmagrath, Rossinver.

Ponsonby **Tottenham**: NL MS. 10162, printed rental, 1802, mainly larger tenants, covering townlands in the civil parishes of Clooneclare and Rossinver

Owen **Wynne**: NL MSS. 5780–2, rentals and expense books, 1737–68, major tenants only; NL MSS. 5830–31, rent ledgers 173853, 1768–73, major tenants only, indexed, NL MSS. 3311–31, a rental and two rent ledgers, yearly from 1798 to 1825, with all tenants; covering townlands in the civil parishes of Clooneclare, Cloonlogher, Killanummery, Killasnet, Rossinver.

Placenames

Townland maps, Londonderry Inner City Trust

CO. LIMERICK

Census returns and substitutes

1569	Freeholders, NL Pos. 1700
1570	Freeholders and Gentlemen in Co. Limerick, JNMAHS, 1964
1586	Survey of leaseholders on the Desmond estates, NA M.5037
1641	Book of Survey and Distribution, NL MS. 973
1654–56	Civil Survey, Vol. IV, NL I 6551 Dublin
1660	Rental of lands in Limerick City and County, NL MS. 9091
1664	Askeaton Hearth Money Rolls, *North Munster Archaeological and Historical Society Journal*, 1965
1673	Part of Limerick city (estates of the earls of Roscommon and Orrery) with occupiers' names and valuation, NL Pos. 792

1746–1836	Freemen, Limerick City, *North Munster Archaeological and Historical Society Journal*, 1944/5, NL Pos. 5526
1761	Limerick City Freeholders, NL MS. 16092; County freeholders, NL MS. 16093
1766	Abington, Cahircomey, Cahirelly, Carrigparson, Clonkeen, Kilkellane, Tuogh. NA 1A 46 49; Protestants in the parishes of Croagh, Kilscannel, Nantinan and Rathkeale, *The Irish Ancestor*, 1977
1776	Freeholders entitled to vote, NA M 1321–2
1776	Voters' List, NA M.4878
1793	'Two Lists of People Resident in the Area of Newcastle in 1793 and 1821', *The Irish Ancestor*, Vol. 16, No. 1 (1984)
1798	Rebel Prisoners in Limerick Jail, JNMAHS, Vol. 10 (1), 1966
1813	Chief inhabitants of the parishes of St Mary's and St John's, Limerick, *The Irish Ancestor*, Vol. 17 No. 2. (1985)
1816–28	Freeholders, GO 623
1821	Fragments for Kilfinane District, JNMAHS, 1975
1821	Some extracts. Thrift Abstracts, National Archives.
1821	'Two Lists of People Resident in the Area of Newcastle in 1793 and 1821', *The Irish Ancestor*, Vol. 16, No. 1 (1984)
1820s/30s	Tithe Books
1829	Limerick Freeholders, GO 623
1835	Parish of Templebredin, JNMAHS, 1975
1835–39	List of inhabitants of Limerick taking water (Waterworks accounts) NL Pos. 3451
1840	Freeholders, Barony of Coshlea, NL MS. 9452
1846	Survey of Households in connection with famine relief, Loughill, Foynes, Shanagolden areas, NL MS. 582
1851	Some extracts. Thrift Abstracts, National Archives
1851/2	Griffith's Valuation. Alphabetical index to householders, on microfiche, National Archives
1870	Rate Book for Clanwilliam barony, NA M 2434
1901	Census
1911	Census

Local history

Countess of Dunraven, *Memorials of Adare*, Oxford, 1865
Cromwellian Settlement of Co. Limerick, *Limerick Field Journal*, Vols 1–8, 1897–1908, NL Ir. 794205 l 1
Dowd, Rev. James, *Limerick and its Sieges*, Limerick, 1896
Dowd, Rev. James, *St Mary's Cathedral Limerick*, 1936
Dwyer, Philip, *The Diocese of Killaloe*, Dublin, 1878
Ferrar, John, *A History Of the City of Limerick*, Limerick, 1767

Ferrar, John, *The History of Limerick, Ecclesiastical, Civil and Military from the earliest records to the year 1787*, Limerick, 1787

Fitzgerald, P. and McGregor, J. J., *The history, topography and antiquities of the city and county of Limerick*, Dublin, 1826–27

Hamilton, G. F., *Records of Ballingarry*, Limerick, 1930, NL Ir. 94144 h 2

Hayes, R., *The German Colony in County Limerick*, Reprint, from *The North Munster Antiquarian Soc. Journal*, Limerick, 1937

Lee, Rev. Dr C., 'Statistics from Knockainy and Patrickswell parishes, 1819–1940'. *Journal of the Cork Historical and Archaeological Society*, Vol. 47, No. 165

Lenihan, Maurice, *Limerick, its history and antiquities*, Dublin 1866, NL Ir. 94144 l 1

MacCaffrey, James, *The Black Book of Limerick*, 1907

Meredyth, Francis, *Descriptive and Historic Guide, St Mary's Cathedral*, Limerick, 1887

Nash, Roisin, *A bibliography of Limerick*, Limerick, 1962

Seymour, St John D., *The Diocese of Emly*, Dublin, 1913

Westropp Manuscripts, Royal Irish Academy. Will abstracts mainly for Counties Clare and Limerick

White, Rev. P., *History of Clare and the Dalcassian Clans of Tipperary, Limerick and Galway*, Dublin, 1893

Local journals

North Munster Antiquarian Society Journal, NL Ir. 794105 n 1 (Index 1897–1919, Ir. 7941 n 1)

Old Limerick Journal, NL Ir. 94144 o 2

Limerick Field Journal, NL Ir. 794205 l 1

Lough Gur Historical Society Journal (from 1985)

Directories

1769   John Ferrar, *Directory of Limerick*

1788   Richard Lucas, *General Directory of the Kingdom of Ireland*, NL Pos. 3729

1809   Holden's *Triennial Directory*

1820   J. Pigot, *Commercial Directory of Ireland*

1824   Pigot and Co., *City of Dublin and Hibernian Provincial Directory*, NL Ir. 9141 p 75

1846   Slater's *National Commercial Directory of Ireland*

1856   Slater's *Royal National Commercial Directory of Ireland*

1866   George H. Bassett, *Directory of the City and County of Limerick and of the principal Towns in Counties Tipperary and Clare*, NL Ir. 914144 b 5

1870   Slater's *Directory of Ireland*

1879   George H. Bassett, *Limerick Directory*

1881   Slater's *Royal National Commercial Directory of Ireland*
1886   Francis Guy, *Postal Directory of Munster*, NL Ir. 91414 g 8
1893   Francis Guy, *Postal Directory of Munster*
1894   Slater's *Royal Commercial Directory of Ireland*

Gravestone inscriptions

Ardcanny: *The Irish Ancestor*, Vol. IX, No. 1, 1977
Ardpatrick: *Reflections (. . .) on Ardpatrick*, John Fleming, 1979
Askeaton: IGRS Collection, GO
Athlacca: *Dromin, Athlacca*, Mainchin Seoighe, 1978
Ballingarry: *Records of Ballingarry*, G. F. Hamilton, 1930
Bruree: *Bru Ri: the History of the Bruree District*, Mainchin Seoighe, 1973
Dromin: *Dromin, Athlacca*, Mainchin Seoighe, 1978
Grange: *The Irish Ancestor*, Vol. XII, 1980
Kilbehenny: *The Irish Genealogist*, Vol II, No. 11, 1954
Knockainey (Lough Gur): *Lough Gur Historical Society Journal*, No. 1 1985
Knockainey (Patrickswell): *Lough Gur Historical Society Journal*, No. 2 1986
Nantinan: *The Irish Ancestor*, Vol. XII, 1980
Plassey: GO MS. 622, 85
Rathkeale: *The Irish Ancestor*, Vol. XIV, No. 2, 1982
St Mary's Cathedral: *The Monuments of St Mary's*, M. J. Talbot, 1976
Stradbally: IGRS Collection, GO
Tankardstown: *Bru Ri: the History of the Bruree District*, Mainchin Seoighe, 1973

Estate records

'Description of the estate of John Sadleir in Limerick and Tipperary', JP 3439.

Placenames

Townland Maps, Londonderry Inner City Trust

CO. LONGFORD

Census returns and substitutes

1641   Book of Survey and Distribution, NL MS. 965
1659   Pender's 'Census', Ir. 31041 c 4
1729   Presbyterian exodus from Co. Longford, *Breifny*, 1977/8
1731   Protestants in the parish of Shrule, RCB Library
1747–1806   Freeholders, Registration book, NA M 2745
1766   Protestants in the parishes of Abbeylara and Russough, RCB
            Library, GO 537
*c.*1790   Freeholders NA M 2486–8, NL Pos. 1897
1795–1862   Charlton Marriage Certificates, NA 1A–42–163/4, indexed in
            Accessions, Vol. 37
1796   Spinning-Wheel Premium Lists, microfiche index in National
            Archives, comprising, in the case of Co. Longford, over 3,000 names
1800–1835   Freeholders, GO 444
1820s/30s   Tithe Books
1828–36   Freeholders certificates, NA M.2781
1834   Granard, full census, in Catholic registers, NL Pos. 4237
1838   Householders, Mullinalaghta parish (Scrabby and Columbkill),
            Teathbha, Vol. 1, No. 3, 1973
1854   Griffith's Valuation
1901   Census, indexed in Leahy, David, *Co. Longford and its People*, Dublin,
            Flyleaf Press, 1990
1911   Census

Local history

Brady, G., *In Search of Longford Roots*, Offaly Historical Society, 1987, Ir. 94136
    t 1
Butler, H. T. and H. E., *The Black Book of Edgeworthstown, 1585–1817*, 1927
Cobbe, D., *75 Years of the Longford Leader*, 1972, NL ILB 07
Devaney, O., *Killoe: History of a Co. Longford Parish*, 1981, Ir. 9413 d 1
Farrell, James P., *History of the county of Longford*, Dublin, 1891, Ir. 94131 f 2
Healy, John, *History of the Diocese of Meath*, 2 vols, Dublin, 1908
Leahy, David, *Co. Longford and its People*, Dublin, Flyleaf Press, 1990
Murtagh, H., *Irish Midland Studies*, 1980, Ir. 941 m 58
Stafford, R. W., *St Patrick's Church of Ireland, Granard: Notes of Genealogical and
    Historical Interest*, 1983, Ir. 914131 s 3

Local journals

Ardagh and Clonmacnoise Historical Society Journal (1926–51), Ir. 794105
Teathbha (Journal of the Longford Historical Society), Ir. 94131 t 1

Directories

1824   Pigot and Co., *City of Dublin and Hibernian Provincial Directory*, NL Ir.
        9141 p 75
1846   Slater's *National Commercial Directory of Ireland*
1856   Slater's *Royal National Commercial Directory of Ireland*
1870   Slater's *Directory of Ireland*
1881   Slater's *Royal National Commercial Directory of Ireland*
1894   Slater's *Royal Commercial Directory of Ireland*

Estate records

Adair estate, Clonbroney parish, 1738–67, NL MS. 3859.
Aldborough estate rentals, 1846, NA M.2971.
Newcomen estates: maps of estates to be sold, 20 July 1827, NL Map Room.

Placenames

Townland Maps, Londonderry Inner City Trust
McGivney, J., *Place-names of the Co. Longford*, 1908, 92942

CO. LOUTH

Census returns and substitutes

1600   'Gentlemen of Co. Louth', JCLAS, Vol. 4, No. 4, 1919/20
1641   Book of Survey and Distribution, NL MS. 974
1659   Pender's 'Census', NL Ir. 31041 c 4
1663/4   Hearth Money Roll, JCLAS, Vol. 6, Nos 2 and 4; Vol. 7, No. 3
1666/7   Hearth Money Roll of Dunleer parish, *The Irish Genealogist*, 1969
1683   Louth brewers and retailers, JCLAS, Vol. 3, No. 3
1683   Drogheda merchants, JCLAS, Vol. 3, No. 3
1739–41   Corn census of Co. Louth, JCLAS, Vol. 11, No. 4, 254–86
1756   Commissions of Array, giving lists of Protestants who took the
          oath, NL Pos. 4011
1760   Ardee parish, *The Irish Genealogist*, 1961

1766	Ardee, Ballymakenny, Beaulieu, Carlingford, Charlestown, Clonkeehan, Darver, Drumiskin, Kildermock, Killeshiel, Louth, Mapestown, Phillipstown, Shanliss, Smarmore, Stickallen, Tallonstown, Termonfeckin. NA 1A 41 100; Creggan, NA 1A 46 49; also Nelson, *History of the Parish of Creggan* . . ., NL, Ir. 941 p 43
1782–92	Cess-payers, parishes of Cappagh, Drumcar, Dysert, Moylary, Monasterboice, JCLAS, Vol. 9, No. 1
1791	Landholders, Dromiskin parish, *History of Kilsaran* . . ., J. B. Leslie
1796	Spinning-Wheel Premium Lists, microfiche index in National Archives, comprising, in the case of Co. Louth, over 4,000 names
1798	Drogheda voters list, JCLAS, Vol. XX, 1984
1801	Tithe applotment, Stabannon and Roodstown parishes, *History of Kilsaran* . . ., J. B. Leslie
1802	Protestant parishioners of Carlingford, JCLAS, Vol. 16, No. 3
1802	Drogheda voters list, JCLAS, Vol. XX, 1984
1816	Grand Jurors, NL, Ir. 6551, Dundalk
1821	Freeholders, NL, Ir. 94132 1 3
1820s/30s	Tithe Books
1830–65	Methodist records, Newry Circuit, *Seanchas Ardmhacha*, Vol. 7, No. 2, 1977
1834	Tallonstown parish, JCLAS, Vol. 14
1837	Valuation of towns returning MPs (occupants and property values): Drogheda, Dundalk. *Parliamentary Papers*, 1837, Reports from Committees, Vol. II (i), Appendix G
1837	Marksmen (illiterate voters) in parliamentary boroughs: Drogheda, Dundalk. *Parliamentary Papers*, 1837, Reports from Committees, Vol. II (i), Appendix A
1852	Mosstown and Phillipstown, JCLAS, 1975
1852	Voting electors, NL MS. 1660
1854	Griffith's Valuation
1865	Parliamentary voters, P. 2491
1901	Census
1911	Census

Local history

Bernard, Nicholas (ed.), *The Whole Proceedings of the Siege of Drogheda* [&] *Londonderry*, Dublin, 1736

Conlon, L., *The Heritage of Collon*, 1984, NL, Ir. 94132 c 5

'Cromwellian and Restoration settlements in the parish of Dundalk', JCLAS, Vol. XIX, 1, 1977

D'Alton, John, *The history of Drogheda*, Dublin, 1844, Ir. 94132 d 1

D'Alton, John, *The history of Dundalk*, Dublin, 1864, NL, Ir. 94132 d 2

Duffner, P., *Drogheda: the Low Lane Church 1300–1979*, Ir. 94132 d 7
'Families at Mosstown and Phillipstown in 1852', JCLAS, Vol. XVIII, 3, 1975
Henderson's Post Office Directory of Meath and Louth, 1861
ICA, *A Local History Guide to Summerhill and Surrounding Areas*, NL, Ir. 94132 i 1
Keenan, Padraic, 'Clonallon Parish: its Annals and Antiquities', JCLAS, Vol. X
Kieron, J. S., *An Outline History of the Parish of St Mary's Abbey*, 1980, NL, Ir. 91413 p 12
Leslie, J. B., *History of Kilsaran Union of Parishes*, 1908, NL, Ir. 94132 l 1
L'Estrange, G., *Notes and Jottings concerning the parish of Charlestown Union*, 1912, NL, Ir. 94132 l 2
'Methodist Baptismal Records of Co. Louth, 1829–1865', JCLAS, Vol. XVIII, 2, 1974
McCullen, J., *The Call of St Mary's*, 1984, NL, Ir. 27413 m 8
Murphy, Peter, *Together in Exile*, Nova Scotia, 1991 (Carlingford emigrants to St John's, New Brunswick)
Nelson, S., *History of the Parish of Creggan in Counties Armagh and Louth from 1611 to 1840*, 1974, NL, Ir. 941 p 43
'Notes on the Volunteers, Militia and Yeomanry, and Orangemen of Co. Louth', JCLAS, Vol. XVIII, 4, 1976
'Old Title Deeds of Co. Louth, Dundalk, 1718–1856', JCLAS, Vol. XX, 1, 1981
O'Neill, C. P., *History of Dromiskin*, 1984, NL, Ir. 94132 o 4
Paterson, J. (ed.), *Diocese of Meath and Kildare: an historical guide*, 1981, NL, Ir. 941 p 75
Redmond, B., *The Story of Louth*, 1931, NL, Ir. 9141 p 1
Tempest, H. S., *Descriptive and Historical Guide to Dundalk and District*, 1916, NL, Ir. 94132 t 1
Witherow, Thomas, *The Boyne and the Aghrim*, 1879

Local journals

Clogher Record (Journal of the Clogher Diocesan Historical Society), NL, Ir. 94114 c 2
Co. Louth Archaeological and Historical Society Journal, NL, Ir. 794105 l 2
Journal of the Old Drogheda Society, NL, Ir. 94132 o 3

Directories

1820   J. Pigot, *Commercial Directory of Ireland*
1824   Pigot and Co., *City of Dublin and Hibernian Provincial Directory*, NL, Ir. 9141 p 75
1830   McCabe's *Drogheda Directory*
1846   Slater's *National Commercial Directory of Ireland*

1856   Slater's *Royal National Commercial Directory of Ireland*
1870   Slater's *Directory of Ireland*
1881   Slater's *Royal National Commercial Directory of Ireland*
1886   George H. Bassett, *Louth County Guide and Directory*
1890   Tempest's *Almanack and Directory of Dundalk*, issued annually from this date
1894   Slater's *Royal Commercial Directory of Ireland*

Gravestone inscriptions

Ardee: *The Irish Genealogist*, Vol. III, No. 1, 1956
Ballymakenny: *Seanchas Ardmhacha*, 1983/4
Ballymascanlon: JCLAS, Vol. XVII, No. 4, 1972
Beaulieu: JCLAS, Vol. XX, No. 1
Carlingford: JCLAS, Vol. XIX, No. 2, 1978
Castlebellingham: *History of Kilsaran Union of Parishes in the Co. of Louth*, J. B. Leslie, 1908
Charlestown: *Notes and Jottings concerning the Parish of Charlestown Union*, G. W. C. L'Estrange, 1912
Clonkeen: *Notes and Jottings concerning the Parish of Charlestown Union*, G. W. C. L'Estrange, 1912
Clonmore: JCLAS, Vol. XX, No. 2
Dromiskin: *History of Kilsaran Union of Parishes in the Co. of Louth*, J. B. Leslie, 1908
Faughart: *Tombstone Inscriptions from Fochart*, Dundalgan Press, 1968
Faughart (Urnai): *Urnai*, D. Mac Iomhair, Dundalk, 1969
Dunany and Salterstown: JCLAS, Vol. XX, No. 3 (1983)
Dysert, Grange, and Drumshallon: JCLAS, Vol. XIX, 3 (1979)
Kildemock: JCLAS, Vol. XIII, No. 1
Killanny: *Clogher Record*, Vol. VI, No. 1, 1966
Kilsaran: *History of Kilsaran Union of Parishes in the Co. of Louth*, J. B. Leslie, 1908
Manfieldstown: *History of Kilsaran Union of Parishes in the Co. of Louth*, J. B. Leslie, 1908
Mayne: JCLAS, Vol. XX, No. 4 (1984)
Newtownstalaban: JCLAS, Vol. XVII, No. 2, 1970
Rathdromin: JCLAS, Vol. XIX, No. 1, 1970
St Mary's 'Abbey', Louth: JCLAS, Vol. XIX, No. 4 (1980)
Seatown, Dundalk: *Tempest's Annual*, 1967, 1971/2
Stabannon: *History of Kilsaran Union of Parishes in the Co. of Louth*, J. B. Leslie, 1908
Stagrennon: *Journal of the Old Drogheda Society*, 1977
Tullyallen: *Seanchas Ardmhacha*, Vol. VII, No. 2, 1977

Estate records

'Tenants of Omeath', 1865, JCLAS, Vol. XVII, 1, 1973.
'Details of the Anglesea estate papers in PRONI', JCLAS, Vol. XVII, 1, 1973 (see also JCLAS, XII, 2).
'Drumgooter: A tenant farm in the 18th and 19th Centuries (from a rent roll of the estate of Sir John Bellew)', JCLAS, Vol. XX, 4, 1984.
'Papers from the Roden estate, Clanbrassel estate map, 1785', JCLAS, Vol. XX, 1 1981.
Trench estate rentals, Drogheda, NL MS. 2576.

Placenames

Townland Maps, Londonderry Inner City trust
Townland Survey of Co. Louth—Newtownstalagan, JCLAS, Vol. XIX, No. 1 (1977)
Townland Survey of Co. Louth—Beaulieu, JCLAS, Vol. XIX, No. 4 (1980)
Townland Survey of Co. Louth—Mullacrew, JCLAS, Vol. XX, No. 1 (1980)

CO. MAYO

Census returns and substitutes

1600s	Mayo landowners in the seventeenth century, *R. Soc. Antiq. of Ire. Jnl*, 1962, 153–62
1783	Ballinrobe, *Analecta Hibernica*, Vol. 14
1785–1815	Westport Rent Rolls, *Cathair na Mart*, Vol. 2, No. 1, 1982
1796	Catholics Emigrating from Ulster to Mayo, *Seanchas Ardmhacha*, 1958, 17–50; see also 'Petition of Armagh migrants in the Westport area', *Cathair na Mart*, Vol. 2, No. 1 (Appendix)
1796	Spinning-Wheel Premium Lists, microfiche index in National Archives, comprising, in the case of Co. Mayo, over 5,000 names
1798	List of those who suffered loss in 1798 Rebellion, NL JLB 94107
1818	Tithe Collectors' account book, parishes of Kilfian and Moygownagh, NA M.6085
1820	Protestants in Killalla, NA MFCI 32

1820s/30s Tithe Books
1832   Protestants, Foxford, NL MS. 8295
1841   Some extracts, Newport. Thrift Abstracts, National Archives
1856/7   Griffith's Valuation
1901   Census
1911   Census

Local history

Achill, 15th report of the mission/report of Achill Orphan Refuges (1849), NL Ir. 266 a 8

Crossmolina Parish: An Historical Survey, NL Ir. 94123 c 5

Hayes-McCoy, G. A., *Index to 'The Compossicion Booke of Connoght, 1585'*, Irish Manuscripts Commission, Dublin, 1945, NL Ir. 9412 c 1

Hurley, Rev. Timothy, *St Patrick and the Parish of Kilkeeran*, Vol. 1

Knox, H. T., *Notes on the Early History of the Dioceses of Tuam, Killala and Achonry*, Dublin, 1904

Knox, H. T., *The history of Mayo to the close of the 16th century*, Dublin, 1908, NL Ir. 94123 k 2 (and LO)

McDonnell, T., *Diocese of Killala*, NL Ir. 94123 m 7

MacHale (ed.), *The Parishes in the Diocese of Killala*, NL Ir. 27414 m 6

O'Hara, B., *Killasser: a history*, 1981, Ir. 94123 o 6

O'Sullivan, W. (ed.), *The Strafford Inquisition of Co. Mayo*, NL Ir. 94123 o 4

St Muiredach's College, Ballina, Roll 1906–1979, NL Ir. 259 m 2/Ir. 37941 s 18

Local journals

Cathair na Mart (Journal of the Westport Historical Society), NL Ir. 94123 c 4

North Mayo Historical and Archaeological Journal, Ir. 94123 n 4

Directories

1824   Pigot and Co., *City of Dublin and Hibernian Provincial Directory*, NL Ir. 9141 p 75
1846   Slater's *National Commercial Directory of Ireland*
1856   Slater's *Royal National Commercial Directory of Ireland*
1870   Slater's *Directory of Ireland*
1881   Slater's *Royal National Commercial Directory of Ireland*
1894   Slater's *Royal Commercial Directory of Ireland*

Estate records

LANDLORD

Lord **Altamont**: NA M5788 (2), Rental of the Westport estate, 1787, principally major tenants. The section on Westport town is published in *Cathair na Mart*, Vol. 2, No. 1, along with a rent roll for the town from 1815; covering townlands in the civil parishes of Aghagower, Burriscarra, Burrishoole, Kilbelfad, Kilbride, Kilconduff, Kildacomoge, Kilfian, Killdeer, Kilmaclasser, Kilmeena, Moygownagh, Oughaval.

Earl of **Arran**: NL MS. 14087, leases on the Mayo estate, 1720–1869, mentioning lives in the leases; NL MS. 14086; valuation survey of the Mayo estates, 1850–52, all tenants; covering townlands in the civil parishes of Addergoole, Ardagh, Ballysakeery, Crossmolina, Kilbelfad, Kilcummin, Kilfian, Killala, Kilmoremoy.

Col John **Browne**: NL Pos. 940, account of the sales of the estates of Col John Browne in Counties Galway and Mayo, compiled in 1778, giving names of major tenants and purchasers, 1698–1704, and those occupying the estates in 1778, covering townlands in the civil parishes of Addergoole, Aghagower, Aglish, Ballintober, Ballyhean, Ballyovey, Ballysakeery, Breaghwy, Burrishoole, Cong, Crossmolina, Drum, Islandeady, Kilcommon, Kilgeever, Killeadan, Kilmaclasser, Kilmainemore, Kilmeena, Manulla, Moygownagh, Oughaval, Robeen, Tonaghty, Turlough.

Lord **Clanmorris**: NL MS. 3279, Rental, 1833, all tenants, covering townlands in the civil parishes of Kilcommon, Kilmainemore, Mayo, Robeen, Rosslee, Tonaghty, Toomour.

Domville: NL MS. 11816, Rentals, 1833–36, 1843, 1847, 1851, all tenants, covering townlands in the civil parishes of Killasser, Manulla, Robeen.

Francis Blake **Knox**: NL MS. 3077, Rental of the estates in Counties Galway, Mayo and Roscommon.

Henry **Knox**: NA 5630 (1), Rental, early nineteenth century, all tenants, covering townlands in the civil parishes of Crossmolina, Doonfeeny, Kilfian, Kilmoremoy.

Thomas **Medlicott**: NL MS. 5736 (3), Tithe Applotment Book, Achill; NL MSS. 5736 (2), 5821, Rent rolls, showing lives in leases, 1774, 1776, major tenants only; covering townlands in the civil parishes of Achill, Aghagower, Burrishoole, Kilcommon, Kilmeena, Kilmore.

Sir Neal **O'Donel**: NL MS. 5738 and 5744, leaseholders on the estates, 1775–1859, 1828, giving lives mentioned in leases, mainly major tenants; NL MS. 5736, Rental, 1788, major tenants only; NL MS. 5281, Rental, 1805, major tenants only; NL MS. 5743, Rental, 1810, major tenants only; NL MS. 5281, Rental, 1828, major tenants only; covering townlands in the civil parishes of Achill, Aghagower, Burrishoole, Cong, Kilcommon, Kilgeever, Kilmore, Kilmaclasser.

Sir Samuel **O'Malley**: NA M1457 (published in *Cathair na Mart*, Vol. 6, No. 1), valuation of the Mayo estates, 1845, all tenants, covering townlands in the civil parishes of Aglish, Kilgeever, Kilmeena.

Placenames

Townland maps, Londonderry Inner City Trust

CO. MEATH

Census returns and substitutes

1641	Book of Survey and Distribution, NL MS. 974
1654/6	Civil Survey, Vol. III, NL I 6551, Dublin
1659	Pender's 'Census', NL Ir. 31041 c 4
1766	Protestants in Ardbraccan, RCB Library, GO 537
1770	Freeholders, NL MS. 787–8
1781	Voters List, NA M.4878, 4910–12
1792	Hearth tax collectors account and collection books: parishes of Colp, Donore, Duleek, Kilshalvan, NL MS. 26735; Ardcath, Ardmulchan, Ballymagarvy, Brownstown, Clonalvy, Danestown, Fennor, Kentstown, Knockcommon, Rathfeigh, NL MS. 26736; Athlumney, Danestown, Dowdstown, Dunsany, Kilcarn, Killeen, Macetown, Mounttown, Tara, Trevet, NL MS. 26737; St Mary's Drogheda, NL MS. 26739
1793	Hearth tax collectors account and collection books; parishes of Ardagh, Dowth, Gernonstown, Killary, Mitchelstown, Siddan, Slane, Stackallen, NL MS. 26738
1795–1862	Charlton Marriage Certificates, NA 1A–42–163/4, indexed under men's names in Accessions, Vol. 37
1796	Spinning-Wheel Premium Lists, microfiche index in National Archives, comprising, in the case of Co. Meath, over 3,000 names
1797–1801	Athboy Tithe Valuations, NA MFCI 53, 54
1802–6	Protestants in the parishes of Agher, Ardagh, Clonard, Clongill, Drumconrath, Duleek, Emlagh, Julianstown, Kentstown, Kilbeg, Kilmainhamwood, Kilskyre, Laracor, Moynalty, Navan,

Robertsown, Raddenstown, Rathcore, Rathkenny, Rathmolyon, Ratoath, Skryne, Staffordstown, Stamullen, Tara, Trevett, Templekeran, *The Irish Ancestor*, 1973

1813   Protestant children at Ardbraccan school, *The Irish Ancestor*, 1973

1821   Parishes of Ardbraccan, Ardsallagh, Balrathboyne, Bective, Church-town, Clonmacduff, Donaghmore, Donaghpatrick, Kilcooly, Liscartan, Martry, Moymet, Navan, Newtownclonbun, Rathkenny, Rataine, Trim, Trimblestown, Tullaghanoge. National Archives

1820s/30s Tithe Books

1833   Protestant Cess payers, parishes of Colpe and Kilshalvan

1835   Tubber parish, NL Pos. 1994

*c.*1850   Register of land occupiers, with particulars of land and families, in the Unions of Kells and Oldcastle, NL MS. 5774

1855   Griffith's Valuation

1865   Census of the town and parks of Kells, Headfort papers, NL MS. 25423

1866–73   Stamullen emigrants, with parish records, National Library

1871   Drumcondra and Loughbraclen, transcript in Catholic parish records

1901   Census

1911   Census

Local history

Brady, J., *A short history of the parishes of the diocese of Meath, 1867–1944*, Ir. 94132 b 2

Carty, Mary Rose, *History of Killeen Castle*, Dunsany, 1991

Cogan, J., *Ratoath*, Ir. 9141 p 84

Coogan, O., *Dunshaughlin, Culmullen and Knockmark*, 1988

D'Alton, John, *Antiquities of the County of Meath*, Dublin, 1833

French, Noel, *Trim Traces and Places*

French, Noel, *Navan by the Boyne*

French, Noel, *Athboy, a short history*

French, Noel (ed.), *Nobber, a step back in time*

French, Noel, *Tracing Your Ancestors in Co. Meath*

Healy, John, *History of the Diocese of Meath*, 2 vols, Dublin, 1908

Henderson's *Post Office Directory of Meath and Louth*, 1861, Ir. 914132 m 3

ICA: *A local history guide to the parish of Summerhill and its surrounding areas*, 1981, Ir. 941, p 75

Larkin, Wm, Map of County, 1812, see NL Map Room

Mooneystown Valuation Survey and Field Book, 1838, P 2011

O'Connell, Philip, *The Diocese of Kilmore: its History and Antiquities*, Dublin, 1937

Parish Guide to Meath (1968), Ir. 270 p 2

Paterson, J. (ed.), *Diocese of Meath and Kildare: an historical guide*, 1981, Ir. 941 p 75
Sims, A., *Irish Historic Towns Atlas: Kells*, Dublin, Royal Irish Academy, 1991

Local journals

Annala Dhamhliag, The annals of Duleek (from 1971), NL I 94132 a 1
Seanchas Ard Mhacha (Journal of the Armagh Diocesan Historical Society), NL Ir. 27411 s 4
Riocht na Midhe (Records of the Meath Archaeological and Historical Society), NL Ir. 94132 r 1

Directories

1824   Pigot and Co., *City of Dublin and Hibernian Provincial Directory*, NL Ir. 9141 p 75
1846   Slater's *National Commercial Directory of Ireland*
1856   Slater's *Royal National Commercial Directory of Ireland*
1870   Slater's *Directory of Ireland*
1881   Slater's *Royal National Commercial Directory of Ireland*
1894   Slater's *Royal Commercial Directory of Ireland*

Gravestone inscriptions

Agher: *The Irish Ancestor*, Vol. X, No. 2, 1978
Ardmulchan: 'Monumental Inscriptions from some Graveyards in Co. Meath', N. French (unpub.), National Archives search room
Ardsallagh: 'Monumental Inscriptions from some Graveyards in Co. Meath', N. French (unpub.), National Archives search room
Arodstown: *Riocht na Midhe*, Vol. VI, No. 1, 1975
Athboy: *The Irish Ancestor*, Vol. XII, Nos 1 and 2, 1981
Athlumney: IGRS Collection, GO
Ballygarth: IGRS Collection, GO
Balfeaghan: IGRS Collection, 21, GO
Balsoon: *The Irish Ancestor*, Vol. VII, No. 2, 1976
Castlejordan: IGRS Collection, 89, GO
Castlekieran: IGRS Collection, 39, GO
Churchtown (Dunderry): IGRS Collection, 59, GO
Clady: IGRS Collection, GO
Clonabreany: *Riocht na Midhe*, Vol. VI, No. 2, 1976
Clonmacnuff: IGRS Collection, 70, GO
Cortown: IGRS Collection, 120, GO
Danestown: *Riocht na Midhe*, Vol. V, No. 4, 1974
Donaghmore: 'Monumental Inscriptions from some Graveyards in Co. Meath', N. French (unpub.), National Archives search room

Dowdstown: 'Monumental Inscriptions from some Graveyards in Co. Meath', N. French (unpub.), National Archives search room

Drumlargan: *The Irish Ancestor*, Vol. XII, Nos 1 and 2, 1980

Duleek: *The Irish Genealogist*, Vol. 3, No. 12, 1967

Dunboyne: *The Irish Ancestor*, Vol. XI, Nos 1 and 2, 1979

Dunboyne C. of I.: IGRS Collection, GO

Dunmoe: 'Monumental Inscriptions from some Graveyards in Co. Meath', N. French (unpub.), National Archives search room

Fore: IGRS Collection, GO

Gallow: IGRS Collection, 39, GO

Gernonstown: 'Monumental Inscriptions from some Graveyards in Co. Meath', N. French (unpub.), National Archives search room

Girly (C. of I. and Catholic): 'Monumental Inscriptions from some Graveyards in Co. Meath', N. French (unpub.), National Archives search room

Hermitage: 'Monumental Inscriptions from some Graveyards in Co. Meath', N. French (unpub.), National Archives search room

Hill of Ward: 'Monumental Inscriptions from some Graveyards in Co. Meath', N. French (unpub.), National Archives search room

Kells: *The Irish Genealogist*, Vol. III, No. 12, 1967

Kilcarn: 'Monumental Inscriptions from some Graveyards in Co. Meath', N. French (unpub.), National Archives search room

Kilbride: *Riocht na Midhe*, Vol. VI, No. 3, 1977

Kilcooly (Trim): IGRS Collection, 8, GO

Kildalkey: IGRS Collection, 117, GO

Kilaconnigan: IGRS Collection, 100, GO

Killeen: *Riocht na Midhe*, Vol. IV, No. 3, 1970

Kilmore: *Riocht na Midhe*, Vol. VI, No. 1, 1975

Loughcrew: *The Irish Ancestor*, Vol. IX, No. 2, 1977

Loughsallagh: IGRS Collection, 60, GO

Macetown: IGRS Collection, 7, GO

Maudlin (Trim): IGRS Collection, 3, GO

Moy: *The Irish Ancestor*, Vol. VI, No. 2, 1974

Moyagher: *The Irish Ancestor*, Vol. VIII, No. 1, 1976

Moymet: IGRS Collection, 54, GO

Navan (C. of I.): with Church records, NA Mf CI 45

Oldcastle: *Riocht na Midhe*, Vol. IV, No. 2, 1968

Rathfeigh: IGRS Collection, 42, GO

Rathkenny: 'Monumental Inscriptions from some Graveyards in Co. Meath', N. French (unpub.), National Archives search room

Rathmore: *The Irish Ancestor*, Vol. VII, No. 2, 1975

Ratoath: 'Monumental Inscriptions from some Graveyards in Co. Meath', N. French (unpub.), National Archives search room

Scurlogstown: IGRS Collection, 17, GO

Skryne: 'Monumental Inscriptions from some Graveyards in Co. Meath', N.
French (unpub.), National Archives search room
Stackallen: 'Monumental Inscriptions from some Graveyards in Co. Meath',
N. French (unpub.), National Archives search room
Trimblestown: 'Monumental Inscriptions from some Graveyards in Co.
Meath', N. French (unpub.), National Archives search room
Tullyhanogue: 'Monumental Inscriptions from some Graveyards in Co.
Meath', N. French (unpub.), National Archives search room
Tycroghan: IGRS Collection, 4, GO

Estate records

Balfour tenants, townlands of Belustran, Cloughmacow, Doe and Hurtle, 1838,
JCLAS, Vol. 12, No. 3, 1951.
Newcomen estates, maps of estates to be sold, 20 July 1827, NL Map Room.
Reynell family rent books, 1834–48, NL MS. 5990.
William Barlow Smythe, Collinstown, Farm a/c book, NL MS. 7909.
Trench estate rentals, Drogheda, NL MS. 2576.
Tenants of the Wellesley estate at Dengen, Ballymaglossan, Moyare, Morning-
ton and Trim, 1816, *Riocht na Midhe*, Vol. 4, No. 4, 1967.

Placenames

Townland Maps, Londonderry Inner City Trust
Walsh, P., *Some Place-names in Ancient Meath*, NL I 92941

CO. MONAGHAN

Census returns and substitutes

	Medieval Clones families, *Clogher Record*, 1959
1641	Book of Survey and Distribution, NL MS. 976
1659	Pender's 'Census', NL Ir. 31041 c 4
1663/5	Hearth Money Roll, *A History of Monaghan*, D. C. Rushe
1738	Some Clonea Inhabitants, *Clogher Record*, Vol. 2, No. 3, 1959
1777	Some Protestant Inhabitants of Carrickmacross, *Clogher Record*, Vol. 6, No. 1, 1966

1796   Catholic migrants from Ulster to Mayo, see Mayo
1796   Spinning-Wheel Premium Lists, microfiche index in National
            Archives, comprising, in the case of Co. Monaghan, over 6,000
            names
1821   Thrift Abstracts, see *Clogher Record*, 1991
1820s/30s   Tithe Books
1841   Some extracts. Thrift Abstracts, National Archives.
1843   Magistrates, landed proprietors, 'etc.', NL MS. 12, 767
1847   Castleblayney Poor Law Rate Book, *Clogher Record*, Vol. 5, No. 1,
            1963
1851   Some extracts. Thrift Abstracts, National Archives.
1858/60   Griffith's Valuation, All-Ireland Heritage microfiche index
1901   Census
1911   Census

Local history

Bell, Rev. J. Brian A., *A History of Garmany's Grove Presbyterian Church*, Armagh,
    1970
Carville, G., *Parish of Clontibret*, NL Ir. 941 p 74
Cotter, Canon J. B. D., *A Short History of Donagh Parish*, Enniskillen, 1966
Duffy J. (ed.), *A Clogher Record Album: a diocesan history*, NL Ir. 94114 c 3
Gilsenan, M., *Hills of Magheracloone 1884–1984*, 1985, NL Ir. 94117 g 1
Haslett, A. and Orr, Rev. S. L., *Historical Sketch of Ballyalbany Presbyterian
    Church*, Belfast, n.d.
Leslie, Seymour, *Of Glaslough in Oriel*, 1912
Livingstone, Peadar, *The Monaghan Story*, Enniskillen, 1980
Marshall, J., *History of the Town and District of Clogher, Co. Tyrone, parish of Errigal
    Keerogue, Tyrone and Errigal Truagh in the Co. of Monaghan*, 1930, NL I 94114
McCluskey, Seamus, *Emyvale Sweet Emyvale*, Monaghan, 1985
McKenna, J. E., *Parochial Records*, 2 vols, Enniskillen, 1920
McIvor, John, *Extracts from a Ballybay Scrapbook*, Monaghan, 1974
Monaghan Election Petition 1826, minutes of evidence, NL Ir. 32341 m 52
Monaghan Election Petition 1834, minutes of evidence, NL Ir. 32341 m 50
Mulligan, E. and McCloskey, B., *The Replay: A Parish History: Kilmore and
    Drumsnat*, Monaghan, 1984, NL Ir. 94117 m 10
Na Braithre Criostai Mhuineacháin, *Monaghan Memories*, Monaghan, 1984
O Mordha, P., *The Story of the G.A.A. in Currin and an outline of Parish History*,
    Monaghan, 1986
Rushe, Denis Carolan, *Historical Sketches of Monaghan*, Dundalk, 1895
Rushe, Denis Carolan, *Monaghan in the 18th century*, Dublin and Dundalk, 1916
Rushe, Denis Carolan, *History of Monaghan for two hundred years 1660–1860*,
    Dundalk, 1921

St Macartan's College 1840–1990, Monaghan, 1990
Shirley, Evelyn P., *The History of the County of Monaghan*, London, 1879
Shirley, Evelyn P., *Some Account of the Territory and Dominion of Farney*, London, n.d.
Shirley, Evelyn P., *Lough Fea*, 2 vols, London, 1859, 1869
Swanzy, C. E., *The MacKennas of Truagh*, 1977, NL Ir. 9292 s 20
Swanzy, H. B., *Parish of Clontibret, Co. Monaghan: Record of Vicars and Churchwardens from 1662–1924*, Newry, 1925
Watson, William, *Some Records of the Monaghan Regiment of Militia* [from 1793 to 1871], Monaghan, 1871
Wilkinson, W. R., *Our Good School upon the Hill*, NL Ir. 372 w 10

Local journals

Clogher Record (Journal of the Clogher Diocesan Historical Society), NL Ir. 94114 c 2
The Drumlin, a Journal of Cavan, Leitrim and Monaghan, NL Ir. 05 d 34
Macalla (1976–1979)
Clann MacKenna Journal

Directories

1824   Pigot and Co., *City of Dublin and Hibernian Provincial Directory*, NL Ir. 9141 p 75
1846   Slater's *National Commercial Directory of Ireland*
1852   James A. Henderson, *Belfast and Province of Ulster Directory*, issued also in 1854, 1856, 1858, 1861, 1863, 1865, 1868, 1870, 1877, 1880, 1884, 1887, 1890, 1894, 1900
1856   Slater's *Royal National Commercial Directory of Ireland*
1865   R. Wynne, *Business Directory of Belfast*
1870   Slater's *Directory of Ireland*
1881   Slater's *Royal National Commercial Directory of Ireland*
1894   Slater's *Royal Commercial Directory of Ireland*
1897   *Gillespie's Co. Monaghan Directory and Almanac*

Gravestone inscriptions

Aghabog and Killeevan: *Clogher Record*, Vol. XI, No. 1
Cahans (Presbyterian): Monaghan Ancestral Research Group (see below)
Clontibret (Presbyterian): Monaghan Ancestral Research Group (see below)
Clontibret (C. of I.): Monaghan Ancestral Research Group (see below)
Clontibret: *Clogher Record*, Vol. VII, No. 2, 1974
Clones and Roslea: *Clogher Record*, 1982–84
Clones (St Tighernach's C. of I.): *Clogher Record*, Vol. XIII, No. 1, 1988

Coolshannagh, Monaghan: Monaghan Ancestral Research Group (see below)
Donagh: *Clogher Record*, Vol. II, No. 1, 1957
Drumsnat: *Clogher Record*, Vol. VI, No. 1, 1966
Drumswords (Killeevan Parish): *Clogher Record*, 1985
Edergole (Ematris): Monaghan Ancestral Research Group (see below)
Glaslough: *Clogher Record*, Vol. IX, No. 3, 1978
Killanny: *Clogher Record*, Vol. VI, No. 1, 1966
Killeevan and Aghabog: *Clogher Record*, 1982
Kilmore: *Clogher Record*, 1983 and 1985
Magheross: *Clogher Record*, Vol. V, No. 1, 1963
Mullandoy: *Clogher Record*, Vol. VI, No. 1, 1966
Old Errigal: *Clogher Record*, 1987
Rackwallace: *Clogher Record*, Vol. IV, No. 3, 1962
Tydavnet: *Clogher Record*, Vol. I, No. 1, 1954
Urbleshanny (Tydavnet): Monaghan Ancestral Research Group (see below)
Monaghan Ancestral Research Group, 6 Tully, Monaghan, Co. Monaghan

Estate records

LANDLORD
Anketell estate rentals, 1784–89, *Clogher Record*, Vol. XI, No. 3.
Balfour rentals of 1632 and 1636, *Clogher Record*, 1985.
James **Forster**: Five Rent Rolls, 1803–08, 1812–24, covering townlands in
the parishes Aghabog, Killeevan, Tydavnet, Tyholland, Monaghan An-
cestral Research Group.
Kane: Rentals, 1840–41; Account Books, 1842–44; Arrears, 1848, 1849, 1852;
Rent Receipts, 1851–52; covering townlands in the parish of Tydavnet,
Monaghan Ancestral Research Group.
Ker: Landholders, Newbliss, 1790–*c.*1830, Killeevan civil parish, *Clogher
Record*, 1985.
Rossmore estate: Maps with tenants' names, *c.*1820–1852, Monaghan town
and surrounding areas, Monaghan Ancestral Research Group.
Weymouth estate, Magheross: Survey, major tenants only, Monaghan
Ancestral Research Group.
Wingfield estate: Rentals and arrears, 1852, county and town of Monaghan,
Monaghan Ancestral Research Group.

NO LANDLORD GIVEN
Ballybay estate rentals, 1786, *Clogher Record*, Vol. XI, No. 1.
Castleblayney Rent Book, 1772, *Clogher Record*, Vol. X, No. 3.

Emy and Glaslough estates: Rent Roll, 1752–60, principally major tenants; civil parishes of Donagh and Errigal Truagh, Monaghan Ancestral Research Group.

Monaghan Manor and Lordship: Rent Roll, 1790, principally major tenants.

Placenames

Townland maps, Londonderry Inner City Trust

CO. OFFALY

Census returns and substitutes

1641	Book of Survey and Distribution, NL MS. 972
1659	Pender's 'Census', NL Ir. 31041 c 4
1766	Ballycommon, JKAS, Vol. VII, also GO 537
1770	Voters, NL MS. 2050
1802	Protestants in the parishes of Ballyboggan, Ballyboy, Castlejordan, Clonmacnoise, Drumcullin, Eglish, Gallen, Killoughey, Lynally, Rynagh, Tullamore, *The Irish Ancestor*, 1973
1821	Parishes of Aghacon, Birr, Ettagh, Kilcolman, Kinnitty, Letterluna, Roscomroe, Rocrea, Seirkieran, National Archives
1824	Catholic householders, Lusmagh parish, in Catholic registers
1830	Contributors to new Catholic church in Lusmagh, with Catholic registers
1820s/30s	Tithe Books
1840	Eglish and Drumcullin parishes, in Catholic registers of Eglish (NL Pos. 4175)
1852	Assisted passages from Kilconouse, Kinnitty parish, *Analecta Hibernica*, Vol. 22, 1960
1854	Griffith's Valuation
1901	Census
1911	Census

Local history

Byrne, M., *Durrow and its History*, NL Ir. 9141 p 71
Byrne, M., *Sources for Offaly History* (1977), NL Ir. 94136 b 1

Byrne, M., *Towards a History of Kilclonfert*, NL Ir. 94136 t 1
Byrne, M., *Tullamore Catholic parish: a Historical Survey*, NL r 27414 b 7
Feehan, J., *The Landscape of Slieve Bloom: a study of the natural and human heritage*,
    1979, NL Ir. 91413 f 4
Ferbane Parish and its Churches, NL Ir. 91413 f 4
Finney, C. W., *Monasteroris Parish, 8th May 1778–8th May 1978*, NL Ir. 200 p 23
Gleeson, J., *History of the Ely O'Carroll Territory or Ancient Ormond*, 1915, NL Ir.
    94142 g 1
Meehan, Patrick, *Members of Parliament for Laois and Offaly, 1801–1918*, 1983, NL
    Ir. 328 m 6
Paterson, J. (ed.), *Diocese of Meath and Kildare: an historical guide*, 1981, NL Ir. 941 p 75
Raymond, B., *The Story of Kilkenny, Kildare, Offaly and Leix*, 1931, NL I 9141 p 1

Local journals

Ardagh and Clonmacnoise Historical Society Journal (1926–51), Ir. 794105

Directories

1824   Pigot and Co., *City of Dublin and Hibernian Provincial Directory*, NL Ir.
        9141 p 75
1846   Slater's *National Commercial Directory of Ireland*
1856   Slater's *Royal National Commercial Directory of Ireland*
1870   Slater's *Directory of Ireland*
1881   Slater's *Royal National Commercial Directory of Ireland*
1890   John Wright, *The King's Co. Directory* (reprinted as *Offaly 100 Years Ago*,
        Tullamore, 1989)
1894   Slater's *Royal Commercial Directory of Ireland*

Gravestone inscriptions

Cloonygowan (C. of I.): GO MS. 622, 182
Daingean, Offaly Historical Society Series, No. 4
Edenderry, Offaly Historical Society Series, No. 3
Kilclonfert: in Byrne, *Towards a History of Kilclonfert*, NL Ir. 94136 t 1
Kilmachonna, Offaly Historical Society Series, No. 2
Lusmagh, Offaly Historical Society Series, No. 2
Monasteroris, Offaly Historical Society Series, No. 3
Rahan: Offaly Historical Society Series, No. 1

Placenames

Townland Maps, Londonderry Inner City Trust

CO. ROSCOMMON

Census returns and substitutes

1659   Pender's 'Census', NL Ir. 31041 c 4
1749   Aughrim, Ardcarn, Ballintober, Ballynakill, Baslick, Boyle,
            Bumlin, Cam, Clontuskert, Cloocraff, Cloonfinlough, Cloony-
            gormican, Creeve, Drimatemple, Dunamon, Dysart, Estersnow,
            Elphin, Fuerty, Kilbride, Kilbryan, Kilcolagh, Kilcooley,
            Kilcorkey, Kilgefin, Kilglass, Kilkeevin, Killinvoy, Killuken,
            Kilumnod, Kilmacallen, Kilmacumsy, Kilmore, Kilronan, Kiltoom,
            Kiltrustan, Kilnamagh, Lisonuffy, Ogulla, Oran, Rahara,
            Roscommon, St John's Athlone, St Peter's Athlone, Shankill,
            Taghboy, Termonbarry, Tibohine, Tisrara, Tumna, NA 1A 36 1
1780   Freeholders, GO 442
1790–99   Freeholders, C. 30 lists, NL MS. 10130
1796   Spinning-Wheel Premium Lists: microfiche index in National
            Archives, comprising, in the case of Co. Roscommon, over 3,000
            names
1813   Freeholders, NL ILB 324
1821   Some extracts. Thrift Abstracts, National Archives
1820s/30s   Tithe Books
1836   Voters list, NL Ir. 32341 r 20
1841   Some extracts. Thrift Abstracts, National Archives
1848   Male Catholic inhabitants of the parish of Boyle, NL Pos. 4692
1851   Some extracts. Thrift Abstracts, National Archives
1857/8   Griffith's Valuation
1901   Census
1911   Census

Local history

Athlone: Materials from printed sources relating to the history of Athlone
    and surrounding areas, 1699–1899, NL MSS. 1543–7, including an index
    volume
Beckett, Rev. M., *Facts and Fictions of Local History* (Kiltullagh district), 1929
Burke, Francis, *Lough Ce and its annals: North Roscommon and the diocese of Elphin
    in times of old*, Dublin, 1895, NL Ir. 27412 b 1
Hayes-McCoy, G. A., *Index to 'The Compossicion Booke of Connoght, 1585'*, Irish
    Manuscripts Commission, Dublin, 1945, NL Ir. 9412 c 1
Monaghan, Rev. J., *Records Relating to the Diocese of Ardagh and Clonmacnoise*, 1886
Knox, H. T., *Notes on the Early History of the Dioceses of Tuam, Killala and Achonry*,
    Dublin, 1904

Local journals

Ardagh and Clonmacnoise Historical Society Journal (1926–51), NL Ir. 794105

Directories

1824	Pigot and Co., *City of Dublin and Hibernian Provincial Directory*, NL Ir. 9141 p 75
1846	Slater's *National Commercial Directory of Ireland*
1856	Slater's *Royal National Commercial Directory of Ireland*
1870	Slater's *Directory of Ireland*
1881	Slater's *Royal National Commercial Directory of Ireland*
1894	Slater's *Royal Commercial Directory of Ireland*

Gravestone inscriptions

Aughrim (old): Heritage and Genealogy Society (see below)*
Cam: IGRS Collection, 138, GO
Cloonfinlough: Heritage and Genealogy Society (see below)*
Dysert: IGRS Collection, 103, GO; also Heritage and Genealogy Society (see below)*
Elphin (C. of I. Cathedral): GO MS. 622, 151
Fuerty: Heritage and Genealogy Society (see below)*
Hill St (C. of I.): GO MS. 622, 168
Jamestown: GO MS. 622, 170
Kiltrustan: Heritage and Genealogy Society (see below)*
Kilverdin: Heritage and Genealogy Society (see below)*
Lisonuffy: Heritage and Genealogy Society (see below)*
Roscommon (C. of I.): Heritage and Genealogy Society (see below)*
Strokestown: Heritage and Genealogy Society (see below)*, also GO MS. 622, 174 and 182
Taughmaconnell: IGRS Collection, 71, GO
Tisrara: IGRS Collection, 144, GO

* Co. Roscommon Heritage and Genealogy Society, the County Heritage Centre, Strokestown, Co. Roscommon

Estate records

LANDLORD
Frances **Boswell**: NL Pos. 4937, Rent ledger, *c.*1760–86, major tenants only, covering townlands in the civil parish of Kilronan.
John **Browne**: NL 16 1 14 (8), map of Carronaskeagh, Cloonfinlough parish, May 1811, with tenants' names.

Baron **Clonbrock**: NL MS. 19501, Tenants' ledger, 1801–06, indexed, covering townlands in the civil parish of Taughmaconnell.

Edward **Crofton**: NL MS. 19672, Rent roll, May 1778, major tenants only, covering townlands in the civil parishes of Baslick, Estersnow, Kilbryan, Kilgefin, Killinvoy, Killumod, Kilmeane, Kiltrustan, Ogulla.

Sir Humphrey **Crofton**: NL MS. 4531, Rental, March 1833, tenants' names alphabetically, covering townlands in the civil parish of Tumna.

Sir Thomas **Dundas**: NL MSS. 2787, 2788, Rentals, 1792, 1804, major tenants only, covering townlands in the civil parishes of Boyle, Estersnow, Kilnamanagh, Tumna.

Walker **Evans**: NL MS. 10152, Leases, c.1790, covering townlands in the civil parish of Creeve.

Gen'l (?) **Gunning**: NL MS. 10152, Rental, 1792, major tenants only, covering townlands in the civil parishes of Athleague, Fuerty, Kilcooley.

King: NL MS. 4170, Rent rolls and accounts, 1801–1818, major tenants only, covering townlands in the civil parishes of Creeve, Elphin, Kilmore.

Francis Blake **Knox**: NL MS. 3077, Rentals, 1845–66, covering townlands in the civil parishes of Cloonfinlough, Rahara.

Lord **Lorton**: NL MSS. 3104/5, Lease Books, 1740–1900, including many leases to small tenants, with lives mentioned in the leases, covering townlands in the civil parishes of Ardcarn, Aughrim, Boyle, Creeve, Elphin, Estersnow, Kilbryan, Kilnamanagh.

Charles Manners **St George**: NL MSS. 4001–22, Accounts and rentals (annual), 1842–46, 1850–55, 1861–71, covering townlands in the civil parishes of Ardcarn, Killukin, Killumod.

Rev. Rodney **Ormsby**: NL MS. 10152, Leases c.1803, Grange townland.

Pakenham-Mahon: NL MS. 10152, Rent roll, 1725, major tenants only; NL MS. 10152, rent roll, 1765–68, major tenants only; NL MS. 2597, rent ledger, 1795–1804, indexed; NL MSS. 5501–3, rent ledgers, 1803–1818, 1824–36, part indexed; NL MS. 9473, tenants of Maurice Mahon, c.1817; NL MS. 9471, rentals and accounts, 1846–54; covering townlands in the civil parishes of Bumlin, Cloonfinlough, Elphin, Kilgefin, Kilglass, Kilnamanagh, Kiltrustan, Lisonuffy, Shankill; also NL MS. 9472, rent ledger, 1840–48, Kilmacumsy parish.

Sandford: NL MS. 10152, Rental (major tenants only), 1718; NL MS. 10152, Leases, c.1750; NL MS. 10152, Lands to be settled on the marriage of Henry Sandford, with tenants' names, 1750; NL MSS. 4281–9, Annual Rentals, 1835–45; covering townlands in the civil parishes of Ballintober, Baslick, Kilkeevin, Boyle, Kiltullagh, Tibohine.

Thomas **Tenison**: NL MS. 5101, Rental and Accounts, 1836–40, covering townlands in the civil parishes of Ardcarn and Kilronan.

(No Landlord Given): NL MS. 24880, List of tenants, Moore parish, 1834.

Placenames

Townland maps, Londonderry Inner City Trust

CO. SLIGO

Census returns and substitutes

1632   Strafford survey, 1632, landed proprietors, clergy, tenants and others, alphabetical list
1659   Pender's 'Census', NL Ir. 31041 c 4
1664   Hearth Money Roll, Irish Manuscripts Commission, 1967
1749   Parishes of Aghanagh, Ahamlish, Ballynakill, Ballysumaghan, Drumcliff, Drumcolumb, Killadoon, Kilmacallan, Kilmactranny, Kilross, Shancough, Sligo, Tawnagh, NA 1A 36 1
1790   Voters' list, NL MS. 2169
1795   Freeholders, NL MS. 3136, 1796; NL MS. 2733
1798   Persons who Suffered Loss of Property in the Rebellion, NL JLB 94107
1820s/30s Tithe Books
1832–37   Registered voters, Sligo borough, *Parliamentary Papers*, 1837, Reports from Committees, Vol. II (2)
1858   Griffith's Valuation
1901   Census
1911   Census

Local history

Farry, M., *Killoran and Coolaney: a local history*, 1985, NL Ir. 94122 f 1
Finn, J., *Gurteen, Co. Sligo, its history, antiquities and traditions*, 1981, NL Ir. 94122 p 1
Hayes-McCoy, G. A., *Index to 'The Compossicion Booke of Connoght, 1585'*, Irish Manuscripts Commission, Dublin, 1945, NL Ir. 9412 c 1
McDonagh, J. C., *History of Ballymote and the Parish of Emlaghfad*, 1936, NL Ir. 94122 m 1
McGuinn, J., *Curry*, 1984, NL Ir. 94122 m 8

McTernan, J. C., *Historic Sligo* ('a bibliographical introduction to the antiquities, history, maps and surveys, MSS., newspapers, historic families, and notable individuals of Co. Sligo'), 1965, NL Ir. 94122 m 4

O'Rourke, T., *History and Antiquities of the Parishes of Ballysadare and Kilvarnet*, 1878, NL I 94122 (including histories of the O'Haras, Coopers, Percevals and other families)

O'Rourke, T., *History of Sligo, town and county*, Dublin, 1889

Monahan, Rev. J., *Records Relating to the Diocese of Ardagh and Clonmacnoise*, 1886

Knox, H. T., *Notes on the Early History of the Dioceses of Tuam, Killala and Achonry*, Dublin, 1904

Petition by Sligo Protestants, 1813, NL P. 504

Wood-Martin, W. G., *History of Sligo* (3 vols), NL Ir. 94122 w 1

Wood-Martin, W. G., *Sligo and the Enniskilleners, from 1688–91*, Dublin, 1882

Local journals

Ardagh and Clonmacnoise Historical Society Journal (1926–51)

Directories

1820 J. Pigot, *Commercial Directory of Ireland*
1824 Pigot and Co., *City of Dublin and Hibernian Provincial Directory*, NL Ir. 9141 p 75
1839 *Directory of the Towns of Sligo, Enniskillen, Ballyshannon, Donegal, etc.*
1846 Slater's *National Commercial Directory of Ireland*
1856 Slater's *Royal National Commercial Directory of Ireland*
1870 Slater's *Directory of Ireland*
1881 Slater's *Royal National Commercial Directory of Ireland*
1889 *Sligo Independent County Directory*
1894 Slater's *Royal Commercial Directory of Ireland*

Gravestone inscriptions

Calry: IGRS Collection, GO
St John's, Sligo (C. of I.): *Church and Parish of St John*, Tyndall, Ir. 2741 p 20
Sligo Abbey: IGRS Collection, GO

The County Heritage Centre, Stephen St, Sligo, has transcribed and indexed the gravestone inscriptions for all but ten of the graveyards and churches in the county.

Estate records

Landlord

Francis **Boswell**: NL Pos. 4937, Rental, *c*.1760–1786, major tenants only, covering townlands in the civil parishes of Ahamlish, Drumrat.

Cooper family: NL MSS. 3050–3060, eleven volumes of rentals and rent ledgers, 1775–1872, major tenants only; NL MS. 3076, rental 1809/10, major tenants only; NL MSS. 9753–57, rentals and accounts, major tenants only; covering townlands in the civil parishes of Achonry, Ahamlish, Ballysadare, Ballysumaghan, Drumcolumb, Drumcliff, Killery, Killaspugbrone, Kilmacallan, Kilmorgan, Kilross, Tawnagh, Templeboy.

Sir Malby **Crofton**: NA M938X, rental, 1853, with all tenants; NA M940X, leases on the estate, including many small tenants, and mentioning lives in the leases; covering townlands in the civil parishes of Dromard, Templeboy.

Sir Thomas **Dundas**: NL MSS. 2787, 2788, rentals, 1792, 1804, major tenants only, covering townlands in the civil parishes of Aghanagh, Drumrat, Emlaghfad, Kilcolman, Kilfree, Kilglass, Kilmacallan, Kilmacteigue, Kilmactranny, Kilmoremoy, Kilshalvey, Skreen.

Lord **Lorton**: NL MSS. 3104, 3105, lease books, 1740–1900, including many leasees to small tenants, with lives mentioned in leases, covering townlands in the civil parishes of Aghanagh, Drumcolumb, Kilfree, Killaraght, Kilmacallan, Kilshalvey, Toomour.

Charles **O'Hara** the younger: NL Pos. 1923, Rent roll, *c*.1775, all tenants, giving lives named in leases, covering townlands in the civil parishes of Achonry, Ballysadare, Killoran, Kilvarnet.

The Earl of **Strafford** (and others): NL MS. 10223, estate rentals, 1682 and 1684, major tenants only (includes a large part of Sligo town), covering townlands in the civil parishes of Ahamlish, Ballysadare, Ballysumaghan, Calry, Cloonoghill, Dromard, Drumcliff, Kilfree, Killoran, Kilaspugbrone, Kilmacallan, Kilmacowen, Kilmacteigue, Kilross, St John's, Skreen, Templeboy, Toomour.

Owen **Wynne**: NL MSS. 5780–5782, rentals and expense books, 1737–68, major tenants only; NL MSS. 5830–1, rent ledgers, 1738–53, 1768–73, major tenants only, indexed; NL MSS. 3311–13, a rental and two rent ledgers, yearly from 1798 to 1825, with all tenants; covering townlands in the civil parishes of Ahamlish, Ballysadare, Calry, Drumcliff, Killoran, St John's, Tawnagh, Templeboy.

Placenames

Townland maps, Londonderry Inner City Trust

CO. TIPPERARY

Census returns and substitutes

1595   Freeholders, NL Pos. 1700

1635   Census of Newport and Birdhill, NL Pos. 1561

1641   Book of Survey and Distribution, NL MS. 977

1641–63   Proprietors of Fethard, *The Irish Genealogist*, Vol. 6, No. 1, 1980

1653   Name of soldiers and adventurers who received land in Co. Tipperary under the Cromwellian settlement, *The Cromwellian Settlement of Ireland*, John Prendergast, Dublin, 1922

1654   Civil Survey, Vols I and II, NL I 6551, Dublin

1659   Pender's 'Census', NL Ir. 31041 c 4

1666/7/8   Three Hearth Money Rolls, *Tipperary's Families*, T. Laffan (ed.), Dublin, 1911, NL Ir. 9292 l 11

1703   Minister's money account, Clonmel, *Analecta Hibernica*, 34

1750   Catholics in the parishes of Barnane, Bourney, Corbally, Killavanoge, Killea, Rathnaveoge, Roscrea, Templecree, Templetouhy, *The Irish Genealogist*, 1973

1766   Athassel, Ballintemple, Ballycahill, Ballygriffin, Boytonreth, Brickendown, Bruis, Clerihan, Clonbeg, Cloneen, Clonoulty, Clonbolloge, Clonpet, Colman, Cordangan, Corrogue, Cullen, Dangandargan, Drum, Dustrileague, Erry, Fethard, Gaile, Grean, Horeabbey, Killardry, Killbrugh, Killea, Kilconnel, Kilfeacle, Killavanoge, Knockgrafton, Killnerath, Kiltynan, Lattin, Magorban, Mealiffe, Newchapel, Pepperstown, Railstown, Rathcoole, Relickmurry, Redcity, Shronell, St John's Cashel, St Patricksrock, Solloghodmore, Templebeg, Templemore, Templeneiry, Templenoe, Tipperary, Toom, NA 1A 46 49; Ballingarry, Uskeane, GO 536

1776   Voters lists, NA M.4910–12, 4878; Freeholders, NA M.1321–2, GO 442

1799   Census of Carrick-on-Suir, NL Pos. 28

1813   Valuation of Roscrea, NA MFCI 3

1821   Clonmel, National Archives, m 242^2

1821   Modreeny, extracts, GO MS. 572

1828   Clonmel, houses and occupiers, *Parliamentary Papers*, Reports from Committees, Vol. 11 (2), 1837

1820s/30s   Tithe Books

1832–37   Registered voters, Clonmel and Cashel boroughs, *Parliamentary Papers*, 1837, Reports from Committees, Vol. II (2)

1835   Parish of Templebredin, JNMAHS, 1975

1835   Newport and Birdhill, NL P. 1561

1837   Protestant parishioners, Clogheen union, 1837, 1877, 1880, *The Irish Ancestor*, Vol. 17, No. 1, 1985
1851   Griffith's Valuation, alphabetical index to householders, All-Ireland Heritage microfiche, National Archives
1901   Census
1911   Census

Local history

Atlas of the parishes of Cashel and Emly, 1970, ILB 94143 a 3
Burke, William P., *History of Clonmel*, Waterford, 1907, Ir. 94142 b 1
Callanan, M., *History of 4 Tipperary Septs—O'Kennedys, O'Dwyers, O'Mulryans, O'Meaghers*, 1933, Ir. 9292 c 16
Coffey, G., *Evicted Tipperary*, Ir. 330 p 22
Cotter, James, *Tipperary*, New York, 1929
Dwyer, Philip, *The Diocese of Killaloe*, Dublin, 1878
Feehan, J., *The Landscape of Slieve Bloom: a study of the natural and human heritage*, 1979, Ir. 91413 f 4
Fitzgerald, S., *Cappawhite and Doon*, Ir. 9141 p 43
Flynn, Paul, *The book of the Galtees and the golden vale: a border history of Tipperary, Limerick and Cork*, Dublin, 1926, Ir. 94142 f 2
Gleeson, J., *History of the Ely O'Carroll Territory or Ancient Ormond*, 1915, Ir. 94142 g 1
Gleeson, J., *Cashel of the Kings*, Dublin, 1927
Gorman (ed.), *Records of Moycarkey and Two-Mile-Borris*, 1955, Ir. 94142 g 4
Hayes, W. J., *Tipperary Remembers*, 1976, Ir. 914142 H 9
Hemphill, W. Despard, *Clonmel and the surrounding country*, 1860
Kenny, M., *Glankeen of Borrisoleigh: a Tipperary Parish*, 1944, Ir. 94142 k 2
McIlroy, M., *Gleanings from Garrymore* (Townland), n.d.
Neely, W. S., *Kilcooley: land and parish in Tipperary*, 1983, Ir. 94142 n 1
O'Dwyer, M. and L., *The Parish of Emly, its history and heritage*, Emly, 1987
Power, V. Rev. P., *Waterford and Lismore: A Compendious History of the Dioceses*, Cork, 1937
Pyke, D., *Parish Priests and Churches of St Mary's, Clonmel*, 1984, Ir. 274 p 40
Ryan, C. A., *Tipperary Artillery, 1793-1889*, 1890, Ir. 355942 t 1
Sheehan, E. H., *Nenagh and its Neighbourhood* (including many family records), n.d.
Watson, Col S. J., *A Dinner of Herbs: a history of Old St Mary's Church, Clonmel*, Clonmel, 1988
Whelan, K. and Nolan, W., *Tipperary: History and Society*, Dublin, 1985
White, James (ed.), *My Clonmel Scrap Book*, n.d.
White, Rev. P., *History of Clare and the Dalcassian Clans of Tipperary, Limerick and Galway*, Dublin, 1893

Local journals

North Munster Antiquarian Society Journal, NL Ir. 794105 n 1 (Index 1897–1919, Ir. 7941 n 1)

Eile (Journal of the Roscrea Heritage Society), Ir. 94142 e 1

Cois Deirge, Ir. 94142 c 4

Clonmel Historical and Archaeological Society Journal, Ir. 94142 c 2

Directories

1788   Richard Lucas, *General Directory of the Kingdom of Ireland*, NL Pos. 3729

1820   J. Pigot, *Commercial Directory of Ireland*

1824   Pigot and Co., *City of Dublin and Hibernian Provincial Directory*, NL Ir. 9141 p 75

1839   T. Shearman, *New Commercial Directory for the Cities of Waterford and Kilkenny, Towns of Clonmel, Carrick-on-Suir, New Ross and Carlow*

1846   Slater's *National Commercial Directory of Ireland*

1856   Slater's *Royal National Commercial Directory of Ireland*

1866   George H. Bassett, *Directory of the City and County of Limerick and of the principal Towns in the Counties of Tipperary and Clare*, NL Ir. 914144 b 5

1870   Slater's *Directory of Ireland*

1881   Slater's *Royal National Commercial Directory of Ireland*

1886   Francis Guy, *Postal Directory of Munster*, NL Ir. 91414 g 8

1889   George H. Bassett, *The Book of County Tipperary*

1894   Slater's *Royal Commercial Directory of Ireland*

Gravestone inscriptions

Ballyclerihan: IGRS Collection, 145, GO

Holy Cross (C. of I.): GO MS. 622, 176/7

Kilmore: *The Irish Genealogist*, Vol. II, No. 10, 1953

Kiltinane: GO MS. 622, 144

Knigh: National Archives, search room

Littleton: GO MS. 622, 171

Newchapel: IGRS Collection, 101, GO

Uskeane: *The Irish Genealogist*, Vol. III, No. 2, 1957

Estate records

Description of the estate of John Sadleir in Limerick and Tipperary, JP 3439.

Newcomen estates: maps of estates to be sold, 20 July 1827, NL, Map Room.

Placenames

Townland Maps, Londonderry Inner City Trust

CO. TYRONE

Census returns and substitutes

1612–13	'Survey of Undertakers Planted in Co. Tyrone', *Historical Manuscripts Commission Report*, 4 (Hastings MSS.), 1947, 159–82
1630	Muster Roll, NL Pos. 206, PRONI T.808/15164
1631	Muster Roll, PRONI T.934
1654/6	Civil Survey, Vol. III, NL I 6551, Dublin
1660	Poll Book, NL Pos. 206
1661	Books of Survey and Distribution, PRONI T.370/C and D.1854/1/23
1664	Hearth Money Roll, NL MSS. 9583/4; also *Clogher Record*, 1965, *Seanchas Ardmhacha*, 1960/61 and PRONI T.283 D/2
1665	Subsidy roll, 1665, 1668, NL Pos. 206; PRONI T.458/1
1666	Hearth Money Roll, PRONI T.307
1699	Protestants in the parishes of Drumragh, Badoney and Cappagh, GO Sources Box 6
1740	Protestants, Derryloran and Kildress, RCB Library, PRONI T.808/15258
1766	Aghalow, Artrea, Carnteel, Clonfeacle, Derryloran, Donaghendry, Errigal Keerogue, Kildress, NA 1A 46 49, PRONI T.808/15264–7
1795–98	Voters List, Dungannon barony, PRONI TYR5/3/1
1796	Catholic migrants from Ulster to Mayo, see Mayo
1796	Spinning-Wheel Premium Lists, microfiche index in National Archives, comprising, in the case of Co. Tyrone, over 11,000 names
1821	Some extracts, Aghaloo. Thrift Abstracts, National Archives
1820s/30s	Tithe Books
1834	Valuation of Dungannon, *Parliamentary Papers*, 1837, Reports from Committees, Vol. II (i), Appendix G
1834	Clonoe (Coalisland), NL Pos. 5579
1851	Griffith's Valuation
1901	Census
1911	Census

Local history

Ardtrea Parish Ordnance Survey Memoir, 1833–36, NL Ir. 914112 o 6

Belmore, Earl of, *Parliamentary Memoirs of Fermanagh and Tyrone, 1613–1885*, Dublin, 1887

Donnelly, T. P., *A History of the Parish of Ardstraw West and Castlederg*, 1978, NL Ir. 94114 d 6

Drumquin . . . A Collection of Writings and Photographs of the Past, NL Ir. 91411 p 10

Duffy J. (ed.), *A Clogher Record Album: a diocesan history*, NL Ir. 94114 c 3

Hutchison, W. R., *Tyrone precinct: a history of the plantation settlement of Dungannon and Mountjoy to modern times*, Belfast, 1951

Johnson and Preston, *Methodism in Omagh . . . over two centuries*, NL Ir. 27411 p 5

Marshall J., *History of the Town and District of Clogher, Co. Tyrone, parish of Errigal Keerogue, Tyrone, and Errigal Truagh in the Co. of Monaghan*, 1930, NL I 94114

Marshall, J., *Vestry Records of the Church of St. John, parish of Aghalow*

O'Daly B., 'Material for a history of the parish of Kilskeery', *Clogher Record*, 1953/4/5

Rutherford, J., *Donagheady: Presbyterian Churches and Parish*, 1953, NL Ir. 285 r 7

Shearman, H., *Ulster*, London, 1949 (incl. bibliographies)

Tyrone Almanac and Directory, 1872, NL Ir. 914114 t 2

Local journals

Seanchas Ard Mhacha (Journal of the Armagh Diocesan Historical Society), NL Ir. 27411 s 4

Clogher Record (Journal of the Clogher Diocesan Historical Society), NL Ir. 94114 c 2

Derriana (Journal of the Derry Diocesan Historical Society), NL Ir. 27411 d 4

Duchas Neill, Journal of the O'Neill Country Society (from 1987)

Directories

1819 Thomas Bradshaw, *General Directory of Newry, Armagh, Dungannon, Portadown, Tandragee, Lurgan, Waringstown, Banbridge, Warrenpoint, Rostrevor, Kilkeel and Rathfryland*

1820 J. Pigot, *Commercial Directory of Ireland*

1824 Pigot and Co., *City of Dublin and Hibernian Provincial Directory*, NL Ir. 9141 p 75

1842 Matthew Martin, *Belfast Directory*

1846 Slater's *Directory*

1852 James A. Henderson, *Belfast and Province of Ulster Directory*, issued also in 1854, 1856, 1858, 1861, 1863, 1865, 1868, 1870, 1877, 1880, 1884, 1887, 1890, 1894, 1900

1856 Slater's *Royal National Commercial Directory of Ireland*

1865 R. Wynne, *Business Directory of Belfast*

1870 Slater's *Directory of Ireland*

1881 Slater's *Royal National Commercial Directory of Ireland*

1887 *Derry Almanac*, annually from this year

1894 Slater's *Royal Commercial Directory of Ireland*

Gravestone inscriptions

Clogher: *Clogher Cathedral Graveyard*, John Johnstone, 1972
Donaghacavey: *Clogher Record*, Vol. VII, No. 2, 1970
Drumglass: *Seanchas Ardmhacha*, Vol. VII, No. 2, 1974
Kilskeery: *Clogher Record*, Vol. VIII, No. 1, 1973

Irish World (26 Market Square, Dungannon, Co. Tyrone, BT70 1AB) has transcribed and computerised the inscriptions of more than 300 graveyards in the six counties of Northern Ireland, principally in the four western counties of Armagh, Derry, Fermanagh and Tyrone.

Placenames

Townland maps, Londonderry Inner City Trust

CO. WATERFORD

Census returns and substitutes

1542–1650	Freemen of Waterford, *The Irish Genealogist*, Vol. 5, No. 5, 1978
1641	Book of Survey and Distribution, NL MS. 970
1641	Houses and tenants, Waterford City, National Archives, Quit Rent Office Papers; also JCHAS, Vol. 51, 1946
1662	Subsidy Roll of Co. Waterford, *Analecta Hibernica*, Vol. 30
1663	Waterford City inhabitants, including occupations, JCHAS, Vol. 51
1664–66	*Civil Survey*, Vol. VI
1766	Killoteran, NA 1A 46 49
1772	Hearth Money Roll for parts of Co. Waterford, *Waterford and South-East of Ireland Archaeological and Historical Society Journal*, Vol. XV, 1912
1775	Gentry of Co. Waterford, *Jnl of the Waterford and S.E. Ire. Arch. Soc.*, Vol. 16, No. 2, 1913
1776	Killoteran parish, NA 1A 46 49
1777–96	Births, Marriages and Deaths from Waterford newspapers, *The Irish Genealogist*, 1973, 1980, 1982

1778	Inhabitants of Waterford City, *Freeman's Journal*, 29 Oct. 1778; 5 Nov. 1778
1792	Leading Catholics of Waterford, *The Irish Ancestor*, Vol. 8, No. 11
1807	Waterford City voters, *The Irish Ancestor*, Vol. 8, No. 11
1821	Townland of Callaghane, parish of Ballygunner, *Decies* 16; Extracts from Waterford City, *The Irish Genealogist*, 1968/9
1820s/30s	Tithe Books
1847	Principal fishermen, Ring. J. Alcock, *Facts from the Fisheries, 1847*
1848/51	Griffith's Valuation, alphabetical index to householders (All-Ireland Heritage)
1901	Census
1911	Census

Local history

Butler, M., *The Barony of Gaultiere*, n.d.

Charter of the Liberties of Waterford, including a list of mayors, sheriffs and bailiffs, 1377–1806, NL I 6551; Kilkenny Council Books of the Corporation of Waterford, 1662–1700, NL Ir. 94141 p 3

Cuffe, Major O. T., *Records of the Waterford Militia, 1584–1885*, (1885), NL 355942

Downey, Edmund, *The story of Waterford to the middle of the 18th century*, Waterford, 1914, NL Ir. 94141 d 1

Egan, P. M., *History, guide and directory of the city and county of Waterford*, Kilkenny, 1891, NL Ir. 94191

Fitzpatrick, Thomas, *Waterford during the Civil War, 1641–53*, 1912

Ochille, F., *The Holy City of Ardmore, Co. Waterford*, Youghal, n.d.

Pender, S., *Waterford merchants abroad*, Ir. 941 p 23

Power, Rev. Patrick, *History of the County of Waterford*, Waterford, 1933

Power V. Rev. P., *Waterford and Lismore: A Compendious History of the Dioceses*, Cork, 1937

Rent and arrears due to the corporation for 1792, NL P 3000

Ryland, R. H., *The history, topography and antiquities of the county and city of Waterford*, London, 1824, NL Ir. 9141 r 1

Smith, Charles, *The ancient and present state of the county and city of Waterford . . .*, Dublin, 1774, NL Ir. 94141 s 1

Waterford Historical Society Proceedings, newspaper cuttings relating to Waterford, in nine vols, NL ILB 94141

Directories

1788	Richard Lucas, *General Directory of the Kingdom of Ireland*, NL Pos. 3729
1809	Holden's *Triennial Directory*

1820   J. Pigot, *Commercial Directory of Ireland*
1824   Pigot and Co., *City of Dublin and Hibernian Provincial Directory*, NL Ir.
        9141 p 75
1839   T. Shearman, *New Commercial Directory for the Cities of Waterford and*
        Kilkenny, Towns of Clonmel, Carrick-on-Suir, New Ross and Carlow
1839   T. S. Harvey, *Waterford Almanac and Directory*
1846   Slater's *National Commercial Directory of Ireland*
1856   Slater's *Royal National Commercial Directory of Ireland*
1866   T. S. Harvey, *Waterford Almanac and Directory*
1869   Newenham Harvey, *Waterford Almanac and Directory*
1870   Slater's *Directory of Ireland*
1873   *Illustrated Waterford Almanack and Directory*, NL Ir. 014141 w 15
1881   Slater's *Royal National Commercial Directory of Ireland*
1886   Francis Guy, *Postal Directory of Munster*, NL Ir. 91414 g 8
1893   Francis Guy, *Postal Directory of Munster*
1894   Slater's *Royal Commercial Directory of Ireland*

Local journals

Decies (Journal of the Old Waterford Society), NL Ir. 9414 d 5
Journal of the Waterford and South-East of Ireland Archaeological Society, NL Ir.
    794105 w 1

Gravestone inscriptions

Affane: *The Irish Genealogist*, Vol. II, No. 9, 1952
Ballygunner Old: IGRS Collection, 56, GO
Ballynakill House: IGRS Collection, 16, GO
Ballynakill C. of I.: IGRS Collection, 40, GO
Churchtown (Dysert): *Decies* 25, 1984
Clashmore: *The Irish Genealogist*, Vol. II, No. 8, 1950
Crook Old: IGRS Collection, 138, GO
Crook R.C.: IGRS Collection, 4, GO
Carbally: IGRS Collection, 153, GO
Drumcannon: IGRS Collection, 86, GO
Dunhill Old: IGRS Collection, 23, GO
Dunmore East C. of I.: IGRS Collection, 123, GO
Faha Chapel of Ease: *Decies* 17, 1981
Faithlegg: IGRS Collection, 166, GO
Fenough: IGRS Collection, 16, GO
Fiddown: GO MS. 622, 150
Guilcagh C. of I.: IGRS Collection, 11, GO
Islandikane: IGRS Collection, 9, GO

Kilbarry: IGRS Collection, 48, GO
Killea Old: IGRS Collection, 94, GO
Killotteran: IGRS Collection, 31, GO
Kill St Lawrence: IGRS Collection, 170, GO
Kilmedan: IGRS Collection, 122, GO
Knockeen: IGRS Collection, 6, GO
Lisnakill: IGRS Collection, 35, GO
Mothel: *Decies*, 38, 39
Newcastle: IGRS Collection, 38, GO
Passage: IGRS Collection, 1, GO
Portlaw C. of I.: IGRS Collection, 7, GO
Rathgormuck: *Decies*, 37
Rathmoylan: IGRS Collection, 10, GO
Reisk: IGRS Collection, 86, GO
Stradbally, *Decies*, Vol. XVI, 1981
Waterford, St Patrick's: *Catholic Record of Waterford and Lismore*, Rev. P. Power, 1916
Whitechurch: *The Irish Ancestor*, Vol. V, No. 1, 1973

Estate records

Rent roll, 1564, NL MS. 9034.
'Tenants of Bellew properties in and adjoining Dungarvan in 1760', *Waterford and South-East of Ireland Archaeological and Historical Society Journal*, Vol. XIX, No. 4, 1911.
'Ballysagart estate, 1849', *Decies* 27, 1984.
'The estate of George Lane Fox' (1857, mainly Kilbarry parish), *Decies* 26, 1984.

Placenames

Townland Maps, Londonderry Inner City Trust
Power, P., *The Place-names of Decies* (1907)

CO. WESTMEATH

Census returns and substitutes

1641	Book of Survey and Distribution, NL MS. 965
1659	Pender's 'Census', NL Ir. 31041 c 4
1666	Hearth Money Roll of Mullingar, *Franciscan College Journal*, 1950
1761–88	Freeholders, NL MSS. 787/8
1763	Poll Book, GO 443
1802–3	Protestants in the parishes of Ballyloughloe, Castletown Delvin, Clonarney, Drumraney, Enniscoffey, Kilbridepass, Killalon, Kilcleagh, Killough, Killua, Killucan, Leney, Moylicar, Rathconnell, *The Irish Ancestor*, 1973
1820s/30s	Tithe Books
1832	Voters, *The Irish Genealogist*, Vol. 5, Nos 2 and 6; Vol. 6, No. 1 (1975, 1979, 1980)
1837	Marksmen (i.e. illiterate voters), Athlone Borough, *Parliamentary Papers*, 1837, Reports from Committees, Vol. II (1), Appendix A
1835	Tubber parish, NL Pos. 1994
1854	Griffith's Valuation
c.1855	Partial census of Streete parish, NL Pos. 4236
1901	Census
1911	Census

Local history

Athlone: Material from printed sources relating to the history of Athlone and surrounding areas, 1699–1899, NL MSS. 1543–7, including an index volume

Clarke, Desmond, 'Athlone, a bibliographical study', *An Leabhar*, No. 10, 1952, 138–9

Clarke, M. V., *Register of the priory of the Blessed Virgin Mary at Tristernagh*, IMC, NL Ir. 271 c 22

Egan, O., *Tyrellspass, Past and Present*, 1986, NL Ir. 94131 e 1

Grand Jurors: genealogies of the grand jurors of Co. Westmeath, 1727–1853, NL Ir. 94131 g 1

Monahan, Rev. J., *Records Relating to the Diocese of Ardagh and Clonmacnoise*, 1886

Irish Midland Studies (1980), NL Ir. 941 m 58

Paterson, J. (ed.), *Diocese of Meath and Kildare: an historical guide*, 1981, NL Ir. 941 p 75

Sheehan J., *Westmeath as others saw it . . . AD 900 to the present*, (1982), NL Ir. 94131 s 5

Stokes, George T., *Athlone, the Shannon and Louth Ree*, Dublin and Athlone, 1897, NL Ir. 91413 s 1
Westmeath Local Studies: a guide to sources, NL Ir. 94131 k 1
Woods, James, *Annals of Westmeath*, Dublin, 1907, NL Ir. 94131 w 1
Upton Papers, Royal Irish Academy: Wills and Deeds mainly relating to Co. Westmeath, NL Pos. 1997

Local journals

Journal of the Old Athlone Society, NL Ir. 94131 o 1
Ardagh and Clonmacnoise Historical Society Journal (1926–51), NL Ir. 794105
Riocht na Midhe (Records of the Meath Archaeological and Historical Society), NL Ir. 94132 r 1

Directories

1820   J. Pigot, *Commercial Directory of Ireland*
1824   Pigot and Co., *City of Dublin and Hibernian Provincial Directory*, NL Ir. 9141 p 75
1846   Slater's *National Commercial Directory of Ireland*
1856   Slater's *Royal National Commercial Directory of Ireland*
1870   Slater's *Directory of Ireland*
1881   Slater's *Royal National Commercial Directory of Ireland*
1894   Slater's *Royal Commercial Directory of Ireland*

Gravestone inscriptions

Athlone: *Athlone Abbey Graveyard Inscriptions*, H. A. Ryan, Longford/Westmeath Joint Libraries Committee, 1987
St Mary's Church of Ireland, with parish registers, NL Pos. 5309
St Peter's Church of Ireland, with parish registers, NL Pos. 5309
Ballyloughloe (Mount Temple): *The Irish Ancestor*, Vol. IV, No. 2, 1972
Carrick (near Mullingar): GO MS. 622, 171
Castletown (Finea): GO MS. 622, 107
Fore: IGRS Collection, 27, GO
Kilcleagh: *Moate, Co. Westmeath, a history of the Town and District*, Liam Cox, 1981
Killua: 'Monumental Inscriptions from some Graveyards in Co. Meath', N. French (unpub.), National Archives search room
Kilomenaghan: *Moate, Co. Westmeath, a history of the Town and District*, Liam Cox, 1981
Moate: *Moate, Co. Westmeath, a history of the Town and District*, Liam Cox, 1981
Mullingar (C. of I.): Dun na Si Heritage Centre, Moate, Co. Westmeath
Stonehall (C. of I.): GO MS. 622, 183
Streete: *Riocht na Midhe*, Vol. IV, No. 3, 1969

Placenames

Walsh, Rev. Paul, *The Place-names of Westmeath*, Ir. 92942 w 1

CO. WEXFORD

Census returns and substitutes

1618	Herald's Visitation of Co. Wexford, GO 48, NL Pos. 8286
1641	Book of Survey and Distribution, NL MS. 975
1654/6	Civil Survey, Vol. IX, NL I 6551, Dublin
1659	Pender's 'Census', NL Ir. 31041 c 4
1665–1839	Free Burgesses of New Ross, *Proceedings of the Royal Society of Antiquaries of Ireland*, Ser. 5, Vol. 1, pt 1 (1890), 298–309
1766	Ballynaslaney, NA 1A 41 100; Protestants in Edermine, GO 537
1776	Freemen of Wexford, *The Irish Genealogist*, 1976
1789	Protestant householders in the parish of Ferns, *The Irish Ancestor*, Vol. 13, No. 2, 1981
1792	Some Protestant householders in the parishes of Ballycanew and Killtrisk, *The Irish Ancestor*, Vol. 13, No. 2, 1981
1798	Protestants murdered in the rebellion, Cantwell, *Memorials of the Dead, Co. Wexford*, Vol. 10, 432; NL Ir. 9295 c 2
1798	List of persons who suffered loss of property in 1798, NL JLB 94107
1820s/30s	Tithe Books
1853	Griffith's Valuation
1861	Catholics in Enniscorthy parish, in Catholic records
1867	Marshallstown, *The Irish Genealogist*, 1985
1901	Census
1911	Census

Local history

Coghlan, P. J., *A directory for the co. of Wexford . . . townlands, gentlemen's seats and noted places*, 1867, NL Ir. 914138

Doyle, Lynn, *Ballygullion, County Wexford*, 1945

Doyle, Martin, *Notes and Gleanings Relating to the County of Wexford*, Dublin, 1868
Flood, W. H. Grattan, *History of Enniscorthy, County Wexford*, n.d.
Griffiths, George, *The chronicles of the county of Wexford*, NL Ir. 94138 g 1
Hay, Edward, *History of the Insurrection of County Wexford in 1798*, Dublin, 1803
Hore, H. J., *The Social State of the Southern and Eastern Counties of Ireland in the Sixteenth Century*, 1870
Hore, P. H., *History of the town and county of Wexford*, London, 1900–11, 6 vols, NL Ir. 94138 h 2
Kirk, Francis J., *Some Notable Conversions in the Co. of Wexford*, (1901)
'Owners of Land of one acre and upwards, Co. Wexford', NL I 6551, Wexford
Shapland Carew Papers and Maps, IMC, NL Ir. 399041 c 5

Local journals

Journal of the Old Wexford Society, Ir. 94138 o 5
The Past (Journal of the Uí Cinsealaigh Historical Society), Ir. 941382 p 1

Directories

1788   Richard Lucas, *General Directory of the Kingdom of Ireland*, NL Pos. 3729
1820   J. Pigot, *Commercial Directory of Ireland*
1824   Pigot and Co., *City of Dublin and Hibernian Provincial Directory*, NL Ir. 9141 p 75
1839   T. Shearman, *New Commercial Directory for the Cities of Waterford and Kilkenny, Towns of Clonmel, Carrick-on-Suir, New Ross and Carlow*
1846   Slater's *National Commercial Directory of Ireland*
1856   Slater's *Royal National Commercial Directory of Ireland*
1870   Slater's *Directory of Ireland*
1872   George Griffith, *County Wexford Almanac*
1881   Slater's *Royal National Commercial Directory of Ireland*
1885   George H. Bassett, *Wexford County Guide and Directory*
1894   Slater's *Royal Commercial Directory of Ireland*

Gravestone inscriptions

Memorials of the Dead, Brian J. Cantwell, Co. Wexford (complete): Vols V to IX, Master Index, Vol. X, Ir. 9295 c 2 and National Archives search room

Estate records

Alcock estate tenants, Clonmore, 1820, NL MS. 10169.
Baron Farnham estate rent books for Bunclody, 1775–1820, NL MSS. 787–8.

Co. Wexford rent lists, eighteenth century, NL MS. 1782.
Shapland-Carew rent books, 1740–63, NA 1A 41 49; see also Local History.

— — — — — — —

CO. WICKLOW

Census returns and substitutes

1641	Book of Survey and Distribution, NL MS. 969
1669	Hearth Money Roll, GO 667; NA m 4909
1745	Poll Book, PRONI 2659
1766	Dunganstown, Rathdrum, Wicklow, Ballynaslaney (Protestants only), GO 537
1792–96	Valuation of Corn Tithes, Newcastle, Co. Wicklow, with tenants' names, NL MS. 3980
1798	List of persons who suffered loss of property in 1798, NL JLB 94107
1820s/30s	Tithe Books
1847–56	Index to the Coolattin estate emigration records, *Journal of the West Wicklow Historical Society*, No. 1, 1983/4
1852/3	Griffith's Valuation, microfiche Index, Andrew Morris
1901	Census
1911	Census

Local history

Black, A. and C., *Guide to Dublin and Co. Wicklow*, 1888
Coleman, James, 'Bibliography of the counties Carlow, Kilkenny and Wicklow', *Waterford and S–E of Ire. Arch. Soc. Jnl*, 11, 1907–8, 126–33
Scott, G. D., *The stones of Bray* (the barony of Rathdown), Dublin, 1913, Ir. 914133 b 2

Local journals

Journal of the West Wicklow Historical Society
Journal of the Old Bray Society
Arklow Historical Society Journal, Ir. 94134 a 1

Directories

1788	Richard Lucas, *General Directory of the Kingdom of Ireland*, NL Pos. 3729
1824	Pigot and Co., *City of Dublin and Hibernian Provincial Directory*, NL Ir. 9141 p 75
1846	Slater's *National Commercial Directory of Ireland*
1856	Slater's *Royal National Commercial Directory of Ireland*
1870	Slater's *Directory of Ireland*
1881	Slater's *Royal National Commercial Directory of Ireland*
1894	Slater's *Royal Commercial Directory of Ireland*

Gravestone inscriptions

Memorials of the Dead, Brian J. Cantwell, Co. Wicklow (complete), Vols I to IV; Master Index, Vol. X, Ir. 9295 c 2 and National Archives search room

Placenames

Townland Maps, Londonderry Inner City Trust
Price, Liam, *The Place-names of Co. Wicklow*, Dublin 1945–58, Ir. 92942 p 3

13

Family Histories

What follows is a full listing of the Irish family history section ('Ir. 9292') of the National Library of Ireland. Part 1 consists of individual works given alphabetically under the principal family treated. No attempt has been made to standardise 'O' and 'Mc', and it may be necessary to check names with and without the prefix. Part 2 lists general works under the author's surname. Although it is probably the largest single collection of Irish family histories, the Ir. 9292 section is by no means comprehensive, and does not include all the material of potential genealogical interest in the Library. It consists of two principal categories, published and privately printed pedigrees and family histories from the nineteenth and early twentieth century, generally relating to the Anglo-Irish, and the results of genealogical research, often carried out by the descendants of emigrants to the US, either in typescript or privately printed. The quality of both categories varies enormously. Also included here are some only of the Library's manuscript holdings.

PART 1

A

Adams: Rev. B. W. Adams, *A genealogical history of the family of Adams of Cavan*, 1903, Ir. 9292 a 7

Alen: H. L. L. Denny, *An account of the family of Alen of St Wolstan's, Co. Kildare*, 1903, Ir. 9292 a 1

Allen: W. E. D. Allen, *David Allen: the history of a family firm, 1857-1957*, Ir. 9292 a 8

Amory: Gertrude Meredith, *The Descendants of Hugh Amory, 1605-1805*, 1901, Ir. 9292 a 2

Anderson: (1) A. L. B. Anderson, *The Andersons of Co. Kilkenny*, 1931, Ir. 9292 a 11

(2) J. G. T Anderson, *Family Descent of Andersons of Flush and Bawn, Sixmile-cross, Co. Antrim*, 1977, Ir. 9292 a 11

Andrews: John Burls (ed.), *9 Generations: a history of the Andrews family of Comber*, 1958, Ir. 9292 a 9

Anketell: *A Short History of the Family of Anketell . . . compiled by one of its members*, 1901, Ir. 9292 a 6

Archdale: Henry B. Archdale, *Memoirs of the Archdales with the descents of some allied families*, Enniskillen, 1925, Ir. 9292 a 3

Ash: Rev. T. Martin (ed.), *The Ash Mss of 1735*, 1890, Ir. 9292 a 4

Aylmers: Sir F. J. Aylmer, *The Aylmers of Ireland*, 1931, Ir. 9292 a 5

B

Bagenal: P. H. Bagenal, *Vicissitudes of an Anglo-Irish Family, 1530-1800*, 1925, Ir. 9292 b 1

Ball: Rev. W. Ball Wright, *Ball Family Records*, 1908, Ir. 9292 b 2

Barrington: Amy Barrington, *The Barringtons: a Family History*, 1917, Ir. 9292 b 20

Barry: (1) A. de Barry, *De L'origine des Bary d'Irlande*, 1900, Ir. 9292 b 13

(2) C. de Bary, *Étude sur l'histoire des Bary-Barry*, 1927, Ir. 9292 b 24

(3) Rev. F. Barry, *Barrymore: records of the Barrys of Co. Cork from the earliest times to the present*, 1902, Ir. 9292 b 19

Barton: F. B. Barton, *Some account of the family of Barton*, 1902, Ir. 9292 b 12

Beamish: C. T. M. Beamish, *A genealogical study of a family in Co. Cork and elsewhere*, Ir. 9292 b 23

Beck: J. W. Beck, *Beck of Ireland*, 1930, Ir. 9292 p 23 (3)

Bernard: *The Bernards of Kerry*, 1922, Ir. 9292 b 3

Bessborough: Earl of Bessborough, *Lady Bessborough and her family circle*, London, 1940, Ir. 9292 b 17

Bewley: Sir E. T. Bewley, *The Bewleys of Cumberland and their Irish descendants*, 1902, Ir. 9292 b 4

Bingham: (1) M. Bingham, *Peers and Plebs: two families in a changing world*, London, 1975, Ir. 9292 b 35

(2) R. E. McCalmont, *Memoirs of the Binghams*, London, 1915, Ir. 9292 b 21

Birch: M. E. Birch, *The Birch genealogy*, Canada, 1978, Ir. 9292 b 44

Blacker: L. C. M. Blacker, *History of the Family of Blacker of Carrickblacker in Ireland*, 1901, Ir. 9292 b 5

Blake: (1) Martin J. Blake, *An Account of the Blakes of Galway*, 1898, Ir. 9292 b 60

(2) Martin J. Blake, *Blake Family Record, 1300–1700*, 1902, 1905, Ir. 9292 b 6

Blayney: E. Rowley-Morris, *The family of Blayney . . .*, 1890, Ir. 9292 b 7

Boleyn: E. G. S. Reilly, *Historical anecdotes of the families of Boleyn, Carey, Mordaunt, Hamilton and Jocelyn . . .*, Newry, 1825, Ir. 9292 b 14

Bolton: C. K. Bolton, *Bolton families in Ireland*, 1937, Ir. 9292 b 15

Bourne: M. A. Strange, *The Bourne families of Ireland*, 1970, Ir. 9292 b 32

Bowen: Elizabeth Bowen, *Bowen's Court*, London, 1944, Ir. 9292 b 18

Boyle: E. M. F. G. Boyle, *Genealogical Memoranda relating to the family of Boyle of Limavady*, 1903, Ir. 9292 b 8

Braden: B. B. Peel, *In search of the Peels and the Bradens*, Edmonton, 1986, Ir. 9292 p 23 (4)

Braly: (1) D. Braly, *A history of the Bralys*, 1975, Ir. 9292 b 38

(2) D. Braly, *The Bralys, a family of the old south and the wild west*, 1980, Ir. 9292 b 50

Brennan: T. A. Brennan, *A history of the Brennans of Idough, Co. Kilkenny*, New York, 1975, Ir. 9292 b 42, 45

Brett: C. E. B. Brett, *Long Shadows Cast Before*, Edinburgh, 1978, Ir. 9292 b 43

Bronte: J. Cannon, *The road to Haworth*, London, 1980, Ir. 9292 b 49

Brooke: R. F. Brooke, *The burning river*, Dublin, 1961, Ir. 9292 b 27

Browne: (1) J. More, *A tale of two houses*, Shrewsbury, 1978, Ir. 9292 b 47

(2) D. Browne, *Westport House and the Brownes*, 1981, Ir. 9292 b 52

Bryan: G. and J. Latterell, *Genealogical information on the Bryan/O'Bryan and Fitzgerald families*, 1981, Ir. 9292 b 54

Bullock: J. W. Beck, *Bullock or Bullick of Northern Ireland*, 1931, Ir. 9292 b 16

Burke: (1) T. U. Sadleir, *The Burkes of Marble Hall*, n.d., Ir. 9292 b 10

(2) E. Burke, *Burke People and Places*, Whitegate, 1984, Ir. 9292 b 55

Butler: (1) *Account of the Family of Butlers . . .*, 1716, Ir. 9292 b 11

(2) 'Journal of the Butler Society', 1968–, Ir. 9292 b 28

(3) W. Clare, *Testamentary Records of the Butler Family*, Peterborough, 1932, Ir. 9292 b 59

Byrne: Mrs D. Byrne, 'Byrne and Kelly Notes' (typescript), 1968, Ir. 9292 b 29

C

Cahalan: D. Cahalan, *Patrick Cahalan 1833–1915, and his relatives in Ireland and America*, Berkeley, 1980, Ir. 9292 c 27

Cairns: H. C. Lawlor, *A History of the Family of Cairnes or Cairns*, 1906, Ir. 9292 c 1

Caldwell: W. H. Greaves-Bagshawe, *The Caldwell family of Castle Caldwell, Co. Fermanagh*, Ir. 9292 c 24

Camac: Frank O. Fisher, *Memoirs of the Camacs of Co. Down*, 1897, Ir. 9292 c 2

Caraher: 'Caraher Family History Society Journal', 1980–, Ir. 9292 c 28

Carlisle: R. H. Crofton, *Ann Jane Carlisle and her descendants*, 1950, Ir. 9292 c 15

Carey: (1) E. G. S. Reilly, *Historical anecdotes of the families of Boleyn. Carey, Mordaunt, Hamilton, and Jocelyn . . .*, Newry, 1825, Ir. 9292 b 14

(2) H. Rudnitzky, *The Careys*, Belfast, 1978, Ir. 9292 c 23

Carson: (1) J. Carson, *Short history of the Carson family*, Belfast, 1909, Ir. 9292 c 3

(2) J. Carson, *The Carsons of Monanton, Ballybay, Co Monaghan*, Lisburn, 1931, Ir. 9292 c 31

Cartland: G. and J. B. Cartland, *The Irish Cartlands and Cartland Genealogy*, Tasmania, 1978, Ir. 9292 c 30

Caulfield: B. Connor, *Clan Cathmhaoil or Caulfield Family*, Dublin, 1808, Ir. 9292 c 4

Charley: Irene Charley, *The romance of the Charley family*, 1970, Ir. 9292 c 21

Chichester: A. and B. Chichester, *History of the family of Chichester*, London, 1808, Ir. 9292 c 18

Clancy: M. Clancy, *Clancy: a brief family history*, US, 1980, Ir. 9292 p 20 (1)

Clayton: J. Paul Ryalands, *Some account of the Clayton family of . . . Doneraile and Mallow*, Liverpool, 1880, Ir. 9292 r 6

Coffey: A. Cuffez, *Coffey Genealogy*, Vols 1 and 2, 1983, Ir. 9292 c 25, 29

Cole: R. L. Cole, *The Cole family of West Carbery*, Belfast, 1943, Ir. 9292 c 13

Coote: *Historical and genealogical records of the Coote family*, 1900, Ir. 9292 c 6

Copinger: W. A. Copinger, *History of the Coppingers or Copingers of Co. Cork*, 1882, Ir. 9292 c 7

Conway: S. T. McCarthy, *Three Kerry Families: Mahonys, Conways and Spotiswoods*, Folkestone, 1923, Ir. 9292 m 7

Corry: Earl of Belmore, *History of the Corry Family of Castlecoole*, 1891, Ir. 9292 c 8

Cox: John H. R. Cox, *Claim of J. H. R. Cox to the Baronetcy of Cox of Dunmanway, Co. Cork* (. . .), 1912–14, Ir. 9292 c 9

Crawford: Robert Crawford, *The Crawfords of Donegal and how they came there*, 1886, Ir. 9292 c 14

Crichton: J. H. Steele, *Genealogy of the Earls of Erne*, London, 1910, Ir. 9292 e 5

Crofton: H. T. Crofton, *Crofton Memoirs: Account of John Crofton of Ballymurray, Co. Roscommon*, 1911, Ir. 9292 c 10

Crozier: R. A. Foulke, *The Crozier family of Dublin and Prince Edward Island*, US, 1979, Ir. 9292 c 26

D

Darbyshire: J. Harris, *The Darbyshire Genealogy*, Knollwood, 1983, Ir. 9292 d 15

Denham: C. H. Denham, *Denhams of Dublin*, Dublin, 1936, Ir. 9292 D 4

Devereux: G. O'C. Redmond, *The family of Devereux of Ballymagir*, 1891, Ir. 9292 d 1

Dignam: H. M. Dignam, *A chronicle of the Dignam family of Ireland and Canada*, Toronto, 1962, Ir. 9292 d 8

Dillon: (1) G. D. F. Dillon, *Lineage of G. D. F. Dillon, gent.*, Ir. 9292 d 9

  (2) *Pedigree of Dillon. Vicounts Dillon*, 1912, Ir. 9292 d 2

  (3) J. J. Dillon, *Claim of the Dillon family of Proudston to the Great Chamberlainship of all England*, 1829, Ir. 9292 d 7

Dineen: R. V. Spear, *The descendants of Redmond Peter Fahey and Cecilia Haverty, and John Sweeney and Mary Dineen, 1810–1894*, US, 1984, Ir. 9292 s 21

Donnelly: R. Fajazakas, *The Donnelly Album*, Ir. 9292 d 10

Downshire: H. McCall, *The House of Downshire*, Belfast, 1881, Ir. 9292 d 3

Downey: L. C. Downey, *A history of the Protestant Downey families of Counties Sligo, Leitrim, Fermanagh and Donegal*, 1931, Ir. 9292 d 13

Ducey: A. C. Ducey, *A family lifeline*, Chicago, 1981, Ir. 9292 d 14

Dundon: T. J. Dundon, *The Dundon Family*, Wisconsin, 1977, Ir. 9292 d 12

Dunlevy: G. D. Kelley, *A genealogical history of the Dunlevy family*, 1901, Ir. 9292 d 5

E

Eager: F. J. Eager, *The Eager family of Co. Kerry*, 1860, Ir. 9292 e 1

Ebel: M. Bingham, *Peers and Plebs: two families in a changing world*, London, 1975, Ir. 9292 b 35

Echlin: J. R. Echlin, *Genealogical memoirs of the Echlin family*, 1881, Ir. 9292 e 2

Edgeworth: (1) Harriet J. Butler (ed.), *The Black Book of Edgeworthstown*, 1917, Ir. 9292 e 3

(2) E. E. McDonald, *The American Edgeworths*, Virginia, 1970, Ir. 9292 e 9

Ellis: W. S. Ellis, *Notices of the Ellises of England, Scotland and Ireland*, 1881, Ir. 9292 e 7

Ellison: H. H. Ellison, *In Search of my Family*, Dublin, 1971, Ir. 9292 e 10

Ely: *Adam Loftus and the Ely Family*, n.d., Ir. 9292 l 17

Emmett: T. A. Emmett, *The Emmett Family*, 1898, Ir. 9292 e 4

Eyre: (1) A. S. Hartigan, *A short account of the Eyre family of Eyre Court*, 1899, Ir. 9292 e 6

(2) I. Gantz, *Signpost to Eyrecourt*, Bath, 1975, Ir. 9292 e 11

F

Fahey: R. V. Spear, *The descendants of Redmond Peter Fahey and Cecilia Haverty, and John Sweeney and Mary Dineen, 1810–1894*, US, 1984, Ir. 9292 s 21

Farnham: *Farnham Descents from Henry III*, Cavan, 1860, Ir. 9292 f 14

Ferrall: R. B. Ferrall, *History of the Ferralls and their American Genealogy*, US, 1981, Ir. 9292 f 18

Filory: S. P. Filory, *Fragments of family history*, London, 1896, Ir. 9292 f 3

Finn: T. M. MacKenzie, *Dromana: Memoirs of an Irish Family*, 1916, Ir. 9292 f 1

Finnegan: C. Fitzgibbon, *Miss Finnegan's Fault*, Ir. 9292 f 8

Fitzgerald: (1) Marquis of Kildare, *Descents of the Earls of Kildare and their wives*, Dublin, 1866–69, Ir. 9292 f 13

(2) M. Estouche, *Heirs and Graces: the claim to the dukedom of Leinster*, London, 1981, Ir. 9292 f 16

(3) J. A. King, *The Irish lumberman-farmer: Fitzgeralds, Harrigans and others*, California, 1982, Ir. 9292 f 17

(4) *The case of Charlotte Fitzgerald and the barony of Roscommon*, 1921, Ir. 9292 f 20

(5) S. Hayman (ed.), *Unpublished Geraldine Documents* (2 volumes), 1870–81, Ir. 9292 g 2

(6) J. A. Gaughan, *The Knights of Glin, a geraldine family*, Dublin, 1978, Ir. 9292 g 17

(7) H. J. Gerrard, *The Meath Geraldines*, 1964, Ir. 9292 p 7 (6)

Fitzwilliam: D. G. Holland, *The Fitzwilliam, O'Brien and Watson families: history and genealogy*, 1973, Ir. 9292 f 11

Fleetwood: Sir E. Bewley, *An Irish Branch of the Fleetwood Family*, 1908, Ir. 9292 f 2

Fleming: (1) L. T. Fleming, *Fleming and Reeves of Co. Cork*, 1975, Ir. 9292 p 12 (4)

(2) Sir William Betham, *History and genealogical memoir of the family of Fleming of Slane*, Dublin, 1829, Ir. 9292 f 10; Ir. 9292 9 7 (10)

Flood: C. R. Patterson, *Flood Family Triad*, US, 1982, Ir. 9292 p 22

Folliots: Sir E. Bewley, *The Folliots of Londonderry and Chester*, 1902, Ir. 9292 f 5

Forbes: John Forbes, *Memoirs of the Earls of Granard*, 1868, Ir. 9292 g 5

French: *Origin of the family of French in Connaught*, Tuam, 1928, Ir. 9292 f 6

French: Rev. H. B. Swanzy, *The Families of French of Belturbet and Nixon of Fermanagh and their Descendants*, 1908, Ir. 9292 f 15

Fulton: Sir T. Hope, *Memoirs of the Fultons of Lisburn*, 1903, Ir. 9292 f 7

G

Galbraith: C. L. House, *The Galbraiths and the Kootenays*, New York, 1969, Ir. 9292 g 26

Galwey: C. J. Bennett, *The Galweys of Lota*, 1909, Ir. 9292 g 1

Gillman: A. W. Gillman, *Searches into the History of the Gillman or Gilman Family . . . in Ireland*, 1895, Ir. 9292 g 3

Goodbody: (1) M. I. A. Goodbody, *The Goodbody Family of Ireland*, Halstead, 1979, Ir. 9292 g 20

(2) M. I. A. Goodbody, *Goodbodys of Clara*, 1965, Ir. 9292 g 12

Gormley: V. R. and T. M. Spear, *Descendants of Bernard Gormley in New Brunswick*, California, 1982, Ir. 9292 g 25

Gowan: J. H. B. Gowan, *The genealogy of the Clan Gowan* (2 volumes), Bucks, 1978, Ir. 9292 g 19

Grace: Sheffield Grace, *Memoirs of the Family of Grace*, 1823, Ir. 9292 g 4

Grady: J. L. Grady, *From Ireland . . .*, 1984, Ir. 9292 g 24

Graves: H. H. G. MacDonnell, *Some Notes on the Graves family*, Dublin, 1889, Ir. 9292 g 18

Green: H. B. Swanzy and T. G. Green, *The Family of Green of Youghal*, 1902, Ir. 9292 g 15

Greene: Lt Col J. Greene, *Pedigree of the Family of Greene*, 1899, Ir. 9292 g 6

Gregory: V. R. T. Gregory, *The House of Gregory*, 1943, Ir. 9292 g 12

Grubb: G. W. Grubb, *The Grubbs of Tipperary*, 1972, Ir. 9292 g 13

Guinness: (1) R. Linn, *Pedigree of the Magennis (Guinness) family of New Zealand and Dublin*, Christchurch, 1897, Ir. 9292 g 7

    (2) F. Mullally, *The silver salver: the story of the Guinness family*, London, 1981, Ir. 9292 g 21

Gunning: I. Gantz, *The pastel portrait: the Gunnings of Castlecoote and Howards of Hampstead*, London, 1963, Ir. 9292 g 23

H

Hagerty: J. L. Grady, *From Ireland . . .*, 1984, Ir. 9292 g 24

Halloran: M. L. Resch, *The descendants of Patrick Halloran of Boytonrath, Co. Tipperary*, Baltimore, 1987, Ir. 9292 r 12

Hamilton: (1) E. G. S. Reilly, *Historical anecdotes of the families of Boleyn, Carey, Mordaunt, Hamilton, and Jocelyn . . .*, Newry, 1825, Ir. 9292 b 14

    (2) E. Hamilton, *Hamilton Memoirs*, Dundalk, 1920, Ir. 9292 h 1

Hanrahan: P. L. Hanrahan, *Hanrahan, family history*, Oregon, 1983, Ir. 9292 h 10

Harrigan: J. A. King, *The Irish lumberman-farmer: Fitzgeralds, Harrigans and others*, California, 1982, Ir. 9292 f 17

Harvey: G. H. Harvey, *The Harvey families of Inishowen, Co. Donegal, and Maen, Cornwall*, Folkestone, 1927, Ir. 9292 h 3

Hassard: Rev. H. B. Swanzy, *Some account of the Family of Hassard*, 1903, Ir. 9292 h 3

Haverty: R. V. Spear, *The descendants of Redmond Peter Fahey and Cecilia Haverty, and John Sweeney and Mary Dineen, 1810–1894*, US, 1984, Ir. 9292 s 21

Hawksby: L. C. Downey, T*he Hawksby family of Leitrim and Sligo*, 1931, Ir. 9292 d 13

Hayes: D. H. Crofton, *The children of Edmonston Park*, Peterhead, 1980, Ir. 9292 h 12

Heffernan: Patrick Heffernan, *The Heffernans and their times*, 1940, Ir. 9292 h 9

Hervey: D. A. Ponsonby, *Call a Dog Hervey*, London, 1949, Ir. 9292 h 14

Higginson: T. B. Higginson, *Descendants of Rev. Thomas Higgenson*, London, 1958, Ir. 9292 h 13, 15

Ho(a)re: Edward Hoare, *Account, from 1330, of the families of Hoare and Hore (. . .)*, 1883, Ir. 9292 h 5

Hogan: M. J. Culligan-Hogan, *The quest for the galloping Hogan*, New York, 1979, Ir. 9292 h 11

Holians: D. Regan, *The Holians, a Galway family in Australia*, 1984, Ir. 9292 r 10

Hollingsworth: Harry Hollingsworth, *The Hollingsworth Register*, 1965 to date, Ir. 9292 h 21

Hovenden: *Lineage of the family of Hovenden (Irish branch) by a member of the family*, 1892, Ir. 9292 h 6

J

Jacob: (1) A. H. Jacob and J. H. Glascott, *Historical and genealogical narration of the families of Jacob*, 1875, Ir. 9292 j 1

   (2) H. W. Jacob, *History of the Families of Jacob of Bridgewater. Twerton and Southern Ireland*, 1929, Ir. 9292 j 4

Jellett: C. S. Gould, *Great trees from little saplings*, New York, 1931, Ir. 9292 j 3

Jephson: Brigadier M. D. Jephson, *An Anglo-Irish Miscellany: Some Records of the Jephsons of Mallow*, 1964, Ir. 9292 j 2

Jocelyn: E. G. S. Reilly, *Historical anecdotes of the families of Boleyn, Carey, Mordaunt, Hamilton, and Jocelyn . . .*, Newry, 1825, Ir. 9292 b 14

Joyce: K. Nutting, *The Joyces of Overflow and Eidsvold*, Brisbane, 1961, Ir. 9292 p 23 (2)

K

Kelly: (1) Turquet de la Boisserie, *Kelly of Nenton*, Ir. 9292 k 8

   (2) P. O'Kelly d'Aghrim, *Annales de la maison d'Hy Many*, La Haye, 1830, Ir. 9292 o 2

   (3) 'Notes on the O'Kellys and other families of Kilkeerin parish, Co. Roscommon' (typescript), Ir. 9292 k 5

   (4) J. D. Williams, *History of the name O'Kelly*, Dublin, 1977, Ir. 9292 p 14 (3)

Keeffe: B. Brodee, *Keeffe and Toner Families in Ireland and the U.S.*, Iowa, 1984, Ir. 9292 b 61

Kennedy: F. M. E. Kennedy, *A family of Kennedy of Clogher and Londonderry, 1600–1938*, Taunton, 1938, Ir. 9292 k 1

Kernans: *The Utica Kernans, descendants of Bryan Kernan, gent, . . . Co. Cavan*, 1969, Ir. 9292 k 7

Kerr: H. C. Kerr, *History of the Gabriel and George Kerr families, and other Kerr families from Enniskillen*, Quebec, 1976, Ir. 9292 k 9

Kirkpatrick: A. Kirkpatrick, *Chronicles of the Kirkpatrick family*, 1897, Ir. 9292 k 3

Kirwan: *Pedigree of the Kirwan family*, Ir. 9292 k 2

Knox: A. K. [*sic*] *Notes on some of the Ranfurly Knoxes*, 1950, Ir. 9292 k 10

L

Lally: D. P. O'Mullally, *History of O'Mullally and Lally Clans*, 1941, Ir. 9292 o 19

La Touche: *Genealogy of the La Touche Family of France*, Strasbourg, 1883, Ir. 9292 l 3

Le Fanu: T. Le Fanu, *Memoir of the Le Fanu Family*, 1924, Ir. 9292 l 4 ,

Lefroy: Sir J. H. Lefroy, *Notes and Documents relating to the Lefroy family (. . .) of Carrickglas, Co. Longford*, 1868, Ir. 9292 l 18

Lenox-Conyngham: M. Lenox-Cunningham, *An old Ulster house, and the people who lived in it*, 1946, Ir. 9292 l 14

Le Poer Trench: 2nd Earl of Clancarty, *Memoir of the Le Poer Trench family*, Dublin, 1874, Ir. 9292 l 5

Leslie: (1) P. Leslie Pielou, *The Leslies of Tarbert, Co. Kerry, and their forebears*, 1935, Ir. 9292 l 12

    (2) Seymour Leslie, *Of Glaslough in the kingdom of Oriel, and of noted men who have dwelt there*, 1913, Ir. 9292 l 6

Levinge: Sir Richard Levinge, *Jottings for the Early History of the Levinge Family*, 1873, Ir. 9292 l 7 and 15

Lindsay: (1) J. C. and J. A. Lindsay, *The Lindsay Memoirs* (Lisnacrieve and Belfast), 1884, Ir. 9292 l 8

    (2) E. H. Godfrey, *The Lindesays of Loughry, Co. Tyrone*, 1949, Ir. 9292 l 16

    (3) Daryl Lindsay, *The leafy tree, my family*, Cheshire, 1967, Ir. 9292 l 21

Lloyd: A. R. Lloyd, *Genealogical Notes*, n.d., Ir. 9292 l 13

Loftus: *Adam Loftus and the Ely Family*, n.d., Ir. 9292 l 17

Londonderry: H. M. Hyde, *The Londonderrys, a family portrait*, London, 1979, Ir. 9292 l 20

Lowther: Sir Edmund Bewley, *Lowthers in Ireland in the 17th century*, 1902, Ir. 9292 l 9

Lynch: (1) E. C. Lynch, *Lynch Record*, New York, 1925, Ir. 9292 l 10

    (2) Martin J. Blake, 'Lynch of Galway', 1912–17, Ir. 9292 l 19

Lyster: E. Alinor-Lyster, *Lyster Pioneers of Lower Canada*, British Columbia, 1984, Ir. 9292 l 22

Mc

McCann: A. Mathews, *Origins of the Surname McCann*, Dublin, 1968, Ir. 9292 m 37 (2)

McCarthy: (1) A. MacCarthy, *A historical pedigree of the MacCarthys of Gleannacrain*, Exeter, 1855, Ir. 9292 m 1

    (2) S. T. McCarthy, *A McCarthy Miscellany*, Dundalk, 1928, Ir. 9292 m 1

    (3) S. T. McCarthy, *The McCarthys of Munster*, 1927, Ir. 9292 m 1

    (4) P. Louis Laine, *Généalogie de la maison McCarthy*, Ir. 9292 m 1

    (5) M. J. O'Brien, *The McCarthys in early American history*, New York, 1921, Ir. 9292 o 25

    (6) J. D. Williams, *History of the Name MacCarthy*, Dublin, 1978, Ir. 9292 w 21 (3)

McClusky: W. H. McClusky, *A tree of four ancient stocks*, Iowa, 1984, Ir. 9292 m 44

McDermot: The McDermot, *The McDermots of Moylurg and Coolavin*, 1985, Ir. 9292 m 58

McDonald: A. B. MacDonald, *A romantic chapter in family history*, 1911, Ir. 9292 m 16

McDonnell: (1) G. Hill, *A historical account of the MacDonnells of Antrim*, Belfast, 1873 (repr. 1978), Ir. 9292 m 2

    (2) A. McDonnell, *The Antrim McDonnells*, Belfast, 1979, Ir. 9292 m 42

    (3) B. W. Kelly, *The Fate of Glengorry*, Dublin, 1905, Ir. 9292 m 41

McGillycuddy: W. B. Mazier, *The MacGillicuddy Papers*, 1867, Ir. 9292 m 3

McGready: S. McGready and S. Jennett, *A Family of Roses*, London, 1971, Ir. 9292 m 35

McGuinness: A. Mathews, *Origins of the Surname McGuinness*, Dublin, 1968, Ir. 9292 m 32 (3)

McGuire: B. Patterson, *Pat and Rose Anne McGuire and their descendants*, Madison, 1980, Ir. 9292 m 53

McKee: R. W. McKee, *The Book of McKee*, Dublin, 1959, Ir. 9292 m 26

McKenna: (1) C. E. Sweezy, *The MacKennas of Truagh*, 1977, Ir. 9292 s 20
   (2) A. Mathews, *Origins of the Surname McKenna*, Dublin, 1968, Ir. 9292 m 37 (3)

McKinney: B. M. Walker, *Sentry Hill: an Ulster farm and family*, Belfast, 1981, Ir. 9292 w 19

McKittrick: F. L. McKittrick, *The McKittricks and the roots of Ulster Scots*, Baltimore, 1979, Ir. 9292 m 45

McLysaght: E. MacLysaght, *Short study of a transplanted family in the seventeenth century*, Dublin, 1935, Ir. 9292 m 18

McNamara: (1) R. W. Twigge, *The pedigree of John McNamara Esq.*, pr. pr. 1908, Ir. 9292 m 19
   (2) E. Forgnes, *Histoire d'un sept irlandais*, 1901, Ir. 9292 m 22

McRory: R. F. Cronnelly, *A History of the Clanna-Rory*, 1921, Ir. 9292 r 1

MacSweeny: P. Walsh, *An account of the MacSweeny families in Ireland*, 1920, Ir. 9292 m 5

M

Madden: (1) F. Madan, *The Madan family and Maddens of England and Ireland*, Oxford, 1930, Ir. 9292 m 15
   (2) T. M. O'Madden, *The O'Maddens of Hy Many*, 1894, Ir. 9292 o 6

Magan: J. Lentaigne, *Pedigree of the Magan family of Ennoe, Co. Westmeath*, Dublin, 1868, Ir. 9292 m 17

Magee: F. J. Biggar, *The Magees of Belfast and Dublin*, 1916, Ir. 9292 m 6

Mahony: S. T. McCarthy, *Three Kerry Families: Mahonys, Conways and Spotiswoods*, Folkestone, 1923, Ir. 9292 m 7

Malenfont: A. V. Malenfont, *Malenfont families*, New South Wales, Ir. 9292 m 51

Marshall: G. F. Marshall, *Marshall of Manor Cunningham*, Fleet, 1931, Ir. 9292 m 21

Martin: (1) A. E. S. Martin, *Genealogy of the Family of Martin of Ballinahinch Castle, Co. Galway*, 1890, Ir. 9292 m 8
   (2) S. Clark, *The genealogy of the Martins of Ross*, Inverness, 1910, Ir. 9292 m 34
   (3) G. V. Martyn, *Historical notes on the Martyns of the west of Ireland*, n.d., Ir. 9292 p 9 (3)

(4) M. J. Blake, *Martyn of Cregans, Co. Clare, 1613–1927*, Ir. 9292 c 19

(5) B. E. Martin, *Parsons and Prisoners*, 1972, Ir. 9292 m 36 and m 39

Massey: *A genealogical account of the Massey family from the time of the conquest*, Dublin, 1890, Ir. 9292 m 28

Maunsell: E. P. Statham, *History of the Family of Maunsell*, 1917, Ir. 9292 m 9

Maxwell: W. G. Maxwell, *The annals of one branch of the Maxwell family*, Malaya, 1959, Ir. 9292 m 27

Meade: H. J. Peet, *Chaumiere papers . . . the descendants of David Meade*, n.d., Ir. 9292 m 23

Meagher: N. A. Meagher, *The Meaghers*, New York, 1980, Ir. 9292 m 47

Meares: M. and G. Meares, *Pedigree of the family of Meares of Co. Westmeath*, Dublin, 1905, Ir. 9292 m 38

Monck: E. Batt, *The Moncks and Charleville House*, Dublin, 1979, Ir. 9292 b 46

Monroe: Horace Monroe, *Foulis Castle and the Monroes of Lower Iveagh*, 1929, Ir. 9292 m 10

Montgomery: (1) W. Montgomery, *The Montgomery Manuscripts, 1603–1706*, Belfast, 1869, Ir. 9292 m 11

(2) E. J. S. Reilly, *A genealogical history of the Montgomerys . . . of Mount Alexander and Grey-Abbey*, 1942, Ir. 9292 m 24

Moore: (1) T. J. G. Bennett, *North Antrim Families*, 1974, Ir. 9292 b 23

(2) J. Hore, *The Moores of Moore Hall*, London, 1939, Ir. 9292 M 20

(3) The Countess of Drogheda, *The family of Moore*, Dublin, 1906, Ir. 9292 m 12

Moran: A. J. Moran, *Your father is a Moran and your mother was a Murphy*, 1987, Ir. 9292 m 61

Mordaunt: E. G. S. Reilly, *Historical anecdotes of the families of Boleyn, Carey, Mordaunt, Hamilton, and Jocelyn . . .*, Newry, 1825, Ir. 9292 b 14

Morris: E. Naomi Chapman, *Memoirs of my Family, together with some researches into the Early History of the Morris Families of Tipperary, Galway, and Mayo*, 1928, Ir. 9292 m 13

Mulock: Sir Edmund Bewley, *The Family of Mulock*, 1905, Ir. 9292 m 14

Murphy: (1) B. and M. Doyle, *Murphy: a family history*, US, 1981, Ir. 9292 m 46

(2) J. D. Williams, *History of the name Murphy*, Dublin, 1977, Ir. 9292 p 14 (1)

N

Nash: (1) E. F. Nash, *The Nash Family of Farrihy Co. Cork, etc.*, Ir. 9292 n 3

(2) A. C. S. Pabst, *Nashes of Ireland*, Ohio, 1963, Ir. 9292 n 9

Nangle: (1) F. R. and J. F. T. Nangle, *A short account of the Nangle family of Downpatrick*, 1986, Ir. 9292 n 8

(2) *A genealogical memoir of the extinct Anglo-Norman Catholic family of Nangle of Garisker, Co. Kildare*, 1869, Ir. 9292 n 2

Neill: I. Wilson, *Neills of Bangor*, Coleraine, 1982, Ir. 9292 n 6

Nesbitt: A. Nesbitt, *History of the family of Nesbitt in Scotland and Ireland*, Torquay, 1898, Ir. 9292 n 1

Nixon: Rev. H. B. Swanzy, *The Families of French of Belturbet and Nixon of Fermanagh and their Descendants*, 1908, Ir. 9292 f 15

O

O'Brien: (1) D. G. Holland, *The Fitzwilliam, O'Brien and Watson families: history and genealogy*, 1973, Ir. 9292 f 11

(2) J. D. Williams, *History of the name O'Brien*, Dublin, 1977, Ir. 9292 p 14 (2)

(3) J. O'Donoghue, *The O'Briens*, 1860, Ir. 9292 o 1

(4) D. O'Brien, *History of the O'Briens*, London, 1946, Ir. 9292 o 24

(5) *Playfair's Family Antiquities* (Earls of Thomond), 2 vols, Ir. 9292 o 29

(6) H. Weir, *O'Brien people and places*, Whitegate, 1983, Ir. 9292 o 44

O'Byrne: (1) *The O'Byrnes and their descendants*, Dublin, 1879, Ir. 9292 o 22

(2) P. L. O'Toole, *History of the clan O'Byrne and other Leinster septs*, Dublin, 1890, Ir. 9292 o 42

O'Cleirigh: P. Walsh, *The O'Cleirigh family of Tir Conaill*, Dublin, 1938, Ir. 9292 o 17

O'Connell: Basil O'Connell, *O'Connell Family Tracts*, Dublin, 1950, Ir. 9292 o 26

O'Conor: (1) Charles O'Conor, *The O'Conors of Connaught*, Dublin, 1891, Ir. 9292 o 2

(2) Roderick O'Conor, *A history and genealogical memoir of the O'Conors of Connaught and their descendants*, Dublin, 1861, Ir. 9292 o 32

(3) Roderick O'Conor, *The Anonymous Claim of Mr Arthur O'Connor*, Dublin, 1859, Ir. 9292 O 33

(4) Roderick O'Conor, *Lineal Descent of the O'Conors of Co. Roscommon*, Dublin, 1862, Ir. 9292 o 34

O'Daly: E. R. O'Daly, *History of the O'Dalys*, New Haven, 1937, Ir. 9292 o 14

O'Dempsey: T. Mathews, *An account of the O'Dempseys*, Dublin, 1903, Ir. 9292 o 3

O'Devlin: J. C. Devlin, *The O'Devlins of Tyrone*, US, 1938, Ir. 9292 o 15

O'Doherty: A. Mathews, *Origins of the Surname O'Doherty*, Dublin, 1968, Ir. 9292 m 37 (4)

O'Donnell: E. T. Cook, *John O'Donnell of Baltimore, his forebears and descendants*, 1934, Ir. 9292 o 13

O'Donoghue: (1) M. O'Laughlin, *O'Donoghues*, 1980, Ir. 9292 p 23 (5)

(2) A. Mathews, *Origins of the Surname O'Donoghue*, Dublin, 1968, Ir. 9292 m 37 (5)

O'Doyne: K. W. Nicholls (ed.), *The O'Doyne Mss*, IMC, Dublin, 1983, Ir. 9292 o 46

O'Dwyer: (1) Sir M. O'Dwyer, *The O'Dwyers of Kilnamanagh*, London, 1933, Ir. 9292 o 4

(2) M. Callanan, *Records of Four Tipperary Septs: the O'Kennedys, O'Dwyers, O'Mulryans, and O'Meaghers*, Galway, 1938, Ir. 9292 o 16

O'Flaherty: A. Mathews, *Origins of the Surname O'Flaherty*, Dublin, 1968, Ir. 9292 m 32 (2)

O'Gowan: *A memoir of the name of O'Gowan or Smith, by an O'Gowan*, Tyrone, 1837, Ir. 9292 o 12

O'Kelly: A. Mathews, *Origins of the Surname O'Kelly*, Dublin, 1968, Ir. 9292 m 32 (1)

O'Kennedy: M. Callanan, *Records of Four Tipperary Septs: the O'Kennedys, O'Dwyers, O'Mulryans, and O'Meaghers*, Galway, 1938, Ir. 9292 o 16

Oliver: H. O. Rea, *Henry (William) Oliver 1807–1888: ancestry and descendants*, Dungannon, 1959, Ir. 9292 o 28

O'Madden: T. M. O'Madden, *The O'Maddens of Hy Many*, 1894, Ir. 9292 o 6

O'Mahoney: (1) J. B. O'Mahoney, *A history of the O'Mahony septs of Kinalmeaky and Iveragh*, Cork, 1912, Ir. 9292 o 20

(2) *The O'Mahony Journal*, Vol. 1, 1971–, Ir. 9292 o 38

O'Malley: *Genealogy of the O'Malleys of the Owals*, Philadelphia, 1913, Ir. 9292 o 21

O'Meagher: (1) J. C. O'Meagher, *The O'Meaghers of Ikerrin*, 1886, Ir. 9292 o 7

(2) M. Callanan, *Records of Four Tipperary Septs: the O'Kennedys, O'Dwyers, O'Mulryans, and O'Meaghers*, Galway, 1938, Ir. 9292 o 16

O'Mullally: D. P. O'Mullally, *History of O'Mullally and Lally Clans*, 1941, Ir. 9292 o 19

O'Mulryan: M. Callanan, *Records of Four Tipperary Septs: the O'Kennedys, O'Dwyers, O'Mulryans, and O'Meaghers*, Galway, 1938, Ir. 9292 o 16

O'Neill:(1) T. Mathews, *The O'Neills of Ulster*, 1907, Ir. 9292 o 8

(2) D. Braly, *Ui Neill: a history of Western Civilization's oldest family*, 1976, Ir. 9292 o 35

(3) Anne O'Neill, *Odds and ends about Shane's castle and some of its inhabitants*, London, 1904, Ir. 9292 o 39

(4) P. Walsh (ed.), *The will and family of Hugh O'Neill, Earl of Tyrone*, Dublin, 1930, Ir. 9292 o 41

(5) M. Westacott, *The Clan Niall in Ireland, 379–1030*, Sydney, 1970, Ir. 9292 n 5

(6) A. Mathews, *Origins of the Surname O'Neill*, Dublin, 1968, Ir. 9292 m 37 (1)

(7) J. D. Williams, *History of the Name O'Neill*, Dublin, 1978, Ir. 9292 w 21 (1)

O'Reilly: (1) E. M. O'Hanluain, *The O'Reillys of Temple Mills, Celbridge*, Dublin, 1940, Ir. 9292 o 18

(2) J. J. O'Reilly, *The history of Breifne O'Reilly*, New York, 1975, Ir. 9292 o 36

(3) J. Carney (ed.), *A genealogical history of the O'Reillys*, 1959, Ir. 9292 o 18

(4) A. Mathews, *Origins of the Surname O'Reilly*, Dublin, 1970, Ir. 9292 o 31 (2)

Orpen: Goddard H. Orpen, *The Orpen Family*, 1930, Ir. 9292 o 9

O'Rourke: (1) J. C. Smith, *The Children of Master O'Rourke*, London, 1978, Ir. 9292 o 37

(2) B. McDermott, *O'Ruairc of Breifne*, 1983, Ir. 9292 o 45

(3) A. Mathews, *Origins of the Surname O'Rourke*, Dublin, 1970, Ir. 9292 o 31 (1)

Osborne: J. Osborne, *The Osbornes of Co. Louth and Nicollot County, Wisconsin,* US, 1978, Ir. 9292 o 40

O'Sullivan: (1) M. R. O'Sullivan, *The Beginning of the O'Sullivan Sept,* New Jersey, 1975?, Ir. 9292 p 12 (5)

(2) M. R. O'Sullivan, *Sullivan Sept: Inter Sept,* Ir. 9292 p 12 (6)

(3) J. D. Williams, *History of the Name O'Sullivan,* Dublin, 1978, Ir. 9292 w 21 (2)

O'Toole: (1) P. L. O'Toole, *History of the Clan O'Toole, and other Leinster septs,* Dublin, 1890 (4 vols), Ir. 9292 o 10

(2) C. P. Meehan, *The O'Tooles, anciently lords of Powerscourt,* Dublin, 1911, Ir. 9292 o 10

(3) C. D. Comte O'Kelly-Farrell, *Notice sur le clan des O'Toole . . .,* La Reole, 1864, Ir. 9292 o 49

(4) L. O'Tuathalain, *Notes of the genealogy of the O'Tuathalains of Cloonyquin, Clontarf, and Clara,* 1985, Ir. 9292 o 47

Ouseley: R. J. Kelly, *The Names and family of Ouseley,* 1910, Ir. 9292 o 11

Owen: H. Owen, *Owen and Perrin family histories,* 1981, Ir. 9292 o 43

P

Palmer: T. Prime, *Some account of the Palmer family of Rahan, Co. Kildare,* New York, 1903, Ir. 9292 p 4

Palatines: (1) R. Hayes, *The German Colony in Co. Limerick,* 1937, Ir. 9292 h 8

(2) Hank Jones, *The Palatine Families of Ireland,* San Leandro, 1965, Ir. 9292 p 6

Patterson: B. Patterson, *Edmund and Margaret (Leamy) Patterson and their descendants,* Madison, 1979, Ir. 9292 p 18

Peel: B. B. Peel, *In search of the Peels and the Bradens,* Edmonton, 1986, Ir. 9292 p 23 (4)

Pentheny: *Memoir of the Ancient Family of Pentheny or De Pentheny of Co. Meath,* 1821, Ir. 9292 p 13

Penrose: C. Penrose, *The Penrose family of Halston, Wheeldrake, and Co. Wicklow,* New York, 1975, Ir. 9292 p 11

Perrin: H. Owen, *Owen and Perrin family histories,* 1981, Ir. 9292 o 43

Pilkington: *Harland's history of the Pilkingtons, from the Saxon times (. . .) to the present,* 1882, Ir. 9292 p 1

Pim: F. B. Pim, *A Pim genealogy,* n.d., Ir. 9292 p 21

Poe: Sir E. T. Bewley, *Origin and Early History of the Family of Poe, with full Pedigrees of the Irish Branch . . .,* 1906, Ir. 9292 p 2

Pooles: Rosemary ffolliott, *The Pooles of Mayfield, Co. Cork and Other Irish Families,* 1956, Ir. 9292 p 5

Power: B. Patterson, *Patrick, Margaret, Jeffrey and Ellen Power and their descendants,* Madison, 1980, Ir. 9292 p 17

Pratt: (1) John Pratt, *The Family of Pratt of Gawsworth, Carrigrohane, Co. Cork*, 1925, Ir. 9292 p 3

(2) John Pratt, *Pratt Family records: an account of the Pratts of Youghal and Castlemartyr and their Descendants*, 1931, Ir. 9292 p 15

R

Ranahans: J. P. M. Feheny, *The Ranahans of Iverus, Co. Cork*, 1987, Ir. 9292 r 14

Rea: (1) H. O. Rea, *Samuel Rea, 1725–1811: his heritage and descendants*, 1960, Ir. 9292 r 6

(2) J. H. Rea, *The Rea Genealogy*, Banbridge, 1927, 1971, Ir. 9292 r 8

(3) *A Belfast Man: memoirs of the Rea family, 1798–1857*, London, 1857, Ir. 9292 r 11

Reagan: Hugh Peskett, 'Presented to the Hon. Ronald Reagan on behalf of . . . Ballyporeen', Ir. 9292 p 19

Reeves: L. T. Fleming, *Fleming and Reeves of Co. Cork*, 1975, Ir. 9292 p 12 (4)

Roberts: E. J. A. Impey, *A Roberts Family, quondam Quakers of Queen's Co.*, 1839, Ir. 9292 r 3

Rochfort: R. R. Forlong, *Notes on the history of the family of Rochfort*, Oxford, 1890, Ir. 9292 r 4

Rudkin: Sir E. T. Bewley, *The Rudkins of the Co. Carlow*, 1905, Ir. 9292 r 2

S

Saunderson: Henry Saunderson, *The Saundersons of Castle Saunderson*, 1936, Ir. 9292 s 10

Savage: G. F. Savage-Armstrong, *The Savages of the Ards*, 1888, Ir. 9292 s 1

Seaver: Rev. G. Seaver, *History of the Seaver Family*, 1950, Ir. 9292 s 12

Segrave: C. W. Segrave, *The Segrave Family, 1066–1935*, 1936, Ir. 9292 s 9

Shannon: J. Shannon (ed.), *The Shannon Saga*, New South Wales, 1972, Ir. 9292 p 9 (1)

Shaw: N. Harris, *The Shaws*, London, 1977, Ir. 9292 s 18

Shirley: E. P. Shirley, *Shirlieana, or Annals of the Shirley Family*, 1873, Ir. 9292 s 2

Sinnett: C. N. Sinnett, *Sinnet genealogy . . . records of Sinnets, Sinnots etc. in Ireland and America*, 1910, Ir. 9292 s 3

Slacke: H. A. Crofton, *Records of the Slacke Family in Ireland*, 1900–1902, Ir. 9292 s 4

Smeltzer: (1) M. R. Smeltzer, *The Smeltzers of Kilcooley and their Irish-Palatine kissing cousins*, Baltimore, 1981, Ir. 9292 s 19

(2) M. R. Smeltzer, *Irish-Palatine Smeltzers around the world*, Baltimore, 1987, Ir. 9292 s 23

Smith: (1) *A memoir of the name of O'Gowan or Smith, by an O'Gowan*, Tyrone, 1837, Ir. 9292 o 12

(2) G. N. Nuttall-Smith, *The chronicle of a Puritan family in Ireland*, Oxford, 1923, Ir. 9292 s 5

(3) *Memoir of the descendants of William Smith in New Hampshire*, 1903, Ir. 9292 s 24

Spotiswood: S. T. McCarthy, *Three Kerry Families: Mahonys, Conways and Spotiswoods*, Folkestone, 1923, Ir. 9292 m 7

Standish: J. Richard Houston, *Numbering the Survivors: a history of the Standish family of Ireland, Ontario and Alberta*, 1980, Ir. 9292 s 22

Stewart: G. Hill, *The Stewarts of Ballintoy, with notices of other families in the district in the seventeenth century*, Ballycastle, 1976, Ir. 9292 p 20 (2)

Stoney: F. S. Stoney, *Some old annals of the Stoney family*, n.d., Ir. 9292 s 11

Stopford: L. O'Broin, *Protestant nationalists in revolutionary Ireland: the Stopford connection*, Dublin, 1985, Ir. 9292 s 15

Stuart: A. G. Stuart, *A genealogical and historical sketch of the family of Stuart of Castlestuart in Ireland*, Edinburgh, 1854, Ir. 9292 s 6

Studdert: R. H. Studdert, *The Studdert Family*, 1960, Ir. 9292 s 13

Sullivan: T. C. Armory, *Materials for a family history of John Sullivan of Bewick, New England and Ardee*, 1893, Ir. 9292 s 7

Sweeney: R. V. Spear, *The descendants of Redmond Peter Fahey and Cecilia Haverty, and John Sweeney and Mary Dineen, 1810–1894*, US, 1984, Ir. 9292 s 21

Synan: (1) Mannanaan Mac Lir [*sic*], *The Synans of Doneraile*, 1909, Ir. 9292 s 17
(2) Rev. J. A. Gaughan, *The family of Synan*, 1971, Ir. 9292 s 16

T

Taaffe: Count E. F. J. Taaffe, *Memoirs of the family of Taaffe*, 1856, Ir. 9292 t 1

Tiernan: C. B. Tiernan, *The Tiernans and other families*, 1901, Ir. 9292 t 2

Tone: F. J. Tone, *History of the Tone family*, New York, 1944, Ir. 9292 t 11

Toner: B. Brodee, *Keeffe and Toner Families in Ireland and the U.S.*, Iowa, 1984, Ir. 9292 b 61

Toolan: L. O'Tuathalain, *Notes of the genealogy of the O'Tuathalains of Cloonyquin, Clontarf, and Clara*, 1985, Ir. 9292 o 47

Trant: S. Trant McCarthy, *The Trant Family*, Folkestone, 1924, Ir. 9292 t 3

Travis/Travers: A. Casey, *Southern Travis, Travers and Traverse families*, 1978, Ir. 9292 t 10

Trench: (1) T. R. F. Cooke-Trench, *A Memoir of the Trench Family*, 1896, Ir. 9292 t 5
(2) Henry Trench, *Trench Pedigree*, 1878, Ir. 9292 t 8

Tweedy: Owen Tweedy, *The Dublin Tweedys: The Story of an Irish Family*, 1956, Ir. 9292 t 9

Tyrrell: J. H. Tyrrell, *Genealogical History of the Tyrrells of Castleknock in Co. Dublin, Fertullagh in Co. Westmeath and now of Grange Castle, Co. Meath*, 1904, Ir. 9292 t 6

U

Ussher: Rev. W. B. Wright, *The Ussher Memoirs . . .*, 1889, Ir. 9292 u 1

W

Wall: Hubert Gallwey, *The Wall family in Ireland, 1170–1970*, 1970, Ir. 9292 w 14

Walsh: (1) *Une famille royaliste irlandaise et française*, Nantes, 1903, Ir. 9292 w 1

(2) M. de Courcelles, *Généalogie de la maison de Walsh*, Paris, 1825, Ir. 9292 w 13

(3) J. C. Walsh, *The lament for John McWalter Walsh, with notes on the history of the family of Walsh, 1170–1690*, New York, 1925, Ir. 9292 w 20

Stoker Wallace: E. G. Brandt, *Memoirs of the Stoker Wallaces*, Chicago, 1909, Ir. 9292 w 25

Warren: C. O'Boyle, *The Warren Saga*, Derry, 1946, Ir. 9292 w 8

Washington: George Washington, *The Irish Washingtons*, 1898, Ir. 9292 w 24

Waters: E. W. Waters, *The Waters or Walter Family of Cork*, 1939, Ir. 9292 w 5

Watson: D. G. Holland, *The Fitzwilliam, O'Brien and Watson families: history and genealogy*, 1973, Ir. 9292 f 11

Wauchope: G. M. Wauchope, *The Ulster Branch of the Family of Wauchope*, 1929, Ir. 9292 w 7

White: John D. White, *The History of the Family of White of Limerick, Knocksentry, etc.*, 1887, Ir. 9292 w 10

Williams: J. F. Williams, *The Groves and Lappan: Co. Monaghan . . . in search of the genealogy of the Williams Family*, 1889, Ir. 9292 w 2

Wilson: A. Wilson, *Fragments that remain*, Gloucester, 1950, Ir. 9292 w 9

Winter Cooke: G. J. Forth, *Report on the English and Irish background of the Winter Cooke family*, 1980, Ir. 9292 w 18

Wogan: Count O'Kelly, *Memoire historique et généalogique sur la famille de Wogan*, Paris, 1896, Ir. 9292 w 3

Wolfe: Major R. Wolfe, *The Wolfes of Forenaghs, Co. Kildare*, 1885, Ir. 9292 w 4, 17, 23

Woods: J. R. Woods and L. C. Baxter, *William and Eliza Woods of Co. Antrim, their descendants, and some allied families*, Baltimore, 1984, Ir. 9292 w 22

Wray: C. V. Trench, *The Wrays of Donegal, Londonderry and Antrim*, 1945, Ir. 9292 w 6

Wyly: D. A. A. Wyly, *Irish Origins: a family settlement in Australia*, 1976, Ir. 9292 w 15, 16

Y

Young: Amy Young, *300 Years in Inishowen, being . . . and account of the Family of Young of Culdaff with short accounts of many other families connected with them*, 1929, Ir. 9292 y 1

Z

Zlatover: M. Berman and M. Zlatover, *Zlatover story: a Dublin story with a difference*, Dublin, 1966, Ir. 9292 z 1

PART 2

Appleton, E. G., *A family tapestry: the interwoven threads of some Anglo-Irish and French families*, Cambridge, 1948, Ir. 9292 a 10

Black, J. A., *Your Irish Ancestors*, London, 1974, Ir. 9292 b 51, 53

The Clans of Ireland, Dublin, 1956, Ir. 9292 c 17

Clare, W., *Guide to copies and abstracts of Irish wills*, 1930, Ir. 9292 c 5

Cronnelly, R. F., *Irish Family History*, n.d., Ir. 9292 c 11

Cronnelly, R. F., *A history of Clan Eoghan*, 1964, Ir. 9292 c 16

Cronnelly, R. F., *A simple guide to Irish Genealogy*, 1966, Ir. 9292 c 12

de Breffny, Brian, *Bibliography of Irish Family History and Genealogy*, Cork, 1974, Ir. 9292 d 10

de Courcy, B. W. (ed.), *A genealogical history of the Milesian families of Ireland*, 1880, Ir. 9292 d 6

Edwards, R. D., *Irish Families: the archival aspect*, Ir. 9292 p 10 (1)

Falley, M. J., *Irish and Scotch-Irish Ancestral Research*, Illinois, 1962, Ir. 9292 f 9

Family Links, Vol. 1, 1981–, Ir. 9292 f 19

Grehan, Ida, *Irish Family Names*, London, 1973, Ir. 9292 g 14

Griffith, M. C., *How to use the records of the Republic of Ireland*, Salt Lake City, 1969, Ir. 9292 p 8 (2)

Henchy P., *Three centuries of emigration from the British Isles: Irish emigration to North America . . .*, Salt Lake City, 1969, Ir. 9292 p 8 (1)

L'Estrange, A. G. K., *Connor and Desmond*, 1897, Ir. 9292 g 16

Gaelic Gleanings, Vol. 1, 1981–, Ir. 9292 g 22

Irish Family History Society Newsletter, Vol. 1, 1978–, Ir. 9292 i 3

Kearsley's Peerage, 1796 (3 vols), Ir. 9292 k 4

Laffan, T., *Tipperary's Families: Hearth Money Rolls, 1665–7*, Dublin, Ir. 9292 l 11

MacCarthy, C. J. F., 'Cork Families' (typescript), 1973, Ir. 9292 p 9 (4)

Mac Giolla Domhnaigh, P., *Some Ulster Surnames*, Dublin, 1923 (repr. 1975), Ir. 9292 p 12 (3)

MacLysaght, E., *Irish Families*, Dublin, 1966, Ir. 9292 m 25

MacLysaght, E., *More Irish Families*, Dublin, 1968, Ir. 9292 m 25

MacLyaght, E., *Supplement to Irish Families*, Dublin, 1970, Ir. 9292 m 25

MacLyaght, E., *Bibliography of Irish Family History*, Dublin, 1981, Ir. 9292 m 52

Magee, Peggy, *Tracing your Irish Ancestors*, US, 1986, Ir. 9292 m 59

Mayo, H. N., *The McDonnell, Simpson, McLaughlin and Arnold families and early paper-making in the U.S. . . .*, 1986, Ir. 9292 p 23 (1)

Mullen, T. H., *The Ulster Clans: O'Mullen, O'Kane, OMellan*, Belfast, 1966, Ir. 9292 m 29

Mullen, T. H., *Roots in Ulster soil: a family history*, Belfast, 1967, Ir. 9292 m 54

Mullen, T. H., *Families of Ballyrashane*, Belfast, 1969, Ir. 9292 m 33

Murphy, H., *Families of Co. Wexford*, Dublin, 1986, Ir. 9292 m 60

Newport Macra an Tuaithe, *Newport Local Names*, 1981, Ir. 9292 p 20 (4)

Ni Aonghusa, Nora, *How to trace your Irish roots*, Dublin, 1986, Ir. 9292 n 10

O'Hart, John, *Historic Princes of Tara*, 1873, Ir. 9292 o 5

Rooney, John, *A genealogical history of Irish families*, New York, 1895, Ir. 9292 r 7

Ryan, J. G., *A guide to tracing your Dublin ancestors*, Dublin, 1988, Ir. 9292 r 15

Smythe-Wood, P. (ed.), *Index to Clonfert and Kilmacduagh Wills*, 1977, Ir. 9292 p
      12 (2)

Sweezy, C. E., *The Irish Chiefs: a directory*, New York, 1974, Ir. 9292 p 10 (6)

Ulster Genealogical and Historical Guild Newsletter (continued as *Familia*), Ir. 9292 u
      3

Ulster Genealogical and Historical Guild: Subscribers' interest list, Ir. 9292 u 2

Williams, A. H. D., *Read about your Irish roots* (16 parts), Ir. 9292 r 13 (1–16),
      covering Burke, Byrne, Carroll, Daly, Doherty, Doyle, Fitzgerald, Kennedy,
      Lynch, Murray, O'Connor, O'Donnell, O'Reilly, Ryan, Smith, Walsh

14

Church of Ireland Parish Records in Dublin Repositories

What follows is a listing of all Church of Ireland parish registers, originals, copies and extracts to be found at present (1991) in Dublin repositories, as well as those which have been published. It is *not* a complete list of all surviving records. In particular, no attempt has been made to cover those records for which copies are only available in the Public Record Office of Northern Ireland, in effect the records of all parishes in the six counties of Northern Ireland which survived 1922, or records which are still only available locally. Only records of baptisms, marriages and burials are included (i.e. no vestry records, preachers' lists etc. are given). Where only extracts from the relevant records are available, this is indicated. Where 'RCBL' appears, the original records are deposited in the Representative Church Body Library. The microfilm copies in the RCBL are from the Public Record Office of Northern Ireland. National Archives 'M' numbers may be either original records or transcripts. National Archives microfilms cover both originals and copies made locally before the originals were deposited in the Public Record Office, and destroyed in 1922. For this reason the National Archives' own list showing records destroyed in 1922 is not always an accurate guide to what is actually available. It should be remembered that for microfilm copies of parish records in the dioceses of Kildare, Glendalough and Meath, particularly those with registers extending up to the 1980s, written permission is required from the local clergyman before the Archives can allow research.

Parish	Baptisms	Marriages	Burials	Location
Co. Antrim				
Belfast Cathedral	–	1874–93	–	RCBL (mf)
also:	–	1745–99	–	IMA, Vol. 12/13
Jordanstown	1878–1974	–	–	RCBL (mf)
Co. Armagh				
Newtownhamilton	1622–1826	1622–1826	1622–1826	NL MS. 2669 (Leslie transcript)
Newry	1784–1864	1784–1864	1784–1864	NL MSS. 2202–34 (Leslie transcript)
Mullaghbrack	1622–1826	1622–1826	1622–1826	NL MS. 2669 (Leslie transcript)
Co. Carlow				
Bilboa	–	1846–1956	–	RCBL
Carlow	1695–1885	1695–1915	1698–1894	RCBL
also:	1744–1816	1744–1816	1744–1816	GO 578 (extracts)
	1698–1835	1698–1835	1698–1835	NA ref. 1073
Cloonegoose	–	1846–1954	–	RCBL
Clonmish	–	1846–1934	–	RCBL
Dunleckney	1791–1837	1791–1957	1791–1837	RCBL
Kellistown	–	1854–1917	–	RCBL
Killeshin (see Carlow)				
Kiltennel	1837–75	1837–1950	1837–1957	RCBL
Lorum	–	1845–1954	–	RCBL
Nurney	–	1845–1954	–	RCBL
Old Leighlin	1781–1813	1790–1855	1781–1813	RCBL
Painstown (St Ann)	1859–1919	1864–1913	–	RCBL
also with Carlow records in NA				
Tullow	1696–1844	1700–1843	1700–1844	RCBL
Wells	1870–1957	1803–1915	1802	RCBL
Co. Cavan				
Annagh (see Cloverhill)	1803–1985	1801–1916	1803–1985	RCBL (mf)
Ashfield (see also Kilsherdoney)	1821–1907	1845–1956	1818–1985	RCBL (mf)
also:	1821–76			NA M.5077–80
Arvagh	1877–1905	1845–1941	1877–1921	RCBL (mf)
Baillieboro (see also Knockbride)	1824–1985	1824–1985	1809–1915	RCBL (mf)
Ballintemple	1880–1955	1845–1952	1880–1971	RCBL (mf)
Ballyjamesduff	1877–1986	1845–1955	1879–1985	RCBL (mf)
Ballymachugh	1816–1932	1815–1901	1816–1986	RCBL (mf)
Billis	–	1851–1900	–	RCBL (mf)

Castlerahan	1879–1986	1846–1956	1879–1982	RCBL (mf)
Cloverhill	1860–1985	1860–1956	–	RCBL (mf)
Crosserlough (Kildrumferton)	1801–78	1801–1949	1803–1938	RCBL (mf)
Denn	1879–1982	1845–1954	1879–1986	RCBL (mf)
Dernakesh	1837–1905	1838–1942	1837–1985	RCBL (mf)
Derryheen	1879–1984	1846–1917	1879–1983	RCBL (mf)
Derrylane	1845–1917	1846–1945	1875–1958	RCBL (mf)
Dowra	1877–91	–	–	RCBL (mf)
Drumgoon	1802–1909	1825–1957	1825–1915	RCBL (mf)
Drumlane (see also Quivy)	1874–1985	1845–1932	1877–1982	RCBL (mf)
Kildallon	1856–1986	1845–1923	1877–1985	RCBL (mf)
Killeshandra	1735–1982	1735–1955	1735–1955	RCBL (mf)
Killoughter (Redhills)	1827–1982	1827–43	1827–1905	RCBL (mf)
Killinagh	1877–1941	–	1877–1956	RCBL (mf)
Killinkere (see also Billis)	1878–99	1845–98	1877–1901	RCBL (mf)
Kilmore	1702–1950	1702–1930	1702–1970	RCBL (mf)
Kilsherdoney (Kildrumsherdan)	1796–1982	1796–1845	1797–1929	RCBL (mf)
Kinawley	1761–1972	1761–1935	1761–1966	RCBL (mf)
Kingscourt	–	1845–1949	–	RCBL
Knockbride	1825–1917	1827–1930	1866–1971	RCBL (mf)
Loughan	–	1880–91	–	RCBL (mf)
Lurgan	1831–1902	1831–1900	1831–1901	RCBL (mf)
Moybologue (Baillieboro)	–	1878–1956	–	RCBL
Mullagh	1877–1984	1946–48	1877–1986	RCBL (mf)
Munterconnaght	1857–1901	1845–99	1857–1901	RCBL (mf)
Quivy	1854–1938	1857–1940	–	RCBL (mf)
Shercock	1881–1979	1846–1955	1881–1976	RCBL (mf)
Swanlinbar	1798–1863	1798–1952	1798–1883	RCBL
Tomregan	1797–1984	1802–1913	1805–1986	RCBL (mf)
Templeport	1837	1845–1954	1878–1906	RCBL
Urney	1804–1940	1804–1946	1804–1916	RCBL (mf)

Co. Clare

Clare Abbey	–	1845–1901	–	RCBL
Clondegad	–	1845–85	1882–1915	RCBL
Clonlea	1879–1947	1845–1946	1877–1951	RCBL
Drumcliff (Ennis)	1744–1870	1744–1845	1744–1869	NA MFCI 1, M5222
Kildysert	1881–1920	1847–1918	1882–1915	RCBL
Kilfarboy	–	1845–1957	–	RCBL
Kilfenora	–	1853–1918	–	RCBL

Kilferagh	–	1845–1954	–	RCBL
also:	1829	1829	–	NA M5244
Kilfinaghty	–	1862–1969	–	RCBL
Killard	–	1848–1933	–	RCBL
Killaloe	1679–1872	1682–1845	1683–1873	NA MFCI 5, M5222
Kilmanaheen	1886–1972	1845–1920	–	RCBL
Kilmurry	1889–1972	1845–1905	1892–1954	RCBL
Kilnaboy	1799–1831	1802–1961	1821–31	RCBL
Kilnasoolagh	1731–1874	1799–1844	1786–1876	NA MFCI 2, 5, M5222
also:	1731–1829	1746–1954	1739–1829	RCBL
Kilrush	1741–1872	1760–1845	1742–1873	NA MFCI 4, 5, M5240, 5235
also:	1741–1840	1766–1841	1742–1841	RCBL
Kilseily	1881–1915	1848–1905	1877–1951	RCBL
Ogonnelloe	1807–70	1807–65	1836–75	NA MFCI 5
Quin	1907–54	1845–1915	1906–27	RCBL

Co. Cork

Abbeymahon	1782–1852	1738–1852	1732–1852	RCBL (transcript)
also:	1827–73	–	–	NA MFCI 18 & 20
Abbeystrewery	1788–1915	–	–	NA MFCI 32
Aghabulloge	–	1808–43	–	O'K, Vol. 14
also:	1808–77	1808–43	1808–79	NA M.5067
Aghada	1730–1921	1730–1915	1730–1924	NA M.6075–77a, 6201, MFCI 20, 30, 36
Ballyclogh	1831–1900	1831–1948	1831–1900	NA M.5047
Ballymartle	1799–1868	–	1800–76	NA M.5081
Ballymodan	1695–1878	1695–1958	1695–1878	RCBL, also NA
Ballymoney	1805–71	1805–54	1805–73	NA MFCI 19
Ballyvourney	–	1845–1935	–	O'K, Vol. 11
Berehaven (Killaconenagh)	1787–1872	1784–1844	1796–1873	NA M.6051, MFCI 25
Blackrock	1828–97	1828–1981	1830–1946	RCBL
also:	1828–72	1828–44	1828–71	NA MFCI 19
Bridgetown & Kilcummer	1859–71	–	–	NA M.5083
Brigown	1751–1870	1775–1848	1775–1871	NA MFCI 21, M6044
Brinny	1797–1884	1797–1844	1797–1884	RCBL (transcript)
also:	1797–1884	1797–1844	1797–1884	NA MFCI 28
Buttevant	1873–1900	–	–	O'K, Vol. 11
Caheragh	1836–71	1837–43	1860–78	NA MFCI 19
Caherlog	–	1870–1955	–	RCBL
Carnaway	–	1845–71	–	RCBL

Carrigaline	1724–1871	1791–1871	1808–79	NA MFCI 19 NA M.6001, 6028
also:	1724–56	1726–92	–	RCBL
Carrigleamleary	–	1848–71	–	*O'K*, Vol. 14
Carrigtohill	1776–1875	1779–1844	1776–1843	NA MFCI 24
also:	–	1848–1955	–	RCBL
Castletownroche	1728–1928	1728–1893	1733–1803	NA M.5048, 5083
Clondrohid	–	1848–84	–	RCBL
also:	–	1848–1984	–	*O'K*, Vol. 11
Clonfert	–	1845–47	–	*O'K*, Vol. 14
Clonmel (Cobh)	1761–1870	1761–1845	1761–1870	NA MFCI 28 & 29
Clonpriest	–	1851–70	–	NA M.5114
Cloyne	1708–1871	1708–1845	1708–1871	NA MFCI 30, M.6072, 6036
Cork City				
Holy Trinity	1664–1871	1643–1845	1644–1885	NA MFCI 21, 22
St Anne	1772–1871	1772–1845	1779–1882	NA MFCI 25, 26, 27; M.6053, 6059
(Garrison Chapel & Foundling Hospital)				
St Luke	1837–74	–	–	NA MFCI 27
St Mary	1802–78	1802–40	1802–78	NA MFCI 22, M6049, 5064
St Nicholas	1725–1870	1726–1845	1726–1870	NA MFCI 23, 24, 25, M.6047
Corkbeg	1836–72	1838–50	1836–74	NA MFCI 36
Cullen	1779–1876	1775–1851	1779–1873	NA MFCI 6
Desertserges	1811–71	1811–45	1811–72	NA MFCI 27, 28
Doneraile	1869–1952	–	–	*O'K*, Vol. 14
Douglas	1789–1818	1792–1893	1790	RCBL
also:	1789–1872	1792–1845	1789–1871	NA MFCI 29
Drimoleague	1802–71	1802–11	1802–72	NA MFCI 31, M6086
Dromtarriffe	–	1849–1913	–	*O'K*, Vol. 11
Dungourney	1850–1954	–	–	RCBL
Fanlobbus	1855–71	–	1853–71	NA M5110
Fermoy	1802–73	1803–45	1805–71	NA MFCI 25
Frankfield	–	1847–1955	–	RCBL
Glengarriff	1863–1913	–	–	NA M5113
Inch	–	1847–1948	–	NA M6077b
Inchigeelagh	1900	1845–65	–	RCBL
Iniscarra	1820–71	1820–44	1820–72	NA MFCI 25
also:	1870–1901	1845–1903	1852–1901	*O'K*, Vol. 14
Inishannon	1693–1844	1693–1911	1693–1844	RCBL
also:	1696–1871	1693–1844	1693–1879	NA MFCI 28, 29
Kilbritain	1832–76	1830–68	–	RCBL (transcript)
Kilbrogan	1752–1871	1753–1845	1707–1877	NA MFCI 29, M6065

Killanully	1831–74	–	1836–77	NA M6029, 6030
Killeagh	1782–1870	1776–1879	1782–1884	NA M5114
also:	1782–1863	1778–1840	1787–1868	RCBL (extracts)
Killowen	1833–74	–	1851–1972	NA MFCI 28
Kilmahon	–	1808–1944	–	NA M6046
Kilroan	1885–1920	1846–1920	–	RCBL
Kilshannig	1731–1877	1731–1846	1731–1876	NA MFCI 18, M6031
also:	1731–1965	1845–1925	1855–1958	O'K, Vols 11, 14
Kinneigh	1794–1877	1814–44	1815–70	NA M6038
Kinsale	1684–1871	1688–1864	1685–1872	NA MFCI 30, 31, M6071
Knockavilly	1837–83	1844–48	–	NA MFCI 28
also:	1837–83	1844–48	1837–83	RCBL (transcript)
Leighmoney	1869–1943	–	–	RCBL
Lislee	1809–90	1809–44	1823–89	NA MFCI, 18, 20, M6041
Macroom	1727–1837	1737–1835	1727–1835	NA M5138
also:	1727–1913	1727–1913	1727–1913	O'K, Vols 8, 14
Magourney	1757–1876	1756–1844	1758–1876	NA M5118
Mallow	1793–1871	1793–1863	1793–1871	NA MFCI 18, 19
also:	1783–1965	1845–1936	–	O'K, Vols 11, 14
Marmullane	1801–73	1797–1843	1801–73	NA MFCI 29, 32
also:	1801–73	1802–1954	1803–73	RCBL
Middleton	1810–83	1811–81	1809–83	NA M5119
also:	1699–1881	1728–1823	1696–1877	RCBL (extracts)
Monkstown	1842–72	1841–44	1842–1903	NA MFCI 30
Murragh	1750–1876	1739–1876	1784–1876	NA MFCI 27, M6056, 6060, 6063
Nohaval	1846–70	–	1846–75	NA M6033, 6039
Rahan	1773–1833	1773–1833	1773–1833	NA, no ref.
also:	–	1847–59	–	O'K, Vol. 14
Rathclaren	1780–1875	1780–1849	1792–1875	RCBL (transcript)
Rathcooney	1750–1871	1749–1849	1750–1853	NA MFCI 24, 25
also:	1750–1897	1749–1854	1750–1853	RCBL
Ringcurran	1793–1870	1793–1829	1849–72	NA MFCI 30, M6070
Rosscarbery (Ross)	1690–1871	1704–1845	1696–1870	NA MFCI 19
Rushbrook	1866–72	–	–	NA M6073
Schull	1826–73	–	–	NA MFCI 25
Templemartin	1845–79	–	1845–79	NA MFCI 24, M6048
Templemichael	1845–53	–	–	RCBL
Templenacarriga	–	–	1883–1932	RCBL
Timoleague	1827–78	–	–	RCBL (transcript)
Youghal	1665–1871	1666–1842	1665–1871	NA MFCI 19, 20, M6034/5, 6042

Co. Derry

Culmore	1867–1920	1865–1935	–	RCBL (mf)
Templemore (Derry Cathedral)	1642–1703	1669–1800	1669–1800	PRS

Co. Donegal

Ardara	1829–1954	1845–1956	1876–1984	RCBL (mf)
Aughanunshin	1878–94	1845–1971	1878–90	RCBL
Burt	1829–1913	1829–1929	1829–1941	RCBL (mf)
Clondahorky	1871–1906	1845–1915	1884–1926	RCBL (mf)
Clonleigh	1872–1983	1845–1956	1877–1984	RCBL (mf)
Convoy	1871–1981	1845–1902	1881–1981	RCBL (mf)
Conwal	1876–1971	1845–1988	1878–1906	RCBL
Craigadooish	–	–	1871–1907	RCBL (mf)
Culedaff	1875–1911	1845–1921	1876–1980	RCBL (mf)
Desertegney	–	1848–1929	1879–1981	RCBL (mf)
Donaghmore	1818–1902	1817–1955	1824–92	RCBL (mf)
Dunlewey	–	1853–82	–	RCBL (mf)
Fahan Upper	1762–1921	1814–1909	1832–1934	RCBL (mf)
Fahan Lower	1817–1980	1818–1939	1822–1983	RCBL (mf)
Gartan	1881–1959	1845–1946	–	RCBL
Glenalla	1871–1983	1871–1951	1906–1981	RCBL (mf)
Glencolumbkille	1827–1984	1845–1954	1828–1975	RCBL (mf)
Gleneely	1872–1981	1859–1954	–	RCBL (mf)
Glenties	1898–1972	–	1898–1982	RCBL (mf)
Gweedore	1880–1980	1855–1952	1881–1982	RCBL (mf)
Inch	1868–1951	1846–1946	1868–1965	RCBL (mf)
Inniskeel	1818–64	1818–64	1818–64	NA M5749
also:	1699–1700	1699–1700	1699–1700	NA M5749
also:	1852–1948	–	1852–1983	RCBL (mf)
Kilcar	1819–1957	1819–1938	1818–1930	RCBL (mf)
Killea	1877–1922	1845–1931	–	RCBL (mf)
Killybegs	1809–1983	1810–1944	1806–1984	RCBL (mf)
Kilteevoge	1818–1979	1845–96	1825–1921	RCBL (mf)
Lettermacaward	1889–1982	–	1890–1981	RCBL (mf)
Leck	1878–1975	1846–1959	1878–1900	RCBL
Meenglass	–	1864–1963	–	RCBL (mf)
Milford	1880–1981	1860–1949	1902–76	RCBL (mf)
Muff	1837–1986	1837–1956	1847–75	RCBL (mf)
Newtowncunningham	1877–1937	1845–97	1820–1955	RCBL (mf)
Raymochy	1844–1986	1845–1982	1878–1986	RCBL (mf)
Stranorlar	1802–70	1821–93	1821–1976	RCBL (mf)
Tullyaughnish	1798–1983	1798–1935	1798–1983	RCBL (mf)
Taughboyne	1820–1983	1836–1906	1836–1982	RCBL (mf)
Templecarn	1825–1936	1825–1906	1825–1905	RCBL (mf)
Templecrone	1878–1982	–	1879–1980	RCBL (mf)

Co. Down

Blaris (Lisburn)	1637–1873	1639–1832	1629–1868	RCBL (mf)

Co. Dublin

Castleknock	1709–1959	1710–1956	1710–1963	RCBL
also:	1768–1865	1768–1865	1772–1865	GO 495 (ph.stat)
Clonsilla	1830–1901	1831–1956	1831–1902	RCBL
also:	1827–65	1827–65	1826–45	GO 495 (ph.stat)
Clontarf	1816–49	1811–52	1812–60	NA MFCI 13, M5967
Cloughran	1782–1870	1738–1839	1732–1870	NA M5084
also:	1870–91	1858–75	1871–1938	RCBL
also:	1782–1852	1738–1852	1732–1852	RCBL (extracts)
Crumlin	1740–1863	1764–1863	1740–1862	NA M5088–91
also:	–	–	1740–1830	IMA, Vol. 12/13
Dunganstown	1782–1984	1787–1862	1783–1954	NA MFCI 79
Finglas	–	–	1664–1729	IMA, Vol. 11
also:	–	–	1877–1956	RCBL
also:	1685–1818	1667–1780	1685–1727	GO 578 (extracts)
Monkstown	1669–1800	1669–1800	1669–1800	PRS, Vol. 6
Mulhuddert	–	1871–1944	–	RCBL
Newcastle Lyons	1768–1982	1773–1859	1776–1982	NA MFCI 88

Dublin City

Arbour Hill Barracks	1848–1922	–	1847–84	RCBL
Baggotrath	1865–1923	1882–1923	–	RCBL
Beggar's Bush Barracks	1868–1922	–	–	RCBL
Christ Church	1740–1886	1717–1826	1710–1866	LC
Donnybrook	1712–1857	1712–1956	1712–1873	RCBL
Donnybrook	–	1712–1800	–	IMA
Female Penitentiary	1898–1907	–	–	RCBL
Free Church	1902–87	–	–	RCBL
Grangegorman	1816–1990	1830–1990	1833–34	LC
Irishtown	1812–1973	1824–1956	1712–1873	RCBL
Kilmainham	1857–1982	1861–1981	–	RCBL
Mission to Seamen	1961–81	–	–	RCBL
Molyneux Chapel	1871–1926	–	–	RCBL
North Dublin Union	1906–18	–	–	RCBL
Pigeon House Fort	1872–1901	–	–	RCBL
Portobello Barracks	1857–69	–	–	RCBL
Richmond Barracks	1857–1922	–	–	RCBL
Rathmines (Holy Trinity)	1850–75	–	–	With St Peter's
Royal Hospital, Kilmainham	1826–79	–	1849–79	LC*
St Aidan	1910–61	–	–	RCBL

St Andrew	–	1672–1800	–	PRS, Vol. 12
also:	–	1672–1819		NA M.5135
also:	1694–1803	1695–1802	1694–1796	TCD MS. 2062 (extracts)
also:	–	1801–19	–	IMA, Vol. 12/13
St Anne	1719–1813	1799–1822	1722–1822	GO 577 (extracts)
also:	–	1719–1800	–	PRS, Vol. 11
also:	1873–1938	1845–1973	1780–1816	RCBL
St Audoen	1672–1916	1673–1947	1673–1885	RCBL
also:	–	1672–1800	–	PRS, Vol. 11
also:	–	–	1672–92	IMA, Vol. 12/13
St Augustine	1911–65	–	–	RCBL
St Bride	–	1845–87	–	RCBL
also:	–	1639–1800	–	PRS, Vol. 11
St Catherine	1699–1966	1679–1966	1679–1898	RCBL
also:	1636–1715	1636–1715	1636–1715	PRS, Vol. 5
also:	–	1715–1800	–	PRS, Vol 12
St George	1784–1875	1794–1956	1824–1908	RCBL
St James	1730–1963	1742–1963	1742–1989	RCBL
also:	1730–1836	1742–1834	1742–1834	NL mf, Pos. 6014
St John	1619–1878	1619–1878	1619–1850	RCBL
also:	1619–99	1619–99	1619–99	PRS, Vol. 1
also:	–	1700–98	–	IMA, Vol. 11
also:	–	–	1620–1850	GO 577
St Kevin	1883–1908	1884–1977	–	RCBL
St Luke	1713–1974	1716–1963	1716–1974	RCBL
also:	–	1716–1800	–	PRS, Vol. 12
St Mark	1730–1971	1730–1971	1733–1923	RCBL
also:	–	1730–50	–	NL MS. 18319
St Mary	1697–1972	1697–1880	1700–1858	RCBL
also:	–	1697–1800	–	PRS, Vol. 12
also:	1831–70	1831–70	1831–70	NA, 1A.45.59
St Mathias	1867–1955	1873–1955	–	RCBL
St Michael	1674–86	1663–1765	1678–1750	RCBL (extracts)
also:	1749–1872	1750–1852	1750–1804	printed in *The Irish Builder*, 1890/91
also:	–	1656–1800	–	IMA, Vol. 11
St Michan	1701–87	1706–1809	1727–45	RCBL (extracts)
also:	1636–1701	1636–1701	1636–1701	PRS, Vols 3, 7
also:	1700–24	–	1700–24	GO MS. 577
also:	–	1700–1800	–	IMA, Vol. 11
St Nicholas Within	1671–1866	1671–1865	1671–1863	RCBL
also:	–	1671–1800	1671–1823	IMA, Vol. 11
also:	–	–	1825–63	IMA, Vols 12/13
St Nicholas Without	1694–1861	1699–1861	1694–1875	RCBL
also:	1694–1739	1694–1739	1694–1739	PRS, Vol. 10

St Patrick	1677–1990	1677–1990	1677–1990	LC
also:	1677–1800	1677–1800	1677–1800	PRS, Vol. 2
also:				GO 701 (extracts)
St Paul	1698–1987	1699–1982	1702–1892	RCBL
also:	–	–	1702–18	IMA, Vol. 12/13
also:	–	–	1719–1821	NA, lA.37.52
also:	–	–	1718–30	GO MS. 577
St Peter	1669–1974	1670–1975	1670–1883	RCBL
also:	1669–1771	1669–1771	1669–1771	PRS, Vol. 9
St Philip, Milltown	1844–76	–	–	LC*
St Stephen	1837–1912	1862–1956	–	RCBL
St Thomas	1750–1931	1750–1957	1762–1882	RCBL
St Victor	1897–1954	1916–56	–	RCBL
St Werburgh	1704–1913	1704–1956	1704–1843	RCBL
also:	–	1627–1800	–	PRS, Vol. 12
Sandymount	1850–61	–	–	RCBL
Santry	1754–1875	1754–1831	1753–1876	RCBL
Trinity	1871–1918	1874–1915	–	RCBL

Co. Fermanagh

Aghalurcher	1867–1983	1845–1924	1870–1927	RCBL (mf)
Aghavea	1857–83	1853–1907	1859–1986	RCBL (mf)
Belleek	1820–1918	1823–1912	1822–50	RCBL (mf)
Cleenish	1886–1947	1845–1934	1886–1922	RCBL (mf)
Clones (Aghadrimsee)	1829–1927	1829–1935	1829–90	RCBL (mf)
Drumkeeran	1873–1944	1845–1904	–	RCBL (mf)
Enniskillen	1667–1789	1668–1794	1667–1781	RCBL (extracts)
also:	1666–1826	1666–1826	1666–1826	GO 578 (extracts)
Garrison	1879–1924	1849–1935	1877–1924	RCBL (mf)
Inishmacsaint	1660–72	1660–72	1660–72	NA M5148
also:	1800–66	1800–66	1800–66	NA M5148
also:	1660–72	1660–72	1660–72	GO 578
Mullaghadun	1819–36	1819–1921	1819–1927	RCBL (mf)
Mullaghfad	1878–1971	1906–62	–	RCBL (mf)

Co. Galway

Ahascragh	1785–1872	1785–1859	1787–1875	NA MFCI 6, M5354
Ardrahan	1804–71	–	1857–79	NA M5253/4
Athenry	1796–1828	1796–1827	1795–1827	NA M5147B
Aughrim	1814–75	1815–42	1822–72	NA MFCI 6
Ballinakill	1775–1814	1792–1928	1803–1951	RCBL
also:	1852–72	–	1852–78	NA MFCI 31
Ballinasloe (Creagh)	1809–73	1808–45	1824–71	NA MFCI 6, M5360

* Registers which survived 1922 in local custody, but whose whereabouts now appear uncertain.

Castlekirke	1879–1925	–	1879–1963	RCBL
Clifden (Omey)	1831–87	1831–44	1832–1900	NA MFCI 35, M6088
Clontuskert	–	–	1843–70	NA M5353
Dunmore	1884–1914	1846–1903	1887–1938	RCBL
Eyrecourt				GO 701 (extracts)
Headford	1888–1941	1845–1920	1885–1975	RCBL
Inniscaltra	1851–76	–	1851–74	NA MFCI 4, M5234
Kilcummin	1812–76	1812–76	1812–76	NA MFCI 33
Kilconla	–	1846–1906	–	RCBL
Killaraght	–	1846–1936	–	RCBL
Killererin	1811–28	1818–28	1818	RCBL (extracts)
Kilmoylan	1866	–	–	RCBL
Loughrea	1808–73	1819–45	1819–72	NA MFCI 5, M5222
Moylough	1762–1804	1828	–	NL MS. 7924
also:	1826–1922	1823–44	1843–1940	RCBL
also:	1827–1922	1826–44	1847–1919	NA MFCI 35
Moyrus	1841–71	1845–75	1844–71	NA MFCI 35
Renvyle	1884–1918	1869–1910	1871–1932	RCBL
Ross	–	1856–1950	–	RCBL
Sellerna	1897–1913	1857–1906	–	RCBL
Taughmaconnell	1852–88	–	1845–79	NA M5279
Tuam	1818–71	1831–40	1829–75	NA MFCI 7, M5351/2

Co. Kerry

Aghadoe	1838–78	1840–61	1838–81	NA M5974
Ballybunion (Liselton)	1840–81	–	1840–75	NA MFCI 17
Ballymacelligot	1817–56	1817–56	1817–56	NA MFCI 17, M5991
Ballyseedy	1830–78	–	1831–78	NA MFCI
Caher	1878–1947	1847–76	–	RCBL
Castleisland	1835–71	1836–48	1836–75	NA M5986
Dromod & Prior	–	1822–42	–	NA M5093
Kenmare	1818–73	1819–1950	1818–49	RCBL
Kilcrohane	–	1846–1930	–	RCBL
Kilgarvan	1811–50	1812–1947	1819–1960	RCBL
Killorglin	1840	1837–40	1837	NA TAB 12/63
Kilmore	1826–1960	1850–1925	–	RCBL
Kilnaughtin	1785–1871	1785–1845	1786–1873	NA MFCI 17
Listowel	1835–72	1835–45	1836–71	NA MFCI 17, M5970
Templenoe	–	1849–1920	–	RCBL
Tralee (Ratass)	1771–1872	1796–1850	1805–80	NA MFCI 14
Valentia	1826–72	–	1826–77	NA M5988/9

Co. Kildare

Athy	1669–1880	1675–1891	1669–1850	NA MFCI 78
Ballinafagh	1876–1954	1851–1957	1877–1964	RCBL
Ballymore Eustace	1838–79	1840–79	1832–79	NA MFCI 86
Ballysax	1830–1939	1841–59	1834–1982	NA MFCI 71
also:	–	1859–1903		NA M5140–5
Castlecarbery	1804–1902	1805–45	1805–48	NA MFCI 66
Celbridge	1777–1977	1777–1975	1787–1882	RCBL
also:	1777–1881	1777–1843	1787–1882	NA MFCI 88
Clane	1802–46	1804–81	1804–1906	NA M5953
also:	–	1850–1956	1906–47	RCBL
Clonaslee	1814–1982	1814–44	1816–1982	NA MFCI 69
Clonsast	1805–1983	1804–57	1806–1983	NA MFCI 63
Curragh Camp &				
Newbridge Garrison¯	1856–98	1890–1914	1869–1912	NA M5050–5
Donadea	1890–1968	1846–1939	1892–1920	RCBL
Edenderry				
(Monasteroris)	1678–1754	1678–1754	1678–1754	NA M5111
Fontstown	1814–40	1811–56	1811–69	RCBL
Kilcullen	1778–1982	1779–1839	1778–1982	NA MFCI 71
Kildare	1801–1962	1801–45	1801–69	NA MFCI 70
Kill	1814–84	1820–44	1814–79	NA MFCI 68
Lackagh	1829–82	1829–64	1829–79	NA MFCI 70
Lea	1830–52	1841	1842–86	RCBL
Leixlip	1778–1879	1781–1876	1778–1879	NA MFCI 90
Maynooth	–	1839–70	–	NA MFCI 42
Monasterevin				
(Harristown)	1666–1917	1799–1883	1802–1983	NA MFCI 67
Naas	1679–1882	1742–1848	1679–1891	NA MFCI 68
Newbridge Garrison	1867–1922	–	–	RCBL
Straffan	1838–81	1838–1950	1841–1940	RCBL
also:	1838–81	1838	1841–1940	NA MFCI 88
Timolin	1802–74	1800–97	1803–1984	NA MFCI 84

Co. Kilkenny

Burnchurch	1881–1942	–	1882–1980	RCBL
Callan	1892–1966	1846–1954	1894–1982	RCBL
Castlecomer	1799–1839	1799–1845	1799–1901	RCBL
Castlecomer Colliery	1838–58	1839–44	–	RCBL
Clonmore	1817–1906	–	1822–1921	NA M5086
Gowran	1885–1977	1845–1956	–	RCBL
Graiguenamanagh	1804–5	1846–1933	–	RCBL
Grangesilva	–	1850–1921	–	RCBL
Kilmocahill	–	1848–64	–	RCBL
Knocktopher	1884–1959	1849–1940	1887–1983	RCBL
Mothel	1810–43	1811–1950	1817–42	RCBL
Powerstown	–	1854	–	RCBL

Rathcool	1836–44	1842	–	RCBL
Rower	1888–1943	1849–1937	1883–1985	RCBL
Shankill	–	1845–1950	–	RCBL
Tiscoffin	–	1853–80	–	RCBL
Thomastown	1895–1965	1845–1949	1870–1987	RCBL
Ullard	–	1857	–	RCBL

Co. Laois (Queen's Co.)

Coolbanagher	1802–90	1802–45	1803–72	NA MFCI 69
Durrow	1731–1841	1731–1836	1731–1836	RCBL (transcript)
also:	1731–41	1731–41	1731–41	NL MS. 2670 (transcript)
also:	1808–75	1808–75	1808–75	NA M5056-8
Mountmellick	1840–1982	1840–56	1840–1982	NA MFCI 69
Lea	1801–90	1801–69	1801–69	NA MFCI 72
Portarlington	1694–1972	1694–1812	1694–1983	NA MFCI 72
Roscrea	1784–1878	1792–1845	1792–1872	NA MFCI 3, M5222
Rosenallis	1801–1976	1801–71	1801–1972	NA MFCI 69

Co. Leitrim

Ballaghmeehan	1877–1985	1859–1986	1877–1986	RCBL (mf)
Carrigallen	1883–1986	1845–1941	1874–1936	RCBL (mf)
Clooneclare	1816–1972	1816–1921	1816–1972	RCBL (mf)
Drumkeeran	1873–1944	1845–1904	–	RCBL (mf)
Inishmagrath	1877–1985	–	1877–1983	RCBL (mf)
Killargue	1877–1985	1859–1986	1877–1986	RCBL (mf)
Killasnet	1877–1984	1846–1950	1863–1956	RCBL (mf)
Killenummery	1884–1961	1845–1905	1856–1945	RCBL (mf)
Newtowngore	1877–1921	1847–1950	1877–1981	RCBL (mf)

Co. Limerick

Abington	1811–98	1813–45	1810–92	NA MFCI 2, M5222
Adare	1845–89	–	–	NL Pos. 1994
Ardcanny & Chapelrussel	1802–48	1802–44	1805–44	NL Pos. 2761
also:	1802–1927	1802–1920	1805–1940	NA M5072-5
Ballingarry	1785–1872	1809–46	1809–75	NA MFCI 16
also:				GO 701 (extracts)
Ballinlanders	–	1852–77	–	RCBL
Bruff	1859–71	–	1859–71	NA M5975/6
Cahernarry	1855–77	–	–	NA M5112
Corcomhide	1805–95	1805–95	1805–95	NA MFCI 16, M5987
Fedamore	1840–91	–	–	NA M5112
Kilfergus	1812–58	1815–43	1836–49	NA MFCI 17

Kilfinane	1804–71	1804–41	1798–1871	NA MFCI 16
Kilmeedy	1805–95	1805–95	1805–95	NA MFCI 16, M5987
Kilscannell	1824–74	1825–59	1860–87	NA MFCI 16, M5987
Limerick City				
Garrison	1858–71	–	1865–71	NA MFCI 17, M5789/80
St John's	1697–1883	1697–1845	1697–1876	NA MFCI 14, 15
St Mary's	1726–1871	1726–1845	1726–1942	NA MFCI 15, M5978
St Michael's	1803–71	1803–45	1803–89	NA MFCI 17, M5991
Mahoonagh	–	–	1861–64	NA M5977
Mungret	1852–56	–	1843–72	NA M5981, 5986
Newcastle	1848–70	–	1848–76	NA M5983/4
Particles	1841–71	–	–	NA MFCI 16, M5987
Rathkeale	1781–1871	1781–1836	1781–1871	NA MFCI 16, M5987, M5120/1
Rathronan	1818–71	–	1824–71	NA MFCI 16, M5987
Stradbally	1792–1881	1787–1844	1791–1850	NA MFCI 3, M5222, M5249–52

Co. Longford

Columbkille	1894–1985	1845–1934	1896–1983	RCBL (mf)
Forgney	1808–1918	1804–71	1804–1914	NA MFCI 61
Shrule	1854–63	–	–	RCBL
Templemichael	1796–1835	1777–1838	1796–1838	NA M5724–6

Co. Louth

Ardee	1799–1868	1802–49	1801–1981	RCBL (mf)
Baronstown	1878–1952	1846–1951	1878–1956	RCBL (mf)
Charlestown	1822–1936	1824–45	1823–80	RCBL (mf)
Clogher	1811–91	1792–1910	1810–1986	RCBL (mf)
Collon	1790–1969	1790–1845	1791–1950	RCBL (mf)
Darver	–	1870–75	–	RCBL (mf)
Drogheda	1654–1886	1654–1956	1653–1864	RCBL (mf)
also:	1747–72	1747–72	1747–72	NA M5127
Dundalk	1729–1924	1750–1929	1727–1985	RCBL (mf)
Dunleer	1787–92	1738–96	1729–95	RCBL (extracts)
Faughart	–	1848–64	–	RCBL (mf)
Heynestown	1865–1984	1855–1951	1871–1983	RCBL (mf
Killincoole	1877–1954	1849–1944	1886–1965	RCBL (mf)
Louth	1889–1904	1849–1944	1886–1965	RCBL (mf)
Omeath	1883–1936	1845–1930	1883–1936	RCBL (mf)

Co. Mayo

Aasleagh	–	1849–1956	–	RCBL
Achill	1854–96	1855–1936	–	RCBL
also:	–	–	1854–77	NA MFCI 33
(see also Dugort)				
Aughagower	1825–92	1828–46	1828–93	NA MFCI 33
Aughaval	1801–87	1802–54	1820–1903	RCBL
also:	1801–72	1802–45	1820–1908	NA MFCI 33
Ayle	1825–92	1828–1904	1828–93	RCBL
Ballinakill	1852–73	–	1852–78	NA MFCI 31
Ballinchalla	1831–35	1832–1917	1831–36	RCBL
Ballinrobe	1796–1912	1809–62	1809–1974	RCBL
also:	1796–1872	1809–46	1809–75	NA MFCI 35
Ballycroy	–	1855–98	1883–1962	RCBL
Ballyovey	1879–1951	1854–1954	1880–1966	RCBL
Ballysakeery	1802–71	1802–63	1802–75	NA MFCI 32
Bulnahinch	–	1854–73	–	RCBL
Castlebar	1835–72	1835–72	1834–67	NA MFCI 33
Castlemore	1890–1911	1847–1908	–	RCBL
Cong	1746–1863	1745–1849	1736–1872	NA MFCI 32
also:	1746–1863	1745–1956	–	RCBL
Crossboyne	1877–1924	1854–1937	1879–1963	RCBL
Crossmolina	1768–1872	1775–1851	1779–1873	NA MFCI 6
Dugort	1838–1864	1838–89	1838–74	NA MFCI 33/4
also:	–	1845–88	–	RCBL
Kilcolman	1877–1932	1846–1949	1878–1969	RCBL
Kilcommon	1921–26	1845–1937	1920–59	RCBL
Killalla	1757–1871	1759–1842	1758–1877	NA MFCI 31/2
Kilmainemore	1744–1927	1744–1891	1744–1958	RCBL
also:	1744–1927	1744–1891	1744–1908	NA MFCI 35, M6088
Kilmeena	1887–1904	1845–1917	–	RCBL
Kilmoremoy	1793–1874	1793–1846	1769–1875	NA MFCI 35/6
Knappagh	–	1855–1952	–	RCBL
also:	–	–	1855–71	NA MFCI 32
Louisburgh	–	1846–1952	–	RCBL
Mayo	–	1849–62	–	RCBL
Turlough	1821–72	1822–56	1822–73	NA MFCI 36

Co. Meath

Agher	1796–1874	1807–39	1798–1875	NA MFCI 51
Athboy	1736–1877	1736–1845	1736–1877	NA MFCI 53/4
Bective	1853–73	–	1857–79	NA MFCI 48
Castlerickard	1869–77	–	–	NA M5137
Clonard	1792–1880	1836–76	1838–90	NA M5232, 5233
also:	–	1846–50	–	RCBL
Clongill	1795–1804	–	1795–1804	NA MFCI 43/4

Drogheda (St Mary's)	1763–1871	1763–1845	1763–1872	NA MFCI 39
Drumconrath	1799–1983	1820–44	1821–98	NA MFCI 45
also:	1799–1826	1820–1956	1821–26	RCBL
Dunshaughlin	1839–74	–	1839–77	NA MFCI 41
Julianstown	1787–1869	1797–1837	1778–1873	NA MFCI 39
Kells	1773–1876	1773–1844	1773–1904	NA MFCI 46/7
Kilmainhamwood	1881–92	1852–76	–	RCBL
Kilmore	–	1834–42	1827–42	NA MFCI 42
Killachonagan (Ballivor)	1853–77	1853–62	1853–63	NA M5117
Loughcrew	1800–21	1800–21	1800–21	NA MFCI 51
Nobber	1828–68	1828–44	1831–61	NA M5062
also:	–	1850–1945	–	RCBL
Oldcastle	1814–84	1815–45	1814–90	NA MFCI 52
Painestown	1833–1917	1835–1919	1834–1908	RCBL
also:	1704–1901	1704–1901	1704–1901	NA MFCI 40/1 (extracts)
Rathcore	1810–1983	1811–35	1810–71	NA MFCI 51
Rathmolyon	1733–1876	1834–56	1834–77	NA MFCI 51
Syddan	1720–1983	1721–1865	1725–1983	NA MFCI 46
also:	1720–1825	1721–1949	1725–1824	RCBL
Trim	1782–1876	1792–1849	1792–1871	NA MFCI 49

Co. Monaghan

Carrickmacross	1797–1984	1798–1920	1831–1981	RCBL (mf)
Cooneen	1872–1975	1887–1935	–	RCBL (mf)
Clones (Aghadrimsee)	1829–1927	1829–1935	1829–90	RCBL (mf)
Clontibret	1864–65	–	–	RCBL (extracts)
Donaghmoine	–	–	1878–1969	RCBL (mf)
Kilmore	1826–1984	1826–1956	1826–1982	RCBL (mf)
Magheracloone	1806–1984	1813–1985	1806–1984	RCBL (mf)
Monaghan	1802–1907	1802–1910	1802–57	RCBL (mf)
Mullaghfad	1878–1971	1906–62	–	RCBL (mf)
Tydavnet	1822–83	1822–1950	1822–67	RCBL (mf)

Co. Offaly (King's Co.)

Ballyboy	1709–48	1709–48	1709	RCBL (transcripts)
Ballyboy	1797–1847	1806–19	1800–68	RCBL (extracts)
Birr	1760–1870	1760–1844	1786–1858	NA MFCI 2, 3, M5221
also:	1760–1806	1762–1804	1792–1856	GO 578 (extracts)
Borrisnafarney	1828–77	1827–51	1827–76	NA MFCI 4
Castlejordan	1702–1839	1707–1840	1704–1840	RCBL
also:	1702–1877	1707–1845	1704–1877	NA MFCI 50
Cloneyburke	1824–1982	–	1834–1983	NA MFCI 72
Clonmacnoise	1828–74	–	1818–1977	NA MFCI 57
Dunkerrin	1825–73	1826–45	1825–73	NA MFCI 4, M5222

Durrow	1816–83	1818–75	1817–83	NA MFCI 55
Ettagh	1825–67	1826–68	1826–73	NA MFCI 4, M5222
Ferbane (Whirry)	1819–75	–	1821–57	NA MFCI 57
also:	1797–1822	1797–1822	1797–1822	NL MS. 4122
Geashill	1713–1905	1713–1846	1713–1907	NA MFCI 65
Kilcoleman	1839–75	–	1839–72	NA MFCI 4, M5235
Killeigh	1808–23	1809–32	1808–35	NA M5115/6
also:	1808–35	1808–35	1808–35	NL MS. 7974 (transcript)
also:	1808–71	1808–82	1808–71	NA MFCI 65
Kinnitty	1850–78	–	1850–83	NA MFCI 57
Roscrea	1784–1878	1791–1845	1792–1872	NA MFCI 3, M5222
Shinrone	1741–1877	1741–1844	1741–1876	NA MFCI 4, M5222
Templeharry	1845–79	–	1845–79	NA MFCI 24, M6048
Tessauran	1819–77	–	1819–77	NA MFCI 57
Tullamore	1805–1902	1805–50	1805–70	NA MFCI 55

Co. Roscommon

Athlone (St Mary's)	1849–1903	1845–90	1849–1901	NL Pos. 5309
also:	1746–1903	1754–1860	1747–1892	NA MFCI 57
(St Peter's)	–	1845–70	–	NL Pos. 5309
Kiltoom	1797–1943	1802–1910	1801–1943	NL Pos. 5309
also:	1797–1943	1802–43	1801–73	NA MFCI 61

Co. Sligo

Ballysadare	–	1845–1954	–	RCBL
Castleconnor	1800–21	1800–21	1800–21	NA MFCI 33
Drumcliff	1805–87	1805–66	1805–58	NA M5094–5107
Easkey	1822–71	1822–45	1822–71	NA MFCI 33
Emlafad	1808–80	1831–73	1831–73	NA MFCI 33
also:	1762–1882	1762–1875	1762–1941	RCBL

Co. Tipperary

Ardfinnan	1877–1937	–	–	RCBL
Ardmayle	1815–71	–	1815–77	NA M5889, 5890
Ballingarry	1816–18	–	–	NA M5131
Ballintemple	1805–71	1805–43	1805–75	NA MFCI 13, M5880, 5931
Borrisnafarney	1828–77	1827–51	1827–76	NA MFCI 4
Cahir	1805–73	1802–48	1825–72	NA MFCI 9, M5366
Carrick-on-Suir	1803–74	1804–65	1803–75	NA MFCI 9

Cashel	1668–1842	1654–1842	1668–1842	NA MFCI 7, M5366
also:	1668–1786	1654–1842	1668–1786	NL Pos. 1390
Castletownarra	1802–72	1803–46	1802–79	NA MFCI 5
Clonmel	1766–1874	1768–1847	1767–1873	NA MFCI 8, 9
also:	1791–1807	–	–	RCBL
Clonoulty	1817–92	1817–92	1817–92	NA MFCI 13
Cloughjordan	1846–72	–	–	NA MFCI 4
Corbally	1834–49	–	–	NA MFCI 4
Donoghill	1856–74	–	1859–78	NA M5887, 5888
Dunkerrin	1825–73	1826–45	1825–73	NA MFCI 4, M5222
Fethard	1804–50	1804–43	1804–50	NA MFCI 12
Holy Cross	1800–80	–	1876–80	NA M5930
Killenaule	1742–1801	–	–	NL MS. 2048 (ph.stat)
Magorban	1804–78	1804–14	1805–73	NA M5278, 5280/1
Mealiff	1851–84	–	–	NA M5930
Modreeny	1842–73	1841–44	1842–1903	NA MFCI 30
Newport (St John's)	1755–1842	1789–1872	1783–1836	NA MFCI 2, M5222
Roscrea	1784–1878	1791–1845	1792–1872	NA MFCI 3, M5222
Templemore	1791–1877	1812–45	1791–1891	NA MFCI 7, M5364
Templetouhy	1787–1835	1793–1835	1794–1834	NA MFCI 7
Terryglass	1809–62	1809–1916	1809–82	RCBL
also:	1809–77	1809–53	1809–77	NA MFCI 3, M5222
Tipperary	1779–1873	1779–1845	1779–1875	NA MFCI 6
Toem	1802–66	1804–45	1803–77	NA M5130
Tubrid	1892–1905	–	–	RCBL
Tullamellin	1818–77	1831–40	1829–75	NA MFCI 7, M5351/2

Co. Tyrone

Barr	1880–1982	1845–1934	1885–1921	RCBL (mf)
Clogherny	1859–75	–	–	NA M5049
Donacavey	1878–1936	1845–1902	1878–1903	RCBL (mf)
Newtownsaville	1877–1901	1860–1935	1877–1933	RCBL (mf)

Co. Waterford

Clonegam	1741–1870	1742–1845	1743–1875	NA MFCI 13, 15
Clonmore	1828–76	–	–	NA M5085
Dungarvan	1741–1875	1741–1875	1741–1875	NA MFCI 10, M5056–8

Kill (St Nicholas)	1730–1864	1730–1864	1730–1864	NA MFCI 8
Killea	1816–54	1816–49	1849–52	NA M5363
Killrossanty	1838–76	1838–41	1843–71	NA M5952
Kilwatermoy	1860–72	–	1858–80	NA M5355, 5350
Lismore	1693–1841	1692–1847	1711–1841	NA MFCI 1, 18, M5222, 5982
Rossmire	1866–71	–	1866–71	NA M5370
Tallow	1829–74	–	1831–73	NA MFCI 9, M5357
Templemichael	1801–72	1804–65	1823–1920	NA M5065/6, 5356
Waterford City				
Holy Trinity	1655–1857	1655–1850	1655–1892	NA MFCI 12, 13
St Olave's	1741–1872	1742–1845	1744–1838	NA MFCI 10, 11, M5366, 5368/9
St Patrick's	1723–1872	1725–1845	1723–1855	NA MFCI 10, 11

Co. Westmeath

Almorita	–	1846–1937	–	RCBL
Ardnurcher	–	1819–76	–	NA MFCI 62
Athlone (St Mary's)	1849–1903	1845–90	1849–1901	NL Pos. 5309
also:	1746–1903	1754–1860	1747–1892	NA MFCI 57
(St Peter's)	–	1845–70	–	NL Pos. 5309
(see also Willbrook)				
Bunowen	1820–1941	1820–1941	1820–1941	NL Pos. 5309
also:	1819–76	–	1829–77	NA MFCI 61
Castletownkinadelan	1850–77	–	–	NA MFCI 54
Collinstown	1838–1963	1818–51	1837–1960	NA MFCI 51
Delvin	1817–1947	1817–50	1817–1943	NA MFCI 51
Drumcree (Kilcumney)	1816–75	–	1816–81	NA M5108/9
Enniscoffey	1881–1953	1845–1925	1891–1976	RCBL
Kilkenny West	1762–83	1762–83	–	NL Pos. 5309
also:	1783–1956	1783–1855	1784–1945	NA MFCI 61
Killucan	1696–1863	1787–1857	1700–1888	RCBL
also:	1696–1786	1696–1786	1696–1786	NL MS. 2049 (ph.stat)
also:	1696–1778	–	1700–72	GO 578
Kinnegad	1892–1917	1845–94	1895–1956	RCBL
Leney	1840–72	–	1860–71	NA MFCI 62
also:	1840–43	–	–	RCBL
Mayne	1808–70	1809–70	1808–70	NA MFCI 51
Moyliscar	–	1845–1956	–	RCBL
Mullingar	–	1845–1956	–	RCBL
Portnashangan	–	1846–1979	1880–1977	RCBL
Rathconnell	–	–	1881–95	RCBL
Stonehall	1814–57	1814–54	1915–54	NA MFCI 62
also:	1878–1941	–	–	RCBL

Willbrook (Moydrum)	1756–83	1763–75	–	NL Pos. 5309
also:	1756–83	–	–	NA MFCI 62

Co. Wexford

Carne	–	–	1815–76	NA M1451
Churchtown	–	–	1835–77	NA M1451
Inch	1726–1866	1726–1887	1726–1896	NA M5059 / 60
also:	1866–1984	–	1896–1984	NA MFCI 82
Killinick	1804–20	1804–20	1805–19	NA M5063
Kilmeaden	1693–1873	1683–1847	1683–1882	NA MFCI 13, M5965
Kilpatrick	–	–	1834–64	NA M1451
Templeshanbo	1827–75	1827–91	1827–91	NA M5729
Whitechurch				GO 701 (extracts)

Co. Wicklow

Aghold	1714–1863	1714–1863	1714–1863	GO 578 (extracts)
Ballinaclash	1839–1989	1843–51	1842–1984	NA MFCI 76
Ballintemple	1823–51	1823–54	–	NA MFCI 76
Blessington	1695–1985	1683–1878	1683–1985	NA MFCI 87
Castlemacadam	1720–1904	1719–1860	1719–1979	NA MFCI 76
Delgany	1666–1985	1666–1845	1666–1985	NA MFCI 75
Donard	–	1848–1955	1888–1965	RCBL
Donoughmore	1720–1888	1720–1856	1720–1929	RCBL
also:	1720–1888	1720–1853	1720–1874	NA MFCI 89
Dunlavin	1697–1934	1697–1956	1697–1934	RCBL
also:	1697–1879	1698–1844	1698–1879	NA MFCI 86
Enniskerry	1662–1874	1662–1852	1662–1874	NL Pos. 5484
Glenely	1808–80	1808–64	1817–71	NA MFCI 77
Kilbride	1834–1970	1845–76	1834–1984	NA MFCI 82
Killiskey	1818–1905	1818–44	1824–77	NA MFCI 83
Newcastle	1698–1954	1697–1846	1699–1881	NA MFCI 85
Powerscourt	1677–1874	1662–1860	1663–1873	NA MFCI 91
Rathdrum	1706–1865	1706–1855	1706–1916	NA MFCI 77
Redcross	1830–52	–	–	NA MFCI 79
Wicklow	1655–1983	1729–1869	1729–1909	NA MFCI 83

15

Research Services, Societies and Repositories

SECTION 1. RESEARCH SERVICES

A. Professional Associations

Two associations of professional researchers exist, the Association of Ulster Genealogists and Record Agents (AUGRA), based exclusively in Northern Ireland, and the Association of Professional Genealogists in Ireland (APGI), with members north and south. Both bodies are principally concerned with upholding research standards, rather than undertaking commercial research in their own right. The secretaries of both associations will supply a list of members on request:

The Secretary, AUGRA, Glen Cottage, Glenmachan Road, Belfast BT4 2NP, Northern Ireland.
The Secretary, APGI, c/o The Genealogical Office, 2 Kildare St, Dublin 2.

B. Research Agencies

The following are research agencies whose staff are members of the two professional associations:

Gorry Research, 16 Hume St, Dublin 2.
Hibernian Research Co. Ltd, P.O. Box 3097, Dublin 6.
    Telephone (01) 966522 (24 hours); Fax 973011 (24 hours)
Historical Research Associates, 7 Lancastrian Street, Carrickfergus BT38 7AB, Co. Antrim, Northern Ireland.

Irish Heritage Association, 162a Kingsway, Dunmurry, Belfast BT17 9AD. Telephone (0232) 629595

Irish Research Services, 111 South Parade, Belfast BT7 2GN, Northern Ireland.

Research Ireland, Fair View, Kindelstown Hill, Delgany, Co. Wicklow.

C. The Irish Genealogical Project

In the early 1980s, as part of a series of government-sponsored youth employment and training schemes in the Republic of Ireland, local history and heritage societies and other interested bodies began to organise the indexing of local parish records. With some exceptions, at the outset little thought was given to the potential value of these records. However, in the mid-1980s, as the number of areas covered by the indexing projects grew, their efforts were co-ordinated by an umbrella body, the Irish Family History Council, later to become the Irish Family History Foundation. An ambitious plan was drawn up under the aegis of this body to transcribe and computerise not only all the parish records of all denominations for the entire country, but also all other sources of major genealogical interest: the Tithe Books, Griffith's Valuation, the civil records of births, marriages and deaths, the 1901 and 1911 census returns, and local gravestone inscriptions. Expanded government funding was secured for this plan, known as the Irish Genealogical Project, and in 1990, with the adherence of four centres in Northern Ireland, the International Fund for Ireland also became involved.

Thirty-five geographical catchment areas have been identified, and, as of mid-1991, centres have been designated for thirty-one of these. Each centre is to computerise the records for its area, and provide a commercial genealogical research service using these records. Ultimately this service will be co-ordinated by two central agencies, north and south, acting as signposts to the relevant centre. The computerised records are to remain exclusively in the custody of the local centres, and it is not envisaged that the public will have direct access to them.

As well as those working in the local heritage centres, the Project also aims to include professional genealogists, in particular the members of the two professional bodies named above. When the computerisation of the records is complete, currently anticipated for 1994, a comprehensive research service will exist, combining the experience and expertise of the professionals with the speed and accuracy of the local databases. For the moment, the situation is less clear, with centres at different points on the road to full computerisation. What follows is a listing of the centres currently involved, together with some comments on their progress.

MEMBER CENTRES OF THE IRISH FAMILY HISTORY FOUNDATION
The comments given on the centres reflect the situation in mid-1991; obviously, as the Project develops their positions will change. The comments concentrate on the indexing of parish records, since this was their first priority and the area in which most progress has been made. Apart from parish records, however, the majority of centres also hold copies of the other major genealogical sources. Not all the centres offer a research service. For the moment, the only centres to carry out full commissioned research are those in Clare, Leitrim, Limerick, Laois/Offaly, Roscommon and Waterford. Most of the centres which have completed a substantial amount of indexing will check the records they have covered, though this varies from centre to centre. Again, as the Project progresses the services offered and fees charged will be standardised.

Catchment Area	*Centre*	*Comment*
Antrim/Down	Ulster Historical Foundation, 66 Balmoral Avenue, Belfast BT9 6NY	The UHF is a long-established, highly reputable research and publishing agency. Its indexing activities as part of the IGP date from 1990 and are, as yet, at an early stage.
Armagh	Armagh Records Centre, Ara Coeli, Armagh BT61 7QY	This was originally part of the archives of the Catholic Archdiocese of Armagh, and has computerised the Catholic records for this area, which also includes parts of Cos Tyrone, Louth and Down.
Carlow	No centre designated as yet	
Cavan	Cavan Heritage & Genealogy Centre, c/o Cavan Co. Library	The centre has indexed, on cards, almost all the Catholic records for the county, as well as Griffith's Valuation and the Tithe Books.

Clare

The Clare
Genealogy Centre,
Corofin,
Co. Clare

One of the longest-
established centres, this
has completed indexing
of all church records for
the county, as well as a
substantial proportion of
the other major sources.

Cork North

Mallow Heritage
Centre,
27–8 Bank Place,
Mallow,
Co. Cork

The centre has completed
the indexing, on card, of
most of the Catholic records
of north Cork and a
substantial proportion of the
Church of Ireland records. At
the moment (1991) two further
centres to cover the rest of
Co. Cork have yet to be
designated.

Derry

Inner City Trust
Genealogy Centre,
8 Bishop St,
Derry BT48 6PW

The centre is long-established
and has completed indexing
of Griffith's, Tithe Books and
emigration records, as well as
almost half the Catholic
records, and a number of
Presbyterian registers.

Donegal

Donegal Genealogical
Committee,
Letterkenny,
Co. Donegal

The various groups
represented on the
Committee have indexed
almost all the Presbyterian
and Church of Ireland
records for the county, and
the Catholic records for the
Inishowen peninsula.

Down

See Antrim

Dublin North

The Fingall
Heritage Centre,

The centre has indexed a
substantial number of the

	10 North St, Swords, Co. Dublin	Catholic records of north Co. Dublin.

Dublin City

	Dublin Heritage Group, Clondalkin Library, Clondalkin, Co. Dublin	The group has indexed church records for West Dublin, and a small proportion of the Dublin City records.

Dublin South

	Dun Laoghaire Heritage Centre, Moran Park House, Dun Laoghaire, Co. Dublin	Indexing of the Catholic records of Dun Laoghaire is complete, with work continuing on the records of adjoining parishes.

Fermanagh/Tyrone

	Irish World, 26 Market Sq, Dungannon BT70 1AB, Co. Tyrone	The efforts of this centre have been concentrated so far on Griffith's, Tithe Books, and gravestone inscriptions; the inscriptions are particularly extensive, covering more than 300 graveyards throughout Northern Ireland.

Galway East

	Woodford Heritage Centre, Woodview House, Woodford, Co. Galway	About half the Catholic records of East Galway have been indexed, along with a small proportion of the Church of Ireland records.

Galway West

	Co. Galway Family History Society, 4 New Docks, Galway	The Society has indexed almost half the Catholic records of west Galway.

Kerry

	No centre designated as yet	KERRY GENEALOGY & VISITOR'S CENTRE (CO KERRY Co LIBRARY, TRALEE, CO KERRY).

Kildare

| | Kildare Genealogical Committee, Co. Library, Newbridge, Co. Kildare | Slightly less than half the Catholic records for the county have been indexed. |

Kilkenny

| | Kilkenny Archaeological Society, Rothe House, Kilkenny | Almost half the Catholic records for the county have been indexed, along with a small proportion of the Church of Ireland records, and a large number of gravestone inscriptions. |

Laois/Offaly

| | Family History Research Centre, Charleville Road, Tullamore, Co. Offaly | Over three-quarters of all church records have been indexed. The centre also holds a large number of other sources, and is very active in local history. |

Leitrim

| | Leitrim Heritage Centre, Co. Library, Ballinamore, Co. Leitrim | The centre has completed indexing of all church records for the county, as well as Griffith's, Tithe Books, and other sources. |

Limerick

| | Limerick Archives, The Granary, Michael St, Limerick | All church records for the county are indexed, along with a wide range of other sources. |

Longford

| | Longford Genealogical Centre, Barrack Road, Longford. | Over half the Catholic records for the county are indexed on cards. |

Louth

See Meath

Mayo North

| | Mayo North Family History Research | Virtually all the church records for north Mayo |

	Centre, Enniscoe, Crossmolina, Co. Mayo	have been indexed.

Mayo South

	Family Research Centre, Town Hall, Ballinrobe, Co. Mayo	Almost all the Catholic and Church of Ireland records for the south of the county are indexed. The centre also has a large collection of indexed school rolls.

Meath/Louth

	Meath Heritage Centre, Trim, Co. Meath	Most of the surviving Church of Ireland records for the area are indexed. The Catholic records completed are mainly for Co. Meath, and come to less than half the total.

Monaghan

	Monaghan Ancestral Research Centre, 6 Tully, Monaghan	The centre has indexed a little less than half the total church records for the county. It also holds a wide range of other sources.

Offaly

See Laois

Roscommon

	Roscommon Heritage & Genealogical Centre, Strokestown, Co. Roscommon	The Centre has virtually completed indexing of Catholic records for the county, and has covered a large proportion of the Church of Ireland records.

Sligo

	Sligo Heritage & Genealogical Centre, Stephen's St, Sligo	Indexing of all church records is complete. The centre has also indexed almost all the gravestone inscriptions for the county.

Tipperary North

Nenagh District Heritage Society, Governor's House, Nenagh, Co. Tipperary	The centre holds indexes to more than half the Catholic and Church of Ireland records for the north of the county.

Tipperary South

Bru Boru Heritage Centre, Cashel, Co. Tipperary	Access to Catholic records is limited, though the centre holds a wide range of other sources.

Tyrone

See Fermanagh

Waterford

Waterford Heritage Survey Ltd, St John's College, Waterford	The Survey has indexed almost all the parishes in the diocese of Waterford and Lismore.

Westmeath

Dun na Si Heritage Centre, Moate, Co. Westmeath	A number of Catholic and Church of Ireland registers have been indexed, but the project is still in its early stages.

Wexford

Tagoat Community Council, Tagoat, Rosslare, Co. Wexford	More than half the Catholic records for the county have been indexed.

Wicklow

Wicklow Heritage Centre, Court House, Wicklow	Almost all the Catholic records in the county have been indexed.

SECTION 2. SOCIETIES

A. Ireland

Dublin Family History Society, c/o 36 College Drive, Templeogue, Dublin 6

Huguenot Society of Great Britain and Ireland, c/o Nora Fahie, 47 Ailesbury Road, Dublin 4

Irish Family History Society, P.O. Box 36, Naas, Co. Kildare
Publishes *Irish Family History*

Irish Genealogical Research Society, 6 Eaton Brae, Orwell Road, Dublin 14
Publishes *The Irish Genealogist*

Irish Heritage Association, 162a Kingsway, Dunmurry, Belfast BT17 9AD
Publishes *Irish Family Links*

North of Ireland Family History Society, 29 Grange Park, Dunmurry, Belfast BT17 OAN
Publishes *North Irish Roots*

Ulster Historical and Genealogical Guild, Ulster Historical Foundation, 66 Balmoral Ave, Belfast BT9 6NY
Publishes *Familia: Ulster Genealogical Review*

B. Abroad

Family History Association of Canada, P.O. Box 91398, West Vancouver, BC V7V 3P1, Canada

Federation of Family History Societies, 96 Beaumont Street, Mile House, Plymouth PL2 3AQ, England

Irish Family Names Society, P.O. Box 2095, La Mesa, CA 92044, USA

Irish Genealogical Research Society, c/o Challoner Club, 59/61 Port Street, Knightsbridge, London SW1X 0BG, England
Publishes *The Irish Genealogist*

Irish Genealogical Society, P.O. Box 16585, St Paul MN 55116, USA
Publishes *Septs*

New Zealand Society of Genealogists, P.O. Box 8785, Auckland 3, New Zealand

The Society of Australian Genealogists, Richmond Villa, 120 Kent St, Sydney, N.S.W. 2000, Australia
Publishes *Descent*

SECTION 3. RECORD REPOSITORIES

A. Northern Ireland

AREA LIBRARIES

North-east Area Library, Demesne Avenue, Ballymena BT49 7BG, Co. Antrim. Telephone (0266) 41531

Southern Area Library, Brownlow Row, Legahory, Craigavon BT65 8DP,
   Co. Armagh. Telephone (0238) 562639
South-East Area Library, Windmill Hill, Ballynahinch BT24 8DH, Co.
   Down. Telephone (0861) 341946
Western Area Library, 41 Dublin Road, Omagh BT78 1HG, Co. Tyrone.
   Telephone (0662) 244821
Belfast Central Library, Royal Avenue, Belfast BT1 1EA. Telephone (0232)
   243233 (Open 9.30 a.m. – 8 p.m. Mon. & Thurs.; 9.30 a.m. – 5.30 p.m.
   Tues., Wed., Fri.; 9.30 a.m. – 1 p.m. Sat.)

OTHER REPOSITORIES
Church of Jesus Christ of Latter-day Saints Family History Centre,
   Hollywood Road, Belfast. Telephone (0232) 643998. (Open Wednesday
   evenings)
General Register Office, Oxford House, 49–55 Chichester St, Belfast BT1
   4HL. Telephone (0232) 235211 (Only the indexes are open for public
   research, and by appointment only)
Linen Hall Library, 17 Donegal Square North, Belfast BT1 5GD.
Presbyterian Historical Society, Room 218, Church House, Fisherwick Place,
   Belfast BT1 6DW. Telephone (0232) 323936 (Open 10 a.m. – 12.30 p.m.
   Mon. – Fri.; 10 a.m. – 12.30 p.m. and 2 p.m. – 4 p.m. Wed.)
Public Record Office of Northern Ireland, 66 Balmoral Avenue, Belfast BT9
   6NY. Telephone (0232) 661621 (Open 9.15 a.m. – 4.45 p.m. Mon. – Fri.)
Society of Friends Library, Meeting House, Railway Street, Lisburn, Co.
   Antrim (Postal queries only)

B. Republic of Ireland

COUNTY LIBRARIES
Carlow: Dublin St, Carlow. Telephone (0503) 31126
Cavan: Farnham St, Cavan. Telephone (049) 31799
Clare: Mill Road, Ennis, Co. Clare. Telephone (065) 21616
Cork: Farranlea Road, Cork. Telephone (021) 546499
Donegal: High Road, Letterkenny, Co. Donegal. Telephone (084) 24950
Dublin: (1) Gilbert Library, 138–142 Pearse St, Dublin 2. Telephone (01)
   777662 (2) Central Library, The ILAC Centre, Henry St, Dublin 1.
   Telephone (01) 734333
Galway: Island House, Cathedral Square, Galway. Telephone (091) 62471
Kerry: Moyderwell, Tralee, Co. Kerry. Telephone (066) 21200
Kildare: Athgarvan Road, Newbridge, Co. Kildare. Telephone (045) 31145
Kilkenny: 6 John's Quay, Kilkenny. Telephone (056) 22021
Laois: County Hall, Portlaoise, Co. Laois. Telephone (0502) 21993

Leitrim: The Courthouse, Ballinamore, Co. Leitrim. Telephone (078) 44012
Limerick: 58 O'Connell St, Limerick. Telephone (061) 318692
Longford: Annelly Car Park, Longford. Telephone (043) 41124
Louth: Crowe St, Dundalk, Co. Louth. Telephone (042) 35457
Mayo: Mountain View, Castlebar, Co. Mayo. Telephone (094) 21342
Meath: Railway St, Navan, Co. Meath. Telephone (046) 21134
Monaghan: The Diamond, Clones, Co. Monaghan. Telephone (047) 51143
Offaly: O'Connor Sq., Tullamore, Co. Offaly. Telephone (0506) 21419
Roscommon: Abbey St, Roscommon. Telephone (0903) 26100
Sligo: The Courthouse, Teeling St, Sligo. Telephone (071) 42212
Tipperary: Castle Avenue, Thurles, Co. Tipperary. Telephone (0504) 21555
Waterford: Lismore, Co. Waterford. Telephone (058) 54128
Westmeath: Dublin Rd, Mullingar, Co. Westmeath. Telephone (044) 40781
Wexford: County Hall, Abbey St, Wexford. Telephone (053) 22211
Wicklow: Greystones, Co. Wicklow. (01) 2874387

OTHER REPOSITORIES

Church of Jesus Christ of Latter-day Saints Family History Centre, Finglas
    Road, Glasnevin, Dublin 11. Telephone (01) 309960 (Open Wednesday
    and Friday (evening), Saturday (morning))
Cork Archives Institute, Christ Church, South Main St, Cork. Telephone
    (021) 277809 (Open 10 a.m. – 1 p.m., 2.30 p.m. – 5 p.m. Mon. – Fri.).
The Genealogical Office: 2 Kildare St, Dublin 2. Telephone (01) 618811
    (Open 10 a.m. – 4.30 p.m. Mon. – Fri.)
The General Register Office, Joyce House, 8–11 Lombard St E., Dublin 2.
    Telephone (01) 711000 (Open 9.30 a.m. – 12.30 p.m., 2.15 p.m. – 4.30 p.m.)
Land Valuation Office: 6 Ely Place, Dublin 2. Telephone (01) 763211 (Open
    9.30 a.m. – 12.30 p.m., 2 p.m. – 4.30 p.m. Mon. – Fri.)
National Archives: Four Courts, Dublin 7. Telephone (01) 783711. Due to
    move to Bishop St, Dublin 8, by January 1992. (Open 10 a.m. – 5 p.m.
    Mon. – Fri.)
National Library: Kildare St, Dublin 2. Telephone (01) 618811 (Open 10 a.m. –
    9 p.m. Mon.; 2 p.m. – 9 p.m. Tues., Wed.; 10 a.m. – 5 p.m. Thurs., Fri.;
    10 a.m. – 1 p.m. Sat.)
Registry of Deeds: Henrietta St, Dublin 1. Telephone (01) 733300
    (Open 10 a.m. – 4.30 p.m. Mon. – Fri.)
Society of Friends Library: Swanbrook House, Morehampton Road,
    Donnybrook, Dublin 4. Telephone (01) 683684 (Open Thursdays 10.30
    a.m. – 1 p.m.)
Representative Church Body Library: Braemor Park, Rathgar, Dublin 14.
    Telephone (01) 979979 (Open 9 a.m. – 1 p.m., 1.45 p.m. – 5 p.m. Mon. –
    Fri.)